FIELDING'S
ALASKA
AND THE YUKON

FIELDING'S BERMUDA AND THE BAHAMAS 1990
FIELDING'S BUDGET EUROPE 1990
FIELDING'S CARIBBEAN 1990
FIELDING'S EUROPE 1990
FIELDING'S MEXICO 1990
FIELDING'S PEOPLE'S REPUBLIC OF CHINA 1990
FIELDING'S SELECTIVE SHOPPING GUIDE TO EUROPE 1990

FIELDING'S AFRICAN SAFARIS
FIELDING'S ALASKA AND THE YUKON
FIELDING'S CALIFORNIA
FIELDING'S EUROPE WITH CHILDREN
FIELDING'S FAMILY VACATIONS USA
FIELDING'S FAR EAST 2nd revised edition
FIELDING'S HAVENS AND HIDEAWAYS USA
FIELDING'S LEWIS AND CLARK TRAIL
FIELDING'S LITERARY AFRICA
FIELDING'S MOTORING AND CAMPING EUROPE
FIELDING'S SPANISH TRAILS IN THE SOUTHWEST
FIELDING'S WORLDWIDE CRUISES 4th revised edition

FIELDING'S
ALASKA
AND THE YUKON

BY
ROBERT W. BONE

FIELDING TRAVEL BOOKS
c/o WILLIAM MORROW & COMPANY, INC.
105 Madison Avenue, New York, N.Y. 10016

Library of Congress Catalog in Card Number: 89-85490

ISBN: 0-688-08309-9
ISBN: 0-340-51207-5 (Hodder & Stoughton)

Printed in the United States of America

First Edition

  2 3 4 5 6 7 8 9 10

Text design by Marsha Cohen/Parallelogram

All maps by Mark Stein Studios

Photograph by Sara A. Bone

A 1954 graduate of Bowling Green University in Ohio, Bob Bone has been writing since the mid-1950s, when he began working on Army training manuals and similar works of literature. He went on to work for the Buffalo (New York) *Courier-Express,* the Middletown (New York) *Daily Record,* the San Juan (Puerto Rico) *Star,* the Honolulu (Hawaii) *Advertiser,* and the London bureau of United Press International.

He was editor-in-chief of *Brazilian Business Magazine* in Rio de Janiero, news editor of *Popular Photography Magazine* in New York, and picture editor on the staff of Time-Life Books.

Bone has been a travel writer since 1968 when he joined the staff of the late Temple Fielding in Mallorca, helping to turn out *Fielding's Guide to Europe* and other books.

Since 1971, he and his wife, Sara, have lived in Honolulu, traveling and writing about Hawaii and other Pacific and Asian destinations. He began the Maverick Guide series of books, and worked with that project for more than a decade.

Bone's articles on Hawaii, Australia, New Zealand, Alaska, and other areas frequently appear in newspapers and magazines all across the U.S.

ACKNOWLEDGMENTS

In the process of researching this guidebook we met scores of friendly, helpful people, not the least of which are those named below. Sara and I want especially to thank the following for their assistance and encouragement.

Barry Anderson, Hilda Anderson, John Gottberg Anderson, Denise Belkoski, Vera Benedek, Dana Brockway, Jeff Brown, Susan Bus, Louis Cancelmi, Juli Chase, Howard Clifford, Gary Danielson, Miriam Dunbar, Kathleen Dunlap, Keith Fernandez, Beatrice Franklin, Bill Hackett, Carol Heyman, Duane Davis Heyman, Kathy Hildre, Karen Hofstad, Cliff Hollenbeck, Nancy Hollenbeck, Chuck Holloway, Karin Hopper, Yvonne Howard, Russ Josephson, Michael Kaelke, Kari Kornfeind, John Kostelnik, Karen Lane, Len Laurance, Steve Lefler, Dee Longenbaugh, George Mason, James Michener, Linda Mickle, Mike Miller, Ava Moon, Dale Northrup, Pat Ockert, Gloria Ohmer, Dick Olson, Dotty Olson, Jeff Osborn, Melissa Ottley, Betty Paige, Brad Phillips, Mary Pignalberi, Bruce Pozzi, Lisa Rallo, Ruth Ray, Ann Reading, Whit Reading, Penny Rennick, Leeta Rice, Morgan Richardson, Archie Satterfield, Gert Seekins, Kevin Shackell, Rich Skinner, Suzanne Stolpe, Gordon Thorne, Ralph Tingey, Victoria Torrilhon, Kimberley Tyner, Lisa Von Bargen, Bob Ward, Susan Ward, Chip Waterbury, Betti Weir, Chuck West, Lois Wirtz, and James Wright.

CONTENTS

THE LAST FRONTIER: AN INTRODUCTION

The history of the United States has often focused on the nation's frontier. The word has quite a different definition in America than it does in Europe. The American frontier is not merely the border between nations. Its special meaning becomes clear when you realize it is a noun used often as an adjective—"a frontier outpost" or "the frontier spirit." The frontier always has been that exciting place on the outskirts of American civilization where men and women of character could prove their mettle in a struggle with the forces of nature.

To many of us, the romantic notion of the frontier disappeared soon after the mid-1800s, when the Spanish were driven out of California and the Indians began to move to reservations. Horace Greeley told us to go West, and so we did. There we met up with the Pacific Ocean, built Disneyland, and that was that.

No one told us to go North. In fact, lots of folks cautioned against it. Yet, in the latter half of the nineteenth century, while many weren't looking, the American frontier took a sharp right turn. A few with the gumption to live on the cutting edge of society followed. Most did not.

There was one big exciting difference with this new frontier— somehow it never quite came to an end. Although a few good roads were built and Hershey bars followed apace, Alaska remains a place where moose are a definite traffic hazard and bears have discovered they love chocolate as much as does any back packer.

You will find out for yourself that in many ways the last frontier is still there today. It's no secret to the sourdoughs who live, work, and play in or near the wilderness areas of Alaska and northern Canada. (Indeed, the "Last Frontier" slogan embossed on Alaska's license plates was the winning phrase in a contest only a few years ago.) It is still waiting to be discovered by millions of us *cheechakos* who have a special appreciation for unbridled nature and a robust past.

The bald eagle, that magnificent symbol of the U.S. itself, has

1

virtually disappeared in the rest of the country, but you'll see many in Alaska. And the vigorous spirit of the gold rush still lingers in Skagway and Dawson City, towns that are living museums of the late 1890s.

At least a few folks still build log cabins in Alaska and the Yukon; they feed their families by fishing, hunting, and trapping. Some of them even pan a little gold on the side. On the other hand, a large number of northerners will have none of this rustic life or will save it for an occasional weekend, preferring the day-to-day security and comfort of 9-to-5 jobs with two cars and a home in the suburbs. You'll meet these in Alaska, too, at the theater or the salad bar.

Despite the large number of mountains, streams, lakes and other unnamed natural features over the landscape, not everyone believes that Alaska and the Yukon Territory of Canada should be considered a frontier. After all, Alaska is the 49th State, admitted to the Union 30 years ago. The Yukon is also largely self-governed, even if it is not quite a province. In general, the political and economic sophistication of the region is at least equal to that of any other location in North America.

Still, if a land which has such a vast storehouse of unexplored and unexploited natural wonders and natural wealth can't be called a frontier, we're not sure just what can be.

THE GREAT LAND

The word *Alaska* comes from an Aleut word which is usually spelled *alyeska* and usually translated as "The Great Land." Its original meaning may have been merely "the mainland." In any case, the more exalted translation is a popular term today. You'll probably run across the Great Land Liquor Store, the Great Land Auto Repair Shop, and perhaps even the Great Land Massage Parlor.

Residents of Alaska and the Yukon believe that unlike the population "Outside," they live in a very special and unusual place. There are conflicts aplenty, often between those who favor development of the area's natural resources and those advocating conservation and more concern for the environment.

Many rugged individualists who have spent their lives defying convention and regimentation are not very keen on the rest of the world discovering attractions and opportunities up north. Others, of course, have whole-heartedly embraced the area's nascent tourist industry. A third bunch is not quite sure where to stand on the issue.

Miami-based newspaper satirist Dave Barry visited Alaska last year and then wrote of the strange Alaskan penchant for calling attention to the state's most fearsome feature by placing huge stuffed bears in airport lounges and hotel lobbies where they can be regarded with proper awe by *cheechakos*—usually poised on hind legs with front paws raised in a warlike challenge. "This struck me as an odd concept, greeting visitors with a showcase containing a major local hazard," Barry wrote. "It's as if the Greater Miami Chamber of Commerce went around setting up glass display cases containing stuffed cocaine smugglers, with little plaques stating how much they weighed and where they were taken. (Which is not a bad idea, now that I think of it.)"

AN IMAGE PROBLEM

As you'll no doubt hear again and again, Alaska has suffered from a bad press ever since it was dubbed "Seward's Folly" and other pejorative terms when the territory was purchased from the Russians in 1867. Even today, there are those who believe the state is composed of little more than vast fields of ice, snow, and Christmas trees, along with a number of wolves and bad-tempered bears.

We thought of this image again and again recently—like when we drove around Fairbanks last July with the windows rolled up and air conditioning on full-blast in an attempt to fight the 95-degree temperatures. No self-respecting furry creature would venture out on a day like that.

Alaska has proved to be a considerable economic asset to the U.S. over the last 100 years. There was the gold rush at the end of the last century. But there have been even greater benefits from the salmon and lumber industries, and later from the rich oil fields on the North Slope.

Alaska has also assumed a strategic importance since World War II. The Japanese were defeated when they tried to gain a foothold on American soil in the Aleutian Islands. During the Cold War, the DEW (Distant Early Warning) Line was enforced from Alaska. Similar defense measures are in effect here today, since Alaska is separated by only a few miles from the Soviet Union. Many new residents of the state were first sent there by the Armed Forces.

THE CONFESSION BOX

We first visited Alaska in February 1982, flying from our home in Honolulu to land in Anchorage smack in the middle of winter. The Fur Rendezvous sled races were under way, and it seemed as if half the population of the state was standing along Fourth Avenue, cheering on the mushers and their dogs. Temperatures were in the teens and 20s, but the sun was shining, and the joyous yelps of impatient huskies echoed along the streets. There was an excitement in the air that was only partly due to the annual event itself. Gradually it became apparent that much of the electricity in the air was caused by the clear, crackling spirit of Alaska in general. It was during that visit that we decided to do a guide to the Great Land. We were unable to begin immediately on an Alaska guide, but we did meet several good people during that first trip, some of whom have become close friends and valuable allies.

We were already in the guidebook business, having started a series of volumes we dubbed *the Maverick Guides* in 1977 for another publisher. There were then Maverick Guides to Hawaii, to Australia, and to New Zealand. (We no longer do these books.) Although we had visited Alaska twice before, the principal research excursion we made for this first edition of *Fielding's Alaska and the Yukon* was a three-month trip in the summer of 1988. You don't need to spend three months up north to have a valuable vacation experience, but when you're going to write about it, the situation is much more demanding.

To do the kind of intensive research we felt was required, we spent three or four times the number of days at any given location than the average traveler. We took several tours, interviewed dozens of tourism professionals, inspected scores of hotels and motels, checked out hundreds of restaurants and shops, and drove thousands of miles over routes varying in quality from superhighways to dirt lanes.

Some familiar with the Great Landscape felt we should not do our research during the hectic days of summer but on the off season, when things are more quiet and people would have more time to talk and show us around. Our position was that since most visitors go north from June through August, we should do so too. Thus we got a genuine feel for the summer scene and saw how well our fellow *cheechakos* were enjoying themselves at different destinations during the height of the season.

We first thought of doing a guide (like others on the market) whose subject matter was enclosed strictly within the borders of the State of Alaska. But we soon saw that any volume which ignored the Yukon Territory of Canada would only tell part of the story and not be nearly as useful to today's travelers.

For one thing, one cannot move by land from Southeast Alaska (the panhandle) to Central Alaska without crossing into and out of the Yukon. More important, Alaskans and Yukoners have a strong affinity for one another which dates back 100 years to the gold rush along the Klondike River, which is, after all, in the Yukon. It's safe to say that today's populations of Whitehorse and Dawson City, although loyal Canadians, also feel physically and culturally close to residents of Alaskan cities like Skagway and Fairbanks. Both groups seem ready and willing to compare their lives favorably to folks who live Outside.

As a result of this, we do have some problems in terminology. This book is mainly about Alaska, but you will soon see that when we speak in a general sense about Alaska, the reference also includes Canada's Yukon Territory. There are times when we attempt to be more specific about which we are talking about, of course. And there are other times when *the Yukon* refers only to the great river of the same name, which flows between both Alaska and the Yukon Territory.

OUR ORDER OF MARCH

This is not required reading, but for those with map in hand and who are curious about our more recent itinerary, here is how we did it:

Sara and I began in Seattle, as many visitors to Alaska have done for more than a century. We decided to forego taking the Alaska Marine Highway ferry from that traditional gateway, and we began driving north through British Columbia. We chose the most interesting route we could find: via the Fraser River Canyon and the Cariboo country of B.C. to Prince George. Then we traveled west over the Canadian Rockies to the ambitious little city of Prince Rupert, proud of its position as an alternate jumping-off place to Alaska.

We put the car and ourselves on the Alaska Marine Highway ferry at Prince Rupert and then used nearly a month to investigate every important port in the Alaskan panhandle—what the Alaskans call "Southeast." This included, in order, Ketchikan, Wrangell, Petersburg, Sitka, Juneau, Haines, and Skagway. We also took several excursions by auto, boat, plane, and train from these same Southeast ports.

At Ketchikan, we flew to Misty Fiords; at Petersburg, we tagged along with the *Sheltered Seas* when she visited Le Conte Glacier; at Sitka, we took a cruise to several nearby scenic islands; at Juneau, we climbed aboard an Exploration Cruise Lines boat to sail up Tracy Arm and then another to go over to Glacier Bay; we also flew via helicopter to land on top of the Mendenhall Glacier. At Haines, we had our first close encounter of the furry kind when we came across a grizzly cub while on a casual drive just outside of town. And at Skagway, we climbed aboard the recently renewed railroad excursion up to the historic White Pass.

We drove from Skagway over the mountains into Canada's Yukon Territory to Carcross and Whitehorse. After visiting there and taking the nearby cruise through Miles Canyon on the Yukon River, we joined the Alaska Highway and turned back into central Alaska, to Fairbanks via Tok and the village of North Pole.

From Fairbanks, we boarded the unusual Royal Hyway Tours excursion by bus where private cars normally can't go—500 miles up the rough "haul road" alongside the Alaska Pipeline, crossing the Arctic Circle, over the Brooks Range, and across the North Slope to the oil fields among the caribou at Prudhoe Bay. After flying back to Fairbanks, we poked around the surrounding area for a week, taking the traditional sternwheeler cruise on the Chena and Tanana rivers. Then we drove via Nenana to Denali National Park, which is centered around majestic Mount McKinley, the highest peak in North America. We took the excursion that led deepest into the park—one that many people are never told about—and had some wonderful wildlife viewing. We also took a helicopter flight over another wild portion of the vast area. Back on the road again, we made a side trip into the seldom-visited and slightly oddball hamlet of Talkeetna, on our way down to Anchorage.

We discovered that we liked Alaska's largest city as much in the summer as we had in the winter. We were in and out of Anchorage for more than two weeks. We made an exhaustive exploration of the tourist facilities in town, and we also used it as a base for several major flight excursions—MarkAir's tours to King Salmon (where Sara cought her coho), Katmai National Park on the Alaska Peninsula, and Kodiak Island. We took the Exploration Tour trip to Nome and Kotzebue and, again with Exploration, traveled far out into the Bering Sea to the Pribilof Islands, easily one of our most fascinating excursions ever. We also made several miscellaneous smaller side trips from Anchorage, including the Alaska Railroad to Whittier and Brad Phillips' famous "26 Glacier Cruise" on Prince William Sound.

When Anchorage folks go on vacation, they often drive down the Kenai Peninsula, so we followed in their tiretracks. We visited the dramatic Portage Glacier and then headed over Moose Pass to explore several atmospheric cities on the peninsula itself, notably the ports of Seward and Homer. Then we retraced our steps somewhat, skirting Anchorage and driving to the twin agricultural towns of Wasilla and Palmer, which together form the heart of the fertile Matanuska Valley.

After visiting the gold mining and ski country at nearby Hatcher Pass, we traveled via Glennallen to the historic coastal port of Valdez, "Alaska's Little Switzerland." There we toured facilities at the end of the same pipeline whose beginning we had seen the previous month at Prudhoe Bay.

Then we shot straight up to Tok again and thence, on a dirt and gravel road, through Chicken to the little town of Eagle, which is perched right on the Yukon River. From Eagle, we took the panoramic Top of the World Highway back into the Yukon to the old gold rush town of Dawson City at the confluence of the Klondike and Yukon rivers.

From Dawson we traveled down the Klondike Highway to Whitehorse again, rejoining the Alaska Highway, which we followed south this time, through such important centers as Watson Lake (with its "Forest of Signs"), Fort Nelson, and the end of that historic road at Dawson Creek. From there we drove back to Prince George where we retraced that portion of our route back to Seattle.

We didn't go anywhere that the average tourist can't get to just as easily, and if you wanted to, you could probably do this kind of trip in a month. We took three just because of the nature of the guidebook business. You can have a great Alaska vacation in two weeks, however, and we feel sure that the following pages will help you to do it.

NO INFLUENCE PEDDLING ALLOWED

Now, what is this guide really about—I mean, behind the scenes? Well, for one important thing, and unlike some other publications you can buy, there is absolutely no advertising in our book. You'll find plenty of strong opinions, though—all of them formed by myself and my wife and observant researcher, Sara. (Whenever we disagree, we'll let you know.) We have no ax to grind, and all the judgments expressed are designed to give you an idea on how best to spend your time and your money on a trip to Alaska and the Yukon.

Since the tourist industry is so aggressive and some travel writers through the ages have reportedly come in for their share of venality, it behooves us to be up front about any influences that may have been directed toward us. So let's face it: Producing entirely independent research for a major guidebook would prove prohibitively expensive for any author not independently wealthy. Which we're not.

We haven't added it all up yet, but our direct personal outlay for this book between June and August 1988, was somewhere in the neighborhood of $15,000 of our own funds, and it will be a good while before we make that back again. We might have done the work for less than half that figure if we had let our arms be twisted or our palms be greased, which we did not. On the other hand, we would surely have had to pay considerably more if we hadn't allowed ourselves to accept at least a little help on the basics.

Although we could have had a considerable number of free hotel rooms and free meals from establishments along the road, we chose to pay for these things ourselves, just as we shelled out for our leased car, the gasoline, and other associated expenses. We sometimes did accept a hotel's professional discount, as travel agents and others in the hospitality industry have done for many years. But most establishments we stayed in never knew what we were doing—except that after we paid the bill, we began asking detailed questions about their operation.

We did accept a few offers for complimentary or discounted short and long tours, partly on the theory that the excursion was going anyway and our participation represented no significant outlay for the company. Some of these tours included a night or two in a hotel and some food. We did a lot of flying and sailing, too. A little of this was free, some was at a discount, but most of it was paid for at full fare.

We also asked for and received some valuable assistance from the Alaska State Division of Tourism. Almost none of that represented any monetary savings. (They did get us a press discount on the state ferry.) Mostly their assistance was in cheerfully and ably fulfilling our request for information, introductions, and general guidance, but without any associated pressures or strings attached.

Every opinion in this book is honestly arrived at, and we have allowed no one to influence or interfere with our manuscript. We feel our standard of ethics will withstand scrutiny and is within the guidelines produced by the Society of American Travel Writers, an organization of which I am proud to have been a member for the past 10 years.

HELP WANTED

What about mistakes, bloopers, literary gremlins, and *faux pas*? We're sure you will find a few genuine Boners (along with a bad pun or two) in this book, since this is, after all, the first edition of a brand new guide. As ubiquitous as we tried to be throughout the Great Land last year, and as diligent as we were in noting down the experiences of other tourists we met along the way, it turned out (as it always does) to be just impossible to do everything we wanted to do. Like the baseball manager who says "wait until next year," the writer of a guidebook always looks forward to correcting items that are wrong, misleading or just plain out of date in subsequent editions of the same volume.

For this reason, we would like to enlist the aid of all readers and fellow travelers: After your own trip to Alaska and/or the Yukon, please write to use in care of the publishers and tell us something of your experiences. Cut out the special pages at the end of this book if you want, or we will happily accept and devour reams of your own stationery. This is your opportunity to contribute something to the next edition of this guidebook and pass on some good advice to future travelers.

We are particularly proud of this book and the opportunity it represents for us to rejoin the Fielding family of travel guides after 18 years. Prior to 1968, my experience was extensive as an employee in newspaper, magazine, and book publishing. But that year, I was seduced by the call of travel book writing by the late Temple Fielding himself, joining his European staff and remaining there until 1971. I am happy that I took my apprenticeship in this special field then, learning of its intricacies in Mallorca at the master's elbow. Temp taught this faithful apprentice how to look at restaurants, how to inspect hotels, and how to recognize watered-down Scotch. In the interest of literary style, he led me away from hackneyed travel adjectives like "picturesque" and "quaint"; he never permitted phrases like the "rosy fingers of dawn" or "a city of contrasts in a land of enchantment."

I remember fondly and gratefully Temp's guidance and patience. I know I have profited from this in nearly every way, and I apologize to his spirit today only for failing utterly to learn to mix a good martini.

THE LIVING LAND OF ALASKA

In a state full of surprises, probably the biggest one of all is simply its immensity. Alaska encompasses more than 586,000 square miles, which makes it one fifth the size of the rest of the U.S.A.—bigger than Texas, California, and Montana, the next three largest states, all rolled into one humongous chunk of real estate.

A favorite textbook trick is to superimpose the map of Alaska over that of the "Lower 48." In this unlikely position, it would stretch from coast to coast and border to border—the panhandle touching the shore of South Carolina while the Aleutian Islands brush Mexico and stretch along the beaches of Southern California. The north coast of Alaska would come up to the northern border of the U.S. at Minnesota. The body of the state would then cover a large part of the Midwest, and if you wanted to play with topography a little more, you could move up a map of Texas and drop it pretty neatly into the Alaska portion of this same map, with a lot left over.

In square miles, Alaska is more than twice the size of Texas and a decade ago, when crews of boisterous Texans came up to Alaska to help build the trans–Alaska Pipeline, Alaskan workers would jokingly threaten them: "We just might split Alaska in half, and that'll make Texas the third largest state instead of only the second!"

Alaskans are also fond of pointing out that theirs is not only the northernmost, but also the westernmost and easternmost of all the states, 180° longitude, which is supposed to mark the division between the Eastern and the Western hemispheres, cuts right through the Aleutians. This makes an obscure Aleutian island (Semisopochnoi), just left of that meridian, supposedly the easternmost point in the country. (The international dateline, which also should follow 180°, has been artificially jogged for international convenience.) By this logic, you might think the westernmost point would turn out to be the next island this side of the 180-degree line in the same chain. Instead, it is considered to be the interesting island called Little Diomede much farther north in the Bering Sea.

The island of Little Diomede is within easy sight of the island of Big Diomede, about three miles away across the Bering Strait. Little Diomede, of course, is American, Big Diomede is part of Soviet Siberia. The strait is frozen solid between the two islands in the winter, and although no one likes to talk about it much, it is crossed informally on occasion by parties of Eskimos hunting polar bears and walruses. A few other Americans who have tried it as a stunt in recent years have been arrested, either by Russian or American authorities.

If you don't subscribe to the 180th meridian point of view on what is west, the westernmost point in the U.S. is Attu Island, at the end of the Aleutians, and the easternmost is certainly a point on the coast of Maine. In any case, a favorite bar bet is sometimes won by those sober enough to know that Nome is farther west than Honolulu.

Alaska also used to cut across four time zones, but all that's been changed. Now, most parts of Alaska have only a single time zone, making it a lot easier for business and government to operate. Alaska Time is one hour earlier than Pacific Coast Time, whether you live in Ketchikan or Kotzebue. St. Lawrence Island and a few outposts at the end of the Aleutians are on Hawaii-Aleutian Time, another hour earlier. The Yukon Territory and British Columbia are on Pacific Time.

For all its vast acreage, Alaska is still amazingly empty, with 99% of the state still unpopulated. It totals a little over a half-million people, or less than one soul per square mile. (At the other extreme, New Jersey somehow manages to support an average of 1000 in the same space.) If you want to win another wager, you can easily show that Alaska is both the largest and smallest state—largest in area and smallest in the number of human beings who call it home.

REGIONAL DESIGNATIONS OF ALASKA

Alaska is also one of the most oddly shaped states in the Union, and we *cheechakos* sometimes have trouble getting a handle on it. It is generally accepted that there are six different geographic areas.

What outsiders often refer to as "the panhandle" Alaskans prefer to call **Southeast.** That's the slim finger of real estate alongside Canada which points toward the rest of the U.S. About 700 miles long, Southeast Alaska consists of about a thousand forested islands (the Alexander Archipelago) and many mountainous peninsulas, all separated by saltwater channels—looking like a "broken jigsaw puzzle," according to one writer. Although Southeast averages about 100 miles in width, it is only 15 miles at the mountainous point where it joins with the major portion of Alaska. There are seven important communities in the panhandle, all of them reached by the state ferry service and sometimes by visiting cruise ships. Among them is *Juneau,* the charming if somewhat hemmed-in capital of the state. Others are *Sitka,* the Russian and first American capital; *Ketchikan,* the wettest and southernmost settlement; *Wrangell,* the only town that was once British; *Petersburg,* settled by Norwegians; and *Haines* and *Skagway,* two Southeast cities that are connected to Canada and the rest of North America by road. (No road goes from Southeast Alaska into the rest of the state without passing through Canada.)

The balance of Alaska is the giant peninsula with the incredibly crenulated shoreline that most readily comes to mind for most who have not yet been to the state. Folks who live in Southeast sometimes call the rest of Alaska simply "the Interior," although traditionally it is divided into the five additional regions with sometimes varying names, and certainly inexact boundaries.

Southcentral is the generally accepted term used to describe that portion which immediately connects with Southeast. It includes the well-populated Kenai Peninsula and Kodiak Island plus the area of Alaska that immediately surrounds Anchorage, the state's largest city. Most of today's paved highways are in Southcentral.

Farther west is the strung-out area that composes the Alaska Peninsula, extending throughout the 200 wind-swept Aleutian Islands which separate the Pacific Ocean from the Bering Sea. It is often dubbed **Southwest Alaska,** and west of Katmai, anyway, it is seldom visited by casual travelers.

Jumping to the extreme north, that portion of Alaska which is generally above the Arctic Circle is usually known simply as the **Arctic,** but sometimes as the Far North or Northern Alaska, and is notably marked by the towns of Barrow and Deadhorse (Prudhoe Bay) on the North Slope. Deadhorse/Prudhoe is the only part of Arctic Alaska that is reached by an overland highway.

The huge portion of the state between the Arctic and Southcentral is often arbitrarily split in two. The eastern part, next to the Yukon Territory, is known as the **Interior,** and Fairbanks is its principal city. If you drive from Fairbanks to Anchorage, you enter Southcentral at about Denali National Park, which is more or less midway between the two cities.

The rest of the state, to the left on your map, is sometimes called the Bering District or **Western Alaska,** and its more well-known settlements are Nome and Kotzebue, both destinations reached only by regular air service—or by dog sled. As the saying goes, "No roads lead to Nome."

Be aware that there are arguments about these approximate boundaries. Some people call the Seward Peninsula part of Western Alaska and others say it's in the Arctic. We make no apologies for any inconsistencies in regional terminology; we didn't make these things up. We do feel obligated to pass them on since they are in general use and so you might know which area people are talking about.

MOUNTAIN MAJESTIES

Alaska also turns out to have the tallest point in North America. The twin-peaked mountain the Indians called Denali ("Great One"), known to most of us as Mount McKinley, is over 20,000 feet high. It is now the centerpiece of Denali National Park (formerly Mt. McKinley National Park).

To some, mountains are the dominant characteristics of Alaska. Although there is plenty of flat and rolling country, there always seem to be mountains on the horizon. There are four main ranges and, conveniently for Alaskan schoolchildren to remember, each is about 600 miles long except for the last, which stretches for a thousand miles farther than that.

Mt. McKinley is only one of several well-known summits in the curving Alaska Range, which separates Anchorage and Southcentral from Fairbanks and the Interior. The Alaska Range also forms a weather barrier that causes temperatures to be milder around Anchorage than the extremes often felt in the Fairbanks area. To the south, it connects with the St. Elias Mountains and the Coast Range, the natural wall which separates Southeast Alaska from Canada and which also ensures that the panhandle communities cannot be connected to the rest of North America by road.

The Brooks Range is the line of mountains north of the Arctic Circle that cut off the rest of Alaska from the treeless tundra of the North Slope. It stretches for 600 miles, from the Arctic Ocean to the Canadian border. The last major group is the Aleutian Range which joins with the Alaska Range at about Katmai National Park and then extends some 1600 miles down the Alaska Peninsula into the Aleutian Islands. The range contains about 80 volcanoes along its length, more than half of them considered active.

The dominant range over in the Yukon Territory is the Mackenzie Mountains, which extend from Alaska's Brooks Range. Generally speaking, they separate the Yukon from the Northwest Territories and eventually join with the Canadian Rockies. Others you may see in the Yukon include the Ogilvie Mountains near Dawson City and the Pelly Mountains near Whitehorse.

Of course there are smaller ranges, and ranges within ranges. In Anchorage you'll hear a lot about the Chugach Mountains, a smaller set of peaks near the city. The famous Wrangell Mountains and the St. Elias Mountains are in the area where the Alaska Range blends into the Coast Range (many are in Wrangell-Saint Elias National Park). There are thousands of mountains in Alaska and the Yukon, many of which no one has ever gotten around to naming.

RIVERS AND LAKES

More than 3000 rivers cut through Alaska alone, by some counts. Most famous, of course, is the **Yukon River,** which begins in a group of lakes just south of Whitehorse in the Yukon Territory. After wandering for nearly 2000 miles, it culminates in three different mouths at the Bering Sea. Much of the Yukon flows through territory that is still wild. In Dawson City you might meet a young woman who runs a dress shop and who, with her husband, once drifted along the entire length of the Yukon. She said the float was really duck soup compared to some other raft excursions in the north.

Rivers were important highways in the history of the north and they still serve that purpose today, even though the genuine old stern-wheelers are only a memory (although you will see a few non-functioning museum pieces). Fairbanks was built near the confluence of the **Chena** and **Tanana** rivers. These, the Yukon, and many rivers of the Interior freeze on the surface in winter time. The town of Nenana on the Tanana River south of Fairbanks is the site of the famous spring breakup lottery called the Nenana Ice Classic. Millions are bet annually on the precise date and time that the ice will break and the Tanana River will begin to flow again.

There are 3 million lakes in the State of Alaska, believe it or not. The largest is **Lake Iliamna,** near Katmai National Park. If it seems to show up as just a little blue blob on the map, remember, that's because the whole darn state is so large. Lake Iliamna measures a mere 3000 square miles, and allegedly hides its own Loch Iliamna Monster.

Lakes are also dotted here and there throughout much of the Yukon. Long, thin **Kluane Lake** borders the Alaska Highway. You'll see the famous **Lake Labarge** (the same poetic "Lake Labarge" on whose "marge" Sam McGee was allegedly cremated) just north of Whitehorse on the Klondike Highway.

GLACIERS

Aside from bears, visitors to Alaska seem to come home talking about glaciers more than anything else (and you'll see a lot more glaciers than you will bears). A trip to many parts of Alaska can easily include a visit to a majestic field of slow-moving ice. Cruises along the Inside Passage or short trips from Juneau visit famous **Glacier Bay,** which boasts a score or more (although it is not on the state ferry route). Another dramatic glacier seen on some Southeast cruises is the *Le Conte* Glacier, between Wrangell and Petersburg. Just south of Anchorage you can easily drive to the *Portage* Glacier, or take a short cruise to see dozens of them on Prince William Sound. There are imposing glaciers that seem to suddenly appear beside the road on the Glenn Highway near Palmer (the *Matanuska*) or on the Richardson Highway near Valdez (the *Worthington*). Landing in Juneau on a clear day gives air passengers a magnificent view of the *Mendenhall* Glacier, just outside the airport (sit on the left).

Glaciers are rivers of ice, but they are not merely rivers which have been frozen into ice. Glaciers really have little to do with cold weather, and you will find few glaciers in the really cold parts of Alaska because it doesn't rain or snow enough there. They are nearly all along the warm, moist coastal areas of Southcentral and Southeast, and you'll see them there winter and summer.

Simply stated, glaciers are created wherever snow-fall exceeds snow-melt. Over time the packed snow becomes an unusually dense type of ice, containing almost no air, and under some circumstances this results in spots which feature a dramatic deep lapis lazuli color, particularly noticeable where some of the glacier has just broken away from the main body, and more so on cloudy days (dense ice absorbs all colors but blue). Because of its high density, glacial ice also doesn't melt in quite the same way as other ice. Lately, Japanese visitors with enough disposable income to throw around have been buying pieces of Alaskan glaciers and shipping them home, where it has become a fad to use it in mixed drinks. It lasts longer, and the resulting snap, crackle, and pop makes it a distinctive cocktail conversation piece.

Alaskans claim they have 28,800 square miles of active glaciers and ice fields—more than in the rest of the inhabited world—and that more than half the state's fresh water is imprisoned in glaciers. One Alaska glacier, the *Malaspina* Glacier, near the tiny Indian village of Yakutat, is larger than the entire state of Rhode Island.

Although they appear static, glaciers are always flowing slowly forward, fed by snow high up and propelled toward lower elevations simply by their own weight. They scour and reshape the landscape as they go, usually into distinctive U-shaped valleys. They are often said to be either "advancing" or "retreating." A retreating glacier is one which melts more quickly at its face than it is replenished by snowfall at the source. An advancing glacier is the opposite. Glacier Bay has been created over the centuries by the most rapid glacial retreat ever recorded, although even there some individual glaciers within the ice field are advancing. The once-dramatic *Columbia* Glacier in Prince William Sound near Valdez has retreated so drastically in the past few years that it is no longer easy to appreciate it from cruise ships, which can no longer approach it closely.

It's difficult to put into words the attraction of glaciers. John Muir, the great naturalist who first explored Glacier Bay, simply dubbed it "a picture of icy wildness unspeakably pure and sublime." In some ways they seem to be a slice of time—like a still photograph of a massive, living, moving thing. And there are so many variations in size, shape, even color. You'll see tidewater glaciers releasing great chunks of ice ("calving") into the ocean, creating a thunderous roar and a massive wave. Some of these icebergs are adopted as temporary floating platforms by eagles and seals. Glaciers often extend farther underwater, and sometimes a large piece breaks off underneath the water and then suddenly bobs to the surface next to an observation vessel. If that happens to you, we guarantee you'll never forget it!

CLIMATE AND SEASONS

"Sure, Alaska has four seasons," the know-it-all will tell you: "June, July, August, and winter." (Another version is "winter, breakup, summer, and September.") For much of Alaska, at least in the population centers, these are merely harmless exaggerations, but a lot of what you hear is just plain false. In fact, there is probably more misinformation blowing around about weather and climate in Alaska than anywhere else in the U.S. Members of the "Great White North" school believe that Alaska is little more than a frozen wasteland, and of course that's incorrect. Then there are others who fall into the enthusiastic no-holds-barred civic booster category. They claim with a straight face that weatherwise, most of Alaska is pretty much, well, like any other state in the temperate zone. That's not true, either.

If you visit Alaska and the Yukon in the summer, you will probably not find yourself in snow at all, although you may see it daily on nearby mountains and hills, perhaps some of it falling overnight. Temperatures can be hot, but mostly they are not. Generally speaking, we try to prepare ourselves for daytime readings that might reach the 80s and 90s, but are most often in the 50s and 60s. Fall does come on fast, however. You may be surprised to see leaves on aspen, willow, and birch trees begin to turn yellow in August.

It can rain a lot, particularly in Southeast and especially in the late summer. Ketchikan is one of the wettest spots on earth as a matter of fact, although even there it can often alternate between rain and sun several times in the same day. They say a lot of Ketchikan's rain falls at night, but then there really isn't much of a night to speak of anywhere up north in the months of June, July, and August. Statistically speaking, throughout Alaska you'll find your driest days in May and June.

If you visit these northern areas in the winter, you could be in for some wonderful experiences. First of all, for those folks brought up on the "nation's icebox" theory, it's a revelation just to find out that you can travel to the area and around the countryside in the winter. Except in extreme and unusual conditions, the planes fly, the trains roll, and the roads are well plowed, if needed. In the major centers, anyway, life goes on pretty much as it does in wintry areas Outside. Hertz in Anchorage does not yet need to operate a rent-a-sled business, even if tour companies do offer some exciting dog mushing experiences.

Temperatures of 40 and 50 below? Sure, that happens all right, usually in the same Interior areas that experience the high extremes in the summer. Fairbanks residents who leave their cars out at night can have problems. Even if they've plugged their electric engine warmer into the house current so the engine block won't crack and the oil won't freeze, they still might find their car clumping away in the morning, driving on "square tires." Alaska's highest and lowest temperature records to date were both set at points on or near the Arctic Circle. It was 100° at Fort Yukon on June 27, 1915. And the official all-time low is 80° below zero set at Prospect Creek on Jan. 23, 1971. (It has certainly been colder than that—probably as recently as 1989 during the "Omega Block" monster cold wave that numbed most of the state in January. Nevertheless, the official National Weather Service thermometers simply won't register anything lower than 80 below!)

Technically, there are three or four climate zones in Alaska, depending on who's counting. The *maritime* areas are the mildest (warm in the summer, cool in the winter), with more than their share of rain or snow. This includes most of Southeast, Southcentral, and Southwest. All three areas are warmed by the Japan Current, a stream of warm water which moves up from the Pacific. And because warm, moist air condenses at higher, cooler altitudes, you can often find new snowfall on nearby mountains even during the summer while residents are running around in shirt sleeves down at sea level. In the Southeast "banana belt," yearly average temperatures are considered comparable to those in Philadelphia. Only rarely do they go down to zero in the winter.

The dry *continental* zone covers most of the Interior and Western Alaska, with high temperature extremes in the summer and low ones in the winter, and not much precipitation at any time of year. (Kids in Fairbanks complain that the dry snow they do get is too fluffy and flimsy to be packed into snowballs.) In areas where the permafrost (permanently frozen ground) does not exist or begins at depths of over four feet below the surface, there is usually room enough for some trees to develop a root system.

Then there's the *Arctic* zone north of the Brooks Range, which is affected mostly by winds blowing across the Polar Ice Cap. It has the least amount of precipitation in the state (8 to 12 inches yearly), but when it does get rain or snow, it hangs around for quite a while. Rain can't soak into the permafrost, and the snow will blow hither and yon without melting until spring. Winter temperatures may drop to a maximum of $-25°$ or so, not as severe as those in the Interior since the Arctic Ocean has a somewhat ameliorating influence on the cold.

Some also describe a narrow *transition* zone, dividing the maritime from the continental areas. Anchorage would fall into that category, since it is protected by the Alaska range from the cold-hot extremes of the continental zone, yet it's much dryer than areas in the maritime zone. The coastal areas of Western Alaska, including Nome and Kotzebue, are also considered to be in the transition zone since they do not experience the extremes of the Interior.

THE MIDNIGHT SUN AND DARKNESS AT NOON

For many the differentiating characteristic of summer and winter in Alaska and the Yukon is simply the amount of light available—apparently too much in the summer and not enough in the winter—caused by the tilt of the earth's axis in relation to the sun. The **Arctic Circle** is a line which defines those areas where the sun refuses to rise above the horizon for at least one 24-hour period in the winter or to completely drop below the horizon for a day or more in the summer.

For most residents of the Arctic Zone (who live considerably above the Arctic Circle), the phenomenon lasts for much longer than a day. In Barrow, for example, after the sun rises on May 10 it doesn't set again until August 2, providing about 80 days of uninterrupted daylight as it circles the horizon. As the old song goes, ''that lucky old sun just rolls around heaven all day.''

However, the northernmost town in the U.S. must look forward to a relatively dark Christmas. After about three months of comparatively normal operations, the Barrow sun comes up for only 16 minutes on November 19 and then refuses to show itself again until January 23. Not that all of these days are completely black, of course. At its lowest point, the sun is only 4½ degrees below the horizon in Barrow. A twilight glow low in the southern sky marks the midday period for most far-northern areas, and there is enough light for most outdoor activities. Also, moonlight is reflected from the surrounding snow, and the dramatic green-and-red shimmering-curtain effect called the Northern Lights can be seen most often in winter skies. These are caused by a complicated series of events involving the ionization of the upper atmosphere. (Incidentally, the Northern Lights should be at their best and brightest in 1989 and 1990, scientists say.)

The Arctic Circle is generally considered to be at 66 degrees, 33 minutes North Latitude. That's less than 100 miles north of Fairbanks, and if you fly or float to the historic village of Fort Yukon (on the Yukon River), you'll be right on the line. Many travelers to Alaska never find themselves that far north, but that doesn't mean they won't experience long summer days or short winter ones. The midnight baseball game celebrating the summer solstice is played at Fairbanks on June 20 or 21. The sun sets about 10 minutes before midnight and rises again at about 2:00 a.m. The light never completely leaves the sky between dusk and dawn—no artificial illumination needed to play ball. Even in Southeast, we usually found ourselves clothespinning the hotel room curtains closed in order to get to sleep.

Many in Alaska and the Yukon say they do not need nearly as much sleep in the summer as in the winter. Some scientists now back that up, claiming that man's mysterious pineal gland makes some chemical adjustment in order to compensate for the additional light the body is exposed to. There seems no end to the tricks played on your psyche by the extended summer daylight. It often seems that Alaskan and Yukon stores are always closed. That's because it's often later than we think it is. We'd drive to a shopping mall without using our headlights and be surprised to find locked doors. Looking at our watch, we'd discover it was after 9 p.m.!

After a summer in Alaska and the Yukon, it was strange to us to return suddenly to the world Outside where the skies were actually dark after dinner. At times it seemed a little like going blind when we discovered we could no longer go sightseeing at midnight. We also realized after returning home that we hadn't noticed a moon in three months.

In Anchorage we also met a charming 8-year-old young lady named Samantha Mason, who was amazed to find that the Fourth of July fireworks could be so colorful—at her grandparents' home in California. She had not previously seen pyrotechnics shot off against a sky which was dark enough to provide a suitable contrast for the display.

If you're going camping in Alaska in the summer, you could save a little weight in your pack. Many Alaskans don't bother bringing a flashlight. (Actually, that's not a good idea since it will be dark under the trees or in your tent.)

VOLCANOES, EARTHQUAKES, AND TIDAL WAVES

Southcentral and Southwest Alaska are situated on the Pacific Ring of Fire (or "Rim" of Fire), the same geologically unstable portion of the earth's crust that has caused many volcanic eruptions and earthquakes in places so widely separated as Japan, Indonesia, New Zealand, and California. Indeed, some consider Alaska to be the most volatile land mass on the globe. The Aleutian chain, especially, is often shaken by seismic tremors, even if most of them are not strong enough to be widely felt. In 1912 a mountain on the Alaska Peninsula blew its top, darkening the sky for days and changing the face of the landscape for a hundred miles around (today the area is Katmai National Park). In 1987 Mt.

Augustine, a volcanic island in nearby Cook Inlet, erupted violently, throwing out ash for several days.

The great Good Friday Earthquake of 1964, centered in Prince William Sound, killed 115 people in Anchorage, Homer, Seward, Valdez, and Cordova. Some of them were along the coast and succumbed to the seismic sea wave (tsunami) which was generated by the quake. One of these giant waves even traveled down to California where it took more lives on a beach in Crescent City.

In 1958 an earthquake created a tsunami that reached 1740 feet high, the largest ever known. It scoured all the dirt and vegetation up to that height on mountains surrounding an obscure coastal inlet (Lituya Bay), in a sparsely populated area of Southeast Alaska west of Glacier Bay. Four square miles of forest completely disappeared, and its effects can still be seen there today—more than 30 years later!

MINERALS, ROCKS, AND NATURAL RESOURCES

Everyone knows about Alaska's *gold,* and despite the tons taken out of the ground around the turn of the century, there is still a lot of the precious metal still in the north country. However, it is generally being mined by the sifting of large quantities of dirt by large companies with large investments in equipment, land, and labor. Any tourist who gives gold panning a whirl will usually come up with a few flakes, but they are not likely to pay for the trip. A few determined prospectors do earn a meager living with small sluice operations while dreaming about coming across a new glory hole. Occasionally it happens.

The state also still has deposits of *copper, nickel, uranium, lead, zinc* and other ores in commercial quantities. Alaska is also the only state currently producing *platinum*.

In recent years, of course, fossil fuels have become the new "black gold" of Alaska, particularly *crude oil,* since the discovery of large deposits at Prudhoe Bay and elsewhere on the North Slope. The trans–Alaska Pipeline carries 2 million barrels of oil per day from Prudhoe Bay for 800 miles to the ice-free port of Valdez. The North Slope does not have the only oil wells, however. Oil is also being recovered from the Kenai Peninsula and from offshore operations including the platforms in Cook Inlet, not far from Anchorage.

Several wells producing *natural gas* are also dotted across the state, and there are plans to build a new trans–Alaska Pipeline to carry gas deposits also pumped from the North Slope. Perhaps half of the unmined *coal* left in the United States may be found in Alaska; a lot of it still buried underneath the North Slope oil fields. Whereas federal law prevents Alaskan oil from being sold abroad, no such restrictions affect gas and coal and these resources are regularly sold to foreign markets like Japan and Korea.

A certain number of precious stones are found in Alaska, although seldom by amateurs. North of the Arctic Circle several types of *jade*—the official state gem—are uncovered, among other places, at a place called Jade Mountain near Kotzebue. (Don't miss the jade staircase in the lobby of the Sheraton Anchorage.) Dedicated rock hounds sometimes do pick up some types of *quartz* (agate, chert, jasper, and flint), and finds of such things as *soapstone* (solid talc used for Eskimo carvings), fragile black *argillite* (used for Haida carvings), *garnet* (found and sold by the Boy Scouts in Wrangell), *sapphire,* and *marble* are common enough.

FORESTS AND FLOWERS

Far and away, the dominant color of Alaska and the Yukon is green—even in winter, since most trees are evergreens. If you don't know one **tree** from another at home, you'll soon learn at least one here—the seemingly ubiquitous *spruce* tree. (We say "seemingly" because of course you won't find trees of any kind in some areas, like the storm-swept Aleutians or on the North Slope tundra. Tundra, from a Finnish word, means "treeless.") Spruce vary from the decorative blue-green Christmas tree-ish Sitka Spruce, a stately specimen which is also the official Alaska state tree, to the spindly black spruce with root systems shallow enough to exist in areas where permafrost lies just a few feet below the surface of the ground. One type of small spruce even manages to survive in muskeg, the acidic bogs found throughout Alaska and northern Canada.

Often battling it out with spruce for dominance of the forests are different types of *hemlock* trees (in the vast majority in Southeast Alaska). Third on the list are the handsome *cedar* trees, favored by Southeast Indians as the raw stock for totem poles. Several types of spruce, hemlock, and cedar form the basis for an active timber industry, especially in the panhandle. Much of it is shipped to Japan.

Other commercial trees include *alpine fir,* a high-altitude evergreen; *aspen* (the "trembling aspen" quivers with the slightest breeze); *balsam,* or balsam poplar; *birch,* which has that distinctive red-brown or creamy white bark; and *cottonwood,* whose fluffy seeds blow all over the place about June. The only Alaska-Yukon native pine tree is the *lodgepole pine,* once used by Indians for their teepees (also called the shore pine). The most common deciduous tree in Alaska is the *alder,* a relative of the birch sometimes used for Indian carvings. Smoke from alder fire has long been popular for cooking or smoking fish and game. Some varieties of *willow* trees (but generally not the "weeping" kind) are found in several parts of the state. Along with aspen and birch, tender willow shoots are also a favorite food for moose. The *mountain ash* is often called Alaska's most colorful tree since it produces bright white flowers in June and July and red berries in the fall.

There are two official national forests in Alaska. The **Tongass National Forest** occupies 80% of the panhandle, virtually every place not taken by community or private property. A total of about 17 million acres, it is the nation's largest. The **Chugach National Forest** stretches along much of the coastline south of Anchorage and counts about 6 million acres. Both are managed by the U.S. Forest Service, which supervises the timber harvest there. The USFS also maintains recreational cabins in these areas that can be rented for $15 a night—one of the best accommodation deals in Alaska, *if* you can get a reservation and *if* you can get to them (usually by chartered plane). There is currently considerable debate, both in Alaska and in Washington, over the amount of logging that should be allowed in the two national forests, particularly the Tongass. As usual it pits environmentalists against industry leaders, both of whom claim to speak for the greater good of the country.

Alaskans seem to love **flowers** more than anyone, and if you visit Anchorage during the summer you'll see hundreds of varieties of brilliant blooms, started during cold weather in hot houses, but now transplanted all over the downtown area. In places where permafrost or other ground problems exist, flower pots are hung from lamp posts, under eaves, and in other unlikely places. Similar projects take place in other towns and cities throughout the state.

Besides the traditional varieties of bright posies you might find anywhere else in the U.S., the state also springs forth with wildflowers during the warm months. Dominating the northern landscape during spring, summer, and fall is the ubiquitous *fireweed,* the official territorial flower of the Yukon. Its lavender/pink blooms start out at the bottom of the stalk and proceed to the top just before summer ends and fall begins. (In a pinch, fireweed is completely edible, but some other flowers and berries are poisonous.) Alaska's state flower is the *forget-me-not,* a five-petaled blue blossom with a gold center that seems to match the colors on the state flag.

Some of the flowers we have found often and enjoy in Alaska include the fluffy white *cotton grass,* the odoriferous yellow bloom called the *skunk cabbage* (which is the first sign of spring in some areas), the purplish *bistort,* the buttercup-like *yellow anemone,* several types of *poppies* (including the Arctic poppy), the *alpine arnica* (and other kinds of arnica), several kinds of *saxifrage,* the pretty but poisonous *lupine* (which means wolf, by the way), the well-named *prickly wild rose,* bright-red bushes of *strawberry blite,* the widely distributed *mountain harebell,* which has small blue bell-shaped blooms, and some kinds of *violet.*

Also, the celery-like *cow parsnip* (also called *pushki*—a Russian word—and often eaten by bears as much as cows), the *alpine azalea,* some types of *primrose,* the snapdragon-like *monkey flower,* many kinds of *lousewort,* the daisy-like *fleabane,* and several others. (If you like close-up flower photography, be sure to keep good notes or you'll never keep your slides straight.) We found it handy to buy a couple of wild-flower handbooks, notably the *Alaska-Yukon Wild Flowers Guide,* published by *Alaska* magazine. We ended up pressing and drying some of our flowers using that book, too. Also recommended is a University of Alaska publication, *Wild Edible and Poisonous Plants of Alaska,* which you can get at a nominal charge from the State Forest Service.

FISH STORIES

You can have all your glaciers, mountains, pipelines, rocks, flowers, and gold nuggets and enjoy them to the fullest. But the fact remains that many who travel to Alaska and the Yukon do so primarily to find something often very rare in civilized areas of the world—wildlife—whether to hunt, to catch, to eat, to photograph, or just to watch.

The fish that dominates life in Alaska is that wonderful—and delicious—specimen called the *salmon.* Generally speaking, salmon hatch in fresh water, move downstream to spend most of their life in the ocean, and then return to their exact birth spot to spawn just before they die. The schools of anadromous salmon battling their way upstream against rapids and waterfalls and other obstacles is one of the most dramatic sights in nature.

Many change color to become brilliant red, pink, copper, or even black as they make their way against the current. Salmon hatched near the head waters of the Yukon River make an incredible 2000-mile return trip home from the Bering Sea, a journey they usually complete in 60 days. (You can watch these hardy creatures climb the fish ladder at Whitehorse.) They also do not feed during the long spawning migration.

There are five different types of salmon in Alaskan waters, even though there are several different confusing names for them. Some of these terms depend on whether they are male or female and on what stage of development they may be in when they are caught. The most magnificent of the salmon is of course the *king,* the official state fish which has been honored also by having an Alaskan town named after it. It is also often called the "chinook," and is prized for its delicious if oily flesh. In Alaska, adult king salmon usually exceed 30 pounds, and the record catch was a 126-pound monster in 1949. Some may not return from the ocean to spawn until they are seven years old.

The second largest salmon is the *coho,* also popularly referred to as the "silver," and its flesh is somewhat drier than either king or sockeye salmon. Mature coho salmon weigh from 10 to 26 pounds.

During the spawning stage, the males develop a particularly ugly hooked snout with large teeth. In the ocean and on the fisherman's hook, they are known as spectacular fighters.

Alaska's third salmon is the *sockeye,* also known as the "red" salmon. It has long been regarded as an important commercial harvest in Alaskan coastal waters, although it's considered a difficult catch for sport fishermen. (The world's largest harvest of sockeye is annually taken from Bristol Bay.) Adult specimens of this glassy-eyed creature have a certain amount of a deep dark-red color on their sides. Mature sockeyes weigh about 4 to 8 pounds, but catches up to 15 pounds have been recorded. A land-locked version of sockeye is called "Kokanee."

Also numerous are the *pink* salmon, also popularly known as "hump backs" or "humpies" because of the distinctive shape on the male at spawning season. They average about 3 to 5 pounds at maturity and have light-colored flesh. The most modest of the Alaskan salmon is generally known as the *chum.* It is usually dried for winter use, and is also called "dog salmon" since it was traditionally fed to sled dog teams during cold weather. They are sometimes given the name "calico salmon" since they boast a green-and-purple pattern on their skin at one point in their life cycle.

Some other types of popular game fish in Alaska include the *Arctic char,* which weigh at least 10 pounds; the *Dolly Varden* ("Dollies"), another type of char usually lighter in color with yellow or red spots (and named after a Dickens character); the *rainbow trout,* also known as the "steelhead" under some conditions; the *cutthroat trout,* named for the red streaks under its chin, which weigh in at between 1 and 4 pounds; the very popular *grayling* (or arctic grayling), recognized by its large sail-like dorsal fin; the *eulachon,* also known as the easier-to-pronounce "hooligan"; the mean-looking *northern pike,* sometimes called the "water wolf"; the light-spotted *lake trout,* or "lakers," for which 20 pounds is considered trophy size; the coarse-scaled *sheefish* ("inconnu"), which also put up quite a fight; and the *burbot,* the only freshwater cod in Alaska.

Bottomfish, a term generally referring to any fish not related to salmon or trout whether it lives on the bottom or not, are also found in Alaska. One of the most delicious catches in the state is the Pacific *halibut,* a type of flounder which can run hundreds of pounds, although most tip the scales at around 50. Some cooks say halibut is just as good frozen as it is fresh, but that's a rationalization. The commercial season is so limited that unless you catch your own, you are unlikely to have fresh halibut. Fortunately there are several fishing charter operations that can help, notably in Homer during the summer. The halibut is the flat fish with an eye which gradually migrates to a position on the same side of the head as its other eye.

Other types of bottomfish caught in Alaska include the tasty *lingcod*, including subspecies called the "red snapper" or "yelloweye rockfish;" the *rockfish*, of which there are several kinds, known by several different names; and *pollock*, another wall-eyed species that is important to commercial fishing.

Visitors to Alaska who want to fish had better hire a guide or learn a lot more than we've been able to go into here. Although much of the best fishing is done from boats, there are special places where you can do just as well from shore. If you're going only for trophy size you can take advantage of the state's "catch and release" program, in which you throw back healthy fish in order not to use up your limit before catching that one just right for the mantle. Fishing guides will take care of the license and other legal folderol. Or information and regulations on both fishing and hunting are available from the Alaska Department of Fish and Game, P.O. Box 3–2000, Juneau, AK 99802–2000; tel. *(907) 465–4270.*

There are other kinds of seafood alive, well, and available in Alaska. One particularly prized monster is the *king crab*, which used to be known as the "spider crab" until the Madison Avenue marketing boys got hold of it. Some harvested from Kodiak have a leg spread of 5 feet and weigh over 25 pounds. For a similar reason, *tanner crab* has been marketed as Alaskan snow crab in recent years. Then there's the *Dungeness crab*, also a delicacy. Lovers of crustaceans also would never let us forge the succulent *Petersburg shrimp*, especially identified with catches made in the Southeast village of Petersburg, but available, in season, at markets and restaurants in many parts of the state.

BIRDWATCHING IN THE NORTH

Alaska's most famous bird is the U.S.A.'s most famous bird, but which is almost impossible to find in the Lower 48. The *North American bald eagle* is healthy and numerous throughout Alaska, particularly in coastal regions, and you'll catch sight of some from the ferry or a cruise ship. The first time you come across one of these magnificent flying creatures at a distance, save your film. You'll probably have a closer encounter later. (Since they are scavengers, the local dump is often a good place to search out baldies.) The larger specimens are generally females. Immature eagles are completely brown and do not boast the white pate seen on the adults.

Often mistaken for a young baldy is an adult *golden eagle*. Look for the dark feathers on the front edge of the wing. (Admirers of the golden eagle say it is a hunter whereas the bald eagle is a scavenger.) You may also see a *white-tailed eagle*, which looks rather like a bald eagle with a hairpiece. A fourth type is called *Steller's sea eagle*.

Other birds of prey in Alaska include several types of *hawks* (okay— falcons, accipiters, harriers, buteos, and ospreys, if you insist on knowing everything) and *owls* (including the ground-nesting snowy owl). The Alaska Natural History Association publishes a handy pamphlet on identifying all these creatures.

The official state bird is the *willow ptarmigan*, a pheasantlike phellow who changes from a summer coat of light brown to a winter one of white. There are also a couple of other ptypes of ptarmigan, ptoo. Like many other visitors, we have had the most fun spotting *puffins*, that decorative big-beaked endomorph sometimes called the "sea parrot." You'll be an expert when you pick up one in your binoculars and can answer the question, "Is it 'horned' or 'tufted'?"

Other winged creatures we like include three or four types of *loons*, which give a plaintive cry; certain *cormorants*, especially those showoffs who stand up and dry their wings by unfolding them like Dracula's cape; several kinds of *geese*, notably the snow goose; lots of *ducks*, most of which we seem to confuse with one another (the King eider duck, with its bulbous orange crown, is a magnificent specimen); the *black oystercatcher* with its bright red bill; some kinds of *plovers* (which rhymes with "lovers"); *sandpipers* of incredible variations; *Steller's jay*, which has rich blue-black feathers and is also known as the "camp robber"; several *gulls*, including the raucous Glaucous and the red-legged kittiwake we found in the Pribilofs (both the kittiwake and the mew gulls are onomatopoetic—names for the sound they make; the *arctic tern*, a pelagic specimen which allegedly migrates the farthest in the world; a couple of *guillemots* (black and pigeon); some *auklets*, which are related to puffins; and a few others whose exact names are still buried somewhere in our notes. You will undoubtedly develop some favorites of your own.

Before leaving the bird category, we must not forget the common northern *raven*, which, if you haven't seen one before, will strike you as just the fattest, blackest, sassiest old crow you ever knew existed. Clever, too—ravens have been known to drop a stone near other feeding birds, then fly in to steal the food after the others flee. The Indians of the Yukon and Southeast Alaska have a particular reverence for the raven, whom they say created the entire world, and you might see both a carved one and a real one on top of a totem. It is also the official territorial bird of the Yukon.

AQUATIC MAMMALS

The biggest mammals of any kind summer in Alaska. The *humpback whales*, and sometimes *killer whales* (Orca), *blue whales* and other whales, may be seen along the inside the Inside Passage or even in Glacier Bay. The *bowhead whale*, known also as the "Arctic right whale," is still fair game for the Eskimos on the north coast of Alaska. The *gray whale* is another warm-weather visitor which must get out of the Arctic before freeze up, as anyone knows who followed the news from Barrow in 1988. *Beluga whales,* a distinctive white variety, often beach themselves when the tide runs out in Cook Inlet, but usually survive until the next incoming tide.

Dolphins are harder to see, but they are also spotted along the Inside Passage or in Prince William Sound. The black-and-white *Dall porpoise* looks much like the killer whale to many of us. Other types of marine mammals include *Steller sea lions,* which you might catch sight of from the Homer-Kodiak ferry; the *northern fur seal,* which you can watch hundreds of at St. Paul in the Pribilofs; the *harbor seal,* which we've seen resting on icebergs near glaciers; the *bearded seal,* the Arctic's largest; the *walrus,* a long-tusked creature hard to spot anywhere except on occasion at St. Lawrence Island; and the *sea otter,* that lovable, bewhiskered creature who floats on its back, sometimes while holding a baby otter on its tummy (look for them on Prince William Sound). Seals, sea otters, and other fur-bearing creatures, once hunted to the brink of extinction, are now protected by the Marine Mammal Protection Act.

BEAR FACTS

Probably most visitors to Alaska, when they think of wildlife let their heart speed up with a mixture of anticipation of and apprehension about their first encounter with a bear. In our own family, Sara sometimes seems to spend most of her waking hours in Alaska either being afraid that she might see a bear or that she might *not* see a bear.

Everyone who comes to Alaska, in the summer anyway, should see at least one bear on at least one occasion. And long before you do, you will probably hear a lot of advice on human/bear etiquette from a National Park ranger or other knowledgeable authority. We won't go into it all here, except to emphasize that the most dangerous thing you can do with a bear (besides trying to pet it, maybe) is to run from it. *Never run from a bear because it will almost surely respond by chasing you. And the bear can run a heck of a lot faster than you, no matter how frightened you are.*

Generally speaking, the approved technique is to talk calmly to the bear while backing slowly away: "Excuse me, Mr. Grizzly. I didn't realize this was your path to the salmon fishing area. Please be my guest and just let me step out of your way." Stuff like that. More than 99 times out of 100, the bear will respond by sniffing haughtily and heading off to take care of his own business, since bears basically are not interested in taking a bite out of a bad-tasting human being. Of course if you get between Mama Bear and her cubs, or if you are carrying something the bear considers delicious, look out. (Rangers and others in authority ask that you continue to hold on to your fish or other food so that the bear will not learn that the presence of humans means something to eat—a technique admittedly designed to help the next guy who comes along. Good luck!) If an attack by a bear does seem imminent, your final recourse is to curl up into the fetal position and play dead.

The best way to see a bear is the way we did it on three occasions last year—from a boat, from a car, or from a bus. We got plenty close enough by using a telephoto lens on the camera. Another valid technique to avoid bears is simply to make plenty of noise and thus avoid a dangerous sudden encounter at close range—an equal surprise for the bear as for you, and a situation in which the bear is apt to react violently. Some people wear small "bear bells" just for this purpose; others carry transistor radios or just sing, whistle, or talk loudly while walking in the wilderness.

Despite everything you hear, there are only three different types of bears in Alaska. The *black bear* is the smallest, relatively speaking, and is not always black, by the way. The "cinnamon bear" is a black bear going through its brown phase. And then there's the "glacier bear," a stage during which the fur appears light blue on bears living in the Glacier Bay area.

Black bears may look harmless, and usually they are, especially in areas where they are used to seeing people. In case you're thinking of shinnying up the nearest spruce, though, it's worth remembering that the forest-dwelling "blackie" is the only kind of Alaskan bear that can climb a tree if it has a mind to.

The much larger *brown bear* is the same animal as a grizzly bear (genus and species *Ursus horribilis*). When they live in the coastal areas of Alaska they are called "browns," and when they live in the Interior they are most often referred to as "grizzlies." The brown bear tends to be somewhat bigger than the grizzly mainly because it eats better with all that nutritious salmon readily available to it while grizzlies must fill up more often on berries. The black bear's greatest enemy is the grizzly in the few places where they exist together. A brownie can kill a blackie with one well-placed slap.

There's an old story in Alaska that goes: "Q: How do I know if it's a black bear or a brown bear? A: Climb a tree. Q: How will that help? A: If it's a black bear, it will follow you. If it's a brown bear, it will knock the tree down."

The biggest brown bears of all are those super-healthy specimens who live in the wilds of Kodiak Island. The so-called Kodiak bear can reach 10 feet or more, standing on his hind legs, and weigh over 1500 pounds. Bullets have been known to ricochet off their two-inch-thick skulls.

Again, brown bears are not always very brown. The three bears we saw in Denali National Park in 1988 were called Toklat bears, and their fur was almost blond or flesh-colored. Brownies or grizzlies are most readily recognized by their prominent shoulder hump, massive head, and rippling muscles. You might see grizzly or brown bears any place in Alaska, and you'll probably see them at Denali; but there are three specific observation areas for more dependable close-up views—(1) at a federal facility at Pack Creek on Admiralty Island, (2) at Brooks Camp in Katmai National Park, and (3) at the state-run McNeil River Sanctuary north of Katmai. You'll find more about these in the chapters that follow.

The only kind of northern bear which actually will hunt man is the *polar bear,* which can reportedly smell a human from 20 miles away. But don't cancel your plane tickets or sell your RV; the polar bear is the one bear you won't see in Alaska—not outside of the Anchorage Zoo, anyway. Polar bears, or *Ursus maritimus,* are literally that—they stay up on the polar ice cap, looking mainly for seals and coming to land very rarely in the coldest months. Unless you join an Eskimo hunting party out of someplace like Barrow or Little Diomede in February, forget it.

By the way, don't become confused by the pig nomenclature when someone begins talking about bears. The males are called boars, and the females are generally referred to as sows.

OTHER WARM-BLOODS

King of the deer family in Alaska is that massive creature that appears to have been designed by a committee, the *moose.* The Alaskan kind is the world's biggest Bullwinkle, standing seven foot high at his shoulder and often weighing more than a large bear—close to a ton, counting the 50-pound set of antlers on the males. Any moose can be dangerous if approached too closely, but avoid particularly any cow with a calf in the spring.

With their long, spindly, easily breakable legs, moose are regularly struck by automobiles. That's why you'll see the "moose fence" along part of the four-lane divided highway between Anchorage and Palmer. (Moose tend to concentrate along roads partly because frequent clearing of the roadway causes regular regeneration of small birch, aspen, and willow trees, all favorite moose food.) Moose and the Alaska Railroad are also often at loggerheads since the train right-of-way provides an accessible trail for the moose to use during the winter (more than 300 are killed along the track from November to April). No doubt many moose also perceive highways as a similar God-given convenience.

Other ungulates (hoofers) include the *caribou,* some of which migrate in large herds north of Fairbanks. There are about 600,000 caribou in Alaska, outnumbering the people population of the state. A domestic cousin is the *reindeer,* with which they will breed given half a chance. Reindeer were introduced from Lapland and Siberia in 1899, and some call a reindeer not much more than a caribou with a broken spirit. Caribou and reindeer are the only deer in which the females grow antlers. Their skin is used for Eskimo parkas. You will also occasionally find a type of *elk* (actually wapiti) on Kodiak Island, and *mule deer* (also known as the Sitka black-tailed deer) in the coastal rain forests of Southeast Alaska and British Columbia. Sometimes confused with each other are the long-haired *mountain goat*, which are white and live high up, and *Dall sheep*, which are about the same color and also head for the steepest hills possible.

Still more fuzzy creatures seen in greater or lesser degrees include the *wolf*, basically a shy and gentle creature (as far as man is concerned anyway—in Alaska he preys on deer, moose, caribou, and mice); the *wolverine*, the world's largest weasel known also as the "skunk bear," and who will attack much larger animals; the *coyote*, which moved to Alaska only during the 20th century; the *Arctic fox*, which changes from blue to white; the *red fox*, which can switch from red to black; the *American buffalo* (bison), an import which you may see from the Alaska Highway near Delta Junction; the *musk ox*, which you'll probably find only on a farm at Palmer; the *beaver*, whose dams and lodges you'll see more often than the builder/proprietor himself; the *muskrat*, whom you might mistake for a beaver except for the rat-like tail; the *porcupine*, sometimes a disastrous traffic hazard for dog sleds; and the *shrew*, known as Alaska's smallest mammal.

You might also see the *marten*, the "American sable" who usually patrols only at night; the *hoary marmot*, which resembles a woodchuck and whistles loudly at any sign of danger; the *lynx*, Alaska's only native cat, feeding mainly on the *snowshoe hare* (which is brown in summer, white in winter, and named for its large hind feet); the *river otter*, certainly a fun-loving creature when you can find them; several types of *lemmings*, some of which are known for their suicide rush into the ocean; the *red squirrel* with its bushy tail; and the often-seen *Arctic ground squirrel*, sometimes called "road puppies" or "parkas" since its pelt is used to make the Eskimo parka ruff. It has an unusual, narrow tail and often asks for a handout in areas frequented by tourists, but not by Eskimos. And what about the *woolly mammoth*? Sorry, you're a few thousand years too late. Alaska has recognized the species, however, by making it the official state fossil.

As far as domestic mammals are concerned, you'll find the same pets in the Upper One as in the Lower 48. You might remember, though, that *sled dogs*, although often well-loved, well-treated, and even named, are basically working animals and usually are not considered pets. (The best sled dogs seem to come from isolated villages where Natives can afford to keep only the best ones.) Sled dogs include those wonderful blue-eyed Siberian huskies, the bushy-tailed Alaskan malamute (solid white ones are considered to be purebreds), or any kind of dogs chosen to pull a sled—even standard poodles. And any sled dog can be called a "husky" in Alaska.

THE INSECT WORLD

Out of all the wildlife in Alaska, you will hear a disproportionately sized lament about its pesky bug life, including the large black *deer fly* (also "horse fly" or "moose fly"), whose buzz is worse than his bite; the *no-see-um* (or "punky"), a tiny gnat that bites and runs before you realize he's ever been to dinner; the *whitesox* ("black fly"), whose itch can last a week; plus of course, that macho *mosquito,* supposed to be larger, tougher, and meaner in Alaska than anywhere else (although macho is probably the wrong word, since it's only the females who draw blood).

Some folks swear by B vitamins, Avon's Skin So Soft, and other "secret" remedies, but the only way to be completely safe from mosquitoes, apparently, is to be dead. They're attracted to us and other animals by carbon dioxide. They're particularly active at twilight, during early morning, and in periods of no wind. Mosquitoes also head for dark colors, particularly dark blue materials, and they're also attracted by perfume. In areas where they occur, we have found that ordinary insect repellent keeps them at bay. Light-colored clothing and an absence of perfume might help, too—if the mosquitoes are following the rules.

THE ALASKAN CHARACTER

Are Alaskans different from other people? Yes and no. Some, of course, are just like any other Americans, with the same hopes, dreams, and aspirations. Many who live in the state consider it only a temporary stopping place in their lives—military families stationed there or those who have come up for a year or so from Texas or Oklahoma to make a pile working in the oil fields. And some, of course, are summer workers employed in tourism, the fish-processing business, or other seasonal activity. But beyond these there is a cadre of residents who like to call themselves the real Alaskans. Alaska tends to have a tremendous tolerance for the rugged individualist who has resisted society's attempts to force him or her to conform. In Alaska, you will still find those who build their own houses and shoot their own meat—along with those who at least like to appear to be that type.

Not surprisingly, most permanent residents of Alaska are Republicans, if they admit to being anything at all. And it might be the only state in the Union in which a bank would pass over the traditional toaster and TV premiums to do what one did last year—reward anyone who bought a certificate of deposit with a brand-new .44-caliber Smith & Wesson revolver.

THE INDEPENDENT CUSS

Some Alaskans seem to go to extremes to look the part. Beards, which have been steadily losing popularity since the '60s in the Lower 48, are still much in evidence in Alaska, winter or summer. Some Alaskans of both sexes seem to abhor new clothes and take a certain satisfaction in being judged a sourdough by wearing threadbare wooly shirts, worn-out jeans, and dirty rubber boots even in the hottest, driest days of summer. We have never seen a restaurant or a hotel turn away a potential patron because they didn't like what he or she was wearing, and we certainly have seen a lot of far-out get-ups at the table next to us.

Many Alaskans seem to carry the same theme to their immediate environment, cluttering up their houses or at least their front and back yards with assortments of nonfunctioning manufactured junk—automobile bodies and parts, rusting oil drums, heavy wooden boxes, old bathroom fixtures, and what-have-you—with little fear that anyone from a neighborhood improvement committee will register even the slightest protest. For many months of the year, even the typical working model of an Alaskan car or truck will seem only one step removed from the junkyard, wearing a semi-permanent coating of mud or dust that makes all vehicles in a parking lot look much alike.

And although it's impossible to generalize, it still seems that a typical Alaskan is a man who damn well doesn't see why he should take off his hat to eat dinner. All this old-fashioned cussedness does not necessarily mean that Alaskan men are into machismo in a big way. Indeed, most seem to demand as much resilience in their women as in themselves. For several reasons, teams led by women have come in first in the annual Iditarod Sled Dog Race, which to some is a symbol of the kind of rugged self-reliance and discipline demanded by life in the north. Alaska has taken this in good humor, and tee shirts and bumper stickers were soon produced with the slogan: "Alaska—where men are men and women win the Iditarod!" And last year the contestants for queen of the Spring Carnival at the village of Fort Yukon all had to make tea—*after* they built a fire, melted snow for water, ran in a snowshoe race, and skinned a snowshoe hare!

There's a mystique that has built up among some Alaskans to the effect that, well, we're all in this together. Usually this manifests itself in a spirit of helpfulness that just won't quit. Tourists who stop along the road just to take pictures or enjoy the view often report that locals soon pull up to see if someone is in trouble and needs help.

The vehicle that stops usually turns out to be a truck. Alaskans seem to prefer four-wheel drives to some kind of sissy sedan. They often look like they've forded about 100 muddy rivers without ever being washed, and usually there's at least one dog in the back. Someone once asked us if there was any symbol of Alaska and the Yukon that particularly stands out in our memory. There is; it's a big dog riding in the back of a pickup.

THE YOUNG AND THE RESTLESS

The population of Alaska is young—with an average age of about 26. After a number of years up north, senior folk have less tolerance for the winters and retire to warmer climes. This means that younger Alaskans sometimes advance more rapidly to positions of authority and responsibility. A newspaper reporter is more quickly promoted to editor; a young lawyer soon finds himself a senior partner in his firm or perhaps a judge. Critics of Alaskan society say that this predominant youthfulness, despite its vigor and inventiveness, deprives the state of the kind of wise and mature judgment that only age can provide. They also say that long-term civic projects suffer since there tends to be less civic spirit among those who do not intend to remain part of the community for the rest of their lives.

Most of this kind of thing may not be visible to the average visitor. What is apparent, however, is that everyone you talk to often seems to be new on the job. Ask your waitress, the bellhop, a taxi driver, or others you meet in Alaska what they were doing this time last year. Chances are they were working someplace else in a different profession—and they may have had a couple of other jobs in the interim.

In many ways, Alaska often seems to be one very large small town. With a population of half a million, and an even smaller number who are more-or-less permanent, you find that citizens of the state all seem to know one another, no matter how spread out they may be. This is particularly true within certain professions. If you meet someone in advertising in Juneau, chances are that they know almost everyone in advertising in Anchorage and around the entire state. Usually it turns out that any two people in a given field have worked with each other or for each other at some point in the past. Virtually every pilot in the state knows every other pilot. The same goes for dog mushers, game hunters, and scores of other specializations.

No doubt the biggest small town in Alaska is Juneau, the state capital. When you think this is a large and impersonal world we live in, remember that in Juneau, the social event of the Christmas season is open house in the governor's mansion.

NATIVE GROUPS

Alaska is a racially diverse state with several different Native groups, potentially confusing to outsiders. These are aboriginal peoples whose ancestors were living in the north long before the Americans, or even the Russians, came to call. Today they add up to about 75,000, or 15% of the state's population. Their culture and artwork are significant aspects of Alaska and the Yukon today. Some experts identify as many as 20 Native languages in Alaska.

The word "native," considered derogatory in many areas of the world, is an honored term in Alaska, at least superficially. For reasons we've never completely understood, it is often considered better form here to lump all these groups together as Natives, rather than more specifically referring to them as Eskimos, Aleuts, Indians, etc. It has to do with the animosity the groups have toward each other and their abhorrence of being misidentified or confused with one another.

Sociologists are worried that the Native population is increasing more rapidly than the population of Alaska in general. This is particularly true in isolated villages and other rural areas where complex social problems like unemployment and chronic alcoholism—as well as suicide and other violent death usually related to alcoholism—are already widespread. Many in these areas depend heavily on government benefits. (Natives are very sensitive about these difficulties, which to a lesser extent are shared by some non-Natives living in Alaska. In any case, be warned that they are subjects better left unraised by any *cheechako*.)

Let's see if we can keep everybody straight, without resorting to drastic measures like footnotes. First, remember that there are three major Native groups: (1) Eskimos, (2) Aleuts (who are probably distantly related to Eskimos), and (3) Indians. Moreover, there are two major groups of Eskimos, two or three types of Aleuts, and several tribes and subtribes of Indians, sometimes divided by language or dialect. There are also variations in the pronunciation and spelling of the names of these groups, which we'll also try to make clear.

Now numbering about 34,000, **Eskimos** include those from the north and northwest who speak Inupiat (Inupiaq), and then those from the southwest who speak Yupik (Yuit). The Yupiks are further subdivided into the Bering Sea Yupik and the Pacific Yupik, and perhaps it is enough to know that there are still more subdivisions under those.

The *Yupik* and *Inupiat* languages are considered to be about as close to each other as English and German. The word "Eskimo" itself is derived from a French phrase meaning raw meat eater, and in Canada it is now rejected as a pejorative term. In fact, the Inupiat-speaking Eskimos living in the Yukon Territory of Canada much prefer to be called *Inuit* instead of Eskimo. (Lately their objection to the term has been spreading to Alaska, and now American Eskimos are beginning to identify themselves more as either Inupiat or Yupik.)

The Canadian Inuit are the only people who build their igloos (temporary hunting shelters) out of ice and snow. These things are virtually unknown in Alaska, and the snowy igloo image is somewhat resented by Alaskan Eskimos. However, intricate ivory carving and realistic maskmaking are arts still carried on by the Eskimos. And do Eskimos really kiss by rubbing noses? Sometimes. Today it's mainly a gesture of affection between mother and child.

Okay. The **Aleuts** were well-established along the treeless, cloudy, and wind-swept Aleutian islands when the Russians arrived, and considered themselves racially and culturally very different from the Eskimos. Some scientists believe that thousands of years before, however, they were indeed the same people.

Due to the influx of Russian fur traders, and the gradual intermixing with Aleuts, today's Aleut language seems to have almost as much Russian in it as words from Native tongues. Aleuts are also predominantly members of the Russian Orthodox church, and many have Russian names. (Related culturally to the Aleuts are the peoples called the *Koniag* from Kodiak Island and the *Chugach* from the Gulf Coast.) Ancient Aleuts are sometimes credited with inventing the sun visor— interesting in an archipelago where the sun seldom shines! Aleut women are still known today for excellent basket making. All together the Aleuts today number about 8000.

Now, the **Indians,** who are genetically very different from Eskimos and Aleuts, include the *Athabascan* (Athapascan) in Central Alaska and the Yukon, who sometimes refer to themselves as "Dene," the Athabascan word for people. Interestingly, their language is similar to that of the Navajo and Apache. (In fact, those tribes are now considered to be Athabascans, descended from those who migrated from Canada several centuries ago to settle farther south.)

The northern Athabascans are divided into several subgroups, some of which, like the Kutchin, the Tutchone, the Han, and the Eyak, are well-known peoples in their own right. The nomadic Athabascans contributed dog mushing and snow shoes to the popular culture of Alaska and the Yukon, and some are also known as expert fiddle players. Among the handicrafts still practiced are excellent beadwork and some fine examples of jewelry made from porcupine quills.

Moving now to Southeast Alaska, there are three historically prosperous and more culturally sophisticated groups of coastal Indians, considered not to be related to the traditionally more poor Athabascan (other than the fact that they are Indians, too). The major group of Southeast Indians is the *Tlingit* (usually pronounced "kling-it"), and there are more than a dozen subgroups of Tlingit known by other names (Chilkoot, Chilkat, Yakutat, etc.). It was the Tlingit who fiercely defended their land and culture against the Russians at Sitka. There are also some inland Tlingit in the southwest corner of Canada's Yukon Territory.

The two other important groups of Southeast Alaska Indians are closely related to the Tlingit but are not subgroups. First, there are the *Haida*. Like the Tlingit, they generally divide themselves culturally between Eagle and Raven clans, along with several subclans also named for various animals. Then there are the *Tsimshian*. Both Haida and Tsimshian hailed originally from British Columbia. The Haida expanded from the Queen Charlotte Islands to the southern half of Alaska's Prince of Wales Island about two centuries ago. The Tsimshian are relatively recent immigrants. Led by an Episcopalian priest, most of the Tsimshian relocated to Metlakatla on tiny Annette Island near Ketchikan only in 1887. Metlakatla is now Alaska's only federal Indian reservation.

It is the Tlingit, Haida, and Tsimshian—the Southeast Indians only—who carve totem poles and create similarly elaborate artistic designs and decorations.

Got it? Whew!

PRE-HISTORY TO 1728

The human history of North and South America begins in Alaska with something that no longer exists. It is sometimes called the Bering Land Bridge or the lost land of Beringia. About 15,000 years ago, during the last great Ice Age, much of the earth's water was tied up in ice, reducing the height of the oceans by several hundred feet, and the land between Alaska and Siberia was exposed. Man and animals migrated across the bridge, which has been estimated at about 60 miles long (the approximate distance between the land masses of Alaska and Siberia) by about 600 miles wide (from north to south). Incidentally, scientists say that during this period Alaska was not covered by ice, whereas much of North America was. It is a pattern destined to be repeated several thousand years from now, which perhaps makes Alaska destined to again become a refuge for man in the distant future.

Anyway, as the millennia wore on and the melting ice again caused the world's oceans to rise, those who had come via Beringia began to populate the Western Hemisphere, a part of the world which became thoroughly forgotten in Europe and Asia.

RUSSIANS AND FURS—1728–83

The first European known to reach the shores of Alaska was a Dane by the name of Vitus Bering, on an exploration voyage for the Russian Czar Peter the Great. He sailed through the strait which now bears his name on his first voyage in 1728. On his second trip, he landed on Kayak Island in 1741. He also sighted and named Mount St. Elias on the Alaskan mainland. However, the adventure turned out to be a disaster; Bering himself and many of his crew died there from malnutrition, scurvy, and other causes.

Those who did return to Russia brought with them samples of the pelts of the Alaskan sea otter. The sight of these fine, dense furs inspired some already notorious gangs of professional hunters called the *promyshlenniki* into organizing new expeditions to the lands where these valuable creatures might be hunted and skinned. For years they ravaged the Aleutian Islands, and these hunters were accused of killing almost as many Aleuts as the otters and seals which drew them there. This was an exaggeration. Some Aleuts apparently died of simple starvation because the men working for the Russians were unable to provide for their own families. Many of these Russian hunters considered the Natives to

be simply a subhuman species, and forced them into slavery. Those
Aleuts who resisted with knives and spears soon found themselves overwhelmed by Russian firepower. On one well-known occasion they lined
up a dozen Aleuts and fired a musket ball into the first, merely to see
how many they could kill with a single shot. (Nine men were felled.)
Many more Aleuts died from exposure to venereal disease and other
illnesses to which they had little or no immunity.

After more than a quarter-century of this kind of exploitation, the
Russians and the Aleuts eventually formed informal alliances which had
the Natives willingly working with them in the fur trade. By this time,
a considerable number of Aleut children had been fathered by the newcomers, and they were even speaking Russian, factors which may have
contributed to their more gracious accommodation.

Although the Russians dominated Alaska during the 18th and early
19th centuries, they were soon not the only Europeans on the scene. On
his last voyage in 1778, British naval captain James Cook visited the
Russian settlement at Unalaska. He also explored the inlet that now
bears his name, passing the present site of Anchorage, on his fruitless
search for the fabled Northwest Passage. There were also visits by Juan
Perez of Spain in 1774, and George Vancouver of England in 1792 and
1794.

RUSSIAN AMERICA—1784–1867

The Russians actually did not set up a permanent colony in Alaska until
1784, when Grigori Shelekhov and his wife Natalia, shrewd merchants
from Irkutsk, arrived with a group of men at Kodiak Island. For years,
Natalia Shelekhov was the only white woman in Alaska.

After returning to Russia, the Shelekhovs hired a new manager for
the colony, Alexander Baranov, an iron-willed businessman destined to
become legendary for his ability to run the fur business and govern
Russian America at the same time. The hard-drinking Baranov became
known as the "Lord of Alaska." (His headquarters at Kodiak is now a
community museum.) The Shelekhovs also sent missionaries of the Orthodox church, with whom Baranov often competed for the hearts and
minds of the Aleuts and the Koniags, the residents of Kodiak Island.
Among other things, the priests disapproved of Baranov's Native wife,
especially since he had left another wife behind in Russia.

In 1799, in order to resist encroachment by British and American
traders in the area, Baranov attempted to establish another settlement
600 miles south, on the island which now bears his name, and then
returned to Kodiak. The new colony (now known as Old Sitka) was
soon massacred by the fierce Tlingit Indians. Five years later Baranov
returned with war surplus weapons from the American revolution, routed
the Indians, and successfully established the town of New Archangel on

a beautiful coastal site which was previously the Tlingit stronghold. The Indians called the site Shee Atika, and the community gradually became better known by an agglutination of that name, Sitka.

In contrast to the sometimes destitute Athabascan Indians of the Interior, the salmon-fed Tlingits were healthy and enjoyed a highly sophisticated culture. They built massive wooden houses; large canoes; imposing, intricately carved totem poles; and wore elaborate, decorative costumes. Chiefs and upper-class Tlingits threw lavish potlatches for one another; these were opulent feasts at which the host was expected to give away virtually everything he owned.

Sitka officially became the capital of the Russian-American Company, Baranov was appointed its governor, and he built his headquarters atop a hill which overlooked the town. Eventually, it became known as Baranov's Castle. The Russians, and the Aleuts they brought with them, gradually managed to get along reasonably well with the troublesome Tlingits. Baranov also made friends and business arrangements with many American and English traders, and the new port prospered for more than half a century. Baranov himself finally retired at 72 in 1818, but died at sea on his way back to Russia.

Another towering figure in Russian America was Father Ivan Veniaminov. He became the Bishop of Alaska and is credited with building St. Michael's Cathedral in Sitka, whose distinctive spire is still seen on the city skyline today. He also successfully inoculated hundreds of Tlingits against a smallpox epidemic. After spending more than four decades in the colony he returned to Russia to become the Metropolitan of Moscow, the highest-ranking official in the Orthodox church. The onion domes on churches in Alaska today indicate that the Russian church is still alive in the 49th State.

A succession of distinguished military men and aristocrats continued to govern the colony. One of them married Baranov's half-Aleut daughter. Another was Baron Ferdinand Wrangell, the first Russian to develop a conservation program to ensure that fur-bearing animals would not disappear from Alaska. In any case, fur production began to drop and lumber, fishing, and other new industries were developed. At one time the Russians even sold Alaskan lake ice packed in sawdust to gold rushers and others in California. In 1824 they signed a treaty with the British which defined the boundary between Canada and Alaska. (The jagged border you see today results largely from lines being drawn from mountain top to mountain top along the coastal range.)

Despite the continued enthusiasm of Alaska's governors, after 1854 Mother Russia began to see that she could not keep up her far-flung colonies. In the wake of her 1856 defeat by the British in the Crimean War, she needed cash to pay her debts. One of the first proposals to sell Alaska to the expansion-minded U.S. was delayed by the American

Civil War. Following that, however, Russian ambassador Edouard de Stoeckl was instructed to sell Alaska for at least $5 million.

After considerable negotiating with President Andrew Johnson's cigar-chewing no-nonsense secretary of state, William H. Seward, the controversial deal was cut for an astonishing $7.2 million in 1867 ($7 million for Alaska itself; $200,000 to purchase a contract the Russians had to ship ice from Sitka to the emerging city of San Francisco). Before Congress finally ratified the sale, the legislative fight resulted in bitter one-liners like "Seward's Ice Box" and other know-nothing slogans which continue to plague Alaska's public image even today.

AMERICAN NEGLECT—1867–83

At Sitka, the "Paris of the Pacific," where upper-class Russians spoke English and French as often as their own language, the aristocratic administrators of Alaska could hardly believe their government had sold the colony out from under them. Princess Maria Maksutova, the governor's wife, wept on October 18 as the flag with the Imperial Double Eagle was lowered and the Stars and Stripes were raised in ceremonies at Baranov Castle.

Free-booting American fur hunters who followed in the wake of the sale all but wiped out the seals and sea otters which had begun to make a comeback under Russian conservation measures. In Sitka, the American general assigned to govern the region summarily threw Russians, Aleuts, and Tlingits out of houses he commandeered for himself and his troops. For the next few decades, Alaska suffered more from just plain neglect than anything else.

One of the biggest problems was the fact that Alaska was neither a state nor a territory, and almost no laws applied to it. No one could buy and sell real estate. Federal law said that juries could be empaneled only from taxpayers. Since no one paid any tax in Alaska there were no juries, and therefore no trials. Similar problems invaded every aspect of Alaskan life.

Some of the first Americans in Sitka were already veterans of the Western frontier, and they set up some laws and elections anyway, even if they were not sanctioned by the federal government. No one in Washington seemed to care what happened to Alaska since the prevailing opinion was that there was nothing up there except a lot of snow and a few Eskimos. With no roads, and no prospects of building any, Alaska was thought of as a thoroughly impenetrable land.

This neglect soon began to take its toll on once-proud Sitka. Complaining of the raucous soldiers who enjoyed almost the only income in the community, many Americans and Russians began to leave. Congress did pass one law to protect the fur seal's breeding grounds in the

Pribilof Islands, but its intent was often ignored by those who killed even pregnant female seals at sea for the lucrative furs without thought of future consequences. In 1877, the Army was pulled out of Sitka in order to help put down an Indian uprising in Montana, leaving only a single U.S. Customs collector in Sitka in charge of the half-million square miles and 40,000 people living in Alaska.

During this period, Alaska seemed to have only one hope, which came in the unlikely five-foot form of Dr. Sheldon Jackson, a Presbyterian missionary who happened to arrive in Sitka the year the Army left. He soon became Alaska's unofficial but effective voice, giving impassioned speeches all over America: "In all that country there is no law. There can be no restraint. The lowest animal passions of the rough miners, trappers, hunters, soldiers, and sailors rage unchecked. The Indian woman is considered the lawful spoil of those men!" Contributions rolled in from churches and schools coast to coast. In 1883 Jackson began spending every winter in Washington, where he became an unofficial but effective lobbyist for legislation that would bring law and order to Alaska. Almost single-handedly he organized a petition campaign that sent thousands of letters from churchgoers all over the country to members of Congress.

A FEW LAWS AT LAST—1884–97

In 1884 the first Organic Act of Alaska gave Alaska the civil and criminal laws of Oregon. It wasn't much, since things were much different in Alaska than in Oregon. The Act also established an education budget and Jackson found himself in charge of hiring teachers and setting up an education program for Native Alaskans. He also divided his time with other projects, like buying a herd of reindeer from Siberia and shipping them to Alaska to help feed the Eskimos.

A few explorers began to map Alaska during the period after the purchase, some for scientific purposes and others for such commercial objectives as the abortive attempt to string a telegraph line through Alaska to Siberia and thence to the rest of Europe. A few of these men became famous—naturalists Robert Kennicott, William Dall, Lt. Billy Mitchell, and the great conservationist John Muir, whose efforts resulted in the preservation of Glacier Bay as a national monument. Exploration also revealed that Fort Yukon, established by Canadians, was far inside U.S. Territory. Surprisingly, the prosperous Hudson's Bay Company packed up and left Fort Yukon without protest, losing their fur monopoly in the area. The company never fully recovered from the move.

Beginning in 1870, veteran miners from California began prospecting in Alaska with no more encouragement than the theory that if the mountains in California held gold, the mountains up north must do so, too. The first gold strike of any consequence was made by Joe Juneau and Dick Harris in 1880. The name of the place where it was found was changed from Rockwell to Harrisburgh, but later changed again by public vote to Juneau after Harris became personally unpopular. Juneau turned out to be Alaska's first boom town, and many poured into the area to seek their fortunes. Like many old prospectors, Harris and Juneau eventually died flat broke. Many of the claims of those who came to Juneau were eventually consolidated into the Alaska-Treadwell Gold Mining Company, the first major mining operation in Alaska.

There were a few more modest strikes in Alaska over the next two decades, both in the relatively accessible panhandle and farther north on tributaries of the Yukon River. But the first real glory hole was yet to come. Although it would not even be found in Alaska, it was destined to drastically affect the history of the territory.

GOLD DAYS—1898–1906

On Friday, July 16, 1897, the steamer *Portland,* out of St. Michael, Alaska, docked in Seattle, Washington. On board, according to the front page of the *Seattle Post-Intelligencer,* were 68 newly rich prospectors and "a ton of gold," all taken from new discoveries along the Klondike River. This story and a similar one in San Francisco confirmed rumors that had been circulated but generally scoffed at for a year, and so began America's last big gold rush.

The initial discovery had been made August 16, 1896, by George Washington Carmack and two Indians, James "Skookum Jim" Mason and Tagish Charlie on Rabbit Creek, later renamed Bonanza Creek. Rabbit/Bonanza was a tributary of the Klondike River which, in turn, was a tributary of the great Yukon River. The area of the gold strike was within Canada, in what is now the Yukon Territory. Founded at the nearby junction of the Klondike and the Yukon, Dawson City rapidly became a classic boom town. Of the 100,000 men who caught the "gold fever" and set out for the gold fields during 1897 and 1898, less than 40,000 actually made it all the way to Dawson. Very few however struck it rich, since nearly all the claims had been taken even before the good ship *Portland* tied up in Seattle. Nevertheless, it served to open up Alaska to public consciousness and to create, as some said, the last great American adventure. Among those attracted were writers like Jack London (*The Call of the Wild*), Rex Beach (*The Spoilers*), and the Canadian bank clerk who became known as the Bard of the Yukon, Robert W. Service (*The Shooting of Dan McGrew*).

Faced with this influx of population, the Yukon was named a separate Canadian territory in 1898 and Dawson City was made its capital, giving it much more government than any place in neighboring Alaska during the period.

There seemed to be five ways prospective millionaires might make their way to the Klondike. One was following the length of the Yukon River from St. Michael to Dawson (City), and another was from Valdez over the St. Elias Mountains. A few found their way to Haines and took the Dalton Trail through the Chilkat Valley. But these were considered extremely arduous or expensive routes, and most chose to sail up the Inside Passage to Skagway and from there take either the steep Chilkoot Trail from nearby Dyea or the almost-as-steep White Pass Trail from Skagway itself. These choices also meant extreme difficulties along the way, and the most successful of the gold rushers were those who abandoned hope of staking a claim for themselves in favor of setting up businesses to supply the miners.

One of these was the infamous Jefferson Randolph "Soapy" Smith, an underworld character and general con man who became the unofficial boss of Skagway. He and his gang of professional card sharks, pickpockets, swindlers, thieves, and gunmen cheated hundreds out of their gold or their grub stakes until he was finally gunned down in a duel with an outraged citizen on July 8, 1899. (Soapy's grave is still a Skagway tourist attraction.) Later that year the White Pass & Yukon Route Railroad was finished, offering easy transportation over the pass to the Canadian town of Whitehorse on the Yukon River. From Whitehorse, riverboat transportation was available during the warm months to Dawson City.

Unlike towns in Alaska which boasted no system of organized justice, Dawson was kept relatively clean, largely through the efforts of the well-disciplined ranks of Canada's North West Mounted Police. But no sooner did Dawson begin to fill up with disappointed gold seekers than another major gold strike was made in Nome, Alaska.

Those who had missed out in Dawson set out almost immediately without waiting for the spring breakup of the Yukon River. During the winter of 1898–99, many of them traversed the frozen Yukon by hiking, by dog sled, or by any other means of transportation they could dream up. One prospector rode an old horse, which died for lack of food along the route. It was the first such animal ever seen by Athabascan Indians, who called it a giant dog. They were still talking about that when another man traveling the 2000-mile river on a pair of ice skates came by—only to be overtaken by another who was riding a bicycle, with fair success, on frozen tires. One contemporary comment: "White man. He sit down, walk like hell!"

With virtually no laws in effect, theft, murder, and other crimes were constant problems in Nome. Then there were the late-comers to the rowdy tent city who tried and almost succeeded in taking the claims away from the trio of original discoverers known as "the Three Lucky Swedes" merely because they were not American citizens. Similar shenanigans were performed later on other claims, one involving a corrupt judge who conspired with influential businessmen to defraud miners from their claims. (One who finally did go to prison was personally pardoned by President McKinley.) Graft did not cease in Nome until the appointment of Judge James Wickersham, an honest man who was destined to play several important roles in Alaskan history.

These incidents were largely forgotten with more gold strikes in Nome—especially the paydirt that began to be found right on the beach that fronted the town. Most of the marketable gold played out by about 1906, but you'll see that a few one-man sluice boxes still work the "golden sands" at Nome.

Another major stampede took place in 1902 when gold was discovered along the Tanana River, sparking yet another boom town called Fairbanks at the confluence of the Tanana and Chena rivers. Fairbanks, however, developed a reputation as a law-and-order town almost immediately. The days when a few men could use their personal whim to run another Nome or another Skagway were over.

RISE OF THE SOURDOUGH—1906–14

Although gold began to be less important in Alaska and order finally began to be established, Americans continued to go to Alaska, not to develop new communities but merely to get rich and get out. Those who did stay, however, began to be known as sourdoughs—fiercely individualistic and self-reliant outdoorsmen (from the fermented yeast-less starter many old-timers carried with them in order to make a favored type of bread and pancakes). The extent of the sourdoughs' civic spirit seemed to be to join a couple of fraternal lodge organizations, notably the Pioneers of Alaska and the Arctic Brotherhood. Even now, some Alaskans claim that one cannot become a sourdough until he has fulfilled three requirements, gently paraphrased here: (a) killed a grizzly, (b) urinated in the Yukon, and (c) slept with a Native woman. Few who loudly quote the definition today can claim to have passed all or any of the tests.

Sourdoughs began to tell tall stories about bears and about themselves, and sometimes about the two together. Like the grizzled old prospector who killed a bear and then made himself a set of dentures out of a hammered tin pan and the bear's teeth. Only then did he sit down to have a meal—thus eating the bear with its own teeth! Another reported he had once escaped the cold in the bush by sleeping inside the body of a freshly killed moose. When he woke up, the carcass had frozen solid, and he was unable to break free—until some helpful wolves came along and gnawed through the animal's corpse.

Less apocryphal is the story of the "Sourdough Expedition," four determined prospectors who set out to conquer Mount McKinley (Denali) in 1910, with no mountain-climbing experience at all. On April 6, two of their number reached the peak they had often seen from their mining camps. Only after returning did they learn that Denali has two peaks, and that they had climbed the one that's about 850 feet shorter. (Some years later a half-Athabascan named Walter Harper first set foot on the taller peak.)

Those destined to make the really big money in Alaska were not Alaskans. They were the large corporations with absentee owners who exploited the territory in the same manner that whalers had, a generation previously. (The American whaling fleet never entirely recovered from an 1871 disaster when 31 ships were overtaken and destroyed by the expanding polar ice cap.)

The San Francisco–based Alaska Commercial Company had bought all the assets of the defunct Russian-America Company. Their profits ran over $1 million a year for decades. The Northern Commercial Company was formed to buy up and operate as much of Fairbanks and its mining operation as possible. And the Alaska Syndicate was a giant conglomerate formed by J. P. Morgan and members of New York's prominent Guggenheim family. They had interests in mining operations, railroads, steamships, and salmon canneries. The Alaska Syndicate became a hated entity in Alaska as it bought up company after company and exerted influence on legal and political leaders.

On August 24, 1912, President Taft signed the Second Organic Act, the home rule bill which officially made Alaska a territory and allowed it to elect its own legislature. Unfortunately, the act also reserved most powers for the federal government in Washington. Alaska's first delegate to Congress, who could speak and introduce bills but not vote, was the same Judge James Wickersham who had cleaned the thieves out of Nome and who won continued fame by fighting the non-resident Alaska Syndicate wherever he could. (His home in Juneau is an important museum attraction for Alaskans today.)

In one of his first addresses on the House floor, Wickersham informed the congressmen: "The exploiters of the wealth of Alaska do not live in Alaska at all. They generally live around 45 Broadway, New York . . . If ever there was a criminal conspiracy in the United States to get the immense resources which belong to the people, it is that of the Alaska Syndicate in Alaska."

FIRST TERRITORIAL DAYS—1912–18

On June 12, 1912, the skies over Southwest Alaska and the surrounding territory on the Alaska Peninsula were blackened for two days, following the massive eruption of Mount Katmai. Since the violent explosion took place in a relatively unpopulated area no people were killed, but for hundreds of miles around plant and animal life was wiped out.

Politically, there was still a feeling that Alaska was slowly being killed simply by being ignored by the rest of the country and abandoned to exploiters and other outside forces—a self-image that has persisted, to a lesser extent, to the present day. In 1901 Sam Dunham had put it in the form of a poem entitled "Alaska to Uncle Sam," which was read in 1912 on the floor of the U.S. House of Representatives:

> Sitting on my greatest glacier,
>> with my feet in Bering Sea,
> I am thinking, cold and lonely,
>> of the way you've treated me.
> Three and thirty years of silence!
>> Through ten thousand sleeping nights
> I've been praying for your coming,
>> for the dawn of civil rights.
> When you took me, young and trusting,
>> from the growling Russian Bear,
> Loud you swore before the Nation
>> I should have the Eagle's care.
> Never yet has wing of Eagle
>> cast a shadow on my peaks,
> But I've watched the flight of buzzards
>> and I've felt their busy beaks.

Nevertheless, there were still "strange things done under the midnight sun," to quote Robert Service. The first Alaska governor appointed after the Second Organic Act, John F. E. Strong, was dismissed after five years' loyal service. That's when everyone discovered he was a Canadian citizen.

The capital was moved from Sitka to Juneau, but in a very real sense, Washington, DC, continued to be Alaska's capital, since the federal government still largely dominated territorial affairs. And due to the continued influence of huge corporations on the national scene, the powers the territory received were far less than those that had been given to the U.S.'s other territories.

For all intents and purposes, Alaska was essentially an island—in fact, numerous islands, reachable from one another and from Outside only by sea. A series of shipwrecks pointed to the fact that surveys were badly needed. Secretary of Commerce William C. Redfield declared in a 1916 speech: "We have had very peculiar habits of surveying up there. We have found many rocks by running merchant ships upon them, and have had the regular habit of naming the rocks after the ships which struck them." Even in the Interior, shallow-draft river boats provided the only modern transportation, and that only during the months when the major rivers were ice-free. Attempts to blaze overland routes through Canada to Alaska were tried, tried again, and then abandoned.

Taking office in 1913, President Woodrow Wilson called for Alaska to be given "full territorial government," but through congressional inaction, it was not to be until several years afterwards. The government did sponsor the Alaska Railroad, however, and construction on the 470-mile Seward-Fairbanks route began in 1915. Delayed partly by World War I but mostly because of bureaucratic problems, it was finally finished in 1923. Warren Harding, the first President to visit Alaska, drove the golden spike. Although it would be some 15 years before the railroad would make any money, its construction did result in a temporary economic boom and in the establishment of a new town on Cook Inlet. Anchorage was destined to become the largest city in Alaska.

By this time, whaling and furs had given way to mining, timber, and especially fishing as Alaska's principal industries. However, commercial fishing, based mainly on the massive salmon runs through Alaska's streams and rivers, provided little employment for the territory. Most of the canneries, whose owners were companies in Seattle or San Francisco, brought in their own seasonal packing crews, usually Chinese who worked hard for very low wages. Even independent Alaskan fishermen were not needed after the canneries established salmon-trapping techniques along the rivers, streams, and fjords which led to the spawning beds.

These sometimes severely depleted the number of fish available, although new fish hatchery programs began to alleviate some of the effects. Eventually the packing crews were also replaced, by a machine which could top, tail, and degut the salmon automatically. They called it "the Iron Chink."

BETWEEN THE WARS—1918–38

Of the technology that began to be felt in Alaska, it was the beginning of the air age that would do more than anything else to open up the territory. It also gave rise to a tradition of skilled bush pilots whose sometimes harrowing exploits were told with as much relish as any sourdough-versus-the-bear story ever heard in Alaska. Formerly isolated communities like Nome and Barrow could now have regular contact with the outside world, no longer dependent on ships or dog sleds for supplies and transportation.

Bush pilots became adept at operating not only with conventional landing gear, but also with pontoons or skis substituted for wheels whenever appropriate. They also learned to land and take off on a dime and developed valuable flying techniques for white-outs and other difficult weather conditions which are still in use.

Over the years incautious aviators have had a way of proving the theory of the "survival of the fittest" in Alaska, some of them coming to a dramatic end or just disappearing, plane and all, into wilderness areas of the Great Land. Thus arose what has become an oft-quoted unofficial credo for Alaskan bush pilots: "There are old pilots and there are bold pilots. But there are no old, bold pilots."

While air travel was taking off in Alaska, it was still up to sled dogs and mushers to play the heroes when Nome suffered a winter diphtheria epidemic in 1925. A plea for help was broadcast by wireless and a relay of mushers and their dogs was set up to rush the life-saving serum from the Alaska Railroad Station in Nenana to Nome. The effort was successful, and today's Iditarod Sled Dog Race between Anchorage and Nome recalls the spirit of this great journey.

Alaska paid more for its transportation of goods and passengers from the Lower 48 than free-market forces would normally have allowed. The passage of the Jones Act of 1920 meant that neither people nor goods could be shipped direct between an American port and Alaska in a Canadian-registered ship. Then U.S.-registered vessels charged perhaps twice as much for the same service. (The Jones Act is still largely in effect today, although with air and road options available its effects are not so restrictive. However, it is the reason that many Alaska cruises still beat some high costs by leaving from Vancouver, B.C., instead of nearby Seattle, Washington.)

Perhaps Alaska's most famous citizen made his claim to fame in 1926. That was the year that Benny Benson, a 13-year-old Aleut, entered the contest to create the official Alaskan Flag. His bold but simple design, a gold Big Dipper constellation on a rich blue background, was named first out of 142 entries. He also sent the following explanation: "The blue field is for the Alaska sky and the forget-me-not, an Alaska flower. The North Star is for the future State of Alaska, the most northerly of the Union. The dipper is for the Great Bear—symbolizing strength." Benson's description was later adapted into a poem which then became the official State Song entitled *Alaska's Flag*. It begins: "Eight stars of gold on a field of blue . . ."

Alaska, which had experienced no economic boom during the 1920s, was less affected by the 1929 stock market crash and the resulting depression. Mine employment (coal and copper) was cut and salmon prices dropped, but many Alaskans, particularly the Native groups, continued to supplement their dollar income by subsistence hunting and fishing. Also, it was still possible to chop down trees and build comfortable log houses on homesteaded land. Some Americans from the Lower 48, discouraged by economic conditions there, actually moved to Alaska on their own hook, thinking to take part in this more basic lifestyle.

Depression-era federal construction projects like roads, bridges, docks, airstrips, and telegraph lines certainly helped the territory. The Civilian Conservation Corps (the CCC) was administered by the Forest Service instead of the Army in Alaska. With an eye toward tourism, the

CCC won the gratitude of Indians by hiring them to restore totem poles in Southeast.

One of the most exciting and controversial of President Roosevelt's projects was the 1935 creation of the Matanuska Valley colony—the relocation of 200 farm families from the poverty-stricken areas of Michigan, Wisconsin, and Minnesota to fertile lands north of Anchorage where an entirely new community was set up for them. The valley stretches approximately from Anchorage to Chickaloon, but is centered largely around Palmer and Wasilla. After several initial hardships, most settled in successfully to their new life. Some lacked the necessary skills, however, and a few complained loudly and publicly about their difficulties. They returned to the Lower 48 (and were replaced by others). For a time the experiment became a political football in Washington, and even today some in Alaska look down on those they call "Colonists."

LAST DAYS OF THE TERRITORY—1939–58

As World War II approached, it was apparent to some that Alaska could play an important role. It took a while for others to realize that Japan was 1000 miles closer to the U.S. mainland via the great circle route through Alaska than it was via Hawaii, and that Germany could easily fly bombers over the North Pole from Scandinavia. As early as 1935, Brig. Gen. Billy Mitchell warned Congress that Japan could and probably would attack the U.S. in Alaska. A few desultory steps were taken to work on new bases—Fort Wainwright was established in Fairbanks, and some Naval bases were set up at Kodiak and in the Aleutians—but when Pearl Harbor, Hawaii, was attacked on Dec. 7, 1941, Alaska was still unprepared. In June 1942, Japan bombed Dutch Harbor in the Aleutian Islands (but not with the stealth they supposed, as their carriers had been detected the previous day), and then invaded two of the islands, Attu and Kiska.

They were not defeated on Attu until a bitter 10-day battle nearly a year later, in which nearly all the Japanese not killed in battle committed suicide. After Iwo Jima, it was the second costliest battle for the U.S. in percentage of casualties during the entire war. A battle on Kiska never materialized; the entire island was evacuated under cover of fog before the Americans landed. In any case, Japan never succeeded in widening its campaign in Alaska. (It was later discovered that the entire occupation was originally intended only as a diversion from the 1942 Battle of Midway.)

One undesirable effect of the war was the forcible moving of American Aleuts from their home islands to other areas of Alaska for the duration. The relocation was said to be for their own safety, but most Aleuts did not want to go and many believed that, like the internment of Japanese-Americans, racism played a role in the policy.

Alaska experienced population and building booms throughout the war. One of the most lasting effects was the dramatic construction in an astonishing eight months of the 1500-mile road then called the Alaska-Canada Military Highway (ALCAN), creating for the first time an overland vehicular passage between Alaska and the Lower 48. A crude dirt and gravel route, it nevertheless served well for a series of convoys of men and materials to the U.S. forces as well as supplies destined for the Soviet Union. (The ALCAN has since been paved and improved, and it is now known as the Alaska Highway between Watson Lake, B.C., and Big Delta, Alaska.)

After peace was declared in 1945, the military presence in Alaska soon took on the duties of the Cold War, due to continued tensions between the U.S. and the Soviet Union. Major air installations, including Eielson at Fairbanks and Elmendorf at Anchorage, became bases for long-range bombers. Along with other bases, an America-Canadian radar net dubbed the Distant Early Warning (DEW) Line was created. In human terms, Yupik Eskimos from Alaska and Siberia, both speaking the same language and some of them living only a couple of miles apart in the Diomede Islands, were no longer allowed to visit each other. Some extended families were thus divided indefinitely.

Communications and roads were improved, and as the demand for suppliers and workers increased, prices for food and housing went through the roof. In addition, oil was discovered on the Kenai Peninsula in 1953. Newcomers to Alaska were not interested in roughing it, and they demanded the same quality of life they would expect in the Lower 48. The overall effect was a heavy flow of military dollars in the '40s and '50s, and Alaska developed and profited as never before.

The idea of statehood for Alaska, first proposed by congressional delegate Wickersham in 1914, was revived with new fervor during the late 1940s. Laws regulating Alaska's major money earners—mining, timber, game, and fishing—were still largely dictated by Washington, and most Alaskans thought that statehood would provide the way, finally, to home rule. It was also believed to be good for business.

Congressional opposition continued for various reasons over the next decade. Some lawmakers thought that if statehood were granted, Alaska should become two or three states due to its physical size, or that some portion of it should remain a territory. No new states had been admitted to the Union since 1912, and by this time it seemed axiomatic that the U.S. consisted of exactly 48 contiguous states.

Statehood for Hawaii was opposed by Democrats, who saw it as a Republican state. And statehood for Alaska was opposed by Republicans, who guessed the state would surely be Democratic. Congressional delegations from both Hawaii and Alaska worked together to secure passage of statehood bills for both territories. Public support for Alaskan statehood was significantly increased by the publication of Edna

Ferber's melodramatic novel *Ice Palace* in 1958, which was written specifically for that purpose. The book was immensely popular and was later made into a film starring Richard Burton.

There was considerable opinion that Alaska would never be able to afford the burdens of statehood. At least some of the opposition to granting statehood to Alaska and Hawaii, both of which contained a large number of non-Caucasians, was certainly racial. Nevertheless, the measure passed in both houses of Congress in the summer of 1958 and was quickly signed by President Eisenhower on July 7 (Hawaii was admitted the following year). William A. Egan, a Democrat, became Alaska's first elected governor.

ALASKA, THE FORTY-NINTH STATE—1959 TO PRESENT

Alaska was officially proclaimed a state on Jan. 3, 1959, but its troubles were far from over. Economic growth was slow and it was soon apparent that new taxes were on the horizon. A state constitution was set up, providing for both a house and senate, along with local governmental bodies consisting of boroughs and cities.

But a national consciousness of Alaska began to develop, certainly a favorable harbinger for increased tourism. When John F. Kennedy launched his run for the White House, he did it with a 1960 speech at the agricultural fair in Palmer.

Despite its statehood, the federal government retained extensive control and influence throughout Alaska. The new state also discovered it suffered from regionalism, particularly competition between Southeast and the rest of Alaska, along with arguments on lower levels as to who would get roads and other civic improvements. A movement began which sought to move the capital from Juneau to Anchorage or at least somewhere else in the Interior, an issue that was not laid to rest until recently. In 1966, Anchorage developer Walter J. Hickel, a Republican, was elected governor, a post he resigned two years later when President Nixon named him Secretary of the Interior. Nixon fired him in 1970.

One of the most severe earthquakes in modern history, and the worst ever recorded in North America, struck Southcentral Alaska on March 27, 1964, causing extensive damage in Anchorage and near devastation in coastal cities such as Homer, Seward, and especially Valdez. Known as the "Good Friday Earthquake," it measured 8.7 on the open-ended Richter Scale and caused property damage of more than $200 million. Also, 131 persons were killed, surprisingly few considering the severity of the tremor. Resulting tsunamis (sea waves) caused further death and destruction in Alaska and as far south as Oregon and California. Dramatic evidence of the disaster can still be seen today in several places in Alaska.

But the event which was to have the greatest continuing effect on the history and prosperity of Alaska took place on March 13, 1968. A drill belonging to the Atlantic-Richfield Company (ARCO) broke through into a reservoir of oil on the North Slope, near Prudhoe Bay. It was soon apparent that this would be the richest deposit of "black gold" ever found, an estimated 9.6 billion barrels. The following year the state received the down payment from several oil companies on $900 million worth of oil leases. It was soon obvious that the entire state, and everyone living in it, would benefit in some way from exploitation of the new oil fields. Meetings and conferences were held and several decisions were arrived at concerning how best the money might be used.

The state income tax was abolished, and parking meters were removed from the streets of Anchorage, but two forward-looking projects were still outstanding. One was the construction of the trans–Alaska Pipeline which was needed to get the oil to a year-round ice-free port on the Gulf of Alaska. And since Native groups managed to block the passage of the pipeline over their lands, one effect led to another—the creation of the Alaska Native Claims Settlement Act (ANCSA).

Until then, the descendants of the original inhabitants of Alaska— the Eskimos (Inupiats and Yupiks), the Aleuts, and the Indians (Athabascan, Tlingit, Haida, and Tsimshian)—received very little of the money made in Alaska. Although desultory attempts at making amends had been tried over the years, most Alaskans now admitted that Native lands and hunting and fishing rights had been trampled on for two centuries. Natives and whites in Alaska had always agreed that reservations were not the answer.

After considerable wrangling, ANCSA was passed by the federal government in 1971, giving all Alaskans who could prove at least one quarter Native blood the title to a total of 44 million acres and a payment of $962.5 million in return for giving up their aboriginal land claims. The complex act also set up 13 regional corporations to manage the money—a dozen different areas in Alaska plus a corporation for Natives living outside the state. (Within these corporations were more than 200 village corporations, each holding titles to the particular land of each town.) Each individual member received 100 shares of stock in the larger corporations, and under the law all are prohibited from selling this stock until 1991.

Some of the corporations bought entire businesses inside and outside Alaska. Five even joined together to found a new bank. Many Natives were employed by the corporations in which they also have investments. All in all, some of these corporations have done well, making large sums of money. Others have not. Today there is considerable discussion as to whether or not Alaska's Natives will continue to be able to control their destiny as 1991 approaches and they begin to be deluged with offers to buy their stock.

Another provision of ANCSA, which had nothing directly to do with Natives, was the so-called "D2" section, which withdrew more than 100 million acres of land from public domain status and placed it all in conservation areas. Considerable bitterness still exists against this federal "land grab" among many Alaskans who claim their state continues to be "locked up" by Washington. Conservation in general will probably continue to be an issue in the state as development interests speak of "uselessly removing valuable land from productive purposes" and "prohibiting the economic livelihood of many Alaskans," and environmentalists talk of "preserving wilderness against reckless exploitation for the benefit of future generations."

After defeating opposition from environmental and Native groups, the long-awaited construction of the trans–Alaska Pipeline began in the spring of 1974. For three years, crews labored in near isolation for very high wages to construct the 48-inch diameter conduit that runs for nearly 800 miles from Prudhoe Bay to the tanker terminal at Valdez. Lots of construction difficulties arose, some of them because the pipeline had to be raised above the ground in areas where the melting of the permafrost could cause damage to a conventional buried line carrying the hot oil. The pipeline also had to withstand air temperatures which varied between 60° below and 100° above zero on a year-round basis. The pipeline now can deliver as much as 2 million barrels of oil a day, and it has also taken its place as one of Alaska's foremost tourist attractions, particularly at its two terminals in Prudhoe Bay and Valdez.

In 1974, the same year the first pipe was laid, Alaska elected as its governor the colorful Jay Hammond, a Republican but an admitted environmentalist. The election was remarkable since Hammond not only defeated two former governors in the primary but also the incumbent, William A. Egan, in the general election. Conservation measures are seen as basically anti-development in Alaska, usually identified with meddling by the federal government and such outside do-gooder influences as the Sierra Club and Greenpeace. Hammond was reelected in 1978, demonstrating to some that Alaskans no longer strictly voted their pocketbooks. They were also becoming concerned with the quality of life and the future of the 49th State.

Also in 1978, President Carter used the 1906 Antiquities Act to designate more than 100 million acres of Alaska as national monuments, wildlife refuges, and other areas closed to future development. The following year the state unsuccessfully filed suit to halt some of this designation. Environmental-versus-development battles, often between the federal government and state interests, have continued on one level or another up to the present day.

In 1980, the state legislature enacted Hammond's plan to set aside some of the state's oil money by establishing the Alaska Permanent

Fund. Beginning in 1982, dividends from this fund began to be mailed annually to all Alaskan residents. The first checks that year totaled $1000 for each man, woman, and child resident in the state for at least six months.

Hotel man William Sheffield, a Democrat, was elected governor of Alaska in 1982. His administration was plagued with charges of political favoritism, however. At the same time, world oil prices began to tumble, bringing on a relative recession from which Alaska has still not recovered. Unemployment began to rise and the price of real estate began to fall. A move to impeach Sheffield failed but in 1986 he became Alaska's first incumbent governor to lose his party's primary. The man who defeated him, Steve Cowper (pronounced "Cooper"), went on to win the general election over the first woman ever nominated for governor. Cooper has announced that he will not run for reelection in 1990.

For the past few years, the biggest controversy in Alaska seems to be the proposed use of ANWR (pronounced vaguely "on-war"), the Arctic National Wildlife Refuge, on the North Slope, east of the Prudhoe Bay oil fields. With an eye toward the eventual drying up of the current supply, petroleum interests want to dig for new oil and gas sources there. Conservationists who vigorously oppose this activity point to the fragile environment surrounding the resident Porcupine Herd of caribou and many other wildlife species they say will be damaged. If you read the papers or watch the news while in Alaska, you will no doubt hear the latest on this volatile issue.

The biggest corruption case in Alaska's history began in 1988 when 11 were charged with bribery, mail fraud, and accepting $9 million in kickbacks from contractors in exchange for favors relating to the building boom on the oil-rich North Slope.

Environmental troubles continue with reports that fish have been contaminated with oil in Valdez, at the end of the great pipeline; and that lead pollution was discovered in Skagway, although blood tests showed there was no immediate threat to the population.

Politics, economic development, and the environment dominate the news in Alaska as they do in many other places. The world at large only heard about Alaska in 1988 once—when three California gray whales were trapped in the ice near Barrow. After a million-dollar effort, and with the help of Russian icebreakers, two were eventually rescued. Many Alaskans looked down their noses at what they felt was the undue attention given this event, and a waste of money and resources on animals whose species is not even biologically endangered. In other circumstances, the California gray whale is even legally hunted by the Eskimos.

Probably the most important event for the average man during 1988 was the emotional visit of a group of Alaskan Eskimos and state officials to the Soviet Siberian town of Provideniya. Alaskan and Siberian Yupiks trace their roots back to common ancestors, and as they traded snapshots and memories, many recalled relatives they had not see in 40 years. In the spirit of Soviet *glasnost,* a joint Siberian-Alaskan reindeer-processing industry may now be in the offing, along with other cultural exchanges and a new passenger airline route between the two areas.

A GLOSSARY OF ALASKANA

Like many areas of the world, Alaska and the Yukon have words, terms, abbreviations, and phrases its residents and frequent visitors know and use regularly. Here is a group of these, without which a *cheechako* probably could never become a sourdough. Since some words have been transliterated from Native languages or Russian, you may run across some variations in spelling. With a few exceptions, this list does not cover names of animals, flowers, minerals, people, annual holidays, etc., which are defined in other chapters.

ABC Islands, the—Admiralty, Baranof, and Chichagoff.
ABL—Alaska Baseball League.
ACT—Anchorage Community Theater.
ACVB—Anchorage Convention and Visitors Bureau.
AFN—the Alaska Federation of Natives, mostly Eskimos and Athabascans. (See also: "ANB.")
ADF&G—Alaska Division of Fish and Game, a state agency.
AK—official U.S. Post Office abbreviation for Alaska.
AMHS—the Alaska Marine Highway System, also known as the Marine Highway or just "the ferry."
ANB—Alaska Native Brotherhood, a large organization of Natives (mostly Tlingit Indians).
ANCSA—Alaska Native Claims Settlement Act of 1971.
ANGTS—Alaska Natural Gas Transportation System, a proposed gas pipeline from Alaska's North Slope across Canada to the Lower 48.
ANS—Alaska Native Sisterhood, the women's branch of the ANB.
ANWR—(pronounced "*on*-war") Arctic National Wildlife Refuge, the center of a controversy regarding new oil and gas exploration on the North Slope. (see also: "Porcupine Herd.")
AOC—Anchorage Organizing Committee. Originally formed to pro-

mote Anchorage as a site for the Winter Olympics, it continues to spearhead winter sports construction projects. It aimed for the 1992 Olympics, then 1994, and now 1998.

APOC—Alaska Public Offices Commission.

APRN—Alaska Public Radio Network.

APSC—Alyeska Pipeline Service Company.

APU—Alaska Pacific University.

ASMI—Alaska Seafood Marketing Institute, a group formed to, among other things, promote "wild" (expensive) Alaska salmon over "soft and wimpy" (cheap) pen-reared salmon.

ATCO container—(pronounced *"at*-co") no-nonsense, all-purpose portable prefabricated building capable of being assembled in many sizes and configurations. The latter-day equivalent of the Quonset hut, it is heavily used in remote areas.

ATU—Anchorage Telephone Utility, the local phone company.

ATV—All-Terrain Vehicle, popular open-air three- or four-wheel transportation in the bush or rural communities.

AVA—Alaska Visitors Association, a tourist industry group.

Ah-Ha—a non-alcoholic drink invented in 1967 by the mayor of Anchorage (now defunct).

Air add-on—an extra fare added to a cruise, which pays for a passenger's return by air to certain U.S. cities (not really an Alaskan term, of course).

Air Crossroads of the World—former nickname for Anchorage, now retired.

Akutaq—see: "Eskimo ice cream."

Alascom—the major long-distance phone company in Alaska.

Alaska—the 49th U.S. state. Also the name of a monthly magazine published in Anchorage.

Alaska Air Mushers—a hot-air balloon club, believe it or not.

Alaska Day—State holiday, observed Oct. 18, commemorating the transfer of Alaska from Russia to the United States (not to be confused with Seward's Day).

Alaska Highway—road generally considered to extend the 1520 miles between Dawson Creek, B.C., and Fairbanks, Alaska (not to be confused with the Alaska *Marine* Highway).

Alaska Marine Highway—formal name for the state ferry system, otherwise known simply as "the ferry."

Alaskaland—a large, historic theme park in Fairbanks.

Alaskan—according to some, it should only be applied to a person who has lived through an entire winter in the state.

Alaskana—collection of books and literature or other items devoted to Alaskan subject matter.

Alaskan horses—jocular term for mosquitoes.

Alaska's Secret Season—upbeat state promotional phrase referring to winter tourism in Alaska.

Alaskon Express—new name for White Pass & Yukon Motorcoaches.

Alexander Archipelago—the islands of Southeast Alaska (the panhandle), mainly the ABC islands.

ALCAN—original name for the Alaska Highway (Alaska-Canada Military Highway).

ALCAN 200—annual 200-mile snowmobile race headquartered in Haines.

Aleuts—Natives originally from the Aleutian Islands.

Alevins—newly hatched salmon. (see: "Fry.")

All-Alaska Logging Championships—two-day lumberjack contest held each June in Sitka.

Alotto—Alaska Non-Profit Lottery.

Alpenglow—a red or orange glow seen on the tops of mountains just before sunrise or after sunset.

Alpine glacier—a glacier high on the slopes of a mountain or plateau; also called a mountain glacier or a hanging glacier.

Alpine skiing—downhill skiing; considerably less work (in our opinion) than the Nordic variety.

Alpirod—European copy of Alaska's Iditarod Sled Dog Race.

Alyeska—(1) an old Aleut word for Alaska traditionally translated as "the Great Land" or sometimes "the mainland." (2) Now also the name of the service corporation for the trans–Alaska Pipeline, as well as (3) a ski resort south of Anchorage.

Anadromous—referring to salmon and other determined fish that fight their way from the sea upriver to spawn in fresh water.

Anchorage Bowl—Nope, not a football game; just the ACVB-preferred term for central Anchorage, that's all.

Anchor-town—slang term for Anchorage, *not* preferred by the ACVB.

Angeyok—see: "Umiak."

Arctic, the—the region above the Arctic Circle in which the average temperature of the warmest month is less than 50° and that of the coldest month is below 32° (according to the U.S. Army in Alaska).

Arctic Circle—66°33′ North Latitude, marking the point above which the sun appears not to set in the summer and not to rise in the winter. (Pilots may caution you to lift your feet when flying over it!)

Argonaut—gold prospector.

Athabascans—Indians of Central Alaska and the Yukon (sometimes spelled Athapascan).

Attakiska—brand of Alaska-made vodka.

Aurora borealis—Latin name for Northern Lights.

B.C.—British Columbia, the Canadian province bordering Alaska. (We know *you* know that, but somebody else might not.)

Bachelors—male fur seals without mates.

Baked Alaska—dessert made of ice cream, cake, and meringue.

Baleen—valuable bristle-covered plume of flexible bone found in the mouths of some whales, such as the bowhead or humpback. Once used for corset stays, now for Eskimo arts.

Banana Belt—Southeast Alaska, and its relatively mild climate (by Central Alaska standards).

Bar bell—(not to be confused with a "bear bell") Don't ring it, unless you're prepared to buy a drink for everyone in the house.

Barabara—Aleut shelter built of driftwood and sod.

Bard of Alaska—according to his publicity, it's Larry Beck, an Anchorage entertainer (not to be confused with the following).

Bard of the Yukon—poetic name for the late Robert W. Service, a Yukon poet whose works are also popular in Alaska.

Barn door—a large fish on the line. (see also: "Ping-Pong paddle.")

Beach seines—fish nets led into the water by boats and later swept back to the beach (as opposed to "purse seines").

Bear bell—a small bell pinned on a hiker in order to warn a bear to keep its distance. It is usually not true that (a) the bear will follow the sound to see what is making it, or (b) that the bell is to be fastened on the bear to warn the hikers!

Bear bread—see: "Chickens of the Woods."

Bear stories—what Alaskans like to tell instead of ghost stories, especially to impress *cheechakos*. (see: "Bear bell.")

Bear trail—just what it sounds like, and while on it they have the right-of-way.

Beavertails—snowshoes.

Berger bits—what the Coast Guard calls small pieces of icebergs.

Bering Land Bridge—continental connection that existed 10,000 years ago and allowed men and animals to cross from Siberia to Alaska.

Bidarka—skin-covered boat built by Aleuts.

Bigger Hammer—a community marching band in Skagway (from: "If you can't do the job, get a bigger hammer").

Billiken—Eskimo carving in ivory of a pointed-head, smiling good-luck figure (although not originated by the Eskimos).

Bima dredge—the giant (14-story) dredge still mining gold offshore at Nome.

Blanket toss—originally an Eskimo technique in which one was tossed into the air from a walrus-skin blanket to see offshore whales; now used as a game (also called "nulukataq").

Blizzard—snow blowing so high and thick that it is impossible to tell if the sky is clear or cloudy.

Block heater—electrical heater attached to the engine block of a car so that it can be warmed in the winter. (See also: "Plug-ins").

Blowhole—the nostril of a whale or dolphin.

Blue Babe—popular name for the 36,000-year-old Alaskan bison found frozen in the permafrost, apparently killed by a lion.

Blue Canoe—any Alaska State ferry, from its predominate dark blue color (also: "Big Blue Canoe").

Blue clouds—sardonic term used by rain-soaked southeasterners for breaks in the clouds.

Blue ticketing—during territorial days, an alternative to a jail sentence when the perpetrator was given a one-way ticket to Seattle.

Boar—a papa bear.

Bola—Eskimo weapon for snaring small birds in flight.

Bolshaya Zemlya—Russian name for Alaska (the "Great Land").

Bonspiel—a curling match.

Boomer—somewhat derogatory term for a developer (opposite of a "Greenie"). Also a very temporary Alaskan resident, only up for high wages.

Booties—worn by sled dogs on their feet to prevent damage to their delicate pads for long trips or under adverse conditions.

Bore tide—a strong tide which comes in as a two- to six-feet-high wave in Cook Inlet and the Turnagain Arm near Anchorage.

Boreal forest—hardy, a slow-growing vegetation and trees which have adapted to harsh conditions just short of Alpine tundra areas. (see also: "Taiga.")

Borough—Alaskan equivalent of a county—only much larger.

Braga—fiery Russian drink fermented from fruit, yeast, and sugar, still popular in the Aleutians.

Breaching—said of a whale leaping completely clear of the water (incorrect: "broaching").

Breaking trail—mushing through new snow.

Breakup—spring thaw when river ice begins to crack and flow again in late April or early May; a muddy, slushy period, unloved by Alaskans, when those who have the money fly to Hawaii.

Brim Frost—annual military cold-weather exercise in Alaska—cancelled in 1989, at least, because of cold weather.

Bucs—an Anchorage baseball team, one of two Anchorage members of the ABL.

Buffalo gnats—same as "Whitesox."

Bugling—mating call of the male elk (which has nothing to do with horns).

Bunny boots—oversized rubber boots with air spaces, designed for warmth in extremely low temperatures; also called "vapor barrier boots" and sometimes "Mickey Mouse boots."

Burls—unusual bumps on a log of spruce, considered quite attractive when sanded down and finished like a piece of furniture.

Burning Hills of Suntrana—underground coal fires which have been burning for years in the bush near the town of Healy.

Bush—the remote areas of Alaska and northern Canada. (This nice short word, normally popular with Alaskan newspaper headline writers, has been causing some confusion since the last presidential election.)

Bush baby—an Alaskan who has grown up in the sticks.

Bush pilot—one who flies in rural areas using small planes sometimes equipped with floats or skis.

Bush Pipeline—radio program sending personal messages to people who cannot be reached by phone.

Button blanket—Tlingit and other Southeast Indian blankets in which the design is created by sewing on scores or hundreds of bright buttons (originally pieces of shells).

Button blanket chief—high-caste Tlingit.

By-catches—other species of fish and shellfish accidentally caught up in halibut trawl nets.

CIRI—Cook Inlet Region, Inc., a large native corporation specializing in real estate.

Cabin fever—a form of stir-craziness caused by spending too much time indoors during the winter. (see also: "SAD.")

Cabineering—illegal possession and building on government land; squatting.

Cache—a place to store food safe from animals out in the bush—usually represented in caricature as a log dog house on stilts.

Cake ice—flat ice floes.

Calving—breaking off of large chunks of ice from the face of a glacier.

Cama-i!—(pronounced "chah-*my*") a Yupik Eskimo greeting of friendship.

Candle ice—long ice crystals with tips sharp enough to cut leather—a hazard to sled dog feet. Also called "Needle ice."

Candlefish—eulachon (hooligan) fish, whose flesh is so oily that it can be burned.

Cat—any bulldozer (not necessarily a Caterpillar).

Cdn$** or **C$—abbreviations sometimes used for Canadian dollars.

Central Alaska—We could find no agreed-upon term for that portion of Alaska north of the panhandle, so we have called it "Central Alaska" occasionally in this volume (so sue us); generally speaking, it includes the Interior, the Arctic, Western, Southcentral, and sometimes Southwest.

Cervids—the deer family, including elk, moose, caribou, etc.

Chai—Russian word for tea, still used several places in Alaska.

Chain, the—usually refers to the Aleutian Island chain.

Challenge of the North—another term for the Yukon Quest.

Cheechako—newcomer to the north, or tenderfoot, from a Chinook Indian word (and possibly a mispronunciation of "Chicago"?).

Chickens of the Woods—type of edible orange mushroom or fungi.

Chilkat—subtribe of Tlingit Indians from the Haines area.

Chilkat blanket—Tlingit robe originally of goat skin wool and cedar bark, but today also made of heavy felt.

Chinook—(1) A strong, southerly warm wind, similar to the mistral or *fohn*. (2) A popular brand of Juneau-manufactured beer named Chinook Alaskan Amber. (3) A type of pidgin language. (4) An Indian tribe. (5) Another word for king salmon. (6) Probably something else we've forgotten.

Chip seal—paving used on some portions of the Alaska Highway in Canada (also called BST, bitumen surface treatment), crushed gravel with oil.

Chuck—"Skookum chuck." (See: "Skookum.")

Chum—"Dog salmon" (food for man's best chum).

Cirque—glacial depression; a natural amphitheater.

Class system—a way of rating rivers for rubber rafting purposes. Class I is the calmest; class V is the roughest.

Clear-cut—logging operation which removes all trees, old and young, from a forested area—a highly controversial technique, since it takes a spruce forest about 150 years to grow back.

Clingssiiks—in Yupik Eskimo folklore, tiny magical people (similar to the Irish leprechaun).

Coho—another name for Silver Salmon.

Colonists—Matanuska valley farmers (or their descendants) who were relocated to Alaska in the 1930s as an anti-Depression measure.

Color—a tiny quantity of gold, giving evidence of more to be found. ("Color in my pan!" the prospector shouted.)

Come haw!—command to dog team to make a complete 180-degree turn to the left (opposite of "Come gee!").

Country, the—term used by gold prospectors of '98 to describe the strange north land in Alaska and the Yukon in which they found themselves struggling for their existence.

Crampons—metal spikes attached to shoes to give traction on ice.

Creek robbing—illegal use of nets by stretching nets entirely across a stream in order to catch migrating salmon.

Creoles—applied by Russians to the children of Native women and Russian men.

Crevasse—fissure or rift on the top surface of a glacier.

Cribs—small houses, each usually with a single room, used by "ladies of the evening" during the gold rush (seen in Skagway and Dawson).

Crossbeak, Bonnet, and Bone—neither an Alaskan law firm nor a comedy act related to yours truly, but the names given to whales caught in the ice at Barrow last year. (See also: "Operation Breakthrough.")

Cruisers—passengers on cruise ships.

Cry of the Wild Ram—outdoor August dramatic production in Kodiak, based on Russian days in Kodiak and Sitka.

D2 controversy—arising from section D2 in the ANCSA which set aside a considerable section of land for preservation, prohibiting development.

DEC—Department of Environmental Conservation (State of Alaska).

DEW Line—Distant Early Warning Line, an American-Canadian radar network designed for protection during the Cold War.

Damp town—neither "wet" nor completely "dry," a municipality that has voted to ban liquor sales but not liquor possession.

Deadfall—crude trap for small animals made by propping up a heavy log over the bait.

Deadhead—partially or wholly submerged log, a hazard to navigation (sometimes also called a "sleeper").

Denali—Athabascan name for Mt. McKinley, "the big one." Also Denali National Park, centered around the mountain.

Devil dance—Native dance celebrating end of one year and the beginning of the next.

Devil's club—a thorny vine or shrub which catches you in the forest, used by Indians in olden days to beat suspected witches.

Dimples—tiny holes in beach sand used as a guide by clam hunters.

Dip netting—a small net bag with a handle used to scoop fish from the rivers.

Dog logs—detailed training records of a dog team, kept by the musher.

Dog salmon—chum salmon, usually dried and fed to sled dogs.

Doughnut hole, the—a relatively small international zone in the Bering Sea where fishing is currently unregulated by either the U.S. or the Soviet Union.

Down South—(or "Southern") yet another term for the less fortunate area called the "Lower 48" or "Outside."

Dredge—large floating mechanism for scooping up paydirt and sifting for gold or other mineral content.

Duck shoes—low-cut version of "Sitka slippers."

Dwt.—abbreviation for "pennyweight." (See: "Troy ounce.")

Effie—partial remains of a 21,000-year-old woolly mammoth found in the permafrost along Fairbanks Creek, now on display at the UAF museum (named for the FE Company; see below).

Eskers—sand or gravel ridges deposited by a stream running under a glacier.

Eskimo—members of the Inupiat or Yupik Native groups living in Alaska and Canada (from the French meaning "raw meat eater"; see also: "Inuit").

Eskimo ice cream—cold concoction made from seal oil, tundra berries (or chopped meat), and snow; also called something like "yech-attack" (okay, "akutaq," if you insist on accuracy).

Eskimo Scouts—white-uniformed unit of the Alaska National Guard which patrols the border closest to the Soviet Union.

Everclear—brand of pure white grain alcohol, about 180 proof.

FCVB—Fairbanks Convention and Visitors Bureau. (CVBs are established in several Alaska municipalities.)

FE Company—sometimes referred to as the "Old FE Company"; FE stands for Fairbanks Exploration, the corporation which once did all the gold mining in the Fairbanks area.

FIT—Free and Independent Traveler (as opposed to those on group tours, cruises, etc.), a travel industry term.

Faro—card game, particularly popular during Gold Rush days. Also the location of the lead-zinc mines in the Yukon.

Feeder ferries—short routes on the Alaska Marine Highway, such as the shuttles between Ketchikan and Hollis.

Ferryliners—a somewhat exalted term the Alaska Division of Tourism prefers to call the nine ships in the state ferry system.

Fiddleheads—edible portion of a certain fern.

Fingerlings—young salmon (about the size of a finger).

Fish burner—jocular name for a sled dog (husky).

Fish ladder—artificial setup for salmon, to bypass dams and other obstructions on their way home to their spawning grounds.

Fish wheel—wooden device powered by river current and built by Indians for scooping up salmon; allegedly invented by Chinese, Portuguese, or Scandinavians.

Five a.m. to 8 a.m.—the three hours bars and other liquor outlets must be closed by state law.

Fjord—steep, deep coastal channels carved by ancient glaciers, or sometimes the depths between submerged mountains.

Float trip—cruising down the river on a rubber raft.

Floaters—dead bodies which surface in a river or channel after breakup.

Floatplane—airplane equipped with pontoons for landing on and taking off from water.

Flukes—a whale of a tail, or is it the tail of a whale?

Fly-in fishing—chartering a float plane to get to remote fishing camps or other areas in the bush (relatively less expensive in Canada).

Forgotten War, the—the Aleutian campaign during World War II.

Freddy's—Fred Meyer, a chain store.

Freeze up—opposite of breakup; when a river freezes completely over and appears to stop flowing.

Frost heaves—Up-thrusting of ground or road pavement caused by freezing and thawing of moist soil.

Frostbite—tissue damage from extreme cold.

Fry—juvenile salmon (older stage than alevins or fingerlings).

Fur Rendezvous—annual winter carnival held in February in Anchorage, also called ''Fur Rondy'' and nicknamed the ''Mardi Gras of the North.''

GCI—Alaska's second long-distance telephone company.

Gam—a large pod of whales.

Gill netting—fixed-net trapping technique which catches fish in relatively smaller quantities that simply swim into the net and get caught by their gills. In general, fresh gill net-caught fish are preferable to those caught en masse in seine nets.

Glacial flour—fine rock powder created by glacier action, which gives distinctive color or cloudiness to many rivers.

Glacier bear—gray- or blue-gray-colored fur phase in the development of a black bear.

Glacier Pilots—an Anchorage baseball team, one of two Anchorage members of the ABL.

Glory hole—''Mother lode''—center of a gold vein. Also the name of a soup kitchen in Juneau.

Gold Kings—Fairbanks hockey team.

Gold rush—a psychological stampede which took place several times in the history of Alaska and the Yukon when gold was discovered, principally in 1897 and 1898.

Golden Circle Route—promotional name for the 360 miles of road from Haines through Kluane National Park and Whitehorse to Skagway (or the reverse).

Golden Heart City, the—Fairbanks.

Golden Stairs—steepest portion of the Chilkoot Pass out of Dyea (named during the Gold Rush of 1898).

Goldpanners—Fairbanks baseball team.

Gone Siwash—once applied to white men who began living with Indians, etc. (from Canada's Siwash Tribe).

Good Friday Avalanche—avalanche which killed between 43 and 63 on the Chilkoot Trail near Dyea on April 3, 1898.

Good Friday Earthquake—the great Alaska earthquake of March 27, 1964, in which 115 died.

Good Samaritan Law—an Alaskan statute allowing you to render aid in an emergency without fear of being sued later.

Grape jelly—routine, trite, hackneyed.

Great Alaska Shootout—Thanksgiving invitational inter-collegiate championship basketball tournament in Anchorage.

Greenie—somewhat derogatory term for an environmentalist.

Gridiron—(or "grid") simple dry dock for fishing boats; holds them upright while the tide is out.

Growler—a small iceberg (from the noise it makes going by the hull of a ship).

Grub stake—supplies or money given to a prospector in return for a share of his profits.

Gulf Coast—refers to the coast of the Gulf of Alaska, of course (Homer, Seward, Valdez, etc.)—not the Gulf of Mexico.

Gumbo—Canadian/Yukon term for a sticky type of mud.

Gussak—Eskimo slang for "white man"—from the Russian word "cossack" (also spelled "kass'aq").

Haida—Indian tribe generally living in British Columbia and on Prince of Wales Island in Southeast Alaska (related to but not to be confused with Tsimshian or Tlingit).

Halibut jacket—wool checked or tweed jacket, sometimes in red or green, favored by fishermen in Southeast.

Hanging glacier—see: "Alpine glacier."

Hangtown fry—oysters and eggs, a goldminer's breakfast.

Harem—several female fur seals managed by a single bull.

Haul Road—another term for the Dalton Highway leading from Fairbanks to Deadhorse (Prudhoe Bay).

Hawk—a cold wind from the north.

Headbolt heater—see: "Block heater."

Headlight protectors—clear plastic covers installed by some on their cars to prevent gravel from breaking headlights.

Highliners—champion commercial fishermen.

Hike!—(or "Hi!") starting command sometimes used for a dog sled team (See also: "Mush").

Hoarfrost—frozen dew.

Hooligan—tiny fish; smelt (probably because it was easier to say than "eulachon," the original word).

Hootch—homemade alcoholic beverages (from a Chinook word, "hootchenoo").

Horizontal rain—windy, rainy conditions in Ketchikan, usually in October.

Hot pepper aerosol—a pink, tear-gas-like substance used by some rangers and researchers to ward off attacking bears without harming them.

Houseposts—carvings similar in design and appearance to totem poles, used inside Tlingit buildings as center posts and corner posts.

Huckety-buck—slang term for swift, corresponding to "quick as the Dickens" or perhaps "lickety-split."

Humpie—humpbacked or pink salmon (after reaching fresh water).

Humpback Whales—besides the whales, also the athletic teams at UAS.

Husky—any sled dog, but also a particular breed (Siberian Husky).

Hyderized—a tradition perpetuated in the bars of Hyder, Alaska, involving drinking Everclear chased with water (not recommended by us).

Hypothermia—subnormal body temperature—last stop on the way to freezing to death.

IBC—the Inuit Broadcasting Corp., the northern TV service of the Canadian Broadcasting Corp.

Ice Age—otherwise known as the Pleistocene Epoch, the glacial period about 600,000 years ago.

Ice bridge—temporary bridge or causeway across a frozen river; it gives way at spring breakup.

Ice cap—more-or-less permanently frozen ocean extending outwards from the polar region (also sometimes refers to the head area of a glacier).

Ice dam—temporary blocking of a stream or river by pieces of ice, which can cause severe flooding until it melts or is forceably removed.

Ice field—a large mass of thick ice, generally feeding several glaciers at the same time.

Ice fog—microscopic particles of ice formed from freezing fog (made worse by air pollution).

Iceberg—floating ice that has calved from a nearby glacier.

Icebergia—one of several disparaging terms applied to Alaska by contemporary critics of the Alaska Purchase (others included "Polaria," "Walrussia," "Seward's Folly," etc.).

Icecrete—mixture of sand, gravel, and water poured into forms and frozen.

Iceworm—a very tiny black worm that lives in glacier ice (not mythical, as some believe).

Iditarod—originally the name of a town and a trail; now refers to the annual 1000-mile dog sled race (the "Last Great Race") from Anchorage to Nome (beginning first Saturday of March).

Iditaski—world's longest-distance cross-country ski race (210 miles).

Igloo—Eskimo camping or emergency hunting shelter, usually made from wood or whalebone in Alaska, or occasionally from snow in northern Canada. Also a local chapter of the Pioneers of Alaska, and an airline shipping container.

Illegitimus non carborundum—Latin motto on the masthead of the Nome *Daily Nugget* meaning "Don't let the bastards get you down."

Intertidal invertibrates—creatures like starfish, sea urchins, etc., that live along the shoreline.

Inuit—another word for Eskimo; the term preferred by Canadian Inuit (Inupiat), who consider the word "Eskimo" to be pejorative.

Inupiat—Eskimos inhabiting Northern Alaska (including Barrow, Nome, and Kotzebue) and the northern Yukon; sometimes spelled "Inupiaq." (see also: "Yupik.")

Inside Passage—waterways and channels which serve as highways for shipping in Southeast Alaska.

Interior—what residents of Southeast Alaska sometimes call all the rest of the state. The term is narrower up north, referring to Fairbanks and much of central and eastern Alaska, but not areas to the north, west, or south.

Interpreter—U.S. Forest Service term for a ranger who gives lectures, such as those on board the state ferries traveling through the Tongass National Forest.

Iron Chink—early salmon-processing machine which replaced the need for battalions of Chinese labor in the canning factories.

Iron dog—see: "Snowmachine."

Jacks—small male salmon.

Japan Current—warm water that raises temperatures and causes rains in Southeast and Southcentral Alaska.

Jingler—sled dog wearing bells to let pedestrians, etc., know exactly where they are during dark, foggy days in northern villages.

Johnsonrude—Eskimo word for any outboard motor.

KGB—Ketchikan Gateway Borough (non-Communist and harmless).

KVA—Klondike Visitors Association (Dawson).

Kames—gravel hills caused by glacial action.

Kashim—community house of Eskimos or Athabascans (a Siberian word).

Kayak—small (one-man) Eskimo skin boat.

Kenai twitch—snagging fish (illegal).

Ketchikan tuxedo—jeans and a tee shirt or jeans and a raincoat.

Kettles—small lakes formed by melting glaciers.

Kicker—small motor for temporary installation or backup on a skiff.

Kil own—flat sealskin drums Eskimos beat from the underside with a stick.

Kilometer—approximately six tenths of a mile; important when considering distances in Canada, the Canadian portion of the Alaska Highway, etc.

Klondike, the—mistakenly thought by the stampeders of 1898 to be a large general region in Alaska and the Yukon where gold could be picked up off the ground; actually, a river near Dawson City, Yukon. Also a version of solitaire, and a popular name for a hotel.

Koot's—affectionate term for Chilkoot Charlie's, an Anchorage bar.

Kopuk—popular brand of mountaineering boots.

Kupiak—(pronounced, vaguely, "cup o' yuck") the Inupiat word for coffee.

Kuspuk—type of light, brightly colored Eskimo women's parka, sometimes worn over a conventional parka to protect it in winter or worn alone in summer.

Kutchin—tribe or subgroup of Athabascan Indians split between the U.S. and Canada (Alaska and the Yukon).

Labret—lip or cheek ornament of ivory, used by Eskimos and some Indians.

Land of the Midnight Sun—nickname sometimes used for Alaska.

Layering—technique for dealing with changing cool, cold, and colder temperatures by taking off and donning clothes in layers.

Lead dog—first dog in a team, who follows the musher's commands.

Leads—channels of open water between ice floes.

Let's go!—starting command for a dog team used by mushers who do not use "Hike" or "Mush."

Lighter—small boat to carry cruise ship passengers to shore if the ship doesn't want to pay the high dock fees at some ports (sometimes necessary because of shallow water).

Line, the—former red light district in Ketchikan (Creek Street).

Line out!—musher's command to straighten up his line of dogs.

Liter—metric measurement in which gasoline is sold in Canada, approximately the size of an American quart.

Little Drook—costumed cossack cartoon character, the symbol of the Sitka Visitors Bureau (nothing to do with a "little drunk"); it is an approximate translation of the Russian word for "friend."

Lode—See: "Mother lode."

Log cabin—often refers to the local tourist information center, many of which are in log cabins throughout the state.

Longliners—commercial fishing boats that troll for halibut and other bottomfish.

Lower 48—sometimes "South 48" or similar, used in Alaska to refer to the 48 contiguous or conterminous states of the U.S., i.e., all states except Alaska and Hawaii. (See also: "Outside.")

Luge—a racing sled.

MV—Motor Vessel, as in the MV *Malaspina*, a state ferry.

Malamute—(or Alaskan malamute) a particular type of sled dog, named for an Eskimo tribe ("Yukon King" was a malamute).

Malling—believe it or not, a term used in Juneau for visiting a shopping mall.

Marge—obscure word for shoreline, perhaps used nowhere other than in Robert W. Service's *Cremation of Sam McGee*.

Mariculture—farming of freshwater and saltwater fish, a current controversy in Alaska.

Marine Highway—see "Alaska Marine Highway."

Mat-Su—popular abbreviated term for the area including the adjoining Matanuska and Susitna Valleys north of Anchorage.

Mat-Su Miners—nothing to do with mining; a baseball team from the above vicinity.

Matanuska Maid—brand of dairy products, originally all from cows in the Matanuska Valley (also called "Mat Maid").

Mickey Mouse boots—see: "Bunny boots."

Midnight sun—poetic reference to 24-hour summer sunshine above the Arctic Circle.

Midnight Sun Cross-Country Marathon—annual Fairbanks-to-Anchorage wheelchair race.

Milepost—short white pole occasionally set up along some major highways indicating the distance from that highway's beginning (kilometer posts in Canada). Also an annual road atlas published in Seattle detailing highway services and other motorist information in Alaska, the Yukon, British Columbia, etc.

Milepost Zero—Dawson Creek, B.C. (beginning of the Alaska Highway).

Milt—sperm of salmon.

Miners—Mat-Su's baseball team.

Missed too many boats—in the old days, at least, an Alaskan suffering from mental problems because of continued isolation.

Mr. Whitekeys—see: "Spamtones."

Moil—Hard work, another obscure disservice by Robert Service, used in disposing of the hapless McGee (see: "Marge").

Moose gooser—whimsical term for the Alaska Railroad.

Moose nuggets—just what you might think they are, except that some misguided souls have turned them into handicraft items.

Moraine—three types: *terminal* moraines are rock debris (till) under or in front of a glacier; *medial* moraines are black streaks on a glacier surface caused by debris; and *lateral* moraines are formed by debris on the sides of a glacier.

Mother lode—gold from the main vein in solid rock. (See also: "Glory hole.")

Motionless dancing—sometimes used to describe Eskimo dances in which participants seldom lift their feet.

Motorcoach—what Canadians prefer to call a tour bus.

Mounties—see: "RCMP."

Mudflats—extremely dangerous areas exposed at low tide along Turnagain Arm (near Anchorage) and other rivers, lakes, and inlets. Don't try to walk on them!

Mukluk—type of Eskimo boot made from seal or caribou skin.

Muktuk—whale skin and blubber, considered a delicacy by Eskimos, especially when eaten raw.

Municipal Bear Observation Facility—a tongue-in-cheek reference to the local garbage dump.

Mush—once used as a command to a dog team, but now discarded as not emphatic enough (too mushy?); from the French *marchons,* which means "Let's go." (See also: "Let's go" and "Hike.")

Musher—sled dog driver.

Mushing—traveling by dog sled (Alaska's official state sport).

Muskeg—acidic bog or swampy area, where little else but moss and scrub brush grows; virtually impossible to walk through except when frozen in winter.

NANA Regional Corporation—one of the better-known and most successful Native corporations created by ANCSA (stands for Northwest Alaska Native Association).

NWMP—North West Mounted Police—historical predecessor to today's RCMP.

Nanook—Eskimo word for polar bear; also: "Nanooks," the UAF hockey team.

Native Alaskan—(or "Alaskan Native") generally speaking, refers to Eskimos, Aleuts, and Indians, and not to Caucasians and others who merely were born in Alaska. Curiously, Alaskans often consider it better form to use "Native" rather than specifically identifying each of these groups.

Native Corporations—thirteen business corporations for aboriginal Alaskans financed and set up by ANCSA.

Needle ice—see: "Candle ice."

Nenana Ice Classic—annual lottery on the exact time that the Tanana River breaks up and begins flowing again at Nenana.

Nets—natural circles of stones created by complicated frost heave patterns.

Nicks—ABL baseball team from North Pole, AK.

Nighty-eighters—*(or '98ers)* those who took part in the gold rush of 1898.

No grape jelly—something special, different, or unusual.

No Man's Land—stretch on the Iditarod dog race from Fort Davis to Nome.

No Wake—sign in harbor areas prohibiting vessels from going fast enough to create a wake behind them.

Nomeite—resident of Nome (nope, they're not "Nomans").

Nordic—another term for cross-country skiiing.

North of 60—Canadian term for the Far North (above the 60th Parallel, which marks the southern border of the Yukon).

North Pole—included here because some folks become confused: North Pole, Alaska, is simply a town on the outskirts of Fairbanks. The real North Pole, of course, is out on the ice cap.

North Slope—arctic tundra region north of the Brooks mountain range; also called simply, "the Slope."

North to the Future—Alaska's official state motto.

North Warning System—military radar and communication defense network which is replacing the old DEW Line system in Alaska.

Northern Lights—bright, colorful shimmering effect in the northern sky created by natural electromagnetic forces, seen at night in fall, winter, or spring (also: "Aurora borealis").

Northwest Territories—area of Canada bordering the Yukon on the east.

NorthwesTel—phone company for the Yukon Territory.

No-see-ums—tiny biting gnats, particularly noticeable in late summer.

Nuchalawoya—four-day celebration at Tanana, dating back to a annual meeting between Athabascan chiefs at the site.

Nugget—naturally formed chunk of gold (not counting moose nuggets, which is something different). Also the name of the daily newspaper in Nome.

Nulukataq—see: "Blanket toss."

Nunatak—an "island" of land or rock surrounded by glacial ice (pronounced: "noon attack").

Off Sales—in Canada, a liquor store or bottle shop.

Ohlock—legendary hairy creature of Kodiak (similar to the Bigfoot legend).

Oilers—Kenai Peninsula baseball team.

Oil skins—raincoat and rain trousers.

Old Believers—a Russian-speaking rural group of about 600 in the Kachemak Bay area (Homer) whose beliefs are based on the Orthodox church.

Old man's beard—moss-like lichen that attaches itself to spruce branches in Southeast Alaska (also called "Grandpa's moustache").

Omega Block—the monster mass of cold air from Siberia that numbed Alaska for more than a week in early 1989.

Oogruk—Eskimo word for seal.

Oomingmak—Eskimo word for musk ox.

Oosik—penis bone of the walrus, a popular if expensive conversation piece on the mantle of Alaskan homes, and the subject of a bad joke or two.

Opening—A "halibut opening" or "salmon opening," for example, is a 24-hour period when commercial fishing is allowed for the species involved (generally not affecting sport fishing).

Operation Breakthrough—rescue efforts over 10 days for three ice-trapped whales which put Barrow on the world map in late 1988.

"Out the road"—far out from downtown Juneau, usually out past Auke Bay (there's only one road past that point). Also used in a similar sense in other towns of Southeast.

Outside—anywhere except Alaska and the Yukon (spelled with a capital *O*).

PAC—the Performing Arts Center in Anchorage.

PI, the—short for the *Seattle Post-Intelligencer,* an out-of-state newspaper popular in Alaska.

PSP—Paralytic Shellfish Poison, found in certain clams and mussels (the types harvested commercially are not afiected).

Pack it in, pack it out—concept promoted by USFS and others that whatever you carry ("pack") into a wilderness area you must also take out again.

Palms—the flat parts of moose antlers.

Pan ice—thin, flat, disk-like pieces of ice floating on a river or estuary.

Panhandle—another term for Southeast Alaska.

Panning—looking for gold in a pan of water and dirt, the simplest type of placer mining.

Paris of the North—Dawson City, Yukon, in the old days (1898).

Paris of the Pacific—Sitka, Alaska, in the old, old days (1860s).

Park Strip—ten-block-long by one-block wide park in Anchorage that was once an air strip (actually "Delaney Park Strip").

Parka—Eskimo-style coat, with a hood surrounded by a fur ruff (pronounced "parky" by some old sourdoughs).

Paydirt—soil containing flecks of gold, generally undetectable before placer mining.

Pelagic birds—birds which spend most of their life at sea, several species found on the Pribilof Islands.

People Mover—the Anchorage municipal bus system.

Permafrost—frozen subsoil underlying the Arctic and Interior regions and other parts of the north. In the far north it is "continuous"—underlying everything; further south, as in Fairbanks, it is "discontinuous"—in patches.

Permanent fund—a chunk of money set up in 1976 from oil earnings, from which the state may spend only the interest.

Permanent Fund Dividend program—portion of profits from the above annually distributed to individual Alaska residents.

Petro-Canada—brand of gasoline and other oil products refined and sold in Canada only.

Petroglyphs—mysterious ancient rock carvings in Wrangell and some other locations in Southeast.

Pig—a cleaning plug sent through the trans–Alaska Pipeline from time to time.

Pilot car—vehicle (usually a pickup truck) to follow when negotiating construction areas on the Alaska Highway and other roads, particularly in Canada.

Ping-Pong paddle—a small catch on your fishing line. (see also: "Barn door.")

Pingos—low, rounded hills or mounds created by climatic action against permafrost in some areas; a type of frost heave.

Pioneers—APU basketball team.

Pioneers' homes—state-supported homes for long-time Alaskans over 65.

Pirogi—(or "peroshki") a Russian pie—pastry filled with meat or cheese (often spelled "perogies").

Placer gold—loose gold found by panning or sluicing in sand and gravel.

Plug-ins—electric outlets, provided in some parking spaces, used to plug in block heaters installed on vehicles in the Alaskan Interior and Yukon ("Plug-in Parking").

Pod—a small group of whales, seals, or sea lions.

Poke—miner's bag of money or gold nuggets.

Polar Bear—other than *Ursus maritimus,* it's also a drink made from vodka, Kahlua, and ice cream.

Polar ice cap—the Arctic ice pack at the North Pole and in the ocean north of Alaska.

Polaris—the North Star (Latin), and the largest star on the Alaska flag.

Porcupine Herd—a specific herd of an estimated 165,000 caribou whose calving grounds are in the ANWR area in northeast Alaska.

Postal code—the mishmash of six numbers and letters that is the Canadian equivalent of the zip code.

Potlatch—a large native party, originally it involved extreme generosity on the part of the host.

Prairies, the—what Canadians generally call their midwest—Alberta, Manitoba, etc., where grain is grown.

Prinz Brau—now-defunct brand of Alaskan beer.

Project 92—Alaska-Canada celebration planned for 1992, commemorating the 50th anniversary of the Alaska Highway.

Promyshlenniki—eighteenth-century Russian fur traders and profiteers in Alaska.

Prove up—a final step in establishing title on a homestead after living there five years, building a house, clearing the land, etc.

Puff ball—a type of mushroom.

Pulp mill—a smelly factory which grinds and pulverizes wood in preparation for paper production or other nonwood uses.

Pup—a baby seal.

Purse seines—long, deep fishing nets operated from boats; when hauled up they are closed into a bag by "pursing" the edges.

Qiviut—soft underwool of the musk ox, now woven into scarves and sweaters. (That's a *Q* with no *U*—a great Scrabble word!)

RAHI—Rural Alaska Honors Institute, an intense UAF college-preparatory program for high school students from rural areas.

RATNET—Rural Alaska Television Network.

RCMP—Royal Canadian Mounted Police—the "Mounties" (they're sometimes equipped with radar guns along Yukon highways).

Railbelt—generally speaking, the areas of the Interior and Southcentral (Mat-Su, Nenana, etc.) served by the Alaska Railroad.

Red Dog—rich silver, zinc, and lead deposits, and now a mine, north of Kotzebue. Also a well-known bar in Juneau.

Red Lantern—prize awarded to the last-place musher in the Iditarod Sled Dog Race.

Red tide—sea water containing a large amount of plankton and other microorganisms, poisonous to fish and to people.

Redds—gravel love nests made by female salmon during spawning season.

Reinbou—cross between a reindeer and a caribou (also "carideer").

Rep, the—Alaska Repertory Theater.

Rig—taking a cue from trucker's slang, what an RVer sometimes calls his motor home.

Road kills—bodies of moose or other wild animals killed in an encounter with traffic.

Roadhouse—today any country bar and restaurant that rents a few (usually spartan) rooms; historically one mushing day apart on the trail.

Rock flour—very fine glacier dust.

Roll maneuver—(or "Eskimo roll maneuver") technique used in kayaking for turning upright again after rolling over in the water.

Rookery—breeding place either for birds or fur seals.

Rosemalings—polka dots, hearts, and flowers, a Scandanavian decorating technique used all over Petersburg.

Ruff—the fur lining the edge of a parka hood.

Russian America—name used for Alaska prior to the purchase by the United States.
Russian Christmas—see: "Slaviq."

SAD—Seasonal Affective Disorder; a lethargy brought on by long, dark winters above the Arctic Circle.
SATC—Southeast Alaska Tourism Council; a group to promote tourism in the panhandle, particularly non-cruise-related travel, on behalf of hotels, restaurants, rental cars, etc.
SEACC—Southeast Alaska Conservation Council.
SEADOGS—Southeast Alaska Dogs Organized for Ground Search, a volunteer search-and-rescue team which was sent to help look for victims of the Armenia earthquake in 1988.
SJC—Sheldon Jackson College (Sitka).
SOB—popular designation for the State Office Building in Juneau.
SOME—Special Olympics Mileage Event, sponsored by the Alaska State Police.
Salmon bake—summer outdoor cookout (sometimes called "salmon barbecue" in the Yukon).
Scat—animal droppings, usually bear, in which the temperature and consistency thereof could be vitally important to determining your immediate future.
Sea-Tac—popular name for the airport serving Seattle and Tacoma, Washington (pronounced "see-tack").
Sealaska—large Native corporation in Southeast Alaska.
Seaplane—see: "Floatplane."
Seawolves—UAA basketball, volley ball, hockey, or swimming team.
Seining—salmon fishing with huge nets that are generally for catching open-ocean fish in large, commercial quantities for canning (as opposed to gill netting and other techniques).
Setnetting—commercial salmon harvesting by means of nets anchored along a river, stream, or bay.
Seward's Day—public State holiday on March 28, commemorating the signing of the Alaska Purchase between the U.S. and Russia (not to be confused with "Alaska Day").
Seymour of Anchorage—the name of the dancing moose adopted as a city symbol of the Anchorage Convention and Visitors Bureau.
Shamen—traditional wise man and religious consular of a native village (don't call him a "witch doctor").
Shangri-La of Alaska—self-proclaimed nickname for Homer, Alaska.
Sheffield—defunct Alaska hotel chain; out of habit, many still refer to some hotel in any given town as "the Sheffield" (most became part of the Westmark Chain).

Shelf ice—ice along the banks of a river, the first part to freeze in fall and the last to thaw in spring; also called "Shore ice."

Shore berth—a pier in water deep enough for a ship such as the Alaska ferry to unload passengers and vehicles directly, without lightering.

Sitka slippers—satiric term for black, red, or brown rubber boots used constantly by sourdoughs who don't want to get their feet wet, muddy, or dusty; sometimes called "Wrangell sneakers," "Juneau tennis shoes," "Petersburg pumps," and similar terms.

Siwash—temporary, overnight camp on the trail (also used as a verb: "We had supper and then siwashed").

Ski-Doo—see: "Snowmachine."

Skiff—(from a Chinook word) any small boat ("dinghy" is generally not used in Alaska).

Skijoring—a sport combining cross-country skiing and dog sledding (the dogs wear the harness and you wear the skis).

Skookum—strong, worthy, or stalwart. A skookum chuck is a fast-moving tide through a narrow opening; a skookum house was a jail.

Slack tide—short period of time when the tide is slowly turning, critical in the navigation of some narrow Southeast channels.

Slaviq—Russian Orthodox Christmas Festival, celebrated by some Natives for a week beginning January 7 (also called "Russian Christmas").

Sleeper—see: "Deadhead."

Sleep-off center—facility for drunks, street people, etc., run by the Salvation Army in Anchorage.

Slope—see: "North Slope."

Slough—a shallow drainage area for a stream or inlet. When water is low it can be crossed with caution on foot or by vehicles.

Sluice—riffled trough used to wash out gold from gravel and sand.

Smolt—young salmon on its way downstream to the ocean.

Snag tree—(1) tree dangerously overhanging a stream which could catch a raft in its branches; (2) a dead tree still standing, popular with eagles as a good lookout perch.

Snagging—hooking a fish elsewhere other than in the mouth (usually illegal).

Snow boarding—new northern version of surfing, becoming a popular sport in Alaska (not allowed at some ski resorts).

Snow fog—blinding condition created by blowing snow in high winds.

Snowmachine—usually one word, it is not a machine to *make* snow, as in Southern ski areas, but an Alaskan term for a snowmobile (also "iron dog" or "Ski-Doo" in Alaska, or "sno-go" in the Yukon).

Snowshoe—Athabascan invention that has you walking over drifts on what seems like a couple of tennis rackets.

Soapstone—soft, slippery stone used for carving by Eskimos and others.

Soapy Smith Awards—annual "dubious achievement" list of Alaska happenings over the previous year compiled by the *Anchorage Daily News* in January (named after Skagway's notorious con man).

Sockeye—type of salmon; also called "red salmon."

Solstice—first day of winter (Dec. 21), or of summer (June 22).

Sounding—diving, when referring to whales.

Sourdough—(1) old-timer or long-time resident of Alaska and the Yukon; or (2) a yeasty mixture once carried by prospectors and now prized by anyone, used to make bread or pancakes.

Sour Toe Cocktail—beer mug filled with champagne and garnished with a pickled human toe (invented, generally available, and sometimes even drunk by sober folk in Dawson City, Yukon).

South 48—same as: "Lower 48."

Southcentral—generally accepted term for that portion of Alaska along the Gulf Coast surrounding Anchorage.

Southeast—Alaska's "panhandle," the narrow portion alongside British Columbia.

Southwest—the portion of Alaska that includes the Alaska Peninsula and the Aleutian Islands.

Sow—mama bear.

Spam Can, the—nickname for the Native American Building in Juneau.

Spamtones—a musical group organized by "Mr. Whitekeys," the owner of a bar in Anchorage.

Spenard Action Committee—group of anti-prostitution activists in Anchorage.

Spenard divorce—killing one's spouse.

Square tires—tires on a car that has been left out all night during extremely low temperatures, causing them not to roll smoothly the next morning (usually in Fairbanks).

Squarebanks—used occasionally in Anchorage to refer derogatorily to their rival city in the Interior.

Squaw candy—chewy dried and smoked salmon.

Star of the North—fairly recent sobriquet for Anchorage (which used to be known as "Air Crossroads of the World").

Steelhead—a tough type of sea-run rainbow trout.

Step-on guide—temporary guide from a local area who boards a tour bus to give a more detailed commentary.

Storyknife—Eskimo technique of drawing pictures in the dirt while telling stories or teaching children.

Sundog—a visual effect when bright spots appear around the sun, caused by ice crystals in the air.

Super Shamou—fictional Inuit crime-fighting superhero currently seen on a children's TV program in northern Canada.

Surimi—a minced paste made from pollock or other fish and used to produce imitation crab, shrimp, and other seafood products.

Sweeper—dangerous log, tree, branch, or other obstruction overhanging a river which might knock you off your raft.

Swing dog—animal positioned just behind the lead sled dog.

TAGS—trans–Alaska Gas System, a proposal to build a natural gas line approximately parallel to the TAPS.

TAPS—trans–Alaska Pipeline System (see below).

Taiga—from a Russian word meaning "land of little sticks," referring to spindly spruce trees in the Alaskan interior. (see also: "Boreal forest.")

Tailings—gravel discarded from a gold dredge, sluice box, etc.

Taku wind—gusts of strong cold winds that hit Juneau and vicinity off the glaciers.

Talik—unfrozen areas within the permafrost.

Telecourses—University of Alaska courses taught via television.

Telemarking—a turning technique used in skiing.

Tender—see: "Lighter."

Termination dust—first snowfall of the winter (traditionally, the signal for canneries and other seasonal jobs to terminate).

Territorial agent—in various Yukon communities the person appointed to sell fishing and hunting licenses, etc.

Tesoro—brand of Alaska gasoline refined from crude oil recovered from deposits north of Kenai.

Thunder egg—geological rock formation created by volcanic action.

Tidal flats—see: "Mudflats."

Tidewater—refers to waters of the Inside Passage and other saltwater areas which are not on the open ocean.

Tidewater glaciers—glaciers that flow clear down to sea level so that they calve into saltwater.

Till—glacial debris (see: "Moraine").

Tine—one prong of a moose's antlers.

Tlingit—major group Indians of Southeast Alaska; also their language (see also: "Haida" and "Tsimshian").

Toklat bear—a blondish grizzly.

Tonne—(Canadian) metric ton—about 2204 pounds.

Totem poles—painted and carved sculptures made from cedar trunks by Tlingit and Haida Indians memorializing people, animals, and events.

Trail!—shouted by dog musher when asking for the right-of-way.

Trailhead—beginning of a hiking trail.

Trail of Forty-two—sometimes applied to the construction phase of the Alaska (ALCAN) Highway, which was built in 1942.

Trail of Ninety-eight—the 1898 gold rush trail from Skagway into the Yukon.

Trans–Alaska Pipeline—built 1975–1977 to carry crude oil from Prudhoe Bay 800 miles south to the ice-free port of Valdez (spelled with a small "t," unless it begins a sentence, of course).

Trapline—a system of trails used by a trapper.

Treaty of Cession of Russian America—official name for the Alaska Purchase of 1867.

Tree-huggers—not a very favorable term for environmentalists.

Tree line—can refer either to (1) the mountain elevation above which trees do not grow, or (2) to the latitude north of which the land is treeless.

Tribe—Alaskan or Yukon Natives generally do not like to be asked about what "tribe" they are from. We've included this word merely to suggest that you do not use it.

TRIVIALASKA—question-and-answer game based on Alaskana and other subjects related to Alaska and the Yukon.

Troy ounce—standard for weighing gold, 31.1 grams (slightly more than a normal ounce); further divided into 20 pennyweight.

Trusty Tusty—affectionate nickname for the Alaskan Marine Highway ferry whose official name is the M/V *Tustumena*.

Tsimshian—Indian tribe of Southeast Alaska, generally living on Annette Island (Metlakatla Reservation).

Tsunami—seismic sea wave, often called (incorrectly) a tidal wave.

Tularemia—communicable disease sometimes carried by the snowshoe hare.

Tumwater—Chinook word for waterfall.

Tundra—(from a Finnish word meaning "treeless") an open plain with only low vegetation, soggy in warmer weather.

Tundra Times—statewide Native newspaper.

Turnout—vehicle pulloff area by the side of a road.

Tussock—a tuft of grasses or grass-like plant.

UAA—University of Alaska at Anchorage.

UAF—University of Alaska at Fairbanks.

UAS—University of Alaska Southeast (formerly UA Juneau).

USFS—United States Forest Service (part of the Department of Agriculture).

Ulu—bone-handled, fan-shaped Eskimo knife, sold everywhere as a souvenir. Use with a rocking motion to chop up your celery or carrots (prohibited in hand luggage during air travel).

Umiak—large walrus-skin boat built by Eskimos (sometimes written as "Oomiak," also called "Angeyok").

Up bay—(or "up the bay") term used at Glacier Bay Park Headquarters for the glacier region at the head of the bay ("He's gone up bay").

Upper One—facetious name for Alaska (opposite of "Lower 48").

VPSO—Village Public Safety Officer, sometimes the only legal representative in a rural area of Alaska.

Valley, the—in Anchorage, it refers to the Matanuska Valley around Palmer; in Juneau, it refers to the Mendenhall Valley, near Juneau Airport and the glacier; in Haines, it's the Chilkat Valley.

Valley of the Eagles—promotional name for the city of Haines.

Vapor barrier boots—see: "Bunny boots."

Velkommen!—enthusiastic Norwegian greeting favored by civic boosters in Petersburg.

Velvet—soft, fuzzy skin on the living antlers of caribou, deer, etc.

Virgin forest—one which has never been logged.

Visqueen or **Vizquine**—once a brand name which has become generic for any clear plastic tarp.

WP&YR—White Pass & Yukon Route Railroad (once said to mean: "Wait Patiently and You'll Ride").

Weir—a fence built in a stream to direct salmon into an area where they can be more easily counted.

West Sak—oil field recently discovered near Prudhoe Bay.

Westmark—chain of hotels in Alaska and the Yukon.

Whales, the—the "Humpbacked Whales," the UAS basketball team, believe it or not.

Wheel dogs—the two dogs harnessed directly in front of the sled.

White-out—winter weather condition when overcast sky and ground snow make visibility difficult or impossible, especially for pilots.

Whitesox—also "Blackflies," a type of biting flies.

Williwaw—sudden, very strong gust of wind in coastal maritime areas.

Windchill—combined cooling effect of wind and air temperature—usually much colder than air temperature alone.

Windy City, the—Skagway.

World Eskimo-Indian Olympics—annual Native festival with such championship events as blanket toss, ear pull, knuckle hop, etc., usually held in July in Fairbanks.

Worm—an inexperienced helper on an oil-drilling rig.

XC—symbol for cross-country skiing.

YT—Yukon Territory.

Yukon, the—the Yukon Territory of Canada. Also the Yukon River, which runs for 2000 miles through both the Yukon Territory and Alaska.

Yukon Quest—annual 1000-mile dog-mushing race between Fairbanks, Alaska, and Whitehorse, the Yukon.

Yukoner—resident of Canada's Yukon Territory.

Yupik—Eskimo group which lives in Western Alaska (including Bethel and Dillingham) and Siberia; or the language spoken by this group (also spelled "Yup'ik" and sometimes "Yuit").

Zenith—a kind of toll-free phone number to certain Canadian companies, public agencies, etc., some of which may also be phoned from some areas in Alaska. (e.g."Ask your operator for Zenith 5555.")

Zodiac—a brand name for a type of rubber boat, usually equipped with an outboard motor, often used to explore wilderness areas in Alaska and the Yukon.

COMING INTO THE COUNTRY

A few years ago John McPhee, the talented and prolific writer for *New Yorker* magazine, published a book entitled *Coming Into the Country,* an account of his experiences in the Alaskan bush. This book, along with *Going to Extremes* by Joe McGinniss and of course *Alaska,* the recent novel by James Michener, should be required reading for all who want to know something of the real Far North experience.

But we have borrowed the title of McPhee's classic here to head up a crucial chapter on the necessary nuts-and-bolts planning for visitors to Alaska and the Yukon. It would be helpful to continue reading this chapter with a good map at one hand and a pencil and paper at the other. You're on your own for writing materials, but one map we would recommend is the Rand McNally road map of Alaska ($1.50 at bookstores the last we looked) or the free map produced by the Alaska State Division of Tourism (see later). Some other maps like those published by the National Geographic Society or the Kroll Map Co., etc., are also excellent, but may include too much confusing detail for first-time visitors to the north.

To make them a little easier to find, all telephone numbers in this chapter have been *italicized*.

DECISIONS, DECISIONS

Most travelers to Alaska have several choices to make. The first among these is whether to travel independently—making your own arrangements to drive, fly, or ferry (or a combination of these)—or to take an all-inclusive cruise/tour package offered by the big cruise companies or tour wholesalers.

(a) If you've taken other cruises, and enjoyed them, you might opt for the package. The shipping companies not only pamper you on board their ships, they will also arrange several efficient and logical land tours in combination with the cruise. In many ways, you can get more for your money by wrapping everything up together.

(b) If, like your typical Alaskan, you are an independent kind of a character who enjoys driving your own or a rented car, and you like the freedom of making changes, following up targets of opportunity, and generally catering to your whims, then you obviously would be better off leaving the cruise ships to others. (This doesn't mean you have to do everything yourself; a good travel agent will help you set up an independent trip, too.)

(c) How about a combination deal? Several who travel to Alaska these days give themselves over to a cruise line for a week or so, take a one-way cruise, and then choose to fend for themselves for another week or so prior to flying back home.

The next choice to make is often a selection of one of three important options, whether you are touring in packages or on your own hook: Whether to visit (1) Southeast Alaska, otherwise known as the panhandle, which includes Juneau, the state capital; or (2) Central Alaska and the Yukon, including Anchorage, Fairbanks, and Whitehorse; or (3) both of these areas in the same trip. There's a tendency among some vacationers to make this choice too hurriedly, based solely on one or two factors which may not be entirely relevant to the question:

"We'll be driving our own car or motor home, so that lets out the panhandle because after all, we can't drive over the water."

That's wrong.

"We're not using our car, so I guess we can only afford to see something of Southeast. We'll have to save the rest for another trip."

Not necessarily.

"We'll be taking a cruise, so I guess we'll just have to limit ourselves to wherever the ship goes."

Happily, that's not true either.

With prudent planning driving your car to Juneau, Sitka, Ketchikan, and other major areas in Southeast is as easy as, well, not falling off a log, but driving on and off a ferry boat. Or if you fly into any major airport of Alaska and the Yukon, you can easily fly to any other airport in the north. And if you're taking the ferry boat or a cruise, there are dozens of options open for additional travel by plane, bus, train, rental car, etc., either as part of the cruise plan or entirely on your own.

TIME, THE CRITICAL FACTOR

We believe you should make destination decisions largely according to the time of year you'll be traveling, the amount of time you have to travel, along with the type of transportation available. If you are taking your own car or RV from the Lower 48 and have a month or more to tool around Alaska, by all means plan to see Southeast along with Central Alaska and the Yukon. On the other hand, if you have only a couple of weeks, perhaps you should limit your vacation mainly to Southeast or to some portion of Central Alaska and/or the Yukon.

If you're taking the ferry as a passenger only, without your own wheels, you can do a heck of a lot in two weeks—see the major ports in Southeast, perhaps, and then maybe fly to Anchorage and Fairbanks to cap your trip. If your entire excursion will be by commercial air, you can hit several widely separated cities in two weeks and still have plenty of time for car rental, a train trip to Denali, or local tours at every stop.

WINTER WONDERLAND

Traveling to Alaska during the off season, you may be pleasantly surprised to find that it's easier than you first thought. In most of Southeast Alaska, you will find little if any snow at sea level, and temperatures will probably be higher than you would find in such cities as Chicago or New York during the winter.

In British Columbia, the Yukon, the Alaskan Interior, and in Southcentral Alaska, the major roads are maintained in the winter, including the Alaska Highway. In fact, some experienced drivers prefer to drive some of these routes in the winter. The Interior (Fairbanks, Tok, etc.) can indeed be bitter cold, and travelers there should be prepared for January or February temperatures that can reach $-40°F$ or below. Midwinter temperatures in relatively mild Anchorage and cities on the Kenai Peninsula, however, generally range from a little below to a little above zero.

Despite the efficiency of your car heater, however, if you're driving out of town in cold weather, always travel with boots, gloves, and other winter clothes in the car—enough for all your passengers—even if you don't think you'll use them. If you run into an avalanche or a moose or some other unforeseen difficulty in below-freezing weather, this simple precaution could save lives (many Alaskans keep extra pieces of warm clothing in the car even during the summer months).

As mentioned earlier, moose-car collisions are frequent in Alaska, particularly in winter and spring (almost as many moose are killed by drivers as by hunters). After dark, slow down and check often on the left shoulder of the road, where visibility is poor. And keep your headlights clean.

By far, the major disadvantages of traveling in Alaska in the winter are that the days are shorter, with the sun rising perhaps at 10 a.m. and setting as early as 3 p.m. in some areas of central Alaska; and that some of the traditional "tourist attractions" are closed. The advantages, of course, are that hotel/motel prices are relatively cheap, and that people have more time to be friendly and helpful than they do during the frenetic days of summer.

There is still plenty to do in off season. You'll see the Northern Lights and scenery that is even more dramatic than in the summer. Then take your pick of skiing (cross-country and downhill), dog mushing, snowmobiling, horse-drawn sleighs, skating, snowshoe hikes, hot-spring bathing, ice-hole fishing, winter festivals, and a whole range of genuine original Alaska activities not available after the snow leaves the ground. A few miles from Anchorage, there's a guy who even carves a golf course out of snow and ice every winter. (See "Southcentral Alaska"). You'll still run across moose and some other wildlife, too. And, oh yeah, we almost forgot: You don't have to worry about conflicts with bears or mosquitoes because most of those guys will be asleep. (There are exceptions. In 1988 we discovered there were two or three sluggish mosquitoes on the ski slopes in Juneau! Thankfully, they were not hungry.)

TRANSPORTATION

MOTORING TO ALASKA

In comparison to any other state of the Union, roads are a relative rarity in the far north. Alaska's 11,600 miles of roads are mostly in Southcentral, and fully one fourth of the state's population is not connected by road to the outside world.

New roads are actually controversial in Alaska. Businessmen want to build them so that communities in the state can be as accessible to each other as are towns and cities in the Lower 48. They correctly point out that of Alaska's 151 incorporated communities, 133 are unconnected by conventional roads. Rock-jawed environmentalists are understandably just as determined to prevent the kind of indiscriminate paving they have seen in the rest of the country, so to preserve the state's unique wilderness lifestyle. In any case, there are enough roads today to allow vacation travel to and from the state as well as to a number of communities within it. (By the way, most of the mileages listed in this chapter are approximate.)

How you start your driving trip naturally depends on where you start. If you begin on the West Coast, you might cross into Canada north of Bellingham, WA, and then travel the route through the Fraser River Canyon via Prince George to connect with the Alaska Highway at Dawson Creek.

CANADIAN HIGHWAYS   Travelers from Montana or states or provinces farther east will find a logical route on the **Trans–Canada Highway** and thence through such noteworthy Canadian destinations as Moose Jaw, Calgary, and Edmonton on the way to Dawson Creek.

Another major route is the **Yellowhead Highway** from Edmonton through Prince George to Prince Rupert. If you're interested in catching the Alaska Ferry at Prince Rupert (or at Seattle), see the ferry discussion later on.

A few determined repeat visitors decide to drive to Alaska on the **Cassiar Highway,** certainly a scenic route through the Skeena and Cassiar mountains of British Columbia; it may remind them of the kind of difficult conditions they found on the Alaska Highway a few years ago.

THE ALASKA HIGHWAY   Let's get one thing straight right off the bat. The real **Alaska Highway**—that dreaded wild animal of a road, once known as the ALCAN and about which horror tales have been told since it was first bulldozed through the Canadian and Alaskan wilderness in 1942—has been thoroughly tamed. In 1990 the highway is already a relative pussycat, and in 1992 it is expected to be ready for a major celebration of its 50th anniversary. When we drove the highway southbound recently, it was virtually all paved—or "sealed," as the Canadians sometimes say—and the only parts that weren't were at least under construction. Some of the paving may be a little different than you're used to. One type of surface the Canadians like is something called "chip seal." This starts out as fairly loose gravel on top of an oiled bitumen or asphalt surface, but as traffic begins to grind the gravel into the goop, it gradually begins taking on some of the characteristics of a conventionally paved highway.

There are also portions, both in Canada and in Alaska, that have been adversely affected by "frost heaves," alternate freezing and thawing of the road which creates annoying ridges and valleys in the surface that are generally more uncomfortable than they are dangerous. And of course there are potholes and cracks from time to time that never seem to be repaired as quickly as they develop. In these areas, your only choice is to go slower than you might otherwise prefer.

Technically the Alaska Highway begins in the town of Dawson Creek, B.C.; continues through Watson Lake and Whitehorse in the Yukon; goes through Tok, Alaska; and then ends, after about 1400 miles, in Delta Junction. Most people think of it as continuing on 100 miles farther to Fairbanks, but the portion from Delta Junction to Fairbanks is actually part of the pre-existing Richardson Highway (which runs between Valdez and Fairbanks via Delta Junction). On the Canadian portion of the Alaska Highway, the law requires you to drive with your headlights on (low beam), even during the day.

While you won't find as many roadside services on the Alaska Highway as you do other places, there is little danger that any prudent motorist will run out of gas or have no place to stay overnight. The longest stretch between services is now only 50 miles, which means you will never be more than 25 miles from help. Watch your map carefully and plan ahead for meal and gas stops along the way. In the summer anyway, we sometimes find that we are not averse to traveling longer each day on the road simply because the hours of daylight are so long, but this might not be a good idea for everyone. From Dawson Creek we recommend allowing two or three days to Whitehorse, a full day to a couple of days to see Whitehorse, and then another two or three days to travel to Fairbanks.

Addresses along the Alaska Highway have traditionally been given in milepost numbers (and decimals thereof), now a potentialy confusing system since straightening and re-routing have reduced its actual length, throwing some of these numbers out of whack. A few of these addresses have been changed; most have not. In Canada, of course, these will be calculated by kilometer post. Good luck!

OTHER ALASKA-YUKON HIGHWAYS   Add another couple of days if you will be side-tripping on the southern part of the **Klondike Highway** to Skagway (about 100 miles each way) or on the 150-mile-long **Haines Highway** between Haines Junction and Haines. (With proper planning you can travel only one way on each of these roads by taking the Alaska Ferry between Skagway and Haines, cutting off about 100 miles of the Alaska Highway.)

Out of Whitehorse, if you're going up the northern portion of the **Klondike Highway (Route 2)** for 330 miles to Dawson City, which we highly recommend, add two or three more days to that itinerary. By the way, do not confuse Dawson Creek with Dawson City.

Out of Dawson City (which most folks just call ''Dawson''), the super-scenic **Top of the World Highway (Route 9)** crosses the Yukon-Alaska border, appropriately enough, at a settlement called Boundary and then joins the **Taylor Highway (Route 5)** for a total 175-mile dirt-and-gravel loop to connect with the Alaska Highway near Tok. If you find you're comfortable enough on this road, we would also suggest a 65-mile (3-hour) side trip to Eagle. The Taylor Highway is closed in winter, as is the short portion of the Top of the World Highway on the U.S. side of the border.

Also out of Dawson is the famous **Dempster Highway (Route 8)** which deadheads at the Inuit village of Inuvik far above the Arctic Circle. Here you're talking a 1000-mile round trip, and we don't think most folks would like to attempt the Dempster on their first—or maybe not even on their fifth—trip to the north country. We're saving this one for a later excursion ourselves.

By now you've gotten the idea that highways in these parts are known better by their names than their numbers. There are a few more well-known routes in Central Alaska. North out of Fairbanks, the gravel-surfaced **Dalton Highway,** somewhat better known as the Haul Road, travels almost straight north for 500 miles along the trans–Alaska Pipeline to Deadhorse at the oil fields on Prudhoe Bay. This highway, the only one in Alaska to cross the Arctic Circle, is open to vehicles without special permits only about half way, a little above the last services at a place called Coldfoot. Unlike most others mentioned below, this one is not maintained in the winter.

Other routes north out of Fairbanks include the **Elliott Highway (Route 2)** to Manley Hot Springs and the **Steese Highway (Route 6)** to Circle on the Yukon River. Going southwest from Tok the 325-mile **Glenn Highway (Route 1)** provides the most direct route from the Alaska Highway to Anchorage. Southeast from Fairbanks, the **Richardson Highway** forms a lopsided sort of X with the Glenn (joining with it for a few miles between Gulkana and Glennallen) as it makes its way, for about 370 miles, alongside the southern portion of the trans–Alaska Pipeline to Valdez. (As previously indicated, many think of the Richardson as ending at Delta Junction on the Alaska Highway, but actually it's the other way around.)

Southwest from Fairbanks is the excellent road that folks often call the **Parks Highway (Route 3)** because it goes via Denali National Park and some state parks. Actually the full name is the George Parks Highway, for a former territorial governor. The 360-mile road, through some of the most stimulating scenery in the state, is also the principal route between Fairbanks and Anchorage. It approximately parallels the route of the Alaska Railroad, and no vacationer in Alaska should pass up the chance either to drive it or to take the train. (More on that railroad later.) There is also an unpaved winter-only road, the 135-mile **Denali Highway** which travels the high country (above 2000 feet) between Cantwell on the Parks Highway and Paxson on the Richardson Highway. One of Alaska's most scenic routes, it's open only from mid-May through September.

There are two important routes south of Anchorage on the Kenai Peninsula. The **Seward Highway** makes the 125-mile route alongside the Turnagain Arm to the Portage Glacier and across Moose Pass in the Kenai Mountains to the town of Seward at Resurrection Bay on the Gulf of Alaska. If you take this highway for only 90 miles, there is a cutoff which begins the 135-mile **Sterling Highway** down the length of the peninsula to the seaside village of Homer (about 225 miles from Anchorage). It's worth remembering that during the summer, both the Seward and Sterling highways are often choked with Anchorage weekend traffic, especially on Friday and Sunday nights between 5 p.m. and midnight. Motorists who plan their trip well may be able to take the northern system of the Alaska Ferry between Valdez, Whittier, Seward, Homer, Seldovia, and Kodiak Island. And remember that the Alaska Railroad takes cars for the short trip between Portage and Whittier, which cannot be driven by road.

DRIVING TIPS If you're going to keep pretty much to the **paved streets and roads** in Alaska, there's no reason that any driving machine in good repair should not be suitable transportation. We've done pretty well with sedans and station wagons even on well-maintained dirt and gravel roads. Alaskans who spend a considerable amount of their driving time in the boondocks, usually choose a **four-wheel drive** of some kind, often a pickup truck, preferably one with a winch on the front.

There once was a time when garages that specialized in changing windshields could be assured of a good steady business. This is still true in areas served by gravel roads. There's something about two cars passing each other at high speeds on gravel that tends to send at least one stone rocketing into the face of one of them. If you see the other guy coming toward you like a bat out of hell, better **pull way over** to your right and **slow down** to about zero. Then you've got a shot at not getting hit too hard by flying stones. Some people have special **plastic covers or wire mesh** installed over their headlights to save them from being struck. Others believe in installing screens in front of their grillwork, too. Keep your **windshield washer** filled; and if things start getting dusty, turn on your **heater fan**—that builds up inside air pressure just enough to help keep dust out of the car. (It's a good idea to keep your camera in a plastic bag in dusty conditions.)

Be forewarned that **gasoline** is expensive up north, particularly in Canada—maybe twice the rate you're used to paying in some areas. There's not much you can do to fight it, except to fill up wherever you do run across a good discount price. Generally speaking, gas stations in the country charge considerably more than those in town, where they are surrounded by several competitive stations.

Conventional wisdom is that motorists in Alaska should carry around an **extra fan belt.** That's like flossing your teeth—a good idea, to be sure, although it's something most folks never get around to doing.

Anyone who is going to do considerable driving in Alaska and Western Canada would be well-advised to pick up a copy of the current *Milepost,* an annual magazine-sized motorist's guide published in Seattle. It covers road situations virtually mile by mile in generally accurate, if often confusing and pedantic, detail. Unfortunately it's difficult to separate advertising from objective advice, but it's still worth the outlay of $15 or so for the maps and other driving information. Be sure to get the latest edition, and don't confuse it with the similarly named *Northwest Milepost* which does not cover Alaska.

Anyone driving to Alaska will have to cross at least once and probably twice the Canada-U.S. border and speak with Canadian and American **Customs and Immigration** agents. With the amount of traffic they have to deal with, it's usually a pretty perfunctory process. However be aware that the Canadians are concerned about (a) firearms (mostly not allowed at all), and (b) whether you've got enough money to survive while in Canada.

One Canadian Customs man who had gotten up on the wrong side of bed recently told us that we should have been able to show him $500 in cash and/or travelers' checks, a requirement which certainly seems to be out of date in this electronic age. He said that he had no way of knowing whether our credit cards or bank cards were any good or not (while traveling, we withdraw money from our bank account at home by using our card in automatic teller machines, including those in Canada, that subscribe to the same system). Having given us the scolding, he let us into his country anyway. We have crossed in and out of Canada several times before and since without a lecture or question about money.

Both Canadian and U.S. Customs are sometimes concerned about carved ivory and other products made from endangered animal species. (Alaska's Gov. Steve Cowper recently had to turn over a 16-inch piece of walrus ivory given to him by Soviet dignitaries in neighboring Siberia.) If you're in doubt about any of this, better mail your handicraft purchases back home from Alaska or check it out with a phone call to Customs in advance of reaching the border. Canadian and U.S. Customs both produce pamphlets which they will mail to travelers who are concerned about these problems. Write the Canadians at the Customs and Excise Dept., Connaught Bldg., Sussex Dr., Ottawa, Ont., K1A-0L5, Canada. American requirements can be obtained from the U.S. Customs Service, Washington, DC 20229.

RENTAL CARS AND MOTOR HOMES   If you're not taking your own vehicle to Alaska, you can of course rent one there. Cars can be rented in most major cities, including Anchorage, Fairbanks, Juneau, and virtually any other town that has a street or is on a road. Avis, Budget, Hertz, National, and other well-known companies are represented, along with a group of local outfits. Fares are comparable to those in the Lower 48. You can rent recreational vehicles, too, in Anchorage, Chugiak, Fairbanks, Valdez, Whitehorse, and a few other places. We cover any kind of wheeled vehicle rental in the chapters that follow.

RAILROADS

Sorry, you can't come to Alaska by train and you are unlikely to do so within our lifetime. Alaska has two passenger railroads. One is the **Alaska Railroad,** which runs from Seward through Anchorage and Denali to Fairbanks, with a spur from Portage to Whittier. The ARR traverses some of the most dramatic scenery in the world, especially between Anchorage and Fairbanks. You can travel in the normal cars or in special sightseeing glass-domed cars.

The other train is the historic **White Pass & Yukon Route Railroad.** It once shuttled between Skagway, Alaska, and Whitehorse, the Yukon. Today it is unfortunately limited to sightseeing excursions out of Skagway to a little beyond the Canadian border. Both of these routes are covered in some detail later.

WHAT ABOUT TAKING A BUS?

Independent bus travel to Alaska and the Yukon from the Outside is not terribly convenient, although it can be done. **Greyhound** routes can take you to some Canadian cities, notably Vancouver. From there, you can take **Greyhound Lines of Canada** (formerly Coachways) to Dawson Creek and then up into the Yukon to Whitehorse and Dawson City. Toll-free tel. for Greyhound in the U.S.: *(800) 531–5332.*

Service between Whitehorse and Skagway is available via **Atlas Tours, Ltd.,** a Whitehorse tour bus firm. Another one out of Whitehorse is **Norline Coaches,** which travels to Dawson City and which also may still make a run between Whitehorse and Fairbanks.

The **Alaskon Express** (until 1989 known as White Pass & Yukon Motorcoaches) continues to offer common carrier service between Anchorage, Fairbanks, Haines, Whitehorse, and Skagway. Owned by the same parent company (Holland America), **Westours Ltd.** (Gray Line) has approximately the same route but on guided tours. And **Alaska-Yukon Motorcoaches** (Alaska Sightseeing Co.) sometimes shuttles between Anchorage and Fairbanks with side routes to Valdez, Haines, and Skagway. We'll go into some more bus detail as appropriate in the chapters which follow.

Every now and then, some chartered bus comes up from the Lower 48 for the first time, and they may get along all right. But if you're thinking of bringing up your own Sunday school bus or something similar, note that some drivers unused to narrow roads and frost heaves on the pavement have problems with vehicles that are narrow and have a high center of gravity. Combine that with bad shock absorbers, and you just might not be able to make good time without making your passengers sick on some stretches of road. Most buses that regularly travel through Alaska and the Yukon have been especially modified for these conditions.

THE ALASKA MARINE HIGHWAY SYSTEM

The complex, state-subsidized system, known by almost everyone as simply "the ferry," is actually composed of two systems. The better-known Inside Passage route is served by the **Southeast System.** From a base near Seattle, this voyage winds through the atmospheric wooded islands, mountains, fjords, and inlets and stops at these major ports: Ketchikan, Wrangell, Petersburg, Sitka, Juneau, Haines, and Skagway. Feeder services expand these destinations to several more towns and villages, including Prince Rupert, B.C.

The other is called the **Southwest System,** which mostly serves Southcentral Alaska (don't ask us; we didn't name it!). This system has vessels plying routes between Cordova, Valdez, Whittier, Seward, Seldovia, and Kodiak Island, plus a few runs as far west as Dutch Harbor. Unfortunately, *there is no ferry route between the Southeast and the Southwest Systems.* We'll go into more detail on the Southwest System and its two special ships, the *Bartlett* and the *Tustumena* later in this volume.

The system celebrated its 25th anniversary in 1988. Today there are nine ferries, painted mainly dark blue with gold and white trim, and all named for Alaskan glaciers. Any of these vessels is often affectionately referred to as the "Big Blue Canoe." Each carries both passengers and vehicles. Each has a cafeteria and bar, gift shop, two or more indoor lounges, and a covered solarium up on the top deck. There, regiments of young adults generally prefer to spend the night and sometimes the day wrapped in sleeping bags, blankets, and each other. Elsewhere on the boat, you sometimes will have to step over and around the same people who stretch out to rest on airport lobby floors. There is no doctor on board, although some medical facilities are available.

Now, don't become confused because some references you may have seen still refer to the Ferry's traditional southern terminus as Seattle. That's no longer precisely correct. On October 1, 1989, the port

of Seattle gave up the ferry contract to the proud little port city of
Bellingham, WA—about 80 miles north on Interstate 5 from Seattle
and about 100 miles north of the Seattle-Tacoma (Sea-Tac) Airport—
and some passengers will now have to choose whether to fly on to
Bellingham Airport or take land transportation to the new terminal.
(Bellingham is actually closer to Vancouver, B.C., than it is to Seattle.)
San Juan Airlines and Horizon Air have frequent flights from Sea-Tac
to Bellingham. Seattle has always been a Mecca to many Alaskans who
travel to that city to purchase automobiles and major appliances. We
suspect that most will continue to refer to ''Seattle'' as the beginning
of the ferry line.

Unless current schedules change, the Seattle ferry will make week-
long round trips to Alaska. Leaving the spanking-new Fairhaven Terminal, at the foot of Harris Avenue in Bellingham, every Friday night,
its first stops northbound are almost invariably at Ketchikan, Wrangell,
and Petersburg on Sunday; and it usually makes Juneau, Haines, and
Skagway on Monday, 1000 miles north of its starting point. (Both Haines
and Skagway are connected to the continental road system.)

Then the Ferry reverses direction, leaving Skagway for Haines on
Monday, arriving in Juneau and Sitka on Tuesday, in Petersburg and
Wrangell on Wednesday, and then in Bellingham again on Friday morning. However, since Bellingham is closer by about five hours to Alaska
than Seattle, this schedule could easily change, so you'd better recheck later.

During the summer, this trip is generally made in the handsome
flagship of the Marine Highway System, the 418-foot *Columbia,* which
carries 1000 passengers and about 180 cars, RVs, pickups, or whatever
you have on wheels. Like most of the AMHS vessels, the *Columbia*
looks more like a deep-draft ocean liner than a conventional flat-bottomed
ferry. It also features two- and four-berth cabins and a few handsome
staterooms for high rollers. Alaska tourism folks now prefer to call these
crafts ''ferryliners,'' reflecting the magnificence of the *Columbia* and a
couple of other vessels. In the winter the Seattle-Skagway trip is usually
managed by the old *Malaspina,* which is certainly not our favorite ship,
and in the fall and spring by the *Matanuska,* a much nicer vessel. (The
Malaspina will soon be taken out of service for a $9-million refur-
bishment, more than half of which will be used to remove asbestos
insulation.)

One port the Seattle ferry does not stop at is **Prince Rupert, British Columbia.** Nevertheless, Prince Rupert is a good place to begin an
Alaska ferry trip—if you have a car and want to drive there, as we did
once in 1988. Ferries usually leave Prince Rupert around three times a
week for Ketchikan and points north. Straight through, it's about 30
hours total from Prince Rupert to Skagway, but we would recommend
taking as many stopovers as possible along the way. Try for the *Matan-*

uska or the *Taku,* if you can. (See also "Canadian Ferries," below.)

There are, of course, feeder services to several smaller destinations in Southeast. The little *Aurora* plies between Ketchikan and the Haida Indian village of Hollis on Prince of Wales Island, and the Tsimshian reservation at Metlakatla on Annette Island. It also occasionally sails to Prince Rupert, as well as to Hyder, that unusual Alaskan destination at the end of the Portland Canal, just across from the Canadian town of Stewart. (Some winter Ketchikan-Metlakatla service is also on the 100-foot-long *Chilkat,* oldest and tiniest of the fleet, which may be retired soon.)

Incidentally, we are sometimes asked if it would be a good idea to begin an Alaska Marine Highway auto trip in Hyder/Stewart. Indeed, it would certainly be fun—unless you miss the boat to Ketchikan, which is a distinct possibility if you miscalculate your pace along the highways. That could foul your schedule all the way up the line, and you'd have to hang around Hyder for another week.

The *Le Conte,* as diminutive as the *Aurora,* frequently schedules a 14- to 16-hour run between Sitka and Juneau, stopping for an hour or so each at the isolated settlements of Angoon on Admiralty Island, and Tenakee springs and Hoonah on Chichagof Island. The *Le Conte* also sometimes extends its runs to Ketchikan to the south and clear up to Skagway at the top end of the Lynn Canal, especially in the winter.

We didn't like the only trip we ever made on the *Le Conte.* Besides difficulties with its food and beverage operation, it wasn't clean and there weren't enough lavatories. (Locals sometimes call the long Sitka-Juneau run the "Hell Trip," particularly when they have to share it with high-school sports teams and fans.) We would not normally choose it again—*except* for its unusal itinerary to those tiny Indian villages, which may make it worthwhile. Incidentally, neither the *Aurora* nor the *Le Conte* offer any cabins for rent, but as on all ferries, you still can't go down to your car or RV to sleep.

FARES ON THE FERRY   Rates have not yet been set for the summer of 1990, but here are our guesses as a very general guide: Figure a maximum deck-space **passenger fare** of around $250 between Bellingham and Skagway, the two farthest points on the system. It would be about half that figure if you climbed aboard in Prince Rupert and still got off in Skagway. There are discounts for **children;** those under six sail free. There are no discounts for round trips. Seniors **over 65** travel free in Alaskan waters (ports between Ketchikan and Skagway) during the winter.

Figure another $500 for an **average size car** for the full route. Again, it might cut that amount approximately in half to drive on board at Prince Rupert and off again at Skagway. Now you see why lots of folks choose to board the system in Prince Rupert. Two passengers and a car together would run perhaps $500 that way versus about $1000 to make the whole route for two vacationers and one set of wheels between Seattle and Skagway. Stopping at ports along the way may add about 5% to your total, a relatively negligible amount. Rates are about 15% less in off season (usually Oct. 1 to May 15). Vehicles longer than 15 feet pay proportionately more.

Now if you want a **cabin**—highly advisable for the overnight legs, at least—it will run between $200 and $300 for the full Seattle-Skagway trip, depending on facilities and location, or about half those rates from Prince Rupert to Skagway. Again, figure about 15% less during off season. By the way, the AMHS prefers to call the accommodations "staterooms," although that seems a somewhat exalted term for most facilities. Generally there are two-berth cabins on the inside, far from the daylight, and four-berth ones with portholes on an outside bulkhead. Our own four-berth, white-walled cabin which we took for one overnight leg from Petersburg to Sitka on the *Taku* was clean, comfortable, and unspectacular. We could see through the porthole, although it was not really clear enough for photography and could not be opened.

If you're traveling during the summer, you should have your vehicle reservation and any cabin reservations in hand *six months in advance*. Passengers who seek only deck space are virtually never turned away, even on the most crowded days. (An exception occurs around the spring Gold Medal Basketball Tournament time in Juneau.) Of course standby vehicle space is sometimes possible, but you may be asked to drive off at each port and take your chances again on there being space for you on the next leg of the trip. And there is always a possibility you can rent a cabin for any single leg of the trip after you have boarded. If you're going to take the ferry one way and drive the Alaska Highway the other way, consider ferrying up and then driving back. From the standpoint of getting a car (or cabin) reservation on the boat, it's usually an easier project early in the season than later, and you don't need that kind of problem when it's time to go home.

The Southeast Alaska Tourism Marketing Council recommends leaving your car in Seattle or Prince Rupert and traveling via the ferries as a walk-on during the summer rush, taking short trips between ports close to each other so you may not need a cabin. It also says that car rentals are easily available in each port, and that you can fly back to your own car from any city on up the system. That's true, provided you don't want to continue driving on up to the Yukon and into Central Alaska. The council is concerned largely with non-cruise tourism and the patronizing of hotels, restaurants, rental cars, and similar businesses seldom used by cruise passengers.

The Alaska Marine Highway publishes two **schedules,** a Fall-Winter-Spring and a Summer, which include the latest rates. You may be able to get these from your travel agent. If not, these and other miscellaneous information are available from the Alaska Marine High-way, P.O. Box R, Juneau, AK 99811; or by calling them toll-free at *(800) 642–0066.* Once bookings are made, payment can be by credit card or certified check. (No matter that there is plenty of time for a check to clear or bounce before you actually travel, a personal check is not accepted unless it is from an Alaskan bank!)

You can enjoy some fantastic scenery from the Ferry, especially in the summer, with occasional sightings of bald eagles, whales, seals, and other wildlife on land and in the water. After Prince Rupert, the route lies almost entirely within the **Tongass National Forest** and a U.S. Forest Service lecturer (called an "interpreter") usually comes on board to give free talks to the passengers on nature and history, at least during the high season.

There are lockers to put your things in and safely store them, if you want. Most Alaskans seem to trust their fellow man enough to leave piles of personal goods stacked here and there in the lounges. Some do use the lockers and then save 50 cents simply by not putting the coins in and taking the key!

Some travelers prefer the ferry in the winter, taking pleasure in meeting sourdoughs and other colorful Alaskan "characters" in a much more relaxed and uncrowded atmosphere than in the more hectic days of summer. We spent all of June 1988 on and off the ferry and met enough characters to suit us, although not all of them were Alaskans.

If it looks like the ferry is going to be crowded, and if you are not going to be in a cabin, board the vessel as early as you can. You'll probably want to stake out some good seats in the lounge for whatever leg of the trip you are on, especially at night. You are not permitted to remain in your car, motor home, or any other vehicle while the ship is under way.

CANADIAN FERRIES Ferry boats are a way of life in the Pacific Northwest. You can't quite go to Alaska on a Canadian ferry, but you can still work some into your plans, if you want. For example, you can travel first from Seattle to the Canadian city of Victoria (on Vancouver Island) in about 4½ hours. In the summer, the route is served by **B.C. Steamships,** either by the *Princess Marguerite* or the *Vancouver Island Princess.*

From Victoria, drive the entire length of Vancouver Island (Routes 1 and 19) for about 300 miles up to Port Hardy. There you can drive on board one of the **B.C. Ferries,** probably the *Queen of the North* for a 15-hour cruise via Bella Bella to Prince Rupert. You can then choose to connect with the Alaska Marine Highway System or to travel by land on the Cassiar or Alaska Highway. B.C. Ferries also runs a side trip from Prince Rupert to the Queen Charlotte Islands. Information, bro-chures, and reservations are available from B.C. Steamship Co., Pier

69, Alaska Way, Seattle, WA 98121; tel. *(206) 441–8200,* and from B.C. Ferries, 1112 Fort St., Victoria, B.C. V8V 4V2, Canada; tel. (in Seattle) *(206) 441–6865.* Check carefully the dates of operations of these vessels. We're looking forward to doing this trip ourselves.

BY AIR TO ALASKA

The history of Alaska and the Yukon is, in many ways, the history of the air industry itself, since so much of the country up here has remained virtually inaccessible except by air. You can fly to every place you've ever heard of, along with many locations that nobody seems to have heard of.

Scheduled flights from Outside to major centers like Juneau, Anchorage, and Fairbanks include routes on Alaska Airlines, Delta Airlines, and United Airlines from the Lower 48, along with flights to Anchorage from Honolulu on Hawaiian Airlines. Ask the airlines or your travel agent to check into APEX (advance purchase) and other restricted fares in order to get the best deal.

Anchorage is considered one of the most air-accessible cities in the world, with many foreign airlines using it as a stopover in their over-the-Pole flights between Europe and Asia. These include Air France, British Airways, China Airlines, Japan Airlines, KLM, Korean Airlines, Lufthansa, Sabena, SAS, Swissair, and others. By the Polar or Great Circle route, Anchorage is only nine hours, nonstop from London via Japan Airlines or British Airways, or seven hours, nonstop from New York via China Airlines. It is also only 8½ hours from either Chicago or Dallas or (hold on to your lederhosen) Copenhagen or Amsterdam.

There are a score or more outfits launching flightseeing or charter service, and some of these will be covered in the chapters that follow. Here, now, are some airlines offering scheduled service to, within, and between Alaska and the Yukon Territory:

AIRLINES IN ALASKA

Air B.C.

This small jet airline was not named for the date service began, but for the Canadian province of British Columbia, which it mainly serves. It also offers daily service between Whitehorse and Vancouver, between Prince Rupert and Vancouver, and less frequent service to Seattle. Canada-only toll-free tel. *(800) 663–5824* or in Whitehorse, tel. *(403) 668–4223.*

Air Canada

Flying British Aerospace 146s, Air Canada (a different company than Canadian Airlines International, see below) has occasional flights between Whitehorse and Vancouver, where it connects with its international routes. U.S. toll-free tel. *(800) 422–6232* or Canada toll-free tel. *(800) 663–9100.*

Air North

If you thought Douglas DC3s went the way of goggles and barnstormers, Whitehorse-based Air North may be a prop blast from the past. This diminutive international airline makes low-level hops between Fairbanks, Dawson City, Whitehorse, Watson Lake, and Juneau. Its crew likes to point out the sights to passengers on the p.a. system. Its smaller aircraft include Piper Navajos, Beach 18s, and Cessna 206s. Juneau tel. *(907) 789–2007* or Canada-only toll-free tel. *(800) 661–0407.*

Alaska Airlines

Today a major American western airline based in Seattle, Alaska Airlines has Boeing 727, 737, or jet service north to Ketchikan, Wrangell, Petersburg, Sitka, Juneau, Glacier Bay, Yakutat, Cordova, Anchorage, Fairbanks, Bethel, Nome, Kotzebue, and Prudhoe Bay. It also flies from Seattle to other Lower 48 destinations like San Francisco, Los Angeles, San Diego, Palm Springs, Phoenix, Tucson, and a dozen more. (It also owns a subsidiary commuter company, Horizon Airlines, out of Seattle.)

Some nonstop Alaska Airlines flights are offered between Seattle and Juneau (2½ hours), Juneau and Anchorage (1½ hours), Seattle and Anchorage (3¼ hours), and San Francisco and Anchorage (5 hours).

There's a special "Buy Alaska" policy allowing stopovers in Alaskan cities along the route for $30 each. Seniors over 60 should check into some liberal discount deals, too. (We once saw a $116 ticket go for $40!)

Alaska's cabin crew usually has a fresh-faced *esprit de corps* which seems to reflect that happy face on its vertical stabilizer. We recommend it with a smile ourselves. Toll-free tel. *(800) 426–0333.*

Alkan Air

Using Piper Navajos and Cessna 206s, Alkan Air offers scheduled flights between Whitehorse and Dawson City (1½ hours) and several map-dot communities in the Yukon. Its only flights to Alaska, however, are on charters. In Whitehorse, tel. *(403) 668–2107.*

Bellair

An even smaller airline out of Sitka, Bellair is popular with residents who manage to book cheap seats for its mail runs between towns in that part of the panhandle. Tel. *(907) 747–8636.*

Canadian Airlines International

(Formerly CP Air.) CAI has daily Boeing 737 jet service from Vancouver, B.C., to several northern Canada destinations, including Fort Nelson, Watson Lake, Prince Rupert, and Whitehorse. Nonstop service between Vancouver and Whitehorse takes 2½ hours. U.S. toll-free tel. *(800) 426–7000* or in Whitehorse, tel. *(403) 668–3535* or in Vancouver, tel. *(604) 270–5211.*

Channel Flying

A Juneau-based commuter line, Channel Flying maintains scheduled flights between Juneau and several small airports in Southeast including Hoonah, Angoon, Kake, Elfin Cove, Pelican, and Tenakee Springs. Tel. *(907) 789–3331.*

Delta Airlines

Another major lifeline to the Lower 48, Atlanta-headquartered Delta offers flights from its many destinations all over the country to Juneau, Anchorage, and Fairbanks, including direct flights from New York (one-stop) and nonstops between Salt Lake City and Anchorage (4¾ hours) and between Seattle and Juneau (2¼ hours) on Boeing 727s. It also has intrastate service between Juneau and Fairbanks and between Anchorage and Fairbanks (both nonstop), but for some reason not between Juneau and Anchorage (at this writing). Toll-free tel. *(800) 221–1212.*

Era Aviation

A 45-year-old firm which grew up with Alaska, Era is now associated with Alaska Airlines. It has scheduled Convair commuter flights from Anchorage to several destinations in Southcentral, including Denali, Kenai, Homer, Kodiak, and Valdez. Toll-free tel. *(800) 426–0333* (the Alaska Airlines number).

Fortymile Air

The airline is named for a river, not for its maximum flying distance. Using Piper Comanches, this international route begins at Fairbanks and stops at Eagle, before going on to Dawson City in the Yukon. In Fairbanks, tel. *(907) 474–0518* or in Dawson, tel. *(403) 993–5200.*

Haines Airways

Scheduled service in Piper Navajos between Haines, Glacier Bay, Hoonah, Hobart Bay, and Juneau. Tel. *(907) 766–2646.*

Hawaiian Airlines

Hawaiian flies three times a week between Anchorage and Honolulu sometimes in DC-8s (too cramped in this day and age) and sometimes in Lockheed L1011s (much better, but unfortunately configured for 10-across seating). We have found this 5½-hour route a handy one for us, even though cabin service standards were disappointing and on-time performance has been less than desirable. It also has nonstops between Seattle and Honolulu. Toll-free tel. *(800) 367–5320.*

Hermens Air Express

This is a commuter airline service associated with MarkAir (see below), and sometimes called Hermens MarkAir. Hermens flies smaller float- and wheeled planes out of regional centers such as Kodiak, Una-lakleet, Bethel, King Salmon, Dillingham, etc., to even smaller destinations. We took their amphibian to Brooks Camp in Katmai National Park. Use the MarkAir phone numbers below.

Ketchikan Air Service

It offers frequent hops between Ketchikan and Metlakatla in twin-engine Cessnas. In Ketchikan, tel. *(907) 225–6608.*

L.A.B. Flying Service

Another Alaska Airlines commuter associate, L.A.B. is headquartered in Haines and flies between that city and Skagway, Juneau, and Hoonah. It takes some of Alaska Airlines flight numbers in its Piper Comanches to Gustavus (Glacier Bay). Juneau tel. *(907) 789–9160.*

Larry's Flying Service

This modestly named but well-respected operation serves several outback areas from Fairbanks, including flights to Barter Island and Fort Yukon in twin-engine Piper Navajos. In Fairbanks, tel. *(907) 474–9169.*

MarkAir

Alaska's "other" jet airline, Anchorage-based MarkAir offers flights to many of the same destinations within the state as Alaska Airlines. At the same time it somehow acts as one of Alaska Airlines' commuter services to some other places. It has flights from Anchorage to Fairbanks, Aniak, Barrow, Bethel, Dillingham, Dutch Harbor, King Salmon, Kodiak, Prudhoe Bay, and St. Mary's among others. We have been on MarkAir several times and have found the flights themselves, along with the cabin service, to be smooth and efficient, although the package tours they also run might be a little bumpy. (Drop us a line if you agree or disagree.) MarkAir also sells a one-price Explore Alaska Pass, allowing you to see up to 10 cities on the system within a year. At the moment the pass runs about $700, certainly a good deal if you get to all 10 places. But you'd better recheck that later. Toll-free telephone reservations from *(800) 426–6784* or within Alaska only from *(800) 478–0800.*

Northwest Airlines

Flying nonstop from its Minneapolis headquarters to Anchorage (in 5¾ hours), and also between Anchorage and Seattle (3¼ hours), Northwest offers year-round service on Boeing 727s. It also flies nonstop from Anchorage to Tokyo, and same-plane service between Anchorage and Boston, Newark, Chicago, and Tampa. Toll-free tel. *(800) 225–2525.*

Peninsula Airways

From Anchorage, it flies to Dillingham, Dutch Harbor, King Salmon, and to both of the inhabited Pribilof Islands, St. Paul, and St. George. In Anchorage, tel. *(907) 249–2295.*

Reeve Aleutian Airways

The first time you hear it, it may sound something like "Revolution Airways." But RAA is hardly revolutionary, being more than a half-century old and offering jet prop service in old Lockheed Electras from Anchorage to several airports on the Alaska Peninsula and in the Aleutian Islands, including Cold Bay, Dutch Harbor, Adak, and even out to little Attu. We also flew with them out to St. Paul Island in the Pribilofs. Toll-free tel. *(800) 544–2248,* or in Anchorage, tel. *(907) 243–4700.* (Reeve Aleutian should not be confused with Ryan Air, a trouble-plagued airline you may have heard of and which we do not recommend.)

Southcentral Air

A commuter line associated with United Airlines, it uses some UA flight numbers to fly Piper Navajos to Kenai and other small airports on the Kenai Peninsula. Tel. *(907) 283–7064.*

Temsco Airlines

Temsco offers scheduled commuter service in both sea- and land-based planes, like the Canadian-built De Havilland Otters, from Ketchikan to other small airports in the southern part of Southeast. This includes Metlakatla, Hydaburg, Craig, Klawock, and Thorne Bay. In Ketchikan, tel. *(907) 225–9810.*

Trans Provincial Airlines

An eloquent name has been given to this seaplane outfit headquartered in Prince Rupert. It flies the Gulfstream Aerospace Goose between P.R. and Ketchikan. In Prince Rupert, tel. *(604) 627–1351.*

Trans World Airlines

TWA's "Great Circle" flights take off daily from Boston and St. Louis, plus several nonstops from Seattle to Anchorage, where it stops over on its way to Asian destinations. Toll-free reservations from *(800) 221–2000.*

United Airlines

Along with Delta, TWA, and Northwest, United is another giant of the industry serving Alaska. It launches flights from several Outside cities to and from Anchorage and Fairbanks, but not Juneau. It has several nonstops between Anchorage and either Chicago (6½ hours on a Boeing 767), or Seattle (under 3½ hours on a Boeing 727). Toll-free telephone reservations from *(800) 241–6522.*

Wings of Alaska

Headquartered in Juneau, this sightseeing amphibian operation also makes scheduled runs in their blue-and-white high-winged Cessnas with mail and passengers to several small destinations in Southeast including Skagway, Haines, Juneau, Snettisham, Hobart Bay, Hoonah, Tenakee Springs, Angoon, Excursion Inlet, Gustavus (Glacier Bay), Elfin Cove, Pelican, Sitka, Kake, and Petersburg. Toll-free (within Alaska except Juneau) tel. *(800) 478–WING;* otherwise, *(907) 789–0790.*

Wrangell Air Service

Flying Britten-Norman Islanders, it serves several small communities in the southern part of Southeast, including Wrangell, Petersburg, and Ketchikan. In Ketchikan, tel. *(907) 225–1998.*

Wright Air Service

Using twin-engine Navajos and Beech Barons, and some single-engine planes, Wright Air boasts of scheduled flights to Anaktuvuk, Fort Yukon, and a few other places along with its charters. In Fairbanks, tel. *(907) 474–0502.*

CRUISES—INSIDE AND OUTSIDE THE PASSAGE

In the past few years, the number of posh cruise ships plying the Inside Passage and the Gulf of Alaska during the summer has increased dramatically—all to the good, in some ways. It has sharpened the competition between what was once a small fleet of vessels to the point where all must stay shipshape or fall quickly in the wake of the better operations, in a hectic market which lasts for only about 120 days a year. On the other hand, critics contend that the large number of floating leviathans are beginning to overwhelm facilities in Southeast. In 1979 there were six ships making the summer Inside Passage cruise bringing a total of 46,000 passengers to Southeast Alaska. In 1988 there were 26 ships carrying nearly 210,000 passengers.

When three or more mammoth liners all dock in little Ketchikan on the same day, the place is a madhouse with crowds often walking in the middle of the street; lining up 10 deep in drug stores, cafes, and souvenir shops, etc., and no one seems to have time to talk or listen. There is also talk of limiting the number of large ships annually entering Glacier Bay. (To avoid the worst of the crowds, take cruises in May and early June or in late August and September, or perhaps choose one of the smaller vessels.)

Cruising generally appeals to retired and/or more well-heeled travelers, at least on the larger liners. Young folks sometimes say they feel out of place at captains' cocktail parties, lavish entertainment evenings, tea dances, and black-tie dinners. (One or two cruises brag that they offer a minimum of this kind of folderol.) Some Alaskans welcome cruise ship passengers with open arms. Others who have had some different experiences and do not, believing that by and large cruisers tend to be conceited and demanding. Be sure to ask a lot of questions about your prospective cruise, and try to speak to someone else who has taken it.

Read brochures carefully, and try to ignore the florid prose. Cruises have a habit of trumpeting the lowest fares but showing the facilities in the most luxurious staterooms. They also tend to list as "ports of call" glaciers and fjords where no one really gets off the boat to buy a post card.

Some cruises specialize in round-trip sailing, calling on different ports outward-bound than they do on the way south again. Others are mainly one-way excursions which hit the same cities each way (although they may offer a discount if you want to return with them, too). On these, you can usually begin at either end of the line.

Some cruise ships pull right up to the piers at the various ports. Some will save the high docking fees by anchoring in the bay and lightering their passengers in for sightseeing. (Crews have been known to be less than truthful about the reasons for that, telling patrons their ship is too big for the dock, even when it isn't.) Of course not all cruise ships are large, and some travelers prefer smaller, more intimate vessels which may concentrate more on passenger accommodations and individual exploration opportunities and less on Broadway shows and tuxedos.

Fares vary, but figure an average minimum of about $250 to $300 per person per day—an amount that includes accommodation, transportation, and all meals. So $250 to $300 times a seven-day cruise, for example, means $1750 to $2100 for one, so figure around $3500 to $4200 for a week of cruising per couple. (Some will happily pay $10,000 or more.) In some cases you will shave some significant dollars off your total by reserving a summer cruise before the end of the previous year, or before Jan. 31, called an "early booking discount." You can also save on a per-day basis if you decide to take the cruise both ways, repeating the same itinerary but in reverse.

Most shore excursions are extra, as are tips and other incidentals that are often not so incidental. On the biggest ships accommodations are sumptuous, the food is plentiful and excellent, and the entertainment is first-rate. For more up-to-date information on cruise prices, use the phone numbers listed below, most of which are toll-free. (If you find yourself a real bargain in a cruise, we'd like to hear about it.) If you can okay the outlay, there is certainly no more pampered and luxurious way to see something of Alaska, at least along her dramatic coast line.

Some of these cruise companies, notably Princess Cruises and Holland America Line, also have their own extensive tour operations which don't even involve taking a cruise as part of the deal. And besides these land and/or sea arrangements, any or all of these may be part of a package put together by a tour wholesaler of a completely different name, e.g., Maupintour, Tauck Tours, or Thomas Cook (and remember that wholesalers may push some cruises they're particularly chummy with, ignoring the others).

Even Alaska Airlines acts as a packager for some cruises, working with Holland America, and Delta Airlines has some arrangements with Princess Cruises, at least at this writing. Generally speaking, you will always get a better break on a fly-sail deal than if you simply added the two fares up together. Most cruises are available either as a round-trip on the ship, or sailing one way and flying the other—and it usually doesn't matter which you do first.

Nevertheless, the specifics of things like this change all the time. So, too, do the makeup of the companies themselves. For example, both Princess Cruises and Holland America Line have been buying out other ships, shipping companies, and tour outfits right and left over the past few years. To confuse things even more, almost every time that happens they rename the ships. When Princess bought Sitmar Lines, the old *Fairwind* became the *Dawn Princess,* for example. (All Princess ships become something *Princess.*) When Holland America Line bought the *Homeric,* they changed her name to *Westerdam.* (All Holland America ships become, as one Ketchikan souvenir shop owner put it, ''some dam ship or other.'')

CRUISE LINES IN ALASKA Except as noted, here are some of the cruise outfits that I expect to be in operation by the time you visit. Phone numbers using area code (800) are toll-free (tell them we said to call). Unless otherwise noted, all these cruises cast off from Vancouver, B.C., Canada.

Admiral Cruises
For Alaska Admiral has one very big, boxy, and at least externally unattractive ship called the *Stardancer* (we haven't been on board). Nevertheless, this 1000-passenger vessel has one big advantage for some: At the moment it is the only cruise ship (not counting the ferry) plying the Inside Passage which will also take your car or motor home right on board. You can walk off at Ketchikan or Juneau but only roll off at Skagway. Toll-free tel. *(800) 327–0271.*

Biological Journeys
Using just about the smallest vessel in the business, the company has a series of summertime natural history and whale-watching trips in the panhandle. The 50-foot *Delphinus* offers berths for a maximum of 10 passengers for one week. Tel. *(415) 527–9622.*

Costa Cruises
Miami-based Costa features week-long cruises aboard the 35-year-old 420-passenger medium-sized vessel called the *Daphne.* Most cabins are reasonably large and on an outside bulkhead. A little less formal than some of her competition, her crew is Italian and the atmosphere is reportedly friendly, especially on Roman Bacchanal Night (and you *know* there's gotta be a pizza oven on board someplace). Toll-free tel. *(800) 462–6782* or *(800) 447–6877.*

Cunard Cruises
The well-established British company Cunard is most proud of its longer, 10- to 11-day cruises on the super-luxurious 500-passenger *Sagafjord.* It is not limited to ports in Southeast, but also goes on through the Gulf of Alaska and even up the Knik Arm to Anchorage. It provides

one of the few opportunities to see those areas in between Southeast and Southcentral such as Yakutat Bay. The dignified vessel also boasts that it never over-uses the ship public address system (a rare blessing). Toll-free tel. *(800) 528–6273* or *(800) 221–4770* or in New York, tel. *(212) 661–7777.*

Exploration Cruise Lines

Unfortunately, Exploration went out of business in 1988, apparently for good. We are watching with interest to see what happens to the smaller shallow-draft vessels it used on the Alaska run. These served a special niche in the market that we hope will be picked up efficiently by someone else. Exploration left thousands of creditors, adversely affecting the credibility of the cruise industry in Alaska. (More chapters in this unfortunate sea saga may still be written after our final deadline.) If you think you want a small ship, consider Biological Journeys (above), Special Expeditions, or TravAlaska (below). A good travel agent may have a new alternative which appears after this book is already in print.

Holland America Line

These days Holland America is much identified with summertime mass tourism in Alaska. In fact, it is probably better-known up north than in its country of origin, cutting the touristic horizon in the 49th State like a ¾-ton Kodiak bear. Holland America should have three or four seven-day sailings weekly through the Inside Passage aboard the older *Rotterdam,* the more modern sisters *Noordam* and *Nieuw Amsterdam,* and the recently acquired and much more sleek *Westerdam.* Each of these carries well over 1000 passengers.

The three newer ships keep to ports in Southeast. In 1989 the *Rotterdam* began extending Holland America cruises up to the Gulf Coast with calls at Seward and connections with its tour buses to Anchorage. Passengers who go on to shore adventures in Alaska and the Yukon are taken care of by HA's subsidiary companies: Westours, Gray Line, the Westmark Hotels chain, and other affiliated operations. In late 1988, Holland America was bought by Carnival Cruise Lines, a Caribbean outfit which has announced no changes in HA's operations at this writing. Toll-free tel. *(800) 426–0327* or in Seattle, tel. *(206) 281–1970.*

Princess Cruises

A subsidiary of the old British P&O (Pacific and Orient) firm, Princess' principal port is usually Los Angeles, although it now headquarters its rapidly expanding Alaska operation in Seattle. It recently bought the Sitmar Line, which no longer will have a separate identity on the Inside Passage cruises. Seven- and 10-day round-trip cruises from Vancouver are now offered aboard five or six ships, including the twins called the *Island Princess* and the *Pacific Princess* (the original TV

"Love Boat''); the 1260-passenger *Royal Princess* (those are considered the top three); plus the older *Sea Princess* (formerly known as the *Kungsholm*); the *Sun Princess* (originally the *Spirit of London*); and the *Fair Princess* (formerly the *FairSea*). In 1989, Princess launched some 12-day Alaska cruises from San Francisco aboard the new 1470-passenger *Star Princess,* (nee *Fairmajesty*), another of the prizes acquired in the aforementioned Sitmar deal). Our guess is that another *Princess* will be introduced to society by the time you read these words.

The longer cruises continue north from the panhandle, across Prince William Sound, ending at Whittier, where passengers on sea-land arrangements can take the train into Anchorage. Princess recently bought the Tour Alaska package operation. It also operates Royal Hyway Tours, a sightseeing bus division, and the Midnight Sun Express, glass-domed railroad cars on the Alaska Railroad. In our experience, it's a class act from stem to stern. Toll-free tel. *(800) 421–0522* or in Los Angeles, tel. *(213) 553–1770*.

Regency Cruises

Now featuring two ships, the 22,000-ton 720-passenger *Regent Sea* and the 25,000-ton 810-passenger *Regent Sun,* the New York–head-quartered company offers four-port, seven-day cruises between Vancouver and Whittier (the rail head for Anchorage). The cruises feature port calls at Ketchikan, Juneau, Skagway, and Sitka, besides the usual trips to glaciers, bays, and fjords in between. Toll-free tel. *(800) 457–5566*.

Royal Cruise Line

Not to be confused with the Royal Viking Line (below), the Greek-owned Royal Cruises sometimes launches its 460-passenger *Golden Odyssey* or one of its two larger *Odyssey*s on the one-week Alaska run to Ketchikan, Juneau, Skagway, and across Prince William Sound to end at Whittier, where passengers can catch the train for Anchorage. However, no plans for the Alaska market have been announced for after 1989. Toll-free tel. *(800) 227–4534* or in San Francisco, tel. *(415) 788–0610*.

Royal Viking Line

Along with Cunard, Royal Viking is the only major line we have had any personal experience with, although neither trip was on an Alaska cruise. Ships like the *Royal Viking Star, Royal Viking Sea,* etc., may be boarded in Seattle, Vancouver, or San Francisco for an 11- to 13-day round-trip Inside Passage cruise. The line seems to pride itself on doing something a little special on each voyage. In the summer of 1989, for example, representatives of the Cousteau Society lectured to the passengers. Royal Viking continues to be an elegant operation in the conservative European Tradition. Tel. *(800) 422–8000*.

Sea Venture Cruises

A newer outfit, the company has just one ship so far, the *Sea Venture*. They say it was especially designed for sightseeing in Alaskan waters between Vancouver and Anchorage. Tel. *(800) 426–1004* or *(305) 477–4711*.

Society Expeditions

Highly nature-oriented, this company has featured lectures by naturalists and has traveled beyond the Inside Passage and the Gulf of Alaska to such far out ports as the Aleutian Islands and the Pribilof Islands. The *Society Explorer* decided to skip Alaska in favor of the South Pacific for the summer of '89 and at this writing, plans were not complete for 1990. Tel. *(800) 426–7794* or in Seattle, tel. *(206) 285–9400*.

Special Expeditions

Sven-Olof Lindblad's Special Expeditions normally charters one of the smaller ships of Exploration Cruise Lines to carry about 85 passengers on its 11-day science-oriented cruises through Southeast Alaska in the late spring and early fall. Since the announced bankruptcy of Exploration, however, Special Expeditions may be seeking a different vessel for its tour program. For more information, tel. *(212) 765–7740* in New York City.

TravAlaska Cruises

Also known as Alaska Sightseeing Tours, the company features a different type of cruise aboard a different type of vessel. The 65-foot yacht *Sheltered Seas* carries up to 80 people, but has no staterooms at all. On its 5-day voyages between Ketchikan, Petersburg, Wrangell, and Juneau, passengers put up each night at predesignated hotels. Since all cruising is during the day, no scenery is missed while getting from port to port. Breakfasts and lunches are provided on board, but dinners are ashore.

We tagged along one day when the *Sheltered Seas* explored the Le Conte Glacier out of Petersburg. We had a wonderful time, along with others who had been traveling on the ship for several days (the bartender makes a mean drink called "Glacial Silt"). TravAlaska also has some extensive land operations, so combinations which include flights and land tours can be set up. This operation is still developing, so recheck on the exact arrangements that may be in effect when you go. Toll-free tel. *(800) 426–7702* or in Seattle, tel. *(206) 441–8687*.

World Explorer Cruises

Also into exploring in depth, this San Francisco–based company features 14-day cultural cruises through the Inside Passage and up to

Anchorage aboard the 550-passenger *S.S. Universe*. The ship, which has been a freighter and still functions as a floating college in winter, now calls at nine Alaska ports. It generally caters to a younger, probably less-critical and perhaps less-hedonistic clientele.

The *Universe* has an extensive lecture program, featuring university professors, and World Explorer boasts that it is the only Alaska cruise line offering college credit for a cruise. On a per-day basis, fares have been running lower than average, but you'd better recheck that. Toll-free tel. *(800) 854–3835* or in San Francisco tel. *(415) 391–9262*.

TOURING

TOUR OPERATORS

As we said, large land and air tour operations are also conducted by some of the cruise ship companies above, notably Holland America/ Westours (which is also Gray Line), Princess Cruises/Royal Hyway (which is also Tour Alaska), and TravAlaska/Alaska Sightseeing.

In addition to these, some others with Alaska/Yukon programs include the **AARP Travel Service** (catering to senior citizens), tel. *(800) 448–7010*; **Alaska Travel Adventures** in Juneau, tel. *(907) 789–0052*; **Alaska Travel Bureau,** tel. *(800) 426–0082* or in Seattle, tel. *(206) 624–1477*; **Alaska Wildland Adventures** (natural history safaris), tel. *(800) 334–8730*; **Atlas Tours,** in Vancouver, tel. *(604) 669–1332*; **Maupintour,** tel. *(800) 255–4266*; and **Tauck Tours,** tel. *(800) 468– 2825*. Any of these firms should respond with brochures and further information (although you may have to make your final arrangements through a local travel agent). We have had no personal experience with them and would like to hear from those who have.

TRAVEL AGENTS

It's often hard to choose a travel agent, but we always suggest that you do it in the same way you'd choose a doctor or a dentist—by personal recommendation. In this case, seek advice from someone who has used a good agent to find an enjoyable trip to Alaska and/or the Yukon. Beware of travel agents who try to book you on one all-inclusive tour instead of working with you to find the perfect itinerary, even if you are not "with the program" every step of the way. Alaska is not a foreign country, so you don't need someone holding your hand at every moment. Personally, we like dealing with middle-sized agencies—more than one person in the office, but not one of those giant "name" outfits with desks all over the place.

The agency should be a member of ASTA (the American Society of Travel Agents) or ARTA (the Association of Retail Travel Agents), and will probably have a seal to this effect proudly displayed on his window. The most respected travel agents today also have the initials *CTC* (Certified Travel Counselor) after their names.

LOCAL TOURS

If you're traveling on your own through Alaska and the Yukon, you'll want to be sure you don't miss anything worth seeing and to understand fully some of the nature, history, and culture visible in your surroundings. Since there's less hand-holding than if you were with an organized cruise or tour, you'll have to look for interesting and knowledgeable sources of information.

Reading a book or two helps, but at each destination there are local tours ranging from a one-hour bus ride around town to all-day catamaran cruises to some nearby island. Sometimes it seems that these are set up exclusively to cater to the crowds from the cruise ships, but usually the operation must use these steady groups to keep the business afloat. Almost without exception, "walk-ins" are welcome, too. In fact, some tour outfits seem to prefer the company of those who have deliberately sought them out as a valued Alaska experience.

The best way to find these tours and other on-the-spot visitor information on what to see and do is to hunt up the local CVB—the Convention and Visitors Bureau. You'll find their addresses and phone numbers scattered throughout this volume. And we have gathered information on specific sightseeing and flightseeing opportunities and included them in appropriate sections of the following area chapters.

TIME ZONES

A few years ago, Alaska had no less than four time zones, but it has sensibly now reduced that to two. Since one zone affects only the westernmost of the Aleutian Islands, you can effectively limit that to one. Alaska Time is now one hour earlier than Pacific Time. And yes, believe it or not, Alaska goes to Daylight Saving Time along with the rest of the country every summer—even though it has saved so much daylight it hardly knows what to do with it!

Canada's Yukon Territory is one hour later than Alaska—the same as Pacific Time on the west coast of the U.S. The difference in time zones sometimes becomes important when you want to make border crossings on some roads late at night, when either the Canadians or the Americans may close their Customs station at different times. You can easily recheck these by giving them a phone call first.

TRAVEL THROUGH CANADA

Canadian travel is something you can't avoid if you're going from Southeast up to Central Alaska, or vice versa—unless, of course, you fly. As previously indicated, Canadian and U.S. Customs are usually (but not always) a breeze.

Speed limits and distances will be listed in kilometers (to get a good estimate, we just multiply by six and drop the last zero, i.e. 100 kph becomes 60 mph for all intents and purposes). Gasoline is sold in liters, and a liter is pretty darn close to an American quart (so figure four liters per American gallon).

Canadian money works on the decimal system, the same as American, and even the coins are similar. However, the exchange rate is not at par, and the exact rate can vary daily. A point to remember: While it is easy enough to use American money in Canada (and perhaps even get a 20% or 25% discount from some merchants for it), it is darn near impossible to use Canadian money in the U.S., including Alaska. (Relatively speaking, we Americans are often just too naive or too much in a hurry to think about exchange rates and the like.) Personally, we use our credit cards in Canada and let MasterCard or Diner's Club worry about the exchange rate. We also take Canadian cash from the automatic teller machines in Canada that are compatible with those of our bank back home. (That may be possible for you, too, but recheck this carefully with your bank before you leave on your trip.) In any case, try to spend or exchange your Canadian cash before heading back into the U.S. again.

HOTELS, MOTELS AND B & Bs

One thing you should be very clear on is that if you want the kind of pampering you find in the best Asian and European hotels, you'd better go to Asia or Europe instead of Alaska or the Yukon. For the time being, *the only truly deluxe accommodations you will find in Southeast Alaska will be on board the cruise ships*. The situation is a little better up in Anchorage and Fairbanks where a few establishments can hold their own with operations elsewhere.

Anchorage might be the only city where you run into familiar hotel names—Hilton, Sheraton, Holiday Inn, etc. You will find a few stainless-steel links in the Super-8 motel chain in other parts of Alaska, and sometimes these colorless cubicles turn out to be the cleanest and brightest accommodations for miles around, making up for their more prosaic personality. Their toll-free reservations number is *(800) 843–1991.*

There is one interesting chain of hotels which exists only in Alaska and the Yukon: **Westmark,** owned by the Carnival Cruises/Holland America Line/Westours/Gray Line interests. Unfortunately, almost the only consistency in the Westmarks is their generally up-scale price bracket. They vary in quality or value by several points. In places where they really cater to what the travel industry calls the FIT (free and independent travelers), and where they must also compete with other top drawer establishments—as in Anchorage and Juneau—the Westmarks are excellent, among the best establishments in town. In other locations where they generally exist only to house battalions of tour bus people, like Skagway or Beaver Creek, facilities are mediocre at best. Places like these are geared for mass tourism, and their appeal to FITs is virtually nonexistent. (It doesn't have to be this way, of course; the Westmarks in Tok and Whitehorse for example usually manage to bridge both worlds fairly well.) Several towns or cities have two Westmarks, by the way, so to avoid confusion get the name exactly right. We list the Westmarks' local numbers along with those of other hotels in the area chapters which follow. Its national toll-free reservations number is *(800) 544–0970* or inside Alaska (except from Anchorage), *(800) 478–1111.*

SOURDOUGH SLEEPERS Some Alaskans and Yukoners seem to take a certain amount of pride in roughing it while on the road, and probably some travelers from elsewhere do, too. Just like beards, boots, and dirty jeans, it apparently goes with the rugged bush-and-boondocks image, and there are even some spartan accommodations that freely admit they cater to Alaskans only.

When we began inspecting hotels in preparation for this guide-book, there were even a few establishments that as soon as they found out what we were doing refused to let us see their rooms—something we've never come across before in 20 years of travel reporting. Perhaps they knew that they just would not pass muster for a Fielding guide. In any case, we operate on the theory that if a hotel's sense of public relations is that bad, its desire to furnish comfort and security to its guests is likely to be equally impaired. We make it very clear here that such places are not recommended—at least not by us.

FRILL-LESS FACILITIES An amazing number of establishments do not provide things that are now considered standard in the Lower 48, even in the local Motel 6.

The piece of candy on the pillow is not the point. You can rent plenty of rooms up north with more nos than yesses—i.e., no television, no telephone, no radio, no clock, no closet, no shelves or cloth-ing hooks, no ventilation to speak of, no information in the room about the town or the hotel, no black-out curtains (badly needed in summer), no double-paned windows (badly needed in winter for cold, or at any time to muffle street noise), no wake-up service, no room service, no security locks, no bellhops, and no restaurant or one that closes long before you're ready to have dinner—something you usually find out about too late. Generally speaking, be a little wary of any hotel or motel which is open only during the summer. These tend to scrimp on room telephones, wake-up calls, and other "frills."

As in other areas, watch out for hotels that charge for making col-lect or credit card calls or for calls to toll-free numbers. (We always ask when checking in, and then use the pay phone in the lobby if we decide to stay anyway. Be sure there *is* a pay phone; one hotel in Skag-way, at least, didn't have such an animal.)

We found a large number of dimly lit hotel rooms with tiny win-dows that were certainly overpriced for their dark and dingy rewards. Some cater only to tour groups, and set their rates for walk-ins so high as to discourage the practice. In Ketchikan we stayed in one hotel where the chambermaids were in the habit of entering rooms without knock-ing—a basic no-no in any professional operation. It also had no security lock or chain on the door.

Lack of professionalism has a lot to do with hotel difficulties. In that business, as in many others in Alaska and the Yukon, you may find the owner or manager ran a pizza parlor last year and thought he might take a crack at operating a motel this year. So we take some comfort in the knowledge that when it comes to places to stay, the traveler up north might need a critical guidebook much more than if he had simply spent his or her vacation cruising an interstate in the Lower 48. On the other hand, sometimes an Alaskan room you may think is only marginal turns out to be one of the few decent games in town. We found a few like that, too. On the plus side, some of the amateurishly run places are administered by friendly folks who genuinely would like to please, as long as you make your needs known. A couple of positive features sometimes found in northern accommodations are free coffee in the lobby and free freezer facilities to store any fish you may have caught while in the neighborhood.

By the way, if you don't like TV at breakfast, you may be in for a rough time. Many hotel dining rooms seem to have the tube on in the mornings, especially in the panhandle or other places a long way from population centers. The daily newspapers from Anchorage, Fairbanks, or Seattle don't get in until around noon so management may tune in to CNN, thus serving up opening stock prices on Wall Street as an eye-opener, followed by the latest Middle East crisis with your sourdough pancakes.

BED AND BREAKFAST operations have been increasing in Alaska in recent years. Generally speaking, it is beyond the mission of a large-circulation guide like this one to provide a comprehensive, specific review of tiny places that only offer very few rooms to rent, with bathrooms to share, where meals are taken with the family, etc. Although in a few cases, we have listed a B&B for one reason or another. One directory we've seen is called *Bed and Breakfasts in Alaska: a Directory,* produced by Glacier House Publications (tel. *(907) 272–3286),* P.O. Box 201901, Anchorage, AK 99520, for about $13.95. Listing about 150 B&B operations throughout the state, it is basically advertising. Nevertheless it is revised every couple of years, and it looks like it could be useful to some travelers.

You may also want to make contact with the *Alaska Bed & Breakfast Association—Southeastern Alaska* (tel. *(907) 586–2959),* at P.O. Box 3–6500, Juneau, AK 99802. The Association represents several small operations in towns and cities throughout the panhandle and will handle reservations, etc.

ROOM RATES, ROADHOUSES, AND RVs

Different communities unfortunately have different taxes on hotel rooms—as low as 2% and up to 5% or more (sometimes there's a city tax as well as a "bed tax"). If you're staying long in any one place, it might be a good idea to ask about taxes when making your reservation. Unfortunately we have been unable to gather complete 1990 room rates for these hotels. The prices you see are our best guesses, based on past rates and raises, of the amounts you may be quoted for the summer of 1990. From about October to April, many establishments have winter rates which may be anywhere between 10% and 50% less. As in the Lower 48, sometimes you can ask for and get "corporate rates" if you show a business card, or occasionally "senior rates" if you are over 65 or have a membership card in the AARP (American Association of Retired Persons) or a similar organization.

And, oh yes, here's where you should do as we say, not necessarily as we do: Nail down all your accommodations for peak periods. We try, but sometimes have to change our plans at the last minute, which usually means some inconvenient scrambling from motel to motel during the crazy, hazy days of July and August.

Some addresses you may find for some Alaskan hotels and other tourist facilities have little codes buried in them to tell the businesses where you got their names. This can make for a certain amount of confusion since you may notice that the address varies slightly from one source to another. We're surprised the U.S. Postal Service puts up with it. Anyway, we don't do that ourselves in this volume (unless we've unintentionally picked up the code from somewhere else).

If you're really stuck for a place to stay and you've got your own wheels, you should be aware of an Alaskan/Yukon institution called **roadhouses,** which date back in theory (and sometimes in fact) to Sergeant Preston and the dog-trail days. (Many are considered to be one day's mush apart.) Similar to British country pubs, roadhouses offer a bar, meals, a few overnight rooms for rent, usually with the john down the hall and some other inconveniences. (So far we've found none with an outhouse, although we wouldn't put it past a possibility when far out in the bush!) Also, the local CVB or visitors' center may have a line on an available bed and breakfast operation. (In northwestern Canada, incidentally, there is no such thing as a free-standing bar; liquor laws dictate that any such establishment must also offer at least a few rooms for rent on the premises—even if they are not well advertised, or share a bathroom, etc.)

Those who really save on hotel expenses and who can change their plans with relative abandon are those who carry their room with them— the RVers and intrepid man-handlers of other types of mobile homes who need only to find inexpensive campgrounds with electric, water, and sewer hookups and other such modern facilities. Campers who carry their accommodations rolled up on their backs, of course, will sleep even cheaper.

It is beyond the scope of this book to go into detail on this stuff, so for RVers and tent campers, we particularly recommend *Camping Alaska and Canada's Yukon* by Mike and Marilyn Miller (Pacific Search Press, Seattle). We have no commercial connection with the book, but we do know Mike and Marilyn. They live full-time in Alaska, and we would certainly trust them to the end of the road and beyond. Other standard references on campgrounds and tent/RV subjects throughout North America are produced by the Woodall Publishing Co. (100 Corporate North, Suite 100, Bannockburn, IL 60015-1253). Woodall's tells us their teams inspect campgrounds annually.

If you are considering buying an RV, remember to balance the hotel savings against the price of your vehicle, and figure in the incredibly low gas mileage you'll get in a part of North America that charges so much for this fuel.

DINING OUT AND IN

One thing you'll notice right away. Alaskans and Yukoners tend to eat hearty. It's apparently part of that rugged, outback image to load up with huge plateloads of carbohydrates, especially at breakfast. So you'll find several restaurants serving much more than you felt you needed. Don't be afraid to ask for a doggie bag. We do it all the time, sometimes getting enough for another whole meal in the process.

Prices for restaurants and food run a little higher than some other places in the country. Visitors from major cities like New York or Los Angeles will not notice much difference, but those from other places should budget perhaps 10% more than they would for groceries or meals at home.

If you're hoping to try Eskimo or Indian food, you'll have a hard time finding it outside of a private home. Not counting breakfasts of sourdough pancakes and occasional servings of moose steaks and reindeer sausages, the specialties of Alaska are principally seafood. You'll get some of the best salmon, trout, and halibut there that are available on this earth. Several other kinds of fish are also prepared well, along with saltwater specialties like king crab, Dungeness crab, and Petersburg shrimp.

Coffee is practically a religion in Alaska (another one of those instant wake up/warm up things). Sometimes it comes before you even sit down. Sometimes it comes free, assuming you buy something else in the place to drink it with.

TO TAKE AND NOT TO TAKE

As indicated previously, whenever you travel to Alaska and northern Canada, you will probably find times when it is (a) much warmer than you expected and (b) considerably colder than you thought it would be. Certainly even in the summer we would never think of traveling up north without a warm sweater or jacket along, preferably both. At the same time, we also include at least one pair of shorts and some short-sleeved shirts. In the winter of course, you should be ready to layer on as many things as may be required, depending on how much time you will spend out of doors. If you're staying in the city, then sweaters, overcoats, gloves, scarfs, and a hat, at least, are recommended for winter. In the bush, then parkas or jackets should be down- or fiber-filled. Boots should be waterproof and insulated.

If there are some things you don't have—bunny boots, perhaps, or thermal (long) underwear—don't worry. You can buy it up there, and darn good quality stuff to boot. A raincoat, waterproof jacket, or umbrella is advisable at any time of year, too. So are mosquito repellent (no kidding—we have even dodged mosquitoes on the ski slopes near Juneau), sun glasses, and a good hat with a wide shady brim.

Please, don't go to Alaska without a good pair of binoculars. And don't forget your camera. Remember, too, that wild animals and birds tend to look a lot closer in person than they do later in prints or slides. Ergo, if you're a real photo bug with a 35 mm reflex camera, now is the time to buy that powerful telephoto lens you wanted a good excuse for—200 mm at least, if not a 500 mm. (Show this to your non-camera-laden spouse or parent, if you really think it will help.)

Take plenty of the kind of film you like—maybe twice the amount you think you will use. You may not find the right stuff everywhere you go, and even if you do it will probably cost more, especially in Canada. (Check the expiration date on the box, too, when buying film in the bush.) You may also want to consider using some faster film if you're going to be shooting moose or eagles at high shutter speeds along with your new longer focal-length lens. Take plenty of tape for your video camera, too, especially if it uses the new smaller 8-mm type. We also use a small stereo cassette tape recorder to capture the lectures of tour guides, etc., or sometimes just sound background for the ultimate movie or slide show.

If you are a hunter or fisherman or a dedicated hiker or backpacker, you already know what you need for those activities. If you're unsure, better make a phone call to the Alaska Department of Fish & Game in Juneau (see below). And remember there are strict laws against carrying guns in Canada except under certain circumstances.

Pack a small battery-operated transistor radio, too. It's a way to keep bears at bay, if you'll be walking some distances in the woods. It also provides some comfort if you draw one of those bare hotel rooms with no TV or radio. For the same reason, take an alarm clock, if it's not attached to your radio. Several bleary-eyed Alaska travelers also recommend a sleep mask so you can catch some genuine shut-eye with the midnight sun streaming into your room.

Throw in plenty of 15-cent stamps (if that's still the price) to mail all the I-told-you-so scenic post cards to your unfortunate friends or neighbors who insisted that there's nothing but ice and snow where you'll be going. Post offices always seem to be closed whenever you want to buy stamps, and hotel desks and sundry shops are often out of them. Try to mail all your cards and letters in the U.S. instead of Canada, which seems to have the slowest postal service around. And while we're at it, we also found that long-distance phone calls were much more expensive in Canada, even when we used our telephone calling card from a public phone.

If you're driving, do try to remember that extra fan belt for any long stretches in the wilderness. Since we often like snacking or lunching beside the road, we found a cooler and Thermos to be extremely handy. (We carried condiments like salt and pepper, mustard, ketchup, etc., and bought fresh food in grocery stores and supermarkets.) If you're not driving, try to have everything you need in a form convenient enough that you can carry it all yourself up stairs and for long distances through corridors of the hotels that do not offer porter service.

Don't forget something to throw your vehicle litter in. You can get plenty of good water, but take enough detergent in a squeeze dispenser to help wash the road gunk off your car from time to time, or at least from the windows, especially if you'll be traveling on dirt and gravel roads—and you probably will be, whether you plan to or not.

SOME ADDRESSES AND PHONE NUMBERS

These days the cost of home-based long-distance phone calls around the country has diminished to the point where it hardly makes sense to write lots of letters any more. This is especially true if you can call during off-peak hours and on Saturday and Sunday. If you call Alaska from the eastern and midwest U.S., you can call during the cheaper evening hours and still catch offices in Alaska during the business day. That's why we have given several phone numbers to call to ask for further information.

Of course numbers using the area code (800) are free of charge to the calling party. (In some areas, dial 1 before the area code.) Incidentally, the area code for virtually all of Alaska is (907). The lone exception is little Hyder; due to its unique position adjoining the Canadian village of Stewart, it uses (604), the same code as British Columbia. The area code for the Yukon Territory is (403). Most toll-free (800) numbers in Canada are not accessible from the United States, and vice versa. While you're on the road, remember that some hotels charge for dialing (800) numbers from your room, so check with the desk first.

Your principal source for tourism information to Alaska should be the following: **Alaska Division of Tourism,** P.O. Box E, Juneau, AK 99811; tel. *(907) 465–2010.* Tell them we told you to ask for the latest edition of the *Official Vacation Planner* for Alaska and the Yukon, a multi-color catalog of northern fun. A new one is published in November or December of each year. (Send them $2, if you want it to come via First Class mail.)

Senior citizens traveling to Alaska should get a copy of the latest edition of *Alaska's Senior Citizens' Guide,* a consumer directory listing senior discounts statewide along with organizations and services directed to them. This little yellow booklet is published annually by the Anchorage Telephone Utility and distributed by the non-profit **Older Persons Action Group,** P.O. Box 102240, Anchorage, AK 99510; tel. *(907) 276–1059.* If you will be going into Canada, don't hesitate to write or call **Tourism Yukon,** P.O. Box 2703, Whitehorse, Yukon Y1A 2C6; tel. *(403) 667–5340.* They will also respond with their annual *Vacation Guide* and other valuable literature. Also try **Tourism British**

Columbia, P.O. Box 34971, Seattle, WA 98124–1971; tel. *(206) 623–5937* or its home office at Victoria, B.C. V8V 1X4, Canada; tel. *(604) 387–1642.* There are also Tourism B.C. bureaus in San Francisco: *(415) 981–4780* and in Los Angeles: *(213) 380–9171.* (For better mail service to U.S. addresses contact the Seattle, San Francisco, or Los Angeles offices.)

For fish and wildlife information in Alaska, the **Alaska Department of Fish & Game** can be written to at P.O. Box 3–2000, Juneau, AK 99802; tel. *(907) 465–4112.* (The above Tourism Yukon will provide the same kind of information for that territory.)

Remember that many major municipalities in Alaska have their own CVBs **(Convention & Visitors Bureaus)** which will provide information on their own area. In Anchorage tel. *276–4118;* Barrow tel. *852–5211;* Fairbanks tel. *456–5774;* Juneau tel. *586–1737;* Kodiak Island tel. *486–4782;* Matanuska-Susitna (Wasilla) tel. *745–4840;* Nome tel. *443–5535;* Sitka tel. *747–5940;* Skagway tel. *983–2854;* Valdez tel. *835–2984;* and Wrangell tel. *874–3770* (again, all these are area code 907). Other handy addresses and phone numbers for local visitors centers and other places are listed in the following area chapters.

In addition, for the city of Dawson in the Yukon, call or write the **Klondike Visitors Association,** Box 389, Dawson City, Yukon, Canada Y0B 1G0; tel. *(403) 993–5575.* And for Prince Rupert, the **Prince Rupert Convention & Visitors Bureau,** P.O. Box 669, Prince Rupert, B.C., Canada V8J 3S1; tel. *(604) 624–5637.* (Please don't hold us to those not-exactly-zippy Canadian postal codes; they drive us as nuts as they may do you. We can never be positive exactly when they are letters or numbers, especially between capital *I*s and capital *O*s and ones and zeros.)

THE GATEWAY TOWNS —KETCHIKAN, PRINCE RUPERT B.C., WRANGELL, PETERSBURG

Four communities dominate the southernmost portion of Southeast Alaska below Juneau and Sitka. There is Petersburg, the town settled by Norwegians and where all Alaskans know the world's most delicious shrimp hails from. A little farther south is Wrangell, the only Alaskan municipality that has been under three flags—or perhaps three flags and a totem pole—American, British, Russian, and Tlingit. Almost on the lowest portion of the border separating Canada from Alaska is the city of Ketchikan, which likes to call itself the "Salmon Capital of the World." And then across that international boundary is the proud town of Prince Rupert, British Columbia, whose citizens seem to consider their settlement at least psychologically part of Alaska. Connected to the continental road system as well as to the Alaska Marine Highway, it is an attractive alternate jumping-off place for sea trips to Alaska.

Long before white men appeared, most of these coastal areas were part of three complex Indian societies—the Tlingit, the Tsimshian, and the Haida. Dedicated visitors will learn something of their history in the finely carved cedar totem poles and other distinctive artwork these peoples create even today.

Many totems and other traditional Indian designs of Southeast owe

121

their continued existence to the CCC (Civilian Conservation Corps), which saved many of them during the Great Depression of the 1930s.

Here are details on the four communities:

KETCHIKAN

Some 600 miles north of Seattle, Ketchikan is often the first Alaskan city an Outsider catches sight of—providing he can see it at all. "Alaska's First City" is known by still more sobriquets—"The Rainy City," for example, since it totes up as much as 162 inches of liquid sunshine a year, much of that in October. (It seldom snows in Ketchikan, although ice can be a problem.) Good-natured citizens take their overabundant moisture in stride, laughing: "We don't tan. We rust!"

Ketchikan is also called the "City of Totems" since it has the world's largest collection of carved wooden poles erected by the artistic Tlingit Indians whose culture once dominated the area. Totems illustrate legends and history, trace genealogy, and memorialize important people. You'll even find one Tlingit totem bearing the likeness of Abe Lincoln in a stovepipe hat.

Squeezed into a long, skinny corner of the seemingly unpronounceable island of Revillagigedo, Ketchikan was originally an Indian fishing camp. (Courtesy of early Spanish explorers, the island is approximately enunciated as "reh-vee-yah-gee-*gay*-doh." Most locals shorten it to "Revilla.") There was a brief gold rush in the late 1800s, but timber and fishing soon proved to be the dominant economic forces in the town— along with tourism in later years. Many paved streets and even buildings in the downtown area are built on wooden pilings over the water. Others are on stilts in the hills, and reached by long stairways. Current population is about 7000 in the city or about 15,000 in the entire borough—after Juneau, the panhandle's second largest community.

For those on longer visits, Ketchikan is also the jumping-off place for Prince of Wales Island, the Tsimshian Indian reservation at Metlakatla on Annette Island, seaplane or yacht tours of Misty Fiords National Monument, and cruises up the Portland Canal to the frontier-style villages of Hyder, AK, and Stewart, B.C.

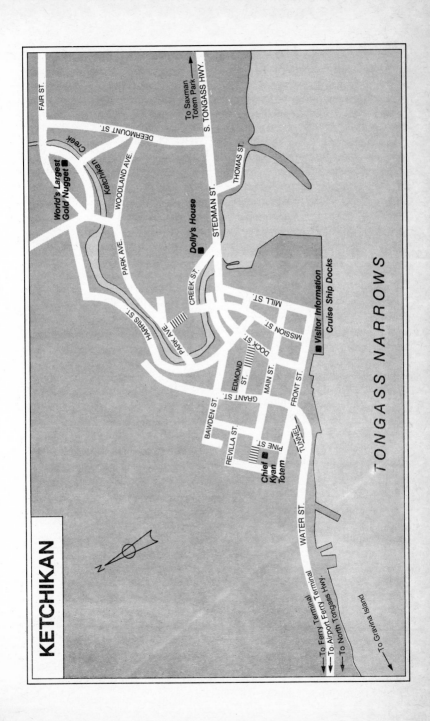

KETCHIKAN

N

TONGASS NARROWS

World's Largest
Gold Nugget ■

Dolly's House ■

Visitor Information ■
Cruise Ship Docks

Chief
Kyan
Totem ■

FAIR ST.

Creek

DEERMOUNT ST.

Ketchikan

WOODLAND AVE.

PARK AVE.

S. TONGASS HWY.

To Saxman
Totem Park

THOMAS ST.

STEDMAN ST.

CREEK ST.

HARRIS ST.

PARK AVE.

MILL ST.

MISSION ST.

DOCK ST.

EDMOND ST.

GRANT ST.

MAIN ST.

FRONT ST.

BAWDEN ST.

REVILLA ST.

PINE ST.

TUNNEL

WATER ST.

To Ferry Terminal
To Airport Ferry Hwy.
To North Tongass Hwy.

To Gravina Island

TRANSPORTATION

Ketchikan is 35–40 hours from Seattle or 6 hours from Prince Rupert, B.C., via the **Alaska Marine Highway System** (tel. *225–6181*). The ferry terminal is two miles north of the main part of town on the only road. If you disembark when things are busy, prepare for a traffic jam in the city center. If you're leaving town with a vehicle, check in the ferry office to be sure you're parked in the correct lane.

Ketchikan is also a hub for feeder ferries to places like Hyder, Annette Island (Metlakatla Reservation), and Prince of Wales Island (Hollis), usually via the 235-foot *Aurora,* which has a cafeteria but no cabins. About three hours away, Prince of Wales Island features several hundred miles of good gravel roads. These trips don't go every day, so recheck at the above phone number for sailing times and dates.

Strange as it may seem, you also have to take a ferry between Ketchikan and the airport, since the latter is on little Gravina Island in the Tongass Narrows. The Ketchikan Airport is only 90 minutes from Seattle on **Alaska Airlines** (tel. *225–2141*); then it's $2 and another 5 minutes or so across the channel to Revillagigedo, and perhaps 10 minutes or more to your hotel. The airport ferries shuttle across every 15 minutes during the summer. There are no sky caps at the airport. (By the way, the airport popcorn is particularly popular with Alaska Airlines flight attendants.)

You'll also find scheduled air service between Ketchikan and Prince Rupert via **Trans Provincial Airlines;** to Wrangell and Petersburg via either **Taquan Air Service** (tel. *225–9668*) or **Wrangell Air Service** (tel. *225–1998*); between Ketchikan and the Metlakatla reservation or Hyder via **Ketchikan Air Service** (tel. *225–6608*); and between Ketchikan and Prince of Wales Island (Hollis) and several smaller airports via **Temsco Airlines** (tel. *225–9810*). Ketchikan Air, Taquan, and Temsco also act as air taxis, available for chartering to forest service cabins and other isolated fishing areas. The Ketchikan Visitors Bureau will help set all that up for you (see "Miscellaneous Addresses and Phones").

The **Ketchikan Airport Shuttle** (tel. *225–5429*), sometimes called the Airporter, continues aboard the ferry boat to the airport itself, so if you have a lot of luggage that may be the way to go. It's about $10 to or from your hotel. The airport ferries are usually met by hotel shuttle vans and all three taxi companies, **Alaska Cab** (tel. *225–2133*), **Sourdough Cab** (tel. *225–6651*), and **Yellow Taxi** (tel. *225–5555*). There is a municipal bus service in Ketchikan operating daily except Sunday within the city limits for $1 per ride.

Rental cars are available from **Avis** (tel. *225–4515*), which has an airport counter, **Holiday/Payless** (tel. *225–6609*), and a little cheaper from **Rent-A-Dent** (tel. *225–5123*). R-A-D is the only one of the three that allows its cars to be taken on the ferry over to Prince of Wales Island, incidentally.

There's only one real road in Ketchikan; it stretches out along the coastline 18 miles north and 13 miles south of town, called North Tongass and South Tongass highways, respectively. (Ketchikan teenagers say they prefer to save up for boats, not cars, in order to get away from their parents!) Within the city limits the road has various names, including Front Street, Mill Street, and Stedman Street, and there are several side streets off these.

Transportation tip: The last time we were cruising Ketchikan, gasoline was at least a nickel a gallon cheaper out at Ward Cove than at the service stations in town.

HOTELS AND MOTELS

Prepare for a shock. We found only two places to stay that were close to modern professional hotel standards. One has so few rooms that normally we might not even mention it (and understandably, you'll often find it full). The second isn't even in town; in fact it's so far out that under other circumstances we might not have listed that one, either. The rest of the lot meet at least our minimum requirements. Ketchikan also levies a hotel room tax (bed tax) of 4% plus a sales tax of 5%. All the hotels and other addresses here may be written at Ketchikan, AK 99901, and all phone numbers begin with 225.

The best accommodations in town are at the **Royal Executive Suites** (tel. *225–1900*), an unprepossessing boxy wooden building built partly on pilings over the water at 1471 Tongass Ave., some distance from the old Ketchikan area. Generally high ceilings; best units with picture-window panoramas of the waterfront; a few large rooms featuring separate living areas, kitchenettes, jacuzzis, etc.; all with solid, restful colors; the usual first-class amenities like cable TV, clock radios, etc.; double rates vary according to size and position, but generally hover in the $100 to $150 range; no restaurant on the premises; catered room service available. There are only a dozen rooms, but for general comfort and facilities, it ranks far above the competition. (Reservations from the hotel at P.O. Box 8331.)

Very good facilities with an excellent restaurant? That would have to be the new, viewful **Salmon Falls Resort** (tel. *225–2752*) on the Behm Canal. Alaskan fishing lodges are usually pretty "rough it" kind of places, but this is a fishing lodge for more than the usual muddy-boot crowd. Unfortunately it's at the end of the north road, some 16 miles from Ketchikan—as far as you can get. But once you do get there, the rooms in the rustic log buildings offer almost anything you might want (except TV, which is a lifestyle they've chosen; and except clothes closets, which seems a little strange). Life seems to center on the octagonal bar/lounge/restaurant, which is building an excellent reputation, especially for salmon. There's a cheery fire on chilly days. And down by the docks, of course, you can arrange any kind of fishing adventure you want. Room rates are expected to be generally in the $100 range. All in all, a good catch. (Reservations toll-free at *(800) 247–9059.*)

Dropping down a notch on our scale of desirability, but perhaps much more convenient, is the local link in the **Super 8 Motel** chain (tel. *225–9088*), near the Plaza Mall. Rooms like those in a thousand and one others—clean enough, but basically uninspired; no views and no dining area; a popular restaurant (Latitude 56) within walking distance; guest laundry available; most doubles in the $80–90 range. (P.O. Box 8818.)

Right across from the state ferry landing, the **Landing Motel** (tel. *225–5166*) tries to run a tight ship at 3434 Tongass Ave. Still known by many locals as the Hilltop, but under a new captaincy that had only just begun when we climbed aboard, a locally popular bar and restaurant on the premises; units with telephone, TV and the usual facilities; most doubles around $75 or $80 or so for your landing here. (Reservations from the hotel at P.O. Box 8515.)

The same crew that is smoothing out the Landing has also taken over the historic old **Gilmore Hotel** (tel. *225–9423*), with its stained glass windows, downtown at 326 Front St. The renovation is a massive undertaking, to be sure, but if they pull it off it could turn out to be fairly comfortable. 42 rooms on three floors with no elevator; old-fashioned high ceilings, of course; TVs, radios, and steam radiators; popular Gilmore Gardens restaurant on the ground floor, which also handles the room service; doubles should be around $75. As with all downtown/bartown hotels, however, residents of the Gilmore must put up with the sounds of late-night revelry on the streets below, particularly on boozy weekends. If you get the right room this one may be for you; but then again, maybe not. (P.O. Box 326.)

Almost next door is the old **Ingersoll Hotel,** which has also been renovated at various times in its history. Some of the rooms are okay, but this is the place we seemed to spend a month in one week. Skipping the depressing details, we judged it an amateurish operation and a difficult experience in several ways. The hotel has one good feature—Charley's, an excellent restaurant for an evening meal (see ''Restaurants and Dining''). We'll be back to eat, but not to sleep.

Surprisingly the same company also has the **Waterfall Resort** (tel. *225–9461*), the highly advertised luxury fly-in fishing establishment over on Prince of Wales Island with American-plan rates of around $500 a day. We can't comment on that since we haven't seen it. (Write P.O. Box 6440 for information.) We also have not yet inspected a couple of fishing lodges on Revillagigedo.

Beyond that, some bed-and-breakfast outfits are registered with **Ketchikan Bed & Breakfast** (tel. *225–8550*), and they can be written at P.O. Box 3213. We haven't seen the **Ketchikan Youth Hostel** (tel. *225–3319*), which is housed in the United Methodist Church only between Memorial Day and Labor Day.

RESTAURANTS AND DINING

For elegant dining, one of the most popular choices is to make the 16-mile trek north to the **Salmon Falls Resort** (tel. *225–2752*). In a wonderful tree, water, and sky setting, the meals, led by salmon and halibut, have been excellent. Prices are stiff, but probably worth it. Reserve always—a day or more in advance, if possible.

Back in town, **Charley's** (tel. *225–5090*), in the Ingersoll Hotel at 208 Front St., is an excellent choice for dinner and perhaps lunch, as long as Calvin is cooking, anyway. Underneath hanging ferns and between mirrored columns, pleasant waitresses offer a good-sized menu. Seafood and steaks are the specialties (try the cajun blackened salmon, perhaps; Sara loved the salmon bisque), and prices are in line with other somewhat dressy choices. Breakfasts are good, too, but they are always served in the bar and we don't like being barraged with sound from a TV they never seem to turn off. At lunch time you may have to compete with the cruise ship gang which often pours in here like flies on a doughnut. (The ships come in about 8 a.m. and leave by around 8 p.m.)

If Charley's is bursting at the seams, the nearby **Gilmore Gardens** (tel. *225–9423*) at 326 Front is a decent possibility. Despite the name, this is not dining *al fresco*. A long narrow room furnished with rattan and wicker, it features a larger-than-life espresso machine at one end. The menu is the usual bill of fare topped off, perhaps, with peanut butter pie, a house specialty.

Somewhat less pretentious but still decent choices for dinner include **The Landing** (tel. *225–5166*), in the motel of the same name at 3434 Tongass Ave., or **Jeremiah's,** the upstairs bar, where food is also served. (You can see the airport in the distance.) Another is **Latitude 56,** in the Ketchikan Bowling Center, next door to the Plaza Mall. Here you can order umpteen different types of hamburgers while listening to the faint sound of pins dropping in the background. (It has no view but its parking lot does!) **Mister C's Gourmet Dining,** 830 Water St., is known more for large servings. You can order fresh shrimp by the pound ("We cook, you peel"). Here's where you might get halibut burgers and reindeer sausage, too.

For lunch only, try very hard to get a reservation at **Kay's Kitchen** (tel. *225–5860*) at 2813 Tongass. Kay has invented many of those special sandwiches and homemade pies, and she still oversees everything herself from a tiny kitchen on the premises. (Usually closed April and May, and Sunday and Monday the rest of the year.) If Kay's is closed or otherwise inconvenient, you can get heroes and other take-out deli sandwiches at **Grandeli's** in the Plaza Mall. We had an excellent pepperoni pie at **Harbor Lights Pizza,** 2531 Tongass, near the ferry terminal. For a case of the late-night hungries, try **Jimbo's Korner Kafe,** 307 Mill St., one of the few Ketchikan Kafes open 24 hours.

ENTERTAINMENT AND NIGHT LIFE

For the moment, there is no regular Indian entertainment on tap in Ketchikan. **The First City Players,** an enthusiastic amateur group, gets together on some Friday evenings during the summer to put on a melodrama called *The Fish Pirate's Daughter*. Last year it was at the Main Street Theatre (tel. *225–4792*), but they seem to have trouble coming up with a new venue every year, so don't count on it. And it almost never hits the boards early enough to catch the ship trade, which is good news for independent travelers, at least. Admission about $10.

Otherwise, there's usually some live musical entertainment at the aforementioned **Charley's.** You'll find R&R (rock 'n' roll) or C&W (country 'n' western) music at bars like the **Rainbird,** 114 Front St., the nearby **Pioneer,** an interesting old bar at 122 Front, or at the **Frontier,** 127 Main St., a very local bar catering mostly to the 20–30 set. One of the most enduring establishments is the **Sourdough** at 301 Front St. There's never a band, but it does feature a tremendous gallery of old photographs, many of them shipwrecks.

The **Totem Bar,** 314 Front St., is out after us *cheechakos*; if you buy a drink in their miniature Mason jar, you can keep the jar. If you're interested in local color, the loggers generally bend their sawing arms at the **Fo'c's'le,** 312 Front St., while the commercial fishermen hang out at the **Arctic,** 509 Water St. (Water Street is built entirely on pilings over the water.) Of course **Jeremiah's,** the bar at the Landing Motel is supposed to be the place to wait for your ship or the ferry to come in.

It sometimes features a small combo, too. Most bars close at 3 a.m., but one that's open late is the **One-O-Eight** at 108 Main St., which stays alive until 5 (some enthusiastic revelers have been known to continue partying in the streets even after that). There are at least two dozen more watering holes in town. If you find some of your own favorites, please let us know.

Special events in Ketchikan include the **Salmon Derby** which takes place on three weekends beginning Memorial Day weekend, the **Logging Carnival** on the weekend of the Fourth of July, the **Alaska Seafest** in August, and the **Blueberry Festival** also in August.

SIGHTS AND SITES

You could hardly go to Ketchikan without seeing totem poles, even if you wanted to. There are two main totem parks: **Totem Bight State Park,** 10 miles north of town and carved out of the South Tongass National Forest, was a partly successful Depression-era attempt to save some of the most beautiful and interesting Tlingit and Haida creations. Take the free brochure you'll find there to fully appreciate the designs. The second is the **Saxman Totem Park,** 2½ miles south of town in the Native village of Saxman. You can get a free pamphlet there, too, in the nearby crafts shop. Check into the carving shed where you may be able to find some of Alaska's most famous totem carvers at work. And if you're not completely totemed out by this time (we weren't), search out the **Totem Heritage Center** (tel. *225–5900*) back in town at 601 Deermount St. There young, knowledgeable volunteers will tell you everything you ever wanted to know about ancient and modern totems. Hours vary; admission about $1.

Many of Ketchikan's steep wooden stairs and boardwalks are named "street" even if no vehicles run on them. Don't miss **Creek Street,** a former red-light district still built on pilings along Ketchikan Creek. When Ketchikan was Alaska's largest city, this area was known as the Barbary Coast of the North, and it's oft-quoted that this was where both the fish and the fishermen went upstream to spawn. At number 24, **Dolly's House,** for 50 years the home of Ketchikan's most famous madam, has been preserved as a museum. Ask to see the trap door where Dolly Arthur got her liquor delivered from the river below the house during prohibition. Admission $2.

From there you can walk to the **fish ladder,** one of those devices to give the fighting salmon an extra boost home; and thence to the **Deer Mountain Fish Hatchery.** Not far away the **Tongass Historical Museum** (tel. *225–5600*) at 629 Dock St. has items from Indian, mining, fishing, and cannery days, including the original Iron Chink you may have read about. Admission about $1. You'll hit several of these sights and several more on a self-guided *Historic Ketchikan Walking Tour.* Get the appropriate map (there are a couple of different versions) from the **Ketchikan Visitors Bureau** (tel. *225–6166*) at 131 Front St., next to the Cruise Ships Dock. (Look for the giant rain gauge.)

SIDE TRIPS

There are three or four popular destinations out of Ketchikan, and all involve either a ferry boat or plane trip. You can fly in 50 minutes or ferry in 150 minutes to **Prince of Wales Island,** the second largest island in Alaska (after Kodiak) and the largest Haida settlement in the state. There are more than a thousand miles of roads and about 10 villages, including Hollis (where the ferry docks) and Klawock and Hydaburg, both of which have dramatic totem parks of their own. *Alaska* magazine declared this year that Red Bay Lake is the best place for cutthroat and rainbow trout fishing anytime and red salmon in July. (Thorne Bay features some interesting on-the-water accommodations at the Floatel, tel. *828–3335,* which were not inspected by us.)

Another side trip is to **Metlakatla,** on Annette Island, and the only genuine federal Indian reservation in Alaska. Metlakatla was founded when a large contingent of Tsimshian Indians, led by an Episcopal priest, moved here from British Columbia a century ago. You'll learn the whole story if you visit Father Duncan's Cottage, now open Monday–Friday as a museum. Rooms are available at the Taquan Inn.

From Ketchikan you can also catch aerial and water tours to the beautifully rugged terrain at **Misty Fiords National Monument,** on the other side of the Behm Canal, next to the Canadian border. There are sheer granite cliffs, 1000-foot waterfalls and, if you're lucky, bears and other wildlife.

Another possibility is the much longer trip to hidden **Hyder,** the "Friendliest Little Ghost Town in Alaska," reached once a week by state ferry (the *Aurora*) from Ketchikan up the long Portland Canal. Often used in feature motion pictures, Hyder is that tiny American community next to the somewhat larger Canadian community of Stewart, which is actually connected to the continental road system. (The only other Southeast Alaskan town that is, besides Haines and Skagway.) Stalwart types might get "Hyderized" at the Glacier Inn, and be sure you get a certificate to prove it! Accommodations are available in the Grand View or the Sealaska Inn in Hyder, as well as at an RV park and campground. (Information from the Stewart-Hyder Chamber of Commerce, Box 306, Stewart, B.C., VOT 1W0, Canada.)

TOURS AND CRUISES

Several tours in and out of town are offered by **Gray Line of Alaska** (tel. *225–6260*), including a four-hour airplane and bus tour to the Indian reservation at Metlakatla for around $100. An hour-long "Ferry Stop-Over Tour" (designed for those on the ferry who are not hanging around town) should cost around $7. **Tour Alaska** (tel. *225–0637*) offers some guided totem park bus tours, and that's a way to learn what totems are all about without all the reading.

An unusual two-hour "Mountain Lake Canoe Adventure" has been set up by **Alaska Travel Adventures** (Juneau tel. *789–0052*), a Juneau company with a branch in Ketchikan. Fare was around $50 the last we looked. The tour is sold mostly to cruise ship passengers, although FITs can join, too. **Southeast Exposure** (tel. *225–8829*) has set up a nature-oriented, three-hour "Sea Kayaking" trip for around $50.

We enjoyed a two-hour cruise along the waterfront with Dale Pihlman's **Outdoor Alaska** (tel. *225–6044*) aboard the M/V *Misty Fjord,* and the lectures by Captain Lee Does and first mate Becky Haddix. Don't miss seeing the bald eagles sitting on the pilings at Harry's Boat Yard. The fare for your visit will probably run around $40. The same company also runs a tour through a local fish-processing plant at around $30, an all-day fly/cruise trip to Misty Fiords National Monument for a fare of around $175, and also some special ocean-going kayak tours.

Flightseeing trips from Ketchikan include one we attempted to Misty Fiords with the snazzy, red-and-yellow 10-passenger seaplanes of **Temsco Airlines** (tel. *225–9810*). We enjoyed the flight, but when the fiords were so misty that our De Havilland Otter couldn't get far enough into the park, they gave everyone on our trip their money back. Walk-in fares are normally about $125 for the 1½-hour tour, which usually includes a landing on one of the lakes.

SPORTS

Ketchikan's biggest sport—if you haven't already guessed—is *fishing,* and record catches of salmon and halibut have been registered there, along with trophy-sized red snapper and lingcod. (Tip: fishermen/photographers sometimes catch the less desirable rock cod, which they later throw out to attract bald eagles into camera range.) Independent anglers can rent skiffs equipped with motors, gas, gaff, and net. Rods and reels, etc., are rentable at bait and tackle shops. A non-resident fishing license cost $10 for three days in 1988.

You can charter a yacht for a half-day, full day or even a week. Many of these are available through Ketchikan Sport Fishing (tel. *225–3293*), 3420 Baranof St., or through the Ketchikan Visitors Bureau (tel. *225–6161*), 131 Front St. The KVB can also refer you to nearby fishing lodges.

Also available are air charters to nearby freshwater lakes or to one of those famous $15-a-night lakeside cabins maintained in the surrounding Tongass National Forest by the U.S. Forest Service (tel. *225–3101*), 3031 Tongass Ave. (That's the cabin reservation phone number in Ketchikan. It's better to book before arriving in the area.) Most of these cabins also include the use of an aluminum skiff. You can rent your own 1.5-hp kicker in town and take it on the float plane if you're going to fly inland to fish for cutthroat or rainbow trout.

For hunters, deer, goats, and bear are fair game, depending on the season, etc. Get the latest on guides from the visitors bureau and on regulations from the Alaska State Department of Fish and Game (tel. *225–7425*) in Ketchikan. The branch is on the second floor at the Prospector Mall, near the Plaza Mall.

Baseball and *softball* are popular games in Ketchikan. The ball park in Bear Valley, across from the Junior High School, sees games played by the Little League as well as adult minor leagues. There's another diamond by the Ketchikan High School at the west end of town. And the game is never called on account of rain.

Bowlers, of course, shoot straight for the 16-lane **Ketchikan Bowling Center** (tel. *225–9011*) at 2050 Sea Level Dr., near the Plaza Mall.

Some Ketchikaners maintain they do go *outdoor swimming* and picnicking on lazy summer days, probably at **Rotary Beach,** a pebbly strip of shoreline 3½ miles south of town (take a blanket). **Settlers Cove,** about 17 miles north of town, is similar. You can find a few genuinely sandy beaches on nearby islands, but only if you have your own boat.

SHOPPING

Unfortunately for Ketchikaners, there is no big department store on the island, not even a Freddy's. However there is a genuine shopping mall, catering both to residents and visitors. It's officially named the Plaza Port West, but apparently since there's no Plaza Port East, it's usually just called the **Plaza Mall,** at 2417 Tongass in the Westend Commercial District. (It's "climate controlled"; meaning enclosed, dry, and cooled or heated as necessary.) Occasionally you'll find a free shuttle bus to the mall from downtown Ketchikan or the ferry terminal. A small building called the **Prospector Mall** is nearby.

Several places specialize in wood carvings (including miniature totems), woven cedar baskets, blankets, pottery, and other Alaskan products (all over the state, look for the polar bear "Made in Alaska" symbol). *Native carvers* are sometimes at work at the **Once in a Blue Moose,** a gift shop at 407 Stedman St. **Nancy's** is the big *Alaskana* shop in the Plaza Mall, and it caters both to locals and tourists. We picked up some Alaskan *books* at the **Voyageur Book Store,** 405 Dock St.

We enjoy the *hodgepodge* of goods in the **Tongass Trading Company,** right next to the cruise dock downtown. They also run the **Outfitter,** at 3232 Tongass, near the ferry dock. Well-known *arts and crafts* galleries include **Scanlon Galleries,** 310 Mission St., **Alaska Legacy Arts,** across the street at 311, and **Grundy's Gallery,** 315 Mill St.

To arrange for *mail-order salmon and other seafood products,* look for the **Silver Lining** (tel. *225–9865*) at 1705 Tongass Ave. It's open daily until 6 p.m. *Canned salmon* and other gift items are also sold at the museum.

MISCELLANEOUS ADDRESSES AND PHONES

In addition to listings already given, here are several more locations in Ketchikan.

- Alaska People's Market (tel. *225–8657*); Mondays, twice a month, Pioneer Hall (314 Pioneer St.)
- Bus information (tel. *225–6151*).

- Cooperative Extension Service, Ketchikan Community College (tel. *225-3290*), 7th and Madison streets.
- Elmo's Hair Design (tel. *225-5447*), Plaza Port West.
- Fire department (tel. *225-9616*), 319 Main St.
- General Hospital (tel. *225-5171*), 3100 Tongass Ave.
- Highliner Dry Cleaners & Laundromat (tel. *225-5308*), 2703 Tongass Ave.
- Police department (tel. *225-6631*).
- Post Office (tel. *225-9601*), next to ferry terminal.
- Public library (tel. *225-3331*), 629 Dock St.
- Sea Mart Supermarket, 2417 Tongass Ave. (open 24 hours).
- Sourdough Liquor Store (tel. *225-2217*), 301 Front St.
- Visitors Bureau (tel. *225-6166*), 131 Front St.

PRINCE RUPERT, B.C.

How Alaskan can you get without being part of Alaska? This spirited little British Columbian coastal city may provide the answer, since it is Canada's northern jumping-off place to reach the Southeast section of the 49th State.

The history of Prince Rupert is a sad one—more what might have been than what was. It was founded by an American visionary who saw this port on Kaien Island, "the third largest natural harbor in the world," as the perfect place for West Coast ocean shipping to connect with Canada's railroads. He went to England in 1912 to line up investors and shipping for the massive project, but chose the S.S. *Titanic* for his return. Charles M. Hays, his plans, and his contracts did not survive. Others bravely carried on, and although the railroad was built, the ships never came and the community never achieved the goals and stature which had seemed its certain destiny. Vancouver soon won the race to become the major Pacific port.

Today Prince Rupert is a solid city of 16,000 or so (over twice the size of Ketchikan), supported mainly by the commercial fishing industry and the local wood pulp mill. Fortunately it is not overwhelmed by tourists, although visitors are warmly welcomed—and not charged as much as elsewhere. There are more similarities than differences between Prince Rupert and Ketchikan. You'll see the same kind of vegetation and wildlife, and it rains about as much too. A CBC correspondent once called Rupert "the city of the drip-dry bald eagle." With cheerful

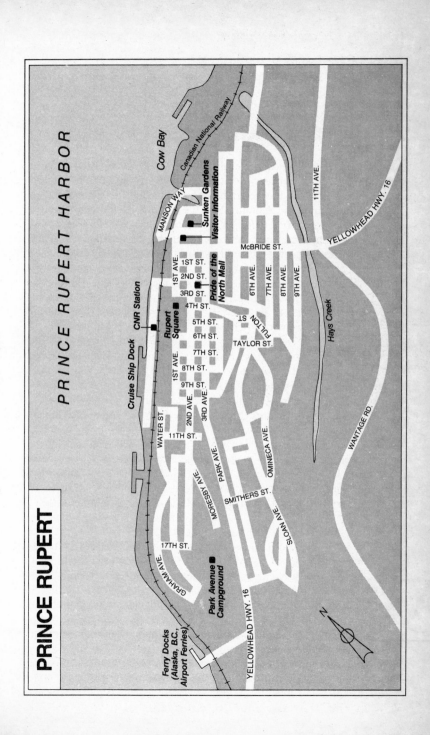

PRINCE RUPERT

PRINCE RUPERT HARBOR

Cow Bay

Canadian National Railway

Manson Way

Sunken Gardens

Visitor Information

McBRIDE ST.

1ST AVE.

1ST ST.

2ND ST.

Pride of the North Mall

3RD ST.

4TH ST.

CNR Station

Cruise Ship Dock

Rupert Square

5TH ST.

Fulton St.

6TH ST.

Taylor St.

1ST AVE.

7TH ST.

8TH ST.

9TH ST.

2ND AVE.

3RD AVE.

Water St.

11TH ST.

Moresby Ave.

Park Ave.

Omineca Ave.

Smithers St.

Sloan Ave.

Hays Creek

11TH AVE.

6TH AVE.

7TH AVE.

8TH AVE.

9TH AVE.

YELLOWHEAD HWY. 16

Wantage Rd.

17TH ST.

Graham Ave.

Park Avenue Campground

Ferry Docks
(Alaska, B.C.,
Airport Ferries)

YELLOWHEAD HWY. 16

N

aplomb, the P.R. folks in P.R. have now dubbed it "the City of Rainbows."

TRANSPORTATION

To answer the question we usually get right off the bat—no, you cannot take a ferry between Seattle (Bellingham) and Prince Rupert. The flagship *Columbia* breezes right on by on her Seattle-Ketchikan leg. But as we indicated in "Coming Into the Country," you can take one of the **B.C. Ferries** (tel. *624–9627*) between Prince Rupert and Port Hardy on Vancouver Island. And then you can take the ferries of the **Alaska Marine Highway** (tel. *627–1744*) for the 100 miles between Prince Rupert and Ketchikan once or twice a week, daily in summer. From Ketchikan, you are positioned to join the rest of the Alaska system. The B.C. and the Alaskan ferry docks are situated within whistling distance of each other in Fairview Bay at the end of Park Avenue. (If you don't have your own vehicle, you'll need a cab or, conceivably, a bus.)

Many motor home owners and other drivers come over the bridge via Canadian Route 16, the scenic Yellowhead Highway, and then take the ferry north. Or you can steam to Prince Rupert with the B.C. Ferry and then drive your car along the Yellowhead to the Cassiar Highway, thence to Stewart/Hyder, which has weekly ferry service to Ketchikan. (As we said earlier, it's a long wait if you miss the boat.) You can also chug into town by train, and it's a popular trip with some excellent scenery along the right-of-way from Jasper. Get on the right track with **VIA Rail** (U.S. toll-free tel. *(800) 872–2648*). That's the passenger branch of Canadian National Railway. You can also show up or leave town on **Greyhound of Canada,** formerly Coachways (tel. *624–5090*), 106 Sixth St.

Prince Rupert has two airports—sort of. Conventional aircraft, like the daily jet flights from Vancouver on **Canadian Airlines International** (tel. *624–9181*) or on **Air B.C.** (tel. *624–4554*), land on Digby Island, which is connected by a 15-minute ferry to Kaien Island. Back in town, Seal Cove handles scheduled seaplane service such as that by **Trans-Provincial Airlines** (tel. *627–1341*) which shuttles to Ketchikan and Stewart/Hyder. **North Coast Air Services** (tel. *627–1351*) regularly hops to Haida settlements in the Queen Charlotte Islands, and also offers charter flights to Alaska.

Rental cars can be had from **Budget** (tel. *627–7400*), 205 Second Ave. West, or **Tilden** (tel. *624–5318*). There is municipal bus service from **Coastal Bus Lines** (tel. *624–3343*) daily except Sunday. The local taxi service is **Skeena Cabs** (tel. *624–2185*).

HOTELS AND MOTELS

There are two outstanding places to stay in Rupert (locals often drop the "Prince" in casual conversation). The cliff-side **Crest Motor Inn** (tel. *624–6771*) is nearly 30 years old, but it has recently been refurbished from top to bottom. 106 fully equipped, warm-toned, wall-papered rooms, all complete with cozy window seats; water-side units with the best views; one of the best dining rooms in town; most doubles in the C$90 range. The Crest has always been a professionally run family operation. If it stays in the same hands, it just might weather well over the next 30 years, too. (Reservations from P.O. Box 277, Prince Rupert, B.C. V8J 3P6.)

Our own stay was nearby at the **Highliner,** which was once called the Coast Highliner (tel. *624–9060*). Almost the only high-rise in town; less personality than the Crest; generally large rooms; some with good views. Due to architectural problems, a restaurant originally planned for the top floor never got off the ground. It's a typical city hotel and a comfortable choice for rates in the C$80 range. (Reservations from 815 First Ave. West, Prince Rupert, B.C. V8J 1B3.)

After those two, things begin slipping downhill. More modest places nearby include the **Drifter Motor Hotel** (tel. *624–9161*), where you may drift into a decent double for around C$60 on your visit. It's at 1080 West Third Ave. Nearby, at No. 909, the **Slumber Lodge Motel** (tel. *627–1711*) also has sleepy rooms at around the same price. The **Moby Dick** (tel. *624–6961*), at 935 Second Ave. West, was once more of a white elephant than a white whale, but it has improved recently. Rooms should be around C$50, although the neighborhood is often noisy into the wee hours.

There are three motels with kitchen facilities, the **Aleeda** (tel. *627–1367*) at 900 Third Ave. West, the **Neptune** (tel. *627–1377*), at 1040 Saskatoon, and the **Parkside** (tel. *624–9131*), at 101 Eleventh Ave. East, next to McDonald's (you can park right outside your front door). The cheapest place in town? That's probably the **Pioneer Rooms** (tel. *624–2334*), a re-formed rooming house at 167 Third Ave. West. You won't get a private bath, but you might get a clean, simple room for around C$25 (no guarantees by us, however). For tent and RV campers, the **Park Avenue Campground** (tel. *624–5861*) is run by the PRCVB at 1750 Park Ave.

RESTAURANTS AND DINING

For the past several years the top dining room in town has been the **Crest Dining Room** (tel. *624–2771*) in the hotel of the same name. Service is elegant at harbor-view tables. Several continental specialties with an emphasis on fresh seafood. Several main dishes are saucy, some are poached, and a few are stir-fried. Allow a couple of hours and figure on spending C$25 or C$30 per person, plus any alcohol. Deservedly popular with the local gentry. (There's also an inside coffee shop on the same premises.)

Other good fish restaurants include **Smile's** (tel. *624–3072*) at 113 George Hills Way on Cow Bay. This place is casual to the extreme at lunch, but at night they bring out some tablecloths and candles. Almost next door is the **Breakers** (tel. *624–5990*), for pub-style dining with a great view of the local yachts. We enjoyed it for lunch. Then out by the ferry terminal, the **Anchorage** (tel. *627–1496*), not much more than a double-wide trailer, has a good nautical reputation although we haven't been in. One of the best bargains for fish 'n' chips (choice of cod or halibut) is the **Green Apple,** a tiny but inexpensive non-alcoholic entry at the corner of Third and McBride, within walking distance of the tourist office. Good hamburgers, too.

In the ethnic file, the best Chinese food in town this year is probably at the **Imperial Palace** (tel. *624–5060*), 611 Third Ave. West. Recently they featured "Singing Herbie" ("Herbie the Halibut" is Rupert's mascot, and they served him still sizzling). For Italian food, the only boat in town is **La Gondola** (tel. *624–2621*), 710 First Ave. West, next to the Rupert Motor Inn. Somewhat Venetian, and the *vista* is *bella* from some tables. Among Greek restaurants, **Rodhos** is the most popular. At 716 Second Ave. West, it also serves steak and pizza.

The only 24-hour restaurant we know about is the **Moby Dick Inn,** which is known for that all-night feature more than it is any other.

ENTERTAINMENT AND NIGHT LIFE

Since many communities up the coast offer a local melodrama or similar entertainment, Prince Rupert has launched its own weekend afternoon variety show, geared mainly to cruise ship passengers. *Pho-*

tographs and Memories is produced at the attractive **Performing Arts Centre** on McBride Ave. The show we saw was okay, but with a lot of historical detail confusing to Outsiders. With a couple of exceptions, the performers were willing but amateurish. Admission C$6.

Nighttime action centers on several bars and cocktail lounges. The bar at the aforementioned **Breakers** appeals to the nautical community at Cow Bay. Three addresses offer live entertainment: **Bogie's,** underneath the Rupert Hotel, appeals to the younger crowd. The **Surf Club** on Second Ave. always has a band—sometimes rock, sometimes country. Then there's the **Belmount,** on Third Ave., which showcases "exotic dancers"—a nice way of saying strippers (once in a while there are exotic men there, too, in this age of equality).

SIGHTS AND SITES

There are at least two "don't misses" in town. The first is a rainy day favorite, the **Museum of Northern British Columbia,** behind the CVB at First and McBride. It is probably the best western Canadian museum north of the Victoria Provincial. Permanent exhibits concentrate on Indians and local history. Check out some of the grandiose blueprints for the city that never were realized. There are also revolving shows in the art gallery, and the shop sells authentic crafts.

The second must is the **Mount Hays Recreation Area,** a wilderness walk at an elevation of about 1800 feet, overlooking the city and the harbor; on a clear day . . . etc.). Drive or cab first to the end of Wantage Rd., whence you reach it via one of those death-defying contraptions Rupertians call "the gondola," which is believably one of the steepest of the type in North America. It's $3 or so round trip, but well worth the fare and the fright. Like going up Jack's beanstalk, you'll find a different world at the top—a sort of alpine meadow, with several different kinds of wildflowers. Boardwalks provide safe passage over the muskeg. There's also a chalet with lounge and restaurant perched on the very edge of this Green Giant land.

During World War II, thousands of American GIs were stationed in the center of town on Acrópolis Hill, which is now known as **Roosevelt Park** in honor of F.D.R.

SIDE TRIPS

About 10 miles out of town, the defunct century-old **North Pacific Cannery** is a large complex that has been turned into a museum and arts-mopheric center near the village of Port Edward. Things were closed the only time we ever made it out there so far, so you're on your own. If you go, let us know.

You can take a plane or a local ferry across Hecate Strait to the **Queen Charlotte Islands**—an eight-hour boat ride, so plan to stay overnight (try the Premier Hotel). The paved road there is actually the last 90 miles or so of the Yellowhead Highway.

TOURS AND CRUISES

A free *walking tour* around the downtown area is offered by the Prince Rupert CVB. Check with the bureau in their office at First and McBride. If you want to ride, the local Gray Line concession is held by **Farwest Bus Lines** (tel. *624–6400*), but it won't go with less than nine people. We know less about **All Tours** (tel. *624–6124*) or **American Sightseeing** (tel. *624–2778*). More small, individual tours can be arranged through **Skeena Taxi** (tel. *624–2185*). For diehard industrial groupies, the PRCVB can also set up tours of the coal terminal and grain-shipping facilities on Ridley Island.

Aerial sightseeing tours are always available from **Trans-Provincial Airlines** (tel. *627–1341*) and sometimes **North Coast Air Services** (tel. *627–1351*). Fares vary depending on aircraft and number of passengers.

SPORTS

As in Ketchikan, the big sport in Prince Rupert is *salt-water sport fishing,* and for the same species and in about the same numbers. The only difference is that it will cost you a lot less in Rupert, apparently since it just isn't as well known. There are only about a dozen charter boats, and they are not falling all over one another. You should be able to charter an entire vessel, carrying up to six people, for the day for around C$500—less than half the cost for the same thing in most of Alaska. And you might not see another fishing boat for the entire day. See the PRCVB for the arrangements or contact **Prince Rupert Charter Operators** (tel. *627–7777*), a lucky number that represents nearly all the boats in town.

If you want to catch a fish, but hate all the work, you can search out **Miller Bay Seafarms,** about 10 km (6 miles) out of town on Route 16. We haven't been there, but allegedly they have stocked a man-made lake with enough fish that you could probably cross the lake walking on their backs. The idea is to rent a rod, catch a fish, pay about 50 cents per inch and then barbecue them right on the spot.

For both *hunting and fishing* information, check with the *Government Agent* (tel. *624–2121*) in the Courthouse at 100 Market Place.

You can rent your own runabout for fishing or just nautical sightseeing from **Seaspray Boat Rentals** (tel. *624–2120*). Look for them at Cow Bay Public Floats.

The **Municipal Golf Course,** a challenging set of links on Wantage Road, has some unusual hazards. Sometimes play must be temporarily suspended when bears appear and begin ambling along the fairway. At other times, the problem is lost balls—apparently stolen by the rather big and bold ravens in the vicinity.

Psst! If you want to really do some serious *wildlife viewing,* go a little past the golf course to the municipal garbage dump. Eagles and ravens abound. Bears sometimes browse for bargains, too.

Bowlers gather at the **Totem Lanes** (tel. *624–3291*), 1241 Prince George St., which has 16 alleys and a cafeteria. Something a little less strenuous? There's a game almost every night at the **Rupert Bingo Centre** (venues vary).

Honestly, there are local sports enthusiasts into all the following activities, and the CVB can tell you how to contact the appropriate clubs: basketball, badminton, guns, boxing, karate, volleyball, hockey, figure skating, flag football, archery, softball, swimming, baseball, skiing, sailing, cricket, curling, judo, soccer, squash, racquet ball, rugby, scuba, water polo, and tennis.

SHOPPING

If you're beginning your Alaska trip at Prince Rupert, we wouldn't suggest you blow your budget for arts and crafts immediately. Nevertheless, there are several good things for sale at the **Museum of Northern British Columbia.** Featured among these are examples of *argillite* *carvings,* which are made only by Haida Indians from the rare, workable black argillite available only on one gradually diminishing mountain in the nearby Queen Charlotte Islands. They don't exactly give it away. The genuine article averages about C$100 per carved inch, although some small medallions go for as low (relatively speaking) as C$50.

An excellent collection of argillite, most of it not for sale, is on display at **Manson's Jewelers,** 528 Third Ave. West (ask to see the obscure case in the corner).

There are things carved from *nephrite,* also known as B.C. jade, the official gemstone of the province. *Wood carvings* are also in demand. Other Indian crafts and jewelry can be found at the museum, at Manson's, and elsewhere. Stores also include **Totem Pole Gifts,** 258 Third Ave. West, and **Harbour Crafts,** 311 Third Ave. West (ask to see the locally made crafts).

Some American travelers are interested in a few British imports, not easily available in the U.S. You might find some excellent *English linens,* among other places, at **Parker's Ladies Wear,** 245 Third Ave. West, and *English bone china* at **Cook's** on Third Ave., along with several other addresses.

The local mall is right downtown, the **Rupert Square Shopping Centre,** 500 Second Ave. The large department store therein is the **Zellers.**

MISCELLANEOUS ADDRESSES AND PHONES

First, here are some miscellaneous facts. McBride Street divides the numbered avenues between east and west, and since most of the commercial area is to the west of McBride, virtually all the addresses we use here are "Avenue West." The Canadian postal code for all addresses in Prince Rupert begins with V8J. Phone numbers, like all those in B.C., are in area code 604.

- Canada Customs (tel. *624–3313*), 417 Second Ave. West.
- Emergencies of all types—dial 911.
- Government Liquor Store, 100 Second Ave. West.
- King Koin Laundry (tel. *624–9934*), 745 Second Ave. West.
- Park Avenue Campground (tel. *624–5637*), 1750 Park Ave.
- Safeway Supermarket, 140 Second Ave. West.
- Lions Club (tel. *624–4570*), P.O. Box 511.
- Shoppers Drug Mart, 501 Third Ave. West.

- Rotary Club (tel. *624–2517*), P.O. Box 225.
- Prince Rupert Convention and Visitors Bureau (tel. *624–5637*), First Ave. and McBride St. (P.O. Box 669), Prince Rupert, B.C. V8J 3S1.
- Public library (tel. *627–1345*), 101 Sixth Ave. West.
- Snappy Photo Centre, 615 Third Ave. West.
- United States Customs (tel. *624–5351*), Alaska Ferry Terminal.
- Women of the Moose (tel. *624–3327*), 745 First Ave. West.

WRANGELL

The next stop north of Ketchikan on the ferry system is the village of Wrangell, which gets about half the annual rainfall of Ketchikan. Disembarking passengers are likely to be greeted by a squad of enthusiastic youngsters learning the principle of free enterprise, their parents standing discreetly to one side, apparently to make sure that none of their competing offspring get too pushy. Back in the 1960s, a piece of property containing a hill and ledge studded with garnets was deeded to the Boy Scouts. Ever since then, the boys and girls of Wrangell have been earning spending money and saving money by chiseling out these hard purple crystals and then selling them to visitors. Some of these junior minors have even printed up their own business cards.

Wrangell, population about 2400, is both a town and an island, and in the past it was held by the Tlingit, the British, and the Russians before it became American along with the rest of Alaska in 1867. In those days there was a brief gold rush on the nearby Stikine (''stickkeen'') River. Life has now settled down to an economy based largely on fishing and lumber—although gold is still important, too, since a rich Canadian mine near the headwaters of the Stikine River has become active and a certain amount of the commercial activity has rubbed off on Wrangell. Like most towns in Southeast, Wrangell is surrounded by the Tongass National Forest, and dedicated explorers and fishermen still escape to the nearby wilderness.

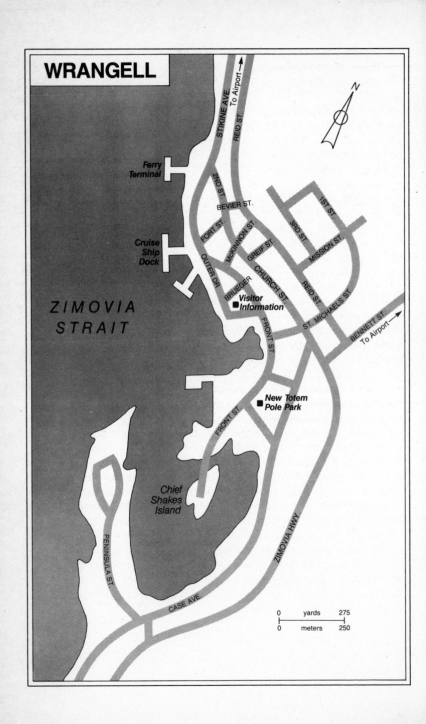

WRANGELL

ZIMOVIA STRAIT

STIKINE AVE.
To Airport

REID ST.

N

Ferry Terminal

2ND ST.

BEVIER ST.

1ST ST.

3RD ST.

MISSION ST.

FORT ST.

McKINNON ST.

GREIF ST.

Cruise Ship Dock

OUTER DR.

CHURCH ST.

REID ST.

BRUEGER

Visitor Information

FRONT ST.

ST. MICHAELS ST.

BENNETT ST.
To Airport

New Totem Pole Park

FRONT ST.

Chief Shakes Island

ZIMOVIA HWY.

PENINSULA ST.

CASE AVE.

| 0 | yards | 275 |
| 0 | meters | 250 |

TRANSPORTATION

You can come into Wrangell on the ferry northbound from Ketchikan and southbound from Petersburg. The Ferry Dock is downtown at the end of Church Street, and ships from the **Alaska Marine Highway** (tel. *874–3711*) tie up at least once a day (one northbound, one southbound)—sometimes more often during the summer (look for the schedule in the *Wrangell Sentinel*). The terminal building opens two hours before the Big Blue Canoe is due; get there before then if your car is on standby.

Wrangell is not on the agenda of most **cruise ships.** The few who do call tie up at City Dock, near the Stikine Inn. During the tourist season, elaborately costumed ''Shady Ladies'' sometimes show up on the docks to greet the visitors. They are not what they appear to be, of course, but rather good-natured Chamber of Commerce volunteers who hand out brochures and answer questions.

About a mile and a half on the other side of town, the Wrangell Airport also has daily northbound and southbound service from **Alaska Airlines** (tel. *874–3308*). The Shady Ladies in gold-rush garb sometimes meet the flights during the summer. There are a couple of charter airlines that also fly scheduled service to Ketchikan or Petersburg: **Diamond Aviation** (tel. *874–2319*) or **Wrangell Air Service** (tel. *874–2369*). There's a fence around the airport now, so there are no more encounters between aircraft and bears or deer on the runway.

There is no municipal bus, but you can call for a taxi from the **Star Cab** (tel. *874–3622*). As for rental cars, you'll have to **Rent-A-Dent** (tel. *874–3322*) or rent nothing at all. Parked at the Thunderbird Hotel, it advertises ''You'll love your Dentley.''

Be careful driving the dirt logging roads, especially if it's been raining. All the locals do it, but you may meet a big truck in a difficult area. You can't quite drive all the way around the 10-by-30-mile island, merely because logging has not quite progressed to that point. Some places you can get to are pretty isolated. If you're going to explore the island countryside, be sure to pick up the newspaperlike **Wrangell Guide** from the visitors center.

HOTELS AND MOTELS

There are a limited number of places to overnight in Wrangell, and it's worth remembering that the city levies a $3-a-day bed tax in addition to the regular 6% sales tax. If you're writing for reservations, Wrangell's zip code is 99929.

The most conveniently comfortable headquarters is the **Stikine Inn** (tel. *874–3388*), downtown at 107 Front St. and within easy reach of the ferry. There is TV and all the mod cons in all 34 rooms, plus a nice view of the water. Our only caveat is to insist on a room in the new wing, which is a fair distance from the popular but noisy bar. Better doubles should be in the $100 range; some others might be $75. The Dock Side coffee shop on the premises is usually fine. (Reservations from P.O. Box 990.)

If you have a car, we recommend the **Roadhouse Lodge** (tel. *874–2335*), four miles out of town on the only highway. We'd like to say "You can't miss it," but you could if you're not keeping your eyes open; it's up a little hill on the left. Dick or Dottie Olson will pick you up and drive you there if you're without your own wheels. Dick also operates a sightseeing bus service, an airport pick-up service, some fishing charter boats, and rents cars to guests. A cozy restaurant and bar are on the ground floor; motel-style rooms are upstairs, the best overlooking the waters of the Zimovia Strait. Doubles around $70. (Reservations from Box 1199.)

Back in town, **Harding's Old Sourdough Lodge** (tel. *874–3613*) caters largely to fellow fishermen who take one of Lloyd Harding's package deals, but it is also open to others for around $75 per room, which includes at least a logger's breakfast (other deals may wrap up all meals), but bathrooms must be shared. The low-level building was partly made from several ATCO containers hooked together; there are no views. The wood-paneled rooms (some non-smoking) are small but well-decorated. The informal lounge/dining area next to the kitchen is cozy, but a new restaurant may be open by now. There's a free guest laundry, plus a sauna and steam bath. (Reservations from P.O. Box 1062.)

Also in town, the **Thunderbird** (tel. *874–3322*) on Front Street is a plain-Jane possibility, but we believe it has much less personality than the other three choices. No restaurant, but there's one next door. Room rates are comparable. Beyond that, there are a couple of tiny bed-and-breakfasts, which we haven't seen. Ask at the visitor center.

RESTAURANTS AND DINING

The choice is small, and you'd better not try to get a meal anywhere after 9 or 10 p.m. In the Stikine Inn, the **Dock Side** (tel. *874–3737*) generally offers good food along with the good views over the city docks. We had an excellent breakfast for reasonable rates. Four miles out at the **Roadhouse** (tel. *874–2335*), Dick or Dottie usually do the cooking themselves. Dinner at around $15 or $16 usually includes salad bar, potatoes, and dessert. While you're waiting, enjoy the veritable museum tacked up on the walls and scattered around the room.

Back in town, the **Hungry Beaver** has only been open sporadically, and it was not when we were hungry. It's on the approximate site of the old Fort Stikine. The **Diamond C Cafe** operates only until 4 p.m. or so, in one corner of an office building on Front Street. We thought it was okay for a nonserious lunch. **Maggie's & Son,** in the nearby red, white, and blue building, specializes in pizza, sandwiches, and ice cream (giant scoops on the cones). The **Snack Shack,** a picnic table and take-out operation, was a teen hangout for years before closing. It may be open again under tough new management soon.

ENTERTAINMENT AND NIGHT LIFE

Unless you arrive during the February Tent City Festival, don't look for Indian dances or Gay 90s melodramas and the like. Wrangell is a small town, and nowadays everybody who has a TV also has either a VCR or a satellite dish.

The only place with a live band is the bar at the **Stikine Inn,** and this is usually action central Tuesday night through Saturday night. Sometimes they get a 5-piece combo in and there's almost no room left for dancers on the floor.

Other than that, let's see—the **Totem Bar** has an electronic dart game (whoop-de-doo). They made a movie starring Joseph Cotten at the **Brig,** and Rosie Greer threw a guy through the rear window for the cameras. Now the Brig has to provide its own entertainment and it's the kind of place where some folks handwrestle to decide who's next at the pool table. A bar for quiet drinking and chatting? We'd go four miles out to our old favorite, the **Roadhouse,** on the Zimovia Highway.

Special events include the **Tent City Winter Festival** in February, the **Salmon Derby** during the last two weeks in May and the **Fourth of July Festival.**

SIGHTS AND SITES

It would be a good idea to get directions at the little A-frame-shaped visitors center near the totem pole and the fork in the road just off Lynch Street. Ask for the newspaper-style *Wrangell Guide,* which outlines a suggested *walking tour* of the downtown area.

The most popular tourist site is **Chief Shakes Island,** a small dollop of land you reach via a wooden bridge from the fishing docks area. For a long time one Chief Shakes or another was the boss around here, and his decorated tribal house with some unusual totem poles have been faithfully restored by the town fathers. The last Chief, Shakes the Eighth, is buried back in town in a patch of weeds.

You can get a 14-page booklet that explains all this at the **Wrangell Museum** (tel. *874–3770*), 122 Second St. The museum is the official repository of much of Wrangell history, but it has limited operating hours. Say hello for us to Patricia Ockert, the director and curator. As the president of the visitors bureau, she also has the answers to lots of other questions. Open 1–4 Monday–Saturday, and usually when cruise ships are in port at other times. Admission $2.

A second museum is **Our Collections** (tel. *874–3646*), on Evergreen Avenue, which was temporarily closed when we searched it out. A family operation, there is no charge to see the miscellaneous memorabilia, and some trinkets are for sale by the owner. It's open only when cruise ships are in or by appointment. Call for directions.

One of Southeast's enduring mysteries is the identity of those who created Wrangell's *petroglyphs,* pictures carved millennia ago in the large rocks down at the beach. They're a little hard to find without some direction, but it's approximately a 15-minute walk along the shoreline north of the ferry terminal. Look for a boardwalk leading down to the beach. Local merchants sell crayons and paper for making rubbings of the designs, and you can get more specific directions from them. (Incidentally, instead of crayons, some visitors like to use scrunched-up fern leaves—a little more difficult but they give a more natural result.)

SIDE TRIPS

The dominant force in the Wrangell area you can't even see from town. The **Stikine River,** whose wide mouth and complex delta of swirls and sloughs are about seven miles away, was once the center for gold mining in the area. In a way, it still is; it extends for more than 330 miles, and all except for the western 30 miles is in Canada. A new gold-mining operation has just begun on the Canadian side of the border.

The Stikine was once an important highway between Canada and the U.S., and some charter flights will go in as far as the 1000-foot-deep **Stikine Canyon** and the small B.C. village of **Telegraph Creek,** the former gold-rush town on its banks. It is also considered the fastest navigable river in North America, and many Wrangell fishermen head for the Stikine River area. So do Wrangell hunters, especially during moose season when they stalk these big beasts from tall trees along the banks. (Everyone seems to have his favorite "moose tree.")

Visitors get to see the Stikine only by chartering boats or planes from Wrangell or Petersburg. The visitors bureau has a list of at least a half-dozen boats, some specializing more in sightseeing, others in fishing.

Both Wrangell and Petersburg like to claim that the **Le Conte Glacier** is in their neck of the Tongass. The southernmost tidewater glacier in North America, it is about 25 miles north of Wrangell, reachable only by chartered boat or plane. When we visited it in June, many of the bergs which had calved from its face were temporary floating birth platforms for mother seals and their pups. The two communities seem to disagree on how that glacier is pronounced. Wrangell folks pronounce the final "e" with a long "a" sound. Petersburgers generally claim, with some reason, that since the man it was named for is French, the "e" is silent.

TOURS AND EXCURSIONS

At the moment the only bus tours in town are run by Dick Olson, proprietor of the **Roadhouse** (tel. *874–2335*), and Dick has it all down to an efficient routine. You won't miss anything, and he'll even help you find and rub down those petroglyphs.

When we were last in town **Diamond Aviation** (tel. *874–2319*) was advertising flightseeing out to Le Conte Glacier at $35 per person. Better recheck that, however, and also see what **Wrangell Air** (tel. *874–2369*) has on tap.

The visitors center has the names of several boat operators who will be glad to set up *sightseeing tours.* Also, you might check with **Aqua Sports** (tel. *874–3811*), also known as Buness Brothers, on Front St.

SPORTS

Well, *fishing* is number one, to be sure; and if you want to go after the abundant salmon or trout in the area, you should check with the state Division of Fish and Wildlife (tel. *874–3215*), in the Kadin Building on Front Street, to get your license and other information. The visitors center has a list of several fishing charter operators. One we've met (but not yet traveled with) is Todd Harding, owner of **TH Charters** (tel. *874–3455*). Other well-known names include John Baker's **Double J Charters** (tel. *874–3225*) and **Bruce Jamieson** (tel. *874–3023*). The midsummer humpbacked salmon run on Anan Creek, 30 miles south of Wrangell on the mainland, is almost legendary. During the run bears, seals, and eagles are there to get in on the action, too.

Fresh-water swimming is available at Pat's Lake and Thom's Lake, right on the island. You might also head five miles out Zimovia Highway to **Institute Beach,** just across from the ruins of the old boarding school there. Visitors are also welcome at the indoor swimming pool on Church St. There's one *tennis court* in the public park out at Shoemaker Bay. The *softball diamond* is there, too. Locals are nuts over *basketball* during the season, and you might catch a game in the Town League. For *shooters,* there's an indoor pistol range in the Public Safety Building (where the police and fire stations and courts are), and an outdoor rifle range out near the airport.

If you're into *hiking,* drop by or call the U.S. Forest Service (tel. *874–2323*), 525 Bennett St., which has up-to-date maps of the trails on Wrangell Island. It will also handle rental of the $15 forest-service cabins in the Tongass.

SHOPPING

As we said, you can buy **garnets** from the kids on the dock. Loose stones about the size of grapes, were in the $3 to $5 range. We preferred those still semi-embedded in the surrounding slate material; so do others, apparently, for these seem to run around $10. If there are no youngsters around, you can sometimes buy some garnets at the **Wrangell Museum,** 122 Second St.

The museum also sells **"Marlinda Dolls"** (about $20) and other Indian products made by Mareleita Wallace. Her home and studio is at 715 Case Ave. Wrangell is a haven for several Southeast artists, some of whose works are also sold in the museum.

The last genuine "Shady Lady" house, dating from 1906, now houses **Sylvia's General Store,** a gift and craft shop at 109 McKinnon St., just off Front St. Looking for gift ideas for the bathroom? You'll find them in the bathroom!

You can buy your petroglyph rubbing supplies and various Alaskana from **Norris Gift Shop** on Front St. (We don't know the number, but Front is only three blocks long.) Photo supplies, books, magazines, etc., are nearby at **Wrangell Drug.**

MISCELLANEOUS ADDRESSES AND PHONES

As we said, all Wrangell zip codes are 99929. All mail pick up and delivery is at the post office on Second Street. All Wrangell telephone numbers begin with 874, and when in Wrangell, you don't need to dial the 874. Dial 01 before area code for long distance calls. (Or 00 for credit card, person-to-person, etc.)

- Cassiar Dry Cleaners (tel. *874–3469*), Front St.
- Fire department (tel. *874–2000*).
- Gramma's Barber Shop (tel. *874–2140*).
- Hair Unlimited (tel. *874–3995*).
- LaDonna's Flowers (tel. *874–3469*).
- National Bank of Alaska (tel. *874–2356*).
- Police department (tel. *874–3304*).
- Southeast Gunsmithing (tel. *874–3170*).

- Thunderbird Laundromat (tel. *874–3322*), Front St.
- Wrangell Convention and Visitors Bureau (tel. *874–3770*), P.O. Box 1078.
- Wrangell Hospital (tel. *874–3356*), Airport Rd., next to the elementary school.
- Wrangell Visitors Center (tel. *874–3901*), near the tall totem pole, Outer Dr.

PETERSBURG

They like to call it "Little Norway," and where other towns in Alaska's Southeast are often gussied up with Indian, Russian, or gold rush themes, little Petersburg (pop. 3200) is the only one which finds itself dressed in the swirly flowered patterns identified with traditional Scandinavia. There are no totem poles, samovars, or mining accoutrements around. The town was carved out of virgin wilderness on Mitkof Island by a group of Norwegian fishermen in the late 1890s. They soon built a profitable cannery, and commercial fishing has remained the backbone of the economy, while some logging also takes place on the island and in neighboring areas.

Like Wrangell, Petersburg is also surrounded by the Stikine Area of the Tongass National Forest, and it also identifies itself with such nearby attractions as the Stikine River and the Le Conte Glacier. Tourism is now part of the economy, but Petersburg is first and foremost just a small town in an atmospheric location—most folks still don't lock their doors; their favorite comic strip is *Haggar the Horrible*. With its Viking/Norwegian theme, clippings seem to be posted on refrigerators and bulletin boards all over town.

TRANSPORTATION

The ferry dock is on Nordic Drive, less than a mile south of town, and ships of the **Alaska Marine Highway** (tel. *772–3855*) tie up at least twice a day, both northbound and southbound. You can sail between Petersburg and Wrangell or Sitka or Juneau. The current schedule is usually printed in the weekly *Petersburg Pilot*.

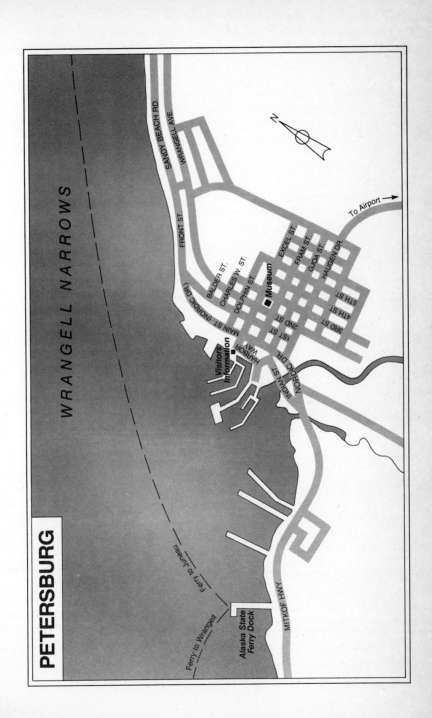

Petersburg Airport is a mile from town on Haugen Drive. Jets of **Alaska Airlines** (tel. *772–4255*) land daily, one northbound and one southbound flight each. Scheduled commuter service between Petersburg, Wrangell, and Kake is offered by **Wrangell Air Service** (tel. *772–3744*) and **Alaska Island Air** (tel. *772–4222*). In the summer only, **Wings of Alaska** (tel. *772–3536*) flies nonstop between Juneau and Petersburg, their southernmost airport. There are also several charter services.

There is no municipal bus service to worry about. One taxi, a van called **City Cab** (tel. *772–3003*), seems to be in fine shape now after a few stop-and-start years. As for car rental, you can get one from **Avis** (tel. *772–4716*) at the Tides Inn. Or for a little less you can try **Rent-A-Dent** (tel. *772–4424*), rentable from the Scandia House.

HOTELS AND MOTELS

If you're writing for reservations, every address in Petersburg is zip coded at 99833. All local phone numbers begin with 772, but from anywhere on the island there's no need to dial anything other than the four numbers that come after that.

Right in town, there are only two choices. At First and Dolphin streets, **The Tides** (tel. *772–4288*) comes in ahead of the competition, at least in the new wing. Ask for the top floor on the harbor side to view the shrimp boats, etc. Some units in the older portion do have kitchenettes, and this may be the only hotel you've seen where you go to sleep watched over by a picture of a salmon steak or a plate full of shrimp, courtesy of the ASMI. That's strange, since it doesn't have a restaurant (although if you check in the middle of the night, they might have a cup of soup available at the front desk). Most doubles should be in the $80 range, and worth it. (Reservations at P.O. Box 1048.)

The Scandia House (tel. *772–4281*), an historic hostelry first built on the main drag in 1905, was totally renovated in 1984. Like the Tides, all units have cable TV, direct dial phones, etc. But despite the Nordic decorations, many of the old rooms made us feel they were more claustrophobic than atmospheric. You may disagree. A sauna and hot tub are available. You can rent cars, boats, and fishing packages right on the premises. Rates are generally in the $70 range. (Reservations from P.O. Box 689.)

Beyond that, about five miles beyond, as a matter of fact, is the out-of-town **Beachcomber Inn** (tel. *772–3888*). A former cannery, it has been turned into a popular summer roadhouse. Upstairs are eight neat bedrooms, some with their own bathroom. Rates were in the $50 range for two, last we knew, but you'd better recheck that. Fine if you have your own wheels, and the food is good, too. (Reservations from P.O. Box 1027.)

Sorry, but we have not inspected the **Rocky Point Resort** (tel. *772–4420*), a fishing camp 11 miles south of Petersburg. Dedicated to dedicated fishermen, it has rates which include all meals, equipment, boats, and everything that goes with ardent and exclusive piscatology. (Details from P.O. Box 1251.)

There are always a couple of bed-and-breakfasts around, and the best way to find the current offering is to ask at the Chamber of Commerce office in the Harbormaster Building down on the docks (see "Miscellaneous Addresses and Phones"). There are also a pair of RV parks, **Glacier** (tel. *772–4680*) at Fourth and Haugen, and **Twin Creek** (tel. *772–3244*), about eight miles out the Mitkof Highway. Campers are accommodated at a site called, believe it or not, **Tent City.**

RESTAURANTS AND DINING

Remember that shrimp, crab, trout, halibut, and salmon are among the specialties everywhere—especially shrimp.

All the locals agree: For dinner only, you can't go wrong at the **Beachcomber Inn** (tel. *772–3888*), which offers fish and steak with a cozy fireplace, good service, and a view over the water. We enjoyed our meal, along with the entertainment which is occasionally on tap.

Also popular, the **Quay** (tel. *772–4600*), pronounced "key," turns out all three meals daily at 1103 Nordic Dr., almost across from the ferry terminal. There generally are a couple of Italian specialties on the menu, but see below for pizza.

In downtown Petersburg, **The Homestead** on Nordic Drive is a regular Chatterbox Cafe, Lake Wobegon-style. Open 24 hours, it's the center for round-the-clock gossip along with your salmon loaf and mashed potatoes or sourdough pancakes. For pizza, the brightest place is probably **Harbor Lights** (tel. *772–3424*), 203 Sing Lee Alley, just across from the Sons of Norway Hall. There's usually a salad bar, too. The other pizza restaurant, **Pellerito's,** across from the ferry, was closed for plastic surgery when we drove up, but it may be wearing its new face by now. They make their own sausage, too—or at least they used to.

For sandwiches and other deli-type selections, go straight to **Helse** off Harbor Way just at the beginning of Sing Lee Alley. If Helse's gates are closed, try **Greens & Grains,** nearby on Nordic Dr. G&G puts some benches outside when the weather is warm. Just across the street is **Joan Mei,** certainly one of the very few Vietnamese, Chinese, American, Tex-Mex takeouts around. It's okay for the type.

Just a cup of coffee and some great pastry? Duck into the little bakery called **Tante's Kitchen** on Nordic Dr. It's mostly takeout, although there are a couple of small tables installed.

ENTERTAINMENT AND NIGHT LIFE

There are a couple of clubs of Norwegian Dancers, mostly women and girls, who perform at the **Beachcomber Inn** and a few other places when the cruise ships are in. Everyone is *velkommen,* of course. Even without the dancers, the Beachcomber often whoops it up with live dance music in the summer.

You'll find more hard rock and busted eardrums at **Kito's Kave,** on Sing Lee Alley. We weren't impressed with the clientele at the **Harbor Bar.**

That's about it, unless you happen to be in town for the **Little Norway Festival** in May, or the **Salmon Derby** in June. Otherwise, you go to the movies then have a pizza. Or stay in, watch TV, and have a pizza.

SIGHTS AND SITES

We enjoy the walk around the **harbor** and its more than 1000 fishing boats as much as anything else in Petersburg itself. It's the home of the largest halibut fishing fleet in North America. A good walk or jog inland and along the shore is on the four-miles-around **Sandy Beach Loop,** which passes a popular eagle-watching area, and if you want to take a slight detour, you might catch a bear in the act of raiding the dump. En route don't miss the boardwalk across the muskeg near the Senior Citizens Center, and which connects at the ball park at the top of Excel St.

Also wander down to the bridge overlooking **Hammer Slough** for some good picture possibilities. Maps detailing these amiable ambles are available weekdays at the Chamber of Commerce at 221 Harbor Way (harbor side of the building), where you also may find Karin Hopper handing out free, no-nonsense advice and literature. You can also easily walk to the **Clausen Memorial Museum,** three blocks up Fram St. from the dock area. A statue and fountain honoring the fishing industry is just outside.

With a car, take a drive out Mitkof Highway, keeping an eye out for blueberries and huckleberries along the side of the road. About 10 miles out, check out the fish ladder at **Falls Creek.** We continued for another seven miles to visit the **Crystal Lake Fish Hatchery.** Visitors are welcome to wander on their own, asking questions of workers tending the vats full of baby salmon. The stuffed owl inside? "It keeps the swallows away," they explained.

SIDE TRIPS

Like Wrangell, Petersburg seems to claim **Le Conte Glacier** as its own, and it is about equally distant from either town. The **Stikine River** is also within striking distance of Petersburg. Unless you're a whale or a dolphin, you probably won't make either site on your own. Check at the Chamber; you might find a group going out on a boat already. Or you can charter one yourself. Aerial tours are usually available, too. (See "Tours and Cruises.")

You can also fly (in a half-hour) or ferry (once a week between Petersburg and Sitka) to the village of **Kake** (pop. 600 or so) on Kuprenof Island. The town boasts the world's largest totem pole—over 132 feet, 6 inches, from head-to-toe—carved to commemorate the state centennial in 1967. (It is perhaps the world's only totem steadied with guy wires.) There is sometimes room at the New Town Inn (tel. *785–3472*), but call or write first.

TOURS AND CRUISES

Those aerial outfits which often make up economical groups for glacier watching include **Alaska Island Air** (tel. *772–4222*), **Nordic Air** (tel. *772–3535*), and **Pacific Wing** (tel. *772–9258*). All are headquartered at the Petersburg Airport on Haugan Dr., about a mile out of town; except for the seaplanes of Alaska Island Air, which has its own dock on Nordic Drive, between town and the ferry.

There is one two-hour bus or van tour, the **Tongass Traveler** (tel. *772–4837*), which usually (no promises) leaves from the Tides Inn at about 1 p.m. When Patti Norheim herself drives the "Patti Wagon,"

the itinerary includes an interesting walk through the family shrimp cannery, and finally everyone stops off at Patti's house for shrimp cocktail.

If you miss the tour and want to guide yourself in detail, pick up
Steve Lefler's *Walking Guide,* sold for $1 at the front desk of the Tides
Inn. Before this litigious age, there used to be a good tour of the large
salmon cannery in town. But eventually somebody slipped on a fish and
sued, and that was the end of that educational experience. (The tourist
experience will continue to be hamstrung in this country until effective
tort reform laws are enacted in all states.)

SPORTS

There is *hunting* for moose, deer, goat, and water birds. Shooters
should aim for the Chamber to get a good guide, and then charter a
plane to the killing fields. Also check at the Alaska Department of Fish
& Game (tel. *772–3801*) at the State Office Building in Sing Lee Alley
(the P.O. Box is 667).

Fish & Game also administers *sportfishing,* of course. All kinds of
salmon are taken, along with halibut, steelhead trout, shrimp, and crab.
You can also get a license at several local stores. At least six charter
boats are available through the Chamber, or you can rent bare boats
(without operator).

If you like to get in the *swim* yourself, and feel that the ocean is
too c-c-cold, the indoor **Melvin Roundtree Memorial Pool** (tel. *772–
3304*), is the pride of the community. It's attached to the elementary
school but open to the public at varying hours.

Like most towns in Southeast, Petersburg goes bananas over *basketball* in the winter and sappy over *softball* during the summer. Basketball is played in the community gym. Both of the ball diamonds are
on Excel St., just past the hospital. Senior citizens mosey over along
that boardwalk to watch the games.

SHOPPING

Petersburg has a 5% municipal sales tax on everything. Just as
Prince Rupert has its argillite, Ketchikan its miniature totems and cedar
baskets, Wrangell its garnets, Petersburg also has its own specialty,
called *rosemaling.* This art form of scrolls and flowers was originally
Norwegian, and you'll find it all over town on shutters and storefronts

(you'll know what we mean when you see it). As far as buying it is concerned, these hand-painted floral patterns will show up on plates, cups, or anything you can carry with you. Lots of women in town do the work, although some are more well-known than others.

There are two fairly large stores in town. **The Trading Union,** on Nordic Dr., calls itself Petersburg's only department store. **Hammer & Wikan** on Nordic at Excel has groceries, hardware, and a large section catering to visitors with rosemaling and other crafts. You might also find a few things next door at **Cash Collection.**

Right in the Sons of Norway Hall in Sing Lee Alley, **Husfliden** (tel. *772–9210*) has *imported arts and crafts* from Norway along with Petersburg rosemaling and other local art works. **Lee's Clothing** features hand-knit Norwegian *sweaters,* and Icelandic sweaters. Between the Chevron and Union Oil docks, **Jewels by the Sea,** an unusual gallery at 806 S. Nordic Dr., features some crafts by local artists, including the owner herself.

MISCELLANEOUS ADDRESSES AND PHONES

- Alaska Marine Highway ferry terminal (tel. *772–3855*).
- Bear Video (tel. *772–3351*), 1103 S. Nordic Dr.
- Bojangles Hair Salon (tel. *772–4276*.
- Chamber of Commerce (tel. *772–3646*), 221 Harbor Way, Harbormaster Building, P.O. Box 649.
- City Police (tel. *772–3838*).
- Emergencies—dial 911.
- Fire department (tel. *772–3838*).
- Nordic Barber Shop (tel. *772–4791*), 223 N. Nordic Dr.
- Petersburg General Hospital (tel. *772–4291*).
- Petersburg Parks and Recreation, P.O. Box 329, City Hall.
- State Police (tel. *772–3100*).
- Quart House Liquor Store (tel. *772–3204*), Main St.
- U.S. Forest Service, Petersburg Ranger District, (tel. *772–3871*), in the Federal Building, P.O. Box 1328.
- U.S. Post Office (tel. *772–3121*), Nordic Dr.
- Viking Travel, Inc. (tel. *772–3818*), P.O. Box 787.

THE CAPITAL CITIES— JUNEAU AND SITKA

Alaska has had two real capitals during its history. Juneau is the more recent, named such by Congress in 1900, although it didn't really begin functioning as the seat of government until six years later. Not counting Kodiak, the first capital of Alaska was Sitka—under the Russians until 1867, and then the Americans.

Both cities were founded in visually attractive surroundings in central areas of the panhandle, and both were fortunate in their history. Unlike many frontier settlements, Juneau never suffered a major fire in its central business district. It has the same street patterns and many of the same buildings it had before the turn of the century. And Sitka, because much modern ''progress'' has passed it by, still radiates the charm of the small coastal town that once led the sophisticated cultural scene in a distant outpost of imperial Russia.

JUNEAU

Juneau still seems an unlikely place for a state capital. Founded because of a gold discovery in 1880, the city still sits under the ruins of a mountain-side mine and mill which closed down a half-century ago. Today portions of that mine may soon be reopened.

Although officially on the mainland, Juneau might as well be an island. It is hemmed into a narrow area between 3600-foot snow-capped peaks and the Gastineau Channel which separates the original city from Douglas Island. From time to time some wag puts up a sign on the

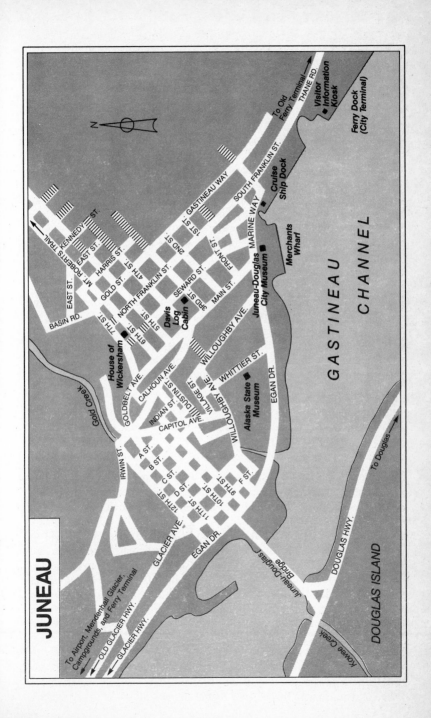

Juneau-Douglas bridge which announces accurately enough: "You are now leaving the North American continent." No roads connect Juneau to the rest of the continent, and it is certainly the country's most isolated state capital after Honolulu.

Houses climb the hills behind Juneau, many of them on stilts and reached by "streets" that are really wooden staircases. The city has extended its boundaries to include Douglas, and it has also spread north to the magnificent Mendenhall, Juneau's dramatic drive-up glacier. Until the recent drop in oil prices, the population of Juneau (including Douglas) was over 30,000. But there are a lot of empty houses around today, and the community now numbers considerably less than that. In any case it is one of the smallest state capitals. On the other hand, since merging with the Borough of Juneau some years ago the city's official boundaries encompass more than 3000 square miles, making it a considerably large municipality.

Some Juneauites divide their year into three seasons. Government is the principal business of Juneau especially during the 120-day legislative session from January to May. Tourism is the big economic activity from May through September. And October through December is sometimes called the quiet season. In any case, there always seems to be plenty to see and do in and around Juneau, including taking some terrific trips to wilderness destinations like the great Glacier Bay or the wildlife experiences on Admiralty Island.

TRANSPORTATION

There is no land transportation to Juneau, and no prospect of any in the immediate future. There is a controversial and expensive proposal to construct a road between Juneau and Skagway, which is at least theoretically feasible.

Once upon a time the **Alaska state ferries** used to tie up right in downtown Juneau, but that story is ended now that those docks are reserved for the cruise ships which come up the channel from the south. (Most liners now sail into Juneau in the morning and leave at about midnight.) Today the Marine Highway's Big Blue Canoes all swing in around Douglas Island from the north and travel only as far south on the strait as the relatively prosaic Auke Bay terminal of the **Alaska Marine Highway System** (tel. *465–3941*), 13 miles north of the main business district.

Although it's a relatively inauspicious entrance for ferry passengers, cruise passengers do get an excellent view on entering the city. When leaving Juneau by car, etc., better phone *789–7453* to see exactly what time the ferry will be departing. Then be sure to get to the terminal in plenty of time to park in the correct lane; vehicles for different destinations are directed into different parts of the hold. Juneau also happens to be the state headquarters for the Marine Highway, and if you need to make reservations or buy tickets, you can see representatives at the main office at 1591 Glacier Ave.

Passengers landing at **Juneau Airport** (JNU on your baggage tags) usually get an excellent view of the Mendenhall Glacier on the left side of the plane, and then enter a modern terminal with a museum-sized display of stuffed animals and birds scattered hither and yon (check out the ''Glacier Bear,'' a light-colored blackie waiting at the base of the escalator).

The modern terminal at 1873 Shell Simmons Dr. is about nine miles from downtown Juneau. The two-story, half moon-shaped structure has commuter airline check-ins on the right (north) side, trunk airlines (Alaska and Delta) in the middle and baggage claim areas on the far left. An attractive bar/restaurant on the upper floor unfortunately overlooks the cars in the parking lot instead of the aircraft on the runway. Gates 2–5 (equipped with covered ramps) are reached from upstairs. Gates for commuter airlines are on the ground floor. Rental car counters are next to the Alaska Airlines check-in, also on the lower level.

A newsstand, gift shop, and a seafood-purchasing facility (''fish packed to fly'') are near the bear at the bottom of the escalator. (Some pilots say ''flying fish'' is no joke, ever since Alaska Airlines collided with one in midair near Juneau a couple years ago. The jet had startled an eagle into dropping his prey, right through the 737's windshield!)

Nonstop flights to and from Fairbanks in the north and Seattle in the south are offered on jets of **Delta Airlines** (tel. *789–9243*). For some reason, however, Delta does not fly Juneau-Anchorage. **Alaska Airlines** (tel. *789–0600*) jets nonstop to or from Anchorage or Seattle, and also several other destinations including Southeast stops like Petersburg, Wrangell, Ketchikan, Sitka, Yakutat, and Gustavus (Glacier Bay)— the latter in a 727–100, with rather narrow seats. (Ouch!) However Alaska Airlines does not serve Skagway and Haines. Juneau is a two-hour jet flight from Seattle.

Some of the smaller though well-established operations represented at JNU include the following: **Alaska Coastal Airlines** (tel. *789–7818*), a charter outfit; **Air North** (tel. *789–2007*), a Canadian airline which has scheduled DC-3 flights to Whitehorse, Dawson, and Fairbanks; **Channel Flying** (tel. *789–3331*), with scheduled service to Hoonah, Angoon, Kake, Elfin Cove, Pelican, and Tenakee Springs; **Glacier Bay Airways** (tel. *789–9009*), which flies schedules between Juneau and Gustavus, Hoonah, and Excursion Inlet; **Haines Airways** (tel. *789–2336*), with scheduled flights to Haines and Skagway; **L.A.B. Flying**

Service (tel. *789–9160*), with scheduled flights to Haines, Skagway, Hoonah, and sometimes Gustavus; **Skagway Air Service** (tel. *789–2006*), with scheduled service between Juneau and Skagway; and **Wings of Alaska** (tel. *789–0790*), with schedules to Snettisham, Hobart Bay, Petersburg, Kake, Angoon, Tenakee Springs, Pelican, Hoonah, Gustavus (Glacier Bay), Haines, and Skagway. Wings has a published schedule of charter fees to several specific USFS cabins in the Juneau area. Generally speaking, most run about $150 to $200 each way.

Alaskans like to tell tall stories about fog preventing landings at Juneau, in which passengers allegedly are flown to Seattle, San Francisco, or other destinations far afield. Over 95% of Juneau's incoming flights are completed without such "overheading." The few that cannot land are usually diverted to Sitka where passengers may spend an unscheduled overnight before continuing to Juneau the following day (if your experience is different, please let us know).

Ground transportation between Juneau and either the airport or the Auke Bay ferry terminal has shuttled between various companies over the past few years. At the moment, two companies are providing the service, at least during the summer. **Mendenhall Glacier Transport** (tel. *789–5460*) was charging about $7 per seat for shuttling from the ferry to the downtown hotels at last report. The **Juneau Shuttle** (tel. *586–2660*), a later entry, is a competitive operation, and it's a distinct possibility that these two may have been reduced to one again by the date of your arrival.

It might not be much more in a taxi, so two or more may prefer to go that way. There are three taxi companies in Juneau. **Taku Taxi** (tel. *586–2121*) and **Capital Cab** (tel. *586–2772*) are both headquartered in downtown Juneau. **Raven Cab** (whose phone number we seem to have left in the back seat) is "out in the Valley" (that's Mendenhall Valley, not far from the airport).

A municipal bus service is run by **Capital Transit** (tel. *789–6901*) daily except Sunday, and you can get separate schedules from the visitor information center (or on the buses themselves) outlining both the express and local service. Unfortunately for visitors, the bus does not run quite as far as either the ferry terminal or the Mendenhall Glacier (you'd have to walk the last mile and a half). The fare is 75 cents.

Although downtown Juneau itself is compact enough to explore on foot, it's a long way from the airport. Roads are spread out quite a bit, so having an automobile is certainly desirable. Three car rental agencies have airport offices, and they may not pick you up from downtown: **Avis** (tel. *789–9450*), **Budget** (tel. *789–5186*), which is also Sears, and **Hertz** (tel. *789–9494*). Less-than-new cars are rented by **Rent-A-Dent** (tel. *789–9000*) and **Rent-A-Wreck** (tel. *789–4111*), both of which are parked near the airport (but they usually pick you up almost anywhere anyway). Other rental cars are available from **National** (tel. *789–9814*),

Holiday Payless (tel. *789–4118*), **Chrysler** (tel. *789–1386*), and **Evergreen Ford** (tel. *789–9386*).

Believe it or not, there are *two* limousine services in town: **Juneau Limousine** (tel. *586–1656*), and **Eagle Limousine** (tel. *789–1354*). We have had no experience with either of them.

~~~~~~

HOTELS AND MOTELS

If you've been staying in hotels throughout Southeast, Juneau may seem like an oasis. Here you will find facilities and services the existence of which are only rumors in most areas of the panhandle. However, be aware that Juneau has a 4% sales tax plus a whopping 7% transient room tax. Look for good discounts off season. All the following addresses may be written to at Juneau, AK 99801. (Be sure to read our general remarks on hotels in ''Coming Into the Country.'')

The best all-around place to stay for the past few years has been the **Westmark Juneau** (tel. *586–6900*), formerly the Sheffield, and before that a genuine Hilton. An ideal location at 51 W. Egan Dr., across from the harbor; lots of parking; a large lobby, by Alaskan standards, with deep green carpeting, wood sculptures, and carved cedar paneling; attractive ground-floor restaurant and giant-screen bar adjoining; 104 recently redecorated rooms in two types—king-size beds on the city side, and double-doubles on the channel side; even more room and extra windows in the ''18 series'' corner units; warm colors; cheerful decorations; plenty of lighting (even in the closets); effective black-out curtains; full-length mirrors; remote-control TVs; reasonably good room service; same-day laundry operation; two non-smoking floors; double rates about $150. Our only caveat: The front rooms are not for slugabeds; the seaplanes across the way begin revving up about 8 a.m. It's probably the top transient address in the panhandle. (Reservations through the Westmark chain or from the hotel.)

With more character, surely, is the 1939-style **Baranof** (tel. *586–2660*), which is now also part of the Westmark chain. Somewhat squeezed in on the narrow corner of Second and Franklin streets; convenient location to the state capitol and government offices; some parking behind the building; small lobby leading into a large lounge in muted men's-club colors, brass, mahogany paneling, marble tables, etc., no doubt appealing to politicos; a painted portrait of old Alex, the ''Lord of Alaska'' himself; dark coffee shop (particularly dim in the non-smoking section); well-regarded fine dining restaurant also on the ground floor; new and larger elevators are going up, or will be soon; widely varying rooms; several painfully small ones in the rear; larger units on the front and side; best rooms with rosewood furnishings, lightly patterned walls, slate blue draperies, remote TVs, but still a little short on shelf space. A grand room-by-room redecorating scheme was under way when we stayed for a week, and all 200 units should be completed by the time you read these words. Doubles probably will hover around the $125 mark. (Reservations through the Westmark chain or from the hotel.)

Many government types also like to dig in at the **Prospector** (tel. *586–3737*) at 375 Whittier St., next to the Alaska State Museum. Up the outside ramp to the portrait of a grizzled geezer; small lobby with stone pillars and a pay phone; somewhat rustic in atmosphere; home of Diggings, a good restaurant; five floors of rooms, most ample with two queen-size beds and knotty pine headboards, many units with kitchenettes; some views over the harbor; good combo tub/showers; cable TV. Most rooms are probably around $90 or $100, by now. When we saw the place some very good suites cost only a little more than regular rooms. (Reservations from the hotel.)

In the same general area the **Driftwood Lodge** (tel. *586–2280*)— a three-story L-shaped structure, has some pleasant if somewhat abbreviated accommodations, many with kitchenettes—at 435 Willoughby Ave., around the corner from the museum. No views, but everything apparently neat and clean; 66 rooms, each reached from an outdoor balcony; a few two-room suites; no proprietary restaurant (but several within easy walking distance, along with a grocery, liquor store, etc.); TV with HBO; guest laundry; free shuttle to the airport or ferry; rates perhaps around $75 for two in 1990, but you can recheck that by phone. (Reservations toll free from the hotel at *(800) 544–2239*.)

Those four are the obvious leaders in the central business district. There are three hotels out by the airport, and a pair of them bear the joint distinction of being the only Juneau accommodations with a swimming pool (indoors and heated, of course, although not terribly large). Not too incidentally, the airport hotels will almost always pick you up without charge from the airport, and many also offer free trips into and out of town from time to time.

The **Juneau Airport TraveLodge** (tel. *789–9700*), is perhaps the more comfortable of the two. Small lobby with a big black bear skin on the wall; 24-hour airport and ferry shuttle; low ceilings; stucco walls; Fernando's, a popular Mexican/American restaurant, on the premises; rooms divided into doubles, queens, and kings; one of the four floors is a non-smoking one; generally good, standard hotel rooms with patterned bedspreads, pictures, round table, no desk, plants, TV; fourth-floor rooms affording a peek over the trees to the Mendenhall Glacier; most rooms should be about the $90 range for two. (Reservations from the hotel at 9200 Glacier Highway.)

The **Best Western Country Lane Inn** (tel. *789–5055*) is a two-story motelish structure, meaning you can drive right up to your door (well, on the ground floor, anyway). Tiny lobby with coffee; small pool and jacuzzi in the solarium behind the front desk; free shuttle to the nearby airport, ferry terminal, the glacier, and downtown; no restaurant (but a fortuitous affiliation with Grandma's, nearby); reasonable rooms with beige walls, but nary a picture seen other than the one on TV; floral bedspreads; blond-wood furniture; complimentary fruit and pastry in the morning; free local phone calls; rates in the $90 range. It may not be the best Best Western, but it's better than some others we've seen. (Reservations through the chain or at the hotel, 9330 Glacier Highway.)

In the same neighborhood, the **Super 8** (tel. *789–4858*) is another chain possibility. There's no restaurant, but it's right next door to McDonald's, for whatever that's worth. Tiny reception area with sea chart of the Gastineau Channel; lobby sometimes dammed with luggage around noon; low ceilings; 75 neat if undistinguished units with all the requisite amenities, not much space to spread out makeup and/or shaving gear; double thermal pane windows muffling aircraft noise when closed; coin-op guest laundry; free shuttle to ferry and airport terminals; double rates around $78.88 or so; singles around $58.88; discounts and other benefits for S-8's VIP Club members. An undistinguished choice, perhaps, but it's a generally efficient operation and good value for the financial outlay. (Reservations through the chain or the hotel at 2295 Trout St.)

Back in town, there are a few establishments with more creaky character than fancy facilities. Parking could be difficult at any of these four. The **Bergmann** (tel. *586–1690*), a free-standing building at the corner of Gold and Third, at first seems not to have changed since its grand opening on Dec. 16, 1913. Lots of flowers outside; lots of frou-frou and ticking clocks marking time inside; Chinese restaurant and Irish bar on the premises; laundry facilities available; many of its 42 rooms recently enlarged and redecorated in Victoriana; all with color TV; but all also with johns "down the hall." Summer rates are expected to be around $60 for two, but that includes the chance to talk to Marguerite Barrett and play with her Siamese cat. (Reservations from the hotel at 434 Third St.)

Dating from the very same year, the **Alaskan Hotel** (tel. *586–1000*) is in the center of the action at 127 Franklin St., and is known more for its atmospheric, old-time bar and the historic personalities who drank there. Nevertheless, there are a few small pink-and-purple rooms upstairs, some with their own plumbing and some without. A guest laundromat and hot tubs are available. Doubles should be around $65 or so. Actually, we prefer one of the six neat and fully plumbed rooms upstairs at the **Silverbow Inn** (tel. *586–4146*), which is known more as a good restaurant, at 120 Second St. Of course they're often full, but we mention it here just in case luck is with you. Rooms are not cheap—

about $70 for one, $80 for two, the last we looked. Non-smokers only.

Down by the cruise docks, another anachronistic address given a new lease on life is the **Inn at the Waterfront** (tel. *586–2050*). Located above an expensive but well-regarded restaurant (the Summit), at 455 S. Franklin, the 21 rooms vary widely in price depending on facilities. (Some accommodations have private baths; some do not.) Despite its gold plumbing fixtures and antique furniture, we generally felt cramped in the parts we inspected. If you go, let us know your reaction. (Reservations from the hotel.)

Sorry, but we didn't particularly go for the well-weathered **Breakwater Inn** and its location as compared to the competition. And the **Tides Motel** may never come in for us at all.

There are at least a half-dozen bed-and-breakfasts around, all listed with the **Alaska Bed & Breakfast Association—Southeast Alaska** (tel. *586–2959*), located in Juneau. Call at the number above or write for details at P.O. Box 3–6500, Juneau, AK 99802.

The ladies at the Davis Log Cabin will be up on campgrounds for RVs and tent campers. During the summer, the U.S. Forest Service maintains the ocean-view **Auke Village Campground,** near the ferry terminal, and the glacier-view **Mendenhall Lake Campground** at Milepost 13.5 on the Glacier Highway. For backpackers, etc., the year-round **Juneau International Hostel** (tel. *586–9559*) is at 614 Harris St. (between Sixth and Seventh streets), Juneau, AK 99801. All AYH rules are observed, and overnight beds may set you back around $10 and an hour of pushing broom in 1990.

RESTAURANTS AND DINING

As in all of Southeast, seafood is the specialty, especially salmon, trout, halibut, crab, shrimp, etc. Don't forget to try Juneau's own brand of beer, Chinook Alaskan Amber, which has been winning prizes lately. It has short production runs, usually costs more than Lower 48 beers, and is often difficult to find outside Juneau. A new light ale has also just been released.

Before we forget, we advise planning to sit down for lunch before 11:45 a.m. or after about 1:15 p.m. in Juneau. That way you'll miss competing with crowds of government workers, almost all of whom have precisely the noon hour during which they must complete their midday repast.

There are two or three standouts in downtown·Juneau in terms of value. Our first choice is the **Fiddlehead** (tel. *586–3150*), named for a scroll-shaped edible fern. It's in its own building at 429 W. Willoughby

Ave., near the state museum. Light wood and papered walls; hanging globes; high ceilings; no view; eclectic menu specializing in seafood dinners in the $15–20 range; beef, pork, and chicken also dependable; some dishes with Chinese and Italian accents; special "light suppers" for under $10; some original salads; open for all three meals—breakfasts and lunch usually excellent; service unfortunately erratic. Many agree it has the best breakfast in the borough too. Due to the nature of our work, we have to try lots of restaurants, but we wouldn't think of visiting Juneau without taking at least one meal at the Fiddlehead.

Swinging from the Fiddle to the Bow, an early day atmosphere, along with excellent victuals, is served up at the 1914-model **Silverbow** (tel. *586–4146*), an historic inn at 120 Second St. Wedded to a bakery, the establishment features fresh bread and pastry in addition to savory seafood with a French accent. Lots of wood, wallpaper, and stained glass in three different rooms; candles on the tables; no view to the outside; summer terrace open on warm days; lunch available Monday– Friday (reserve for that, too). We experienced pleasant, efficient service. Sometimes closed on Sunday or Monday—better recheck on the scene.

Another old reliable is **Diggings** (tel. *586–3737*), often called the "Prospector" by Juneau folk, because that is the name of the hotel into which the Diggings dining room has been dug. This one has a panorama over the channel from some booths and tables, and it's also the place where we first tried the delicious Petersburg shrimp.

Three more pricey dinner places in town are also generally excellent. The first is the **Gold Room** (tel. *586–2660*), the silver-service salon with crystal chandeliers in the Baranof Hotel. You might try the Salmon and Halibut en Braid (filets of both fishes tied together and poached in a brandy sauce), which might set you back about $22.95. Open daily, but from 5 to 10 p.m. only.

Then there's the **Summit** (tel. *586–2050*), strangely named since it's on the ground floor of the Inn at the Waterfront, 455 S. Franklin. You could choose the Alaska abalone for around $25, and there's a long wine list. Over in the Westmark Juneau Hotel at 51 W. Egan Dr., the **Woodcarver** (tel. *586–6900*) has a good variety of goodies, plus a prime rib dinner special every Sunday. When we were last in, there were also several 5- to 7-p.m. specials at lower prices.

There are two heavily advertised salmon bakes in Juneau. At the suggestion of practically everyone, we went to the outdoorsy **Gold Creek Salmon Bake** (tel. *586–1424*). It's in Last Chance Basin, a country setting on the other side of Mt. Roberts from the city, and on the site of an old gold mine. It was fun and the salmon, barbecued over an alder wood fire, was delicious. You can drive there yourself via Basin Road or arrange to take the special free tour bus from the Baranof Hotel at 6 p.m. to get some patter before your platter. Last we heard, it was still all-you-could eat (including one beer or wine) for around $19. After dinner you can pan for gold at no extra charge. The other salmon bake is at the indoor ("No mosquitoes!" they gloat) **Thane Ore House** (tel. *586–3442*). It's competitively priced—or maybe a little more if you also stay to see the entertainment, a gold-rush-style revue. Like Gold Creek, you also get plenty of salad bar, baked beans, beef ribs, and cornbread, and then you can try a little gold panning. We expect to sit down there sometime soon.

Back in Juneau, **Luna's** (tel. *586–6990*), specializes in homemade pastas and other things Italiano. The tablecloths are newsprint, and you get a fistful of crayons to see if you can create something the management deems worth pinning on the walls. We've only been in for a lasagna lunch (about $8.95), but some would-be artists are loyal dinner customers, too. It's down the basement at 210 Seward St.

For lighter lunching, you might try **T.J.'s,** nearby at 230 Seward St., where one end of the bar boasts apparently the biggest projection TV screen in the Great White North. You'll find your fancy burgers here, along with veggie sandwiches. They also feature a sourdough pizza. Despite the nautical atmosphere and great view near the cruise ships, we weren't very impressed with **Fisherman's Wharf,** which might be described as your typical harbor-side greasy harpoon. On warm days sit outdoors for a hot dog, maybe. Maybe.

Speaking of fancy burgers, some swear by the creations turned out by **Mike's** (tel. *364–3271*), in an unlikely location at 1102 Second Ave. over in Douglas. Dating back to before World War I (right, we said "one"), Mike's also has some other good steaks and chops, an excellent salad bar, and a good channel view, they say, but it was closed every time we tried to get there. Better recheck by phone.

While we're still thinking about a Juneau noon, lots of folks like to lunch on the run at one of the streetside carts that suddenly appear at 12 o'clock. The **Hot Dog Lady** who sets up at Third and Seward also has good hamburgers. **Mickey's Bagels** has sandwiches at Front and Seward. And at Fourth and Main, check out **Nimbus Burgers.** (Nimbus is named for a controversial modern sculpture that was finally removed from the corner. The name lives on as a hamburger, which is the way the locals like it.) If you want to sit down for your burger, though, the new **Cookhouse** has opened adjacent to the Red Dog Saloon (see "Entertainment and Night Life").

Juneau boasts not less than four Mexican restaurants, and each seems to have its loyal *afficianados*. Probably the hippist member of the quartet is the **Armadillo Tex-Mex Cafe** (tel. *586–1880*), 431 S. Franklin, at People's Wharf. A giant plate of fajitas served on the red-plastic table cloths should run $10 or so. **Olivias' de Mexico** (tel. *586–6870*), in the basement of the Simpson Building at 222 Seward, is also a budget possibility. Not far away, at 157 S. Franklin, is **El Sombrero** (tel. *586–*

6770). We haven't tried that one on for size, but we have patronized another member of the same family, **Fernando's** (tel. *789–3636*), a hideaway in the TraveLodge at 9200 Glacier Highway, near the airport. Next to a bubbling fountain and two golden *papagayos,* we attacked our enchiladas and chiles with mucho gusto.

And while we're talking about the airport area, a real sleeper is the family-run **Grandma's Farmhouse** (tel. *789–5566*), featuring some of the most delicious down-home staples served by Grandma's charming granddaughters in the specially constructed homestead at 2348 Mendenhall Loop Rd. They have about as good a salad bar as you'll find anywhere plus good ol' American steaks, chicken, real roast turkey and gravy, etc., along with heaps of corn and peas or whatever happens to be in season. Most dinners are in the $15 range—and perhaps worth more. (Psst! When we were there, Grandma's was putting the finishing touches on a small hotel operation which is probably open by now.)

Chinese? We haven't been in, but knowledgeable locals pick up chopsticks at **Canton House** (tel. *789–5075*), at 8585 Old Dairy Rd., out toward the airport. Both mild Cantonese and spicy Szechuan are served. Other Juneauites report Sum Fun Chow at the **Chinese Palace** (tel. *780–4616*) at 5000 Old Glacier Highway.

Pizza? You might try popular if noisy **Bullwinkle's** at 318 Willoughby, across from the State Office Building, in the Mendenhall Mall near the airport. There is also a pizza stand in the Nugget Mall. Also there's the aforementioned Luna's, which sells pizza by the slice.

ENTERTAINMENT AND NIGHT LIFE

Juneau's gold-rush-style production, currently running summers at the Elks Hall (once the state capitol), next door to the Baranof, is the **Lady Lou Revue** (tel. *586–3636*), a musical comedy based partly on characters in Robert Service poems. Produced by the Perseverance Theatre, an accomplished amateur/professional group, the performance costs about $10 and runs for about 1¼ hours. It's good, but if you're heading up to Skagway, Whitehorse, or Dawson, you can catch a similar show later. During the winter, the same theater group turns out other good productions that are less touristy.

Not to be confused with the above, there is also the **Gold Nugget Revue** (tel. *586–1462*), a shorter show produced at the aforementioned Thane Ore House Salmon Bake, with actors portraying Joe Juneau and Richard Harris, cancan dancers, etc. Usually there's one performance a night, at about 6:30 p.m., between the two sittings of the big bake itself. (Don't mix up Gold *Nugget* and Gold *Creek,* a different salmon bake.)

The local Native group is the **Eagle-Raven Dancers.** They perform traditional Tlingit terpsichore for the cruise ship crowd from time to time—perhaps at Gunakadeait Park at Front and Franklin if the weather is good, or under shelter at Marine Park if it's raining hard. Don't count on it at all. But when they do show up it's free, although donations are cheerfully accepted.

Popular and classical musical extravaganzas take place from time to time in Juneau, along with several other kinds of productions. The **Alaska Folk Festival** is held in April, and the **Juneau Jazz and Classics Festival** is usually scheduled in early May. See the staff at the Davis Log Cabin for a calendar of upcoming events.

On the night scene, probably Alaska's most well-known tavern is the **Red Dog Saloon,** which is becoming so popular with tourists that they have to keep reinstalling it in larger and larger red dog houses. The current Red Dog—at least the third in its history—was moved down by the cruise docks and next to the police station in 1988. This is the real mob scene where cheerful *cheechakos* and assorted sourdoughs meet face to fuzz, and it's difficult to know which group is being watched more by the other (except that there are many more of the former during the summer and of the latter during the winter). Sorry, but we only stuck our head in; we don't mind the music and the sawdust, but there was simply too much smoke for our tenderfoot lungs.

Another bar, just as full of local character and characters as the Red Dog (and architecturally more authentic), is the **Alaskan Hotel and Bar** farther up Franklin St. at No. 167. Either may feature a live piano player. The **Penthouse** at No. 175 features hard rock. The **Rendezvous** at No. 184 usually has some good music. The **Imperial Bar,** 241 Front St., was built in 1891 and is allegedly Alaska's oldest saloon. Through an oversight, we haven't been in. But we now skip the **Triangle Club,** 251 Front St., on purpose.

For light rock, pop, and dancing, at least on the weekends, you might try the bar at the **Prospector Hotel.** Bars for just sitting, sipping, and chatting? We'd recommend those at the Westmark (the **Woodcarver Lounge**) and the Baranof (the **Bubbleroom Lounge**), although some locals dismiss them as being a little too yuppie for Alaska. Most taverns and bars close at 2 a.m.

You'll find first-run movies at the **Twentieth Century Theater** on Front St. and the **Glacier Cinema** at 9091 Cinema Dr., off Mendenhall Loop Rd. out in the valley. A more intellectual approach to films is taken at the **Orpheum,** down by the docks at 245 Marine Way. They also sell some great snacks.

For stay-at-homes, Juneau has two television stations. KJUD juggles commercial programming from several networks; local news is on at 6:30 p.m. KTOO is the public broadcasting station. On radio, there are two AM and three FM stations.

SIGHTS AND SITES

Even if you have only a couple of hours or so between planes or ferries, slip out to see Juneau's most impressive natural treasure, the **Mendenhall Glacier.** The 1½-mile-wide, 12-mile-long river of ice flows into Mendenhall Lake next to a visitor center run by the U.S. Forest Service. There the rangers will tell you everything you ever wanted to know about this or any other glacier. Then you can walk right up to the thing, if you want. Be careful not to stand under an ice cliff, of course, but don't miss seeing the glacier.

Visitors to Juneau should stop by the **Davis Log Cabin** (tel. *586–2284*), the information center run by the Juneau Convention and Visitors Bureau (JCVB) at Third and Seward to find out what there is to see and do in and around town. You can pick up a Downtown Juneau Walking Tour map and other historical walking tour brochures there, for example. The cabin itself is a 1980s reproduction of a log church built on the site in the 1890s (unfortunately fronted by one of those ugly green electrical transformer covers that sometimes get in the way of your photographs in Juneau). The JCVB also maintains an information counter at the airport and a summer information kiosk at Marine Park, next to the cruise ship terminal.

Another preliminary stop is the **U.S. Forest Service Information Center** (tel. *586–8751*). Films and interesting displays cover a variety of things to see and do throughout Southeast Alaska, and this is where you buy permits and make reservations for Forest Service cabins, too. It's in the Centennial Hall, downtown on Egan Drive at Willoughby St. (Open daily during the summer; weekdays mid-September to May.)

After the glacier, the most visited site in Juneau is the **Alaska State Museum** (tel. *465–2901*) at 395 Whittier St. You can wander through on your own (with a pamphlet), but taking the free docent tour is better. This is the museum with the famous "eagle tree," which you circle yourself before landing cheek to beak with the eagle on the top floor. If you do this place right, you'll also come away with a new appreciation for Alaska's Native groups, particularly the Indians of Southeast. Serious totem fans might buy a copy of *Totem Talk* by Scott Foster, a necessarily rather tall book describing the two dozen 19th- and 20th-century carved poles to be seen throughout the city. (Open daily during summer; Tuesday–Saturday other times. $1 admission.)

Don't confuse this with the oft-moved **Juneau-Douglas City Mu-**

seum, whose latest home is in the old municipal library at the corner of Fourth and Main (of course, it could move again). Some refer to this facility as the "city mining museum" since it covers a lot about that subject, which is mostly ignored in the state museum.

Walk the streets of Juneau, particularly Franklin Street, from the cruise docks past banner-bedecked **Marine Park** (free Friday night concerts during summer) and several old buildings. The only street left with wooden sidewalks is **Henry Lang Street,** which the locals know better as "Wino Alley." The **Alaska Steam Laundry/Emporium,** the structure with the turret at 174 S. Franklin, was built in 1901 and now houses several shops. The **Alaskan Hotel,** at 167 S. Franklin, was built in 1913 and was the leading hotel before the Baranof was built in 1939.

Don't look for a dome, fountains and a vast front lawn in order to find the **State Capitol,** at Fourth and Main. It's a 1931 Model A six-story city office building that somebody has tried to dignify by slapping four marble pillars on the front. If you wander around inside, you'll see that Alaska could use a newer, larger, more dignified facility. Things are pretty crowded, with Xerox machines in the hallways, etc. If it's Friday at noon, you might like to check out the SOB—the modern **State Office Building,** built on a steep hillside farther along Fourth street. It has some cheerful organ concerts at lunchtime Fridays in its Eighth Floor Lobby (that's one of the "ground floors!") You can also continue along Calhoun Avenue to No. 715, the plantation-style **Governor's Mansion,** which is only open to the public on special occasions. At Sixth and Seward streets, the **Four Story Totem** is well over four stories tall. It's called that simply because its figures tell four stories to totem literates.

Within walking distance of the capitol in the opposite direction is the onion-domed **St. Nicholas Russian Orthodox Church,** at Fifth and Gold. Built in 1894, it is the oldest *original* Orthodox church in Alaska. Also in the neighborhood, at 213 Seventh St., is the **House of Wickersham** (tel. *586–9001*), the last home of the Alaskan statesman Judge James Wickersham, now maintained as a museum (irregular hours; better call first).

Across the bridge to Douglas Island, you can see the side of Mt. Roberts above Juneau and the massive ruins of the **A-J Mine** (and mill), which actually runs right through the mountain. You can no longer approach them, but if you drive around the other side of the mountain (where the Gold Creek Salmon Bake is held), you can wander through lots of old mining ruins (use Walking Tour Brochure #3 produced by the Juneau Parks and Recreation Department, available from the City Museum). In the old days, before American society began to be culturally strangled by everyone suing everyone else, travelers were taken clear through that granite mountain in a level mine shaft which is now closed off to the public. (The high cost of liability insurance now makes that impossible.)

In Douglas itself, there is a hiking trail though the overgrown site of the **Treadwell Mine,** which was closed in 1917 after it was accidentally flooded by the waters of Gastineau Channel (ask at the Davis Log Cabin or the Juneau Museum for the illustrated trail map).

Back on the mainland, if you have a car you can drive "out the road" past the ferry terminal at Auke Bay to several scenic sites. Among these is the **Shrine of St. Therese,** at about Mile 23. There is a causeway out to the little rock church on a tiny island with an excellent view. Another popular church is the **Chapel by the Lake** (tel. *789–7592*) next to the UAS campus, between Auke Lake and Auke Bay. A large picture window frames the Alaskan wilderness and the nearby glacier. The minister has a tough time keeping the attention of his congregation when the neighborhood eagles are putting on a show.

SIDE TRIPS

In the mid-19th century, the great naturalist John Muir overcame some tremendous hardships to find, photograph, and document the "ice mountains" the Indians told him about. Today, if you're on a major Southeast cruise, the chances are you will sail in style and comfort right into the magnificent **Glacier Bay,** the home of 16 active tidewater glaciers and more than 100 alpine glaciers. You can enjoy it all from your deck chair while alternately raising your field glasses to your eyes and a cup of mulled wine to your lips. At the same time you will listen to experts lecture over the public address system.

Non-cruisers have to make independent arrangements, and usually that's done by air or water from Juneau (although you can also easily fly to Glacier Bay from Haines or Skagway). With just a little more effort, they will probably get an even closer look at nature in the raw than those on the luxury liners. In any case remember that *the state ferry does not go to Glacier Bay.*

We won't take the time and space to dwell on all the attractions of the bay, its ice and its wildlife, which will soon become apparent when you get there. Here we will concentrate instead on the logistics of a visit; without some coaching they may be a little hard to find out about.

The tiny village of Gustavus serves as the base came for Glacier Bay National Park, and our advice is (a) if you've been traveling through Southeast on the ferry, then fly to Gustavus round trip from Juneau (about $50 each way) or (b) if you've been traveling by air and have the time to do it, sail to Gustavus and then fly back to Juneau from Gustavus the next day. It takes about three hours on the water to Gustavus or to the spruce/hemlock forest at Bartlett Cove from Juneau. Bartlett Cove is the site of the national park headquarters and the beginning and end of the boat trips "up bay" (perhaps aboard the *Spirit of Adventure,* a big, comfortable catamaran).

Campers and kayakers can arrange to be left off at special sites and later picked up by this boat. Park headquarters is also just a 10-mile bus ride from the airport, and it takes around 20 minutes to jet to or from Juneau via Alaska Airlines. (Propeller services, like Wings, L.A.B., or Glacier Bay Air, take about 40 minutes.)

Even if you catch an early flight into Gustavus and a late flight out, you probably will not be able to make the round-trip bay excursion boat, which was leaving at 7 a.m. and returning around 4 p.m. (The schedules are not set for your visit at this writing, so you'll have to recheck that with the National Park Service.) In any case, you should plan to stay one or two nights. Since the boat trip from Bartlett Cove takes the better part of a day (and costs about $150), save time for at least one walk through the Bartlett Cove rain forest with a ranger (that's free).

We checked in at the **Glacier Bay Lodge** (tel. *697–2225*) the official park concessionaire which has been open late May to late September right at Bartlett Cove (doubles about $125 or dorm space at about $25 per pillow). It was certainly convenient and clean. But it also seemed relatively colorless, the food wasn't great, and we felt like captives isolated so far from the village. A good friend recalls, however, that he was able to order a wake up call in case the Northern Lights were putting on a show after he went to sleep.

Another time, we're going to try the atmospheric old **Gustavus Inn** (tel. *697–2254*), about $125 with meals, or the **Country Inn** (tel. *687–2288*) or one of the other family operated small hotels or B&B operations in town. Many of these establishments provide bicycles for their guests to get around on, incidentally. (Write for information on these as well as on fishing charters, whale-watching trips, and other facilities to the Gustavus Visitors Association, P.O. Box 167, Gustavus, AK 99826.)

An outfit specializing in camping, kayak trips, fishing, etc., in and around Gustavus is **Puffin Travel** (summer tel. *697–2260;* winter tel. *789–9787*), P.O. Box 3. There is also **Glacier Bay Sea Kayaks** (tel. *697–2257*), P.O. Box 26, and **Spirit Walker Expeditions** (tel. *697–2266*), P.O. Box 122. All are at Gustavus, AK 99826.

Almost as popular as Glacier Bay for some travelers is the trip from Juneau up **Tracy Arm,** a special Wilderness Area within the Tongass National Forest. Also marked by icebergs, glaciers, and steep fjords, it nevertheless has a different feeling from Glacier Bay. Unless you're an intrepid outback explorer with your own boat, you can't get there on your own hook. Look for special excursion craft or sightseeing flights out of Juneau to this Alaskan wild kingdom. The future of the cruise we took is in doubt at our deadline, but the Davis Log Cabin should have the latest information.

Wilderness seekers often fly from Juneau to **Admiralty Island,** which boasts a heck of a lot more wild creatures than it does people. In fact, it has the highest recorded density of both brown bears and bald eagles in the world. The Tlingit name for Admiralty traditionally translates as "Fortress of the Bears," and a site called Pack Creek is just about the best place in Southeast for watching brownies during the salmon run ("I got mom and cubs with a 50-mm lens!" enthused one daring camera fan). Access to Pack Creek may soon be restricted, however; check with the Admiralty Island National Monument office in Juneau (tel. *789–3111*) for up-to-date information.

The Tlingit town of Angoon, the only one on the island, is accessible daily by air or about twice a week via the Sitka-Juneau run on the state ferry. Year-round accommodations are available at the **Favorite Bay Inn** (tel. *788–3123*), and perhaps another couple of places.

Some also fly or ferry from Juneau for Sitka to stay for a time on **Chichagof Island,** at the villages of Pelican, Hoonah, or Tenakee Hot Springs. At the latter we took a quick peek at the **Tenakee Inn** (tel. *736–2241*), an acceptable address on the main drag. (Come to think of it, it was the *only* drag!) No private cars are allowed. And near Pelican (pop. 200), floating cabins are available through **Pelican Rentals** (tel. *735–2242*). **Lisianski Lodge** (tel. *735–2227*) also seems interesting. A popular Hoonah hotel (come to think of it, the only Hoonah hotel) is the **Totem Lodge** (tel. *945–3636*). We haven't seen either the Pelican and Hoonah establishments yet. Let us know if you go.

TOURS AND CRUISES

Free *hiking tours* are given Saturday and Wednesday year round by the **Juneau Parks & Recreation Department** (tel. *586–5226*). Stop by the Davis Log Cabin for more information. You can also rent an "Audio Walking Tour"—a tape player and cassette—for a few bucks. It covers most of downtown Juneau. Ask about this at the City Museum. Commercial *guided hikes* are taken out by **Alaska Rainforest Treks** (tel. *463–3466*), P.O. Box 210845, Auke Bay, AK 99821. Rates should be around $95 a day, including lunch, guides, and gear (but bring your own boots).

Slightly less ambulatory than the above are the *Historic Horse 'n'*

Buggy Tours that may or may not be trotted out by the **Juneau Carriage Co.** (tel. *586–6598*) again for 1990. Check for information from the company at 187 S. Franklin St.

Gray Line of Alaska (tel. *586–3773*) runs what they call a *"Ferry Stop-Over Tour"* to Mendenhall Glacier, a one-hour trip designed mainly for ferry passengers who are continuing along the Inside Passage without visiting Juneau for any longer than that. (The tour is okay, if rushed, but the no-stopover idea is a mistake for any first-time visitor.) The fare was around $9 at last report. Pick up the tour on the dock at Auke Bay or see Gray Line at their headquarters in the Baranof Hotel. **Alaska Sightseeing Tours** (tel. *586–6300*) may have some new excursions set up for around Juneau and out to "the Valley" by 1989. Their office is in the Westmark Hotel on Egan Drive.

We have had no experience with **Rosie's Rides,** a taxi tour operation. We do know Rosie keeps changing her phone number. It might be *586–2772, 586–2121,* or *586–2720.* And when we looked again, none of these were listed in the book. *Private tours* are also taken by the **Juneau Limousine Service** (tel. *586–1656*).

Strictly for non-smokers only, **Ptarmigan Ptransport & Ptours** (tel. *586–4146,* and those *P*s are silent) offers a conducted introduction to the city for around $15. Get the details by phone or check at the Silverbow Inn for information. *Passenger-van tours* are also run by **Alaska Up Close** (tel. *789–9544*). The city and Mendenhall Glacier will tote up to around $30 for two hours; the "Juneau Plus" tour, which includes the Shrine of St. Therese and the Chapel by the Lake, etc., may run around $85 for a four-hour experience. The same company also launches some *long-distance nature expeditions,* many designed especially for birders and camera bugs.

A 3½-hour rubber raft *Mendenhall Glacier Float Trip* has been launched by **Alaska Travel Adventures** (tel. *789–0052*). A Juneau-headquartered company, ATA also has operations in Sitka, Ketchikan, and Skagway. For around $75, you can paddle the river (including some mild rapids) and the lake below the glacier and get a "shoreline snack." We haven't gone yet, but it's a popular trip. It also offers a *Goldpanning and Gold Mine Tour,* a 1½-hour van experience through Juneau and then out to Gold Creek Basin. Cost should be around $25. (Less any gold you find, of course!)

For travelers with a good sense of balance and better biceps, there are always one or two Juneau companies specializing in *kayak and canoe tours.* **Alaska Discovery** (tel. *586–1911*) is one. Some go clear to Admiralty Island and other outback locations. See them at or write in advance to 369-G S. Franklin St., Juneau, AK 99801.

The **Glacier Express,** a catamaran excursion to Gustavus (and thence to Glacier Bay) is at least temporarily out of business at this writing. Sorry, but you'll have to update yourself on this one. Ditto for the dinner cruises to Tracy Arm and the Twin Saywer Glaciers from Juneau. (Both were owned by **Exploration/Catamaran Cruise Lines,** which had the bad timing to go belly up just at our deadline.) You *will* need a fast cat or some other speedy vessel in order to get to Tracy Arm in time to take everything in and then get back to Juneau in a day. **Alaska Naturalist & Photography Cruise Tours** (tel. *789–7429*) has announced some Tracy Arm cruises, along with some as far away as Sitka, some involving a return by float plane. Better figure on around $200 for an all-day experience. Call them or write to P.O Box 20424, Juneau, AK 99802.

You can also take a 4½-hour cruise all the way up the picturesque Lynn Canal to Skagway (75 miles each way) operated by **Westours** (tel. *586–3773*), a Holland America/Gray Line subsidiary. Available one-way or round trip, the cruise aboard the *Fairweather* includes a lunch. It takes a straight course and does *not* visit Glacier Bay, although it passes other glaciers and a sea lion rookery en route. Figure around $125 one way or around $200 for a one-day cruise-fly excursion (leaving 9:30 a.m., returning in the evening).

"Flightseeing" trips by seaplane to Glacier Bay, Tracy Arm, and the Juneau Ice Field are launched by **Wings of Alaska** (tel. *789–0790*), usually on charters. Aerial tours by **Channel Flying** (tel. *789–3331*) cover a similar route from its seaplane base at 8995 Yandukin Dr. A smaller seaplane operation, **Taku Glacier Air** (tel. *586–8330*), charges $125 or so for an hour tour over the city and its icy surroundings. Some excursions land at the Taku Lodge for a salmon bake at the foot of the Juneau Ice Field. Get further information from the booth at 2 Marine Way, behind the Fisherman's Wharf restaurant.

On one trip to Juneau, we enjoyed the 45-minute *Mendenhall Glacier Tour* on **Temsco Helicopters** (tel. *789–9501*). We not only got a great eagle-eye perspective flying over the ice river, but actually landed on it, got out, and explored for 15 minutes. Figure $120 or so for this trip in 1990. Temsco sometimes has a longer tour at a greater fare. Chopper tours also lift off via **Era Aviation** (tel. *586–2030*), another well-respected outfit. Its glacier tour was longer but more expensive when we last looked into it.

SPORTS

There are scores of *fishing* charters available. One umbrella outfit which handles reservations for around 40 boats is **Juneau Sportfishing** (tel. *686–1887*), efficiently run by a woman by the name of Suparna. You can write direct to its unusual address at 3–6500 Suite 100, Juneau, AK 99802. *Hunting* excursions are taken out by everyone and his brother, or so it seems. Ask in the Davis Log Cabin for some of the current guides available. You can also charter planes to fishing and hunting areas within the Tongass National Forest. If you're going to get out into the wilderness, be sure to check with the rangers at the U.S. Forest Service (tel. *586–8751*) and stop by their museum-like headquarters and information center in the Centennial Hall on Egan Drive at Willoughby street. The state Department of Fish and Game (tel. *465–4116*) is head-quartered at 1255 W. Eighth St. The Golden North Salmon Derby takes place usually the first weekend in August.

As in all of Southeast, *baseball and basketball* are the big local sports interests. They'll play ball in Juneau even in the sloshiest weather. Basketball fans follow the UAS Humpback Whales, and then don't for-get the big Gold Medal basketball tournament in March.

Believe it or not, there's a nine-hole **Mendenhall Golf Course** (tel. *789–7323*) at the end of Industrial Boulevard in view of the glacier of the same name. With those long summer days, the course is open from 9 to 9. It costs about $5 per round, with club rentals available at around $3.

If you enjoy *skiing,* Juneau boasts an attractive local area with a good selection of bunny slopes, along with intermediate and expert trails, and there's virtually no waiting in lift lines, even on busy weekends. **Eaglecrest** (tel. *586–5284*) is just 12 miles (20 minutes' drive) from Juneau on Douglas Island, and when it's raining in Juneau it just might be snowing up at Eaglecrest (check the snow report at tel. *586–5330*). You'll find two double chair lifts and a platter pull. Besides the base lodge, lessons and boot and ski rentals are available. We had a good time there one March day in 1988. Our only complaint was that because virtually everyone who skis Eaglecrest is local, they all know the trails very well and they're not too well marked for us *cheechakos*. Eaglecrest is generally open from late November until the middle of April. All-day lift rates were around $20.

Like in many other cities, Juneau residents have taken to *running* in recent years. The city Parks and Recreation Department organizes 5- and 10-K runs, plus the Juneau Marathon (¼ and ½) in August. (Run-ning temperatures are usually ideal then—not too cool but not too hot, either.) In August you might find the three-mile "Only Fools Run at Midnight." Most fun for some is the May Day "Mud Run" when ded-icated runners ford the Gastineau Channel, splashing between Juneau and Douglas in water up to their knees!

SHOPPING

Traditional *Indian and Native handicraft items* include sprucewood baskets, moccasins, wood panels, silver jewelry. More recent refinements include things made from salmon skin, which is called *salmon leather* after it's processed; these include belts, wallets, small purses, and the like (one Juneau factory is called, unabashedly, Alas-Skins). You'll find some local ingenuity, too, like marketing *blue topaz jewelry* as "glacial ice," etc. Remember that only items manufactured in Alaska are allowed to use the special logo featuring a white polar bear mom and a little black bear cub. (Additionally, handmade items have an Alaska map logo, and handmade Native goods have a silver hand logo.)

Generally speaking, stores catering to us *cheechakos* seem to get steadily better the farther inland you walk from the cruise docks. Many of the interesting addresses are on Franklin Street, or just off it on Ferry and Front. Most downtown stores normally close around 6 p.m., but many still open as late as 10 p.m. when cruise ships are in. Shopping malls on the outskirts continue until 8 or 9.

Among the better *arts, crafts, and general Alaskana* addresses in downtown Juneau are **Latitude 58,** run by Keil and Moretta Rieger at 170 S. Franklin St.; and **Objects of Bright Pride,** across the street at 165 S. Franklin, has some particularly unusual items. Also there is **George's,** an old timer at 194 S. Franklin, and **Kaill Fine Crafts** at 244 Front St. *Authentic crafts* are also sold in the shop at the **Alaska State Museum** at 395 Whittier St. You can buy *Alaskan gold nugget jewelry* at **Dockside Jewelers** at 145 S. Franklin St.

Everyone up north seems to go for those souvenir enameled or **cloisonne pins,** and many of the best are created in Juneau by Bill Spear of **William Spear Design.** It's at 174 S. Franklin St. right in the turret of the old Emporium Mall, no doubt a terrific location for a business.

More run-of-mill *souvenirs,* perhaps, are available at the **Mt. Juneau Trading Post,** near the corner of Franklin and Front. And **Fit to a T,** at 197 S. Franklin, specializes in Alaskan *T-shirts* and the like. The highly advertised fudge store nearby may be good, but we don't like patronizing any place that has a minimum purchase amount. **Forever in Ivory,** at 231 S. Franklin, has cameos, etc., executed by a woman named Cha, and whose works are sold in several establishments throughout the state. Other high-ticket items include the *leather and fur creations* on the premises at **Nina's Originals,** 221 Seward St. This business was started by the original Nina in 1946 and is now kept going by her daughter (probably nothing much under $1000 there). *Guitars, mandolins, violins,* etc., are made by James E. Hanes at the **String Shop,** 217 Fifth St. East.

Among several *fine art* addresses is the **Rie Munoz Gallery** (tel. *786–2112*), at 210 Ferry Way, featuring the works of Munoz, one of Alaska's best-known living artists, along with two or three others. Several other good Alaskan and Native artists are represented at **Gallery of the North,** upstairs above the Trading Post at 147 S. Franklin St.

There are a couple of excellent *bookstores* downtown: **Big City Books,** 100 N. Franklin St., and **Hearthside Books** just around the corner at 254 Front St. (there's also a branch at the Nugget Mall). Rare and antique books and maps are sold at the **Alaskan Heritage Bookshop,** 174 S. Franklin St. **Southeast Exposure,** at 216 Second St., between Seward and Franklin, is a helpful haven for *camera* bugs—when the boss is in, anyway. (One of the clerks sometimes in charge seemed to us to be either underdeveloped or underexposed.)

Canned, smoked, and frozen *seafood* can be purchased, sent, or ordered from the **Alaska Smoked Salmon Company** (tel. *463–3474*) at 230 S. Franklin St. "If it has anything to do with fish, and is made in Alaska, we probably carry it," they boast. We don't doubt it a bit.

Want a store with real no-nonsense *sourdough clothing* (plaid halibut jackets, etc.) and your basic *fishing and hunting supplies?* That would be the **Alaska Ship Chandlers** at 1050 Harbor Way, just out of the downtown area. They don't get many *cheechakos* there.

There are two main *malls,* both out by the airport. Juneau's major shopping souk, and where all the teenagers hang out, is the **Nugget Mall** nine miles out at 8745 Glacier Highway, just off the Egan Expressway; Lamonts Apparel and Pay-N-Save are the two anchors. Kits Cameras is a well-stocked photo shop in the mall. You'll find the **Mendenhall Mall** just off the Mendenhall Loop Road. On the way to either is the large Juneau branch of **Fred Meyer One Stop Shopping** at 8181 Glacier Highway, just off Egan Drive. With several kinds of stores all wrapped up together, Freddy's sometimes seems almost as good as a mall all by itself.

Newspapers? Hope you can get along without the news with your morning coffee. The Anchorage and Seattle papers come in about noon in Juneau. The Juneau *Empire* publishes afternoons Monday–Friday. Several out-of-town papers are sold at **Percy's Liquor Store** at 214 Front St.

MISCELLANEOUS ADDRESSES AND PHONES

Since Juneau phones have more than one prefix, you'll have to dial all seven numbers again for local calls. (Most begin with 586 or 789.) You'll also find several zip codes—three for Juneau, one for Douglas, another for Auke Bay, etc.

- Alaska State Chamber of Commerce (tel. *586–2323*), 310 Second St., Juneau, AK 99801.
- Alaska State Library (tel. *465–2920*), 8th floor, State Office Building.
- Alaska State Troopers (tel. *789–2161*).
- Bartlett Memorial Hospital (tel. *586–2611*), 3260 Hospital Dr. (off Glacier Highway in Salmon Creek).
- Bus information (tel. *789–6901*).
- Capital City Dry Cleaners (tel. *586–1133*), 281 S. Franklin St.
- City and Borough of Juneau (tel. *586–5279*), 155 S. Seward St., Juneau, AK 99801–1397.
- City Police (tel. *586–2780*).
- Coast Guard Emergency (tel. *586–2680*).
- Convention and Visitors Bureau, Juneau (tel. *586–1737*), 76 Egan Dr., Suite 140, Juneau, AK 99801.
- Cut Above Hair Styling (tel. *586–3555*), 76 Egan Dr.
- Emergencies (tel. 911).
- First National Bank of Anchorage (tel. *586–2550*), 238 Front St.
- Federal Building Switchboard (tel. *586–6106*).
- Juneau *Empire* (newspaper, tel. *586–3740*), 3100 Channel Dr., Juneau, AK 99803–4599.
- Juneau Memorial Library (tel. *586–5249*), top of Municipal Parking Garage, next to Marine Park.
- Mendenhall Laundromat (tel. *789–4224*), Mendenhall Mall.
- Parks and Recreation, Juneau (tel. *586–5226*), Marine View Building.
- Poison information (tel. *586–2627*).
- Pollution incidents, 24 hours (tel. *586–2680*).
- Post Office (tel. *586–7138*), 709 W. Ninth St.
- Time of day (tel. *586–3185*).
- University of Alaska—Southeast (tel. *789–4458*), 11120 Glacier Highway, Juneau, AK 99801.

SITKA

We were recently asked by a couple planning to take the ferry between Skagway and Seattle to choose just one overnight stopover they should make between the two destinations. They wanted to see something historic, yet something substantially different from other destinations in Alaska. Of course we strongly advised against pausing only once along that atmospheric journey. That said, however, the choice was obvious—Sitka, the city the Russians officially named Novo Arkhangelsk (New Archangel), a jewel on the shore of a bay filled with gem-like islands, and surrounded by mountains including a nearby dormant volcano.

While the first crude huts were still being slapped together in San Francisco, Sitka was already billed as the "Paris of the Pacific." The community served as the capital of Russian America for 60 years. After purchase by the U.S., it was also the capital of the District of Alaska for the next 40 years—totaling a century as the dominant center of civilization in Alaska.

After the Americans took control, Sitka's economy underwent a disastrous decline, suffering along with the rest of Alaska from decades of neglect by the federal government and the decline of its fur industry. Following a brief resurgence as a military post during World War II, it has kept alive through lumber, fishing, and tourism. With its respected Sheldon Jackson College and a talent for organizing special events in the arts, Sitka is also becoming known as an intellectual center in Southeast.

TRANSPORTATION

With its shallow shoreline, Sitka has no municipal dock that can accommodate deep-draft vessels. Ocean liners anchor out in Sitka Sound and then lighter in their passengers. Some local cruises on smaller boats pick up their customers right off the ships. Nevertheless, you can still take your car to Sitka on the **Alaska Marine Highway System** (tel. *747–3300*). The ferry docks seven miles away at Old Sitka, a relatively prosaic entrance to Baranof Island. Buses to and from the ferry terminal

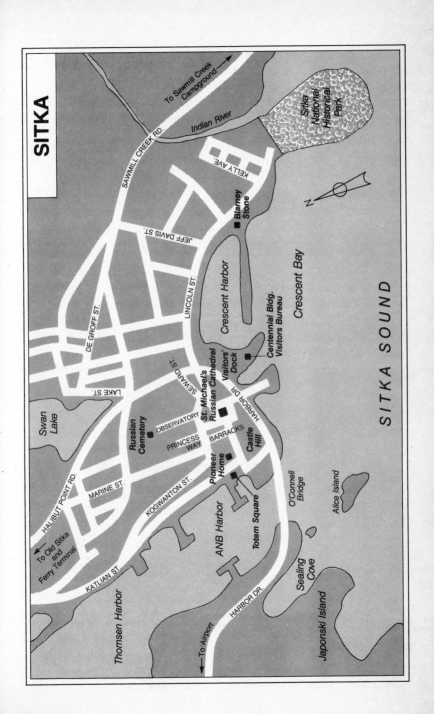

are run by either **Rusty's** (tel. *747–3598*) or **Sitka Tours** (tel. *747–8443*). Figure about $3 into town.

Sitka Sound is directly off the open ocean in the Gulf of Alaska, but the ferries take a tremendously twisted, though extremely scenic, route though the narrows between Chichagof and Baranof Islands in order to make their way between Sitka and Juneau or between Sitka and Petersburg. One of the critical areas is Sergius Narrows, where the vessel almost seems to brush the trees, and passengers are treated to the songs of birds who are just out of reach.

The narrows are subjected to one of the strongest tides in the world, so it must be negotiated in slack periods, only 45 minutes or so every six hours. (It doesn't matter much whether the slack tide is high or low; it's the current the captains worry about.) If, for some reason, the ferry just misses that, it will have to mark time for the next six hours. (See the route outlined with red dashes in the Tongass National Forest map, available free from the Forest Service personnel on board.)

On the Sitka-Juneau run aboard the ferry *Le Conte* (that's the one with no cabins), passengers usually find themselves pausing at the tiny villages of Angoon, Tenakee Springs, Hoonah, and sometimes Pelican (but if these port calls are important to you, be sure to check the most recent schedules). As always, but especially in Sitka, be sure to phone to recheck ferry departure times before you drive all the way out to the terminal.

Air travelers seem to find themselves coming in on the water, too. Actually they land on the airport constructed on Japonski Island. A former World War II military base, the island still houses a large Coast Guard facility. It is connected by the O'Connell Bridge (a good vantage point for photographs) to downtown Sitka.

Sitka Airport is small, modern, and is often wafted with the tempting aroma of pies which are baked at the restaurant. It receives regular jet flights by **Alaska Airlines** (tel. *966–2266*), whose flight attendants often buy those pies to take home to Seattle or Anchorage, plus several charter or ''bush'' services by other outfits. The smaller commuter airlines, which travel to so many other communities in the panhandle, leave all the scheduled services in Sitka to Alaska Airlines. It has three flights north and three south daily during the summer, and two each way during the off season.

There is bus service into town via **Rusty's Airporter** (tel. *747–3598*). You'll find two rental car companies with counters at the airport, **Avis** (tel. *966–2404*) and **Rent-A-Dent** (tel. *966–2552*). Another, parked in town at 713 Katlian St., is **AAA Auto Rental** (tel. *747–3996*), and it should not be confused with the American Automobile Association. There is no airport limosine service, but you will find some taxicabs there and elsewhere in town. They include **Arrowhead** (tel. *747–8888*), **Baranof** (tel. *747–3366*), **Poor Boy's** (tel. *747–5816*), and **Sitka Taxi** (tel. *747–5001*). *Tip:* The taxis in Sitka are not regulated; if you don't like the price you're quoted, offer a lower one.

HOTELS AND MOTELS

There is not a lot of choice in conventional accommodations in Sitka. Figure on 8% tax across the board, too. Write to any of the following at zip code 99835.

Despite some unevenness, the leader is still the **Westmark Shee Atika** (tel. *747–6241*), one link in Alaska's Westmark chain, which is anchored in the center of town. Named after the Tlingit word the Russians agglutinated to "Sitka," it's often better known locally as simply "the Lodge." An Indian mural design dominates the lobby; dark-wood logs and subdued colors, except for the front-desk fluorescents; potted plants lining a conversation pit; wood-burning fireplace; Indian craftsman often working on the weekends; faded engraving of New Archangel; popular Kadata'an cocktail lounge; generally dependable Raven's Room Restaurant; balky elevators; rust-orange rooms with totem designs painted smack onto the walls; some views over the Chevron station toward the harbor; heavy, dark furnishings; cable TV; spotty maintenance and housekeeping on our stay; no luggage rack to be had when we asked for one; bellhops not always on duty, but a self-service cart available; difficult parking. Double rates were around $100, but the hotel makes some spare change by nickel and diming you to death for credit card calls, toll-free numbers, etc. All in all, it's not as mote-free as the Super 8, but its local-landmark personality may make up for a lot. (Reservations through the chain or the hotel at 330 Seward St.)

When the Lodge is loaded, and during the busiest days of summer, they also open the **Westmark Inn** (same phone number), once a separate hotel (the Sheffield), but which everyone now calls "the Annex." It's near the large totem at the end of Lincoln St., next door to the post office substation. The rooms are around $25 less, and not bad at all for the price, although in general the place does have the aura of a building that is often closed. Ask for a harbor view, and you might see eagles swooping over the nearby fishing boats. No restaurant, bar, etc.—for that residents of the Annex have to trudge back to the Lodge. (Reservations as above.)

Some will logically prefer the local link in the venerable **Super 8** (tel. *747–8804*) chain. Two-story, stucco building somewhat away from the center of things at the corner of Lake St. and Sawmill Creek Blvd.; good parking; vaguely pseudo-Tudor architectural style; efficient furnishings; cable TV; free local phone calls (take that, Mr. Westmark!);

air conditioning (unusual in these parts); plain walls; full-length mirrors; light, quilted bedspreads; no closets; minimal shelf space; no views; free coffee; double rates perhaps in the $80 range in 1990. All in all, a typical Super 8—not really "super," but you probably won't "h8" it, either. (Reservations through the chain or from the hotel at 404 Sawmill Creek Blvd.)

After those three, the hotel scene could start getting a little hairy. The old **Potlatch** (tel. *747–8611*), is just a little "out of it" at 713 Katlian St. Some views; cable TV; coin laundry; good wallpaper; new furnishings promised by its new owners; double rates around $70. At that rate, the Potlatch is not exactly a party—but it's a possibility. (Reservations from the hotel.)

Sorry, but when we last saw it, we weren't sure that the musty **Sitka Hotel** (tel. *747–3288*), 118 Lincoln St., met the minimum standards for inclusion in this guide, although the location is certainly more convenient than the Potlatch or the Super 8, and the new owners were promising some improvements. Doubles were around $50. If you find things changed, please clue us in.

There are at least a half-dozen or more bed-and-breakfast operations in town, most of them off the beaten path. Some are pricier than the Westmarks. Unfortunately, they all compete independently rather than organizing through a central agency. We'd just get in trouble listing in a nation-wide guide any place with only a couple of rooms or so. The Sitka Convention and Visitors Bureau will give you an up-to-date list, but you'll have to let your fingers do the dialing after that.

From June 1 through Aug. 31, the **Youth Hostel** (tel. *747–8356*) is open in the basement of the Methodist church at 303 Kimsham St. Figure about $10 per cot per night.

RESTAURANTS AND DINING

Sitka seldom wins any international culinary awards, but there are several establishments serving good, solid meals. The **Raven's Room** (tel. *747–6241*), in the Westmark Shee Atika, is our nomination for the "little girl who had a little curl." Usually the fish is very, very good.

Don't be fooled by the name: **Staton's Steak House** (tel. *747–3396*) is better known for saltwater specialties than it is for beef. Look for it downtown at 228 Harbor Dr. (closed Sunday and Monday). The principal weekend whoop-it-up out-of-town choice is the **Channel Club** (tel. *747–9916*), open daily about three happy miles out Halibut Point Rd. You don't have to wait to eat; everyone gets the salad bar, and the menu is painted on the wall above that. You return to the table with both your salad and your mind made up, and then the server swings by to write down your beef or fish order. We found the steaks and seafood acceptable enough. A few booths have a sea view. The tables are close together, but nobody seems to mind. Noisy and popular.

Also worth remembering is the **Marina** (tel. *747–8840*), downtown again at 205 Harbor Dr. Here is a room specializing in Italian and Mexican dishes, owned and operated by a Chinese woman. Takeouts are also available. Unfortunately it wasn't open when we were in the mood for spicy food. We also never made it to the full-scale Mexican entry **Los Amigos** (which allegedly sells pizza, too) at 1305 Sawmill Creek Rd., next to the new main post office. If you go, let us know.

We found two downtown favorites for lunch. The second-floor **Bayview Restaurant,** in MacDonald's Bayview Trading Company, has American *and* Russian specialties. We actually had a hamburger with borscht on it. For traditionalists, Eastern and Western, there are also such standbys as a piroshki that comes with borscht and salad for perhaps $6.95 or a banana burger for $7.50 or so. (Do not confuse this place with McDonald's.) And is there a "bay view?" You bet. The other noontime winner is the cheerfully operated **Coffee Express** (tel. *747–3343*), also downtown at 104 Lake St., just across from the Shee Atika Lodge. The gourmet coffees are excellent, of course, but so are their creative sandwiches—unusually flavored muffins and buoyant banter, no matter how busy things get. Figure around $7 for a good sandwich with a bowl of homemade soup. (Closed Sunday.) **Revard's** (tel. *747–3449*), a friendly cafe at 324 Lincoln St., is also popular with knowledgeable cheeseburger gourmets.

Probably the best low-budget meals in town are at **Lory's Dockside** (tel. *747–5898*), about a half-mile from the center of town at 619 Katlian St., next to Thomsen Harbor. No atmosphere, unless you count that created by your fellow penny-pinching patrons. A square meal of meat loaf or pork chops will run around $6, including coffee, potato, and soup or salad. No alcohol served. Known too for pies, which were okay, although we still preferred those at the airport.

Fast food? For the occasional Accidental Tourist, there is, indeed, a real **McDonald's** in Sitka, and that should not be mixed up with the local MacDonald's operation downtown. You'll find Ronald and the golden arches at 913 Halibut Point Rd.

ENTERTAINMENT AND NIGHT LIFE

Sitka's most well-known group of entertainers are the **New Archangel Dancers,** a group of talented volunteer women who execute traditional Russian dances while wearing women's and men's costumes. A half-hour show costs $2 and is held at various times in the auditorium in the Centennial Building. The music, however, is recorded. Unfortunately for photographers, they seldom perform outdoors. Held with less regularity are Indian dances, notably by a group called the **Gajaa Heen.** Sometimes you'll find them at the ANB (Alaska Native Brotherhood) Hall on Katlian St. They have no recordings, but then the accompaniment is little more than drum beating anyway. Combined with a pancake breakfast, the fare might be $5, perhaps part of a fundraising effort to send the group on trips, etc. They're nice folks, but if you're going to see the Chilkat Dancers in Haines, you could skip this one.

The **Sitka Summer Music Festival,** featuring classical chamber music, takes place over three weeks each June.

For tippling, toping, and all that, the more popular of the more sophisticated bars is the **Kadata'an Lounge** in the Westmark Shee Atika. Gentle live music gets steadily rockier as the evening—and the beat—goes on.

About two miles out Sawmill Creek Road, the **Kiksadi Club** kicks up its heels until around 2 a.m., serving up hard rock and other modern sounds. *"Local color?"* You'll find all the fishermen, hunters, prospectors, and other tellers of tall tales at the **Pioneer Bar,** 212 Katlian St., near the used-book store. By the way, "Little Drook," has nothing to do with someone being just a bit inebriated; that's the cartoon character Cossack whose name means "friend," and it's the symbol of the Sitka Convention and Visitors Bureau.

SIGHTS AND SITES

Stop first at the **Sitka Convention and Visitors Bureau** (tel. 747–5940) in the Centennial Building, near the harbor, to pick up a map, brochures, etc. The small **city museum** is in the office next door in the same building. Be sure to check out the model of Sitka as it appeared during the days when Smirnoff would have outsold Schlitz hereabouts.

Sitka's horizon has been broken for almost a century and a half by **St. Michael's Cathedral,** the magnificent onion-domed structure built under the direction of Father Ivan Veniaminov, the Russian Orthodox Bishop of Alaska (who later went on to head the church in Russia). The original building on Lincoln Street burned down in 1966. The present one is a faithful replica, and it contains the icons and other artwork that were rescued from the flames. It remains *the* cathedral for the Orthodox church in North America, and services are still conducted partly in Russian. (Open for services and when cruise ships are in; no photography allowed inside; donations accepted.)

Opened in 1988, the restored 1843 **Russian Bishop's House** (tel. *747–6281*), on Lincoln Street just east of the center of town, is now administered as a museum by the National Park Service. It is one of the few original Russian structures in existence in America, and it was still used by the church until 1969. (Open from 8 a.m. to 5 p.m.)

At the east end of Lincoln Street don't miss the 100-acre **Sitka National Historical Park** established on the site of the 1804 Battle of Sitka, the last major clash between the Tlingits and the Russians in this area. The museum building contains several displays on Russian and Indian history, and you sometimes find Indian artists working there in wood, silver, blanket weaving, etc. An easy, two-mile foot trail in the park winds partly through a score of totem poles from all parts of Southeast Alaska. (The legend of each is explained in an attractive Alaska Natural History Association booklet called *Carved History,* sold at the park for $2.) In the second half of August, the walking bridge over Indian River is one of the best places to see pink salmon returning to their spawning grounds. (A salmon, incidentally, is one of the world's few creatures said to be both born an orphan and to die childless.)

Other sights worth seeing include the steep **Castle Hill,** which has 75 breath-defying steps to the top, beginning just off Lincoln Street next to the Harry Race Drug Store. (A new, less-steep trail is on the other side.) This was the site of Baranof's Castle, which burned down in 1894, and the place where Russians cried while Alaska was formally transferred to the U.S. in 1867. Nearby is the **Alaska Pioneers Home,** a retirement institution for genuine old sourdoughs. Note the bronze statue named "the Prospector" just outside, and the nearby totem pole which commemorates the history of Sitka. (See the Russian double-eagle cleverly carved into the pattern?) If you walk up the hill on Marine Street, you can visit the **Russian Cemetery,** where many graves are still marked by Slavic crosses with the slanting bottom crosspiece. There is a replica of one of the original wooden blockhouses there, too.

On the way toward the historical park is the **Sheldon Jackson Museum,** based around the original collection of Presbyterian missionary Jackson himself. Well worth the small admission, the museum is actually on the campus of **Sheldon Jackson College.** The four-year facility enrolls many Native students from all over Alaska, hoping to provide them with a less culture-shocked entrance to the outside world. (Although some Eskimo kids from the open tundra once said they felt "hemmed in" by all those beautiful spruce trees!) It also has a surprisingly large enrollment from out of state. The SJC campus was the temporary home of James Michener in 1987 while he wrote his epic novel, *Alaska*. Students sometimes conduct short morning tours at the college **fish hatchery** (tel. *747–5254*) during the summer. Better recheck the exact time by calling first. Admission $1. Also headquartered on the campus is the ARRC—the **Alaska Raptor Rehabilitation Center** (tel. *747–8662*), which cares for sick and injured hawks and eagles and later returns them to the wild. The facilities can sometimes be visited, but call first.

SIDE TRIPS

Most of what there is to see is within the city limits. Some like to drive seven miles out on the Halibut Point Rd. to find **Old Sitka,** near the ferry terminal. There's not much left of the original site. The colony was moved to New Archangel in 1804 following an Indian massacre. In the opposite direction, you can drive about the same distance to the Japanese-owned **Alaska Pulp Mill** (no tours), and thence to **Blue Lake,** a popular fishing area for rainbow trout. In July and August, look for salmonberries and other wild fruit along the way.

Despite the size of Baranof Island, Sitka is virtually the only settlement on it. Between it and Juneau are two more large islands, **Chichagof Island** and **Admiralty Island.** "Side Trips" of the Juneau portion of this chapter describes these and destinations accessible there by plane or ferry, the villages of Angoon, Hoonah, Tenakee, and Pelican. You can also take a ferry boat or charter a seaplane to **Kake** (pronounced "cake") between Sitka and Petersburg. (See "Petersburg.")

TOURS AND CRUISES

As in many areas of Southeast, tours are sold primarily to the cruise ships, so you may have to search these out yourself if you want to join in the fun. Call the numbers below or check with the tourist office in the Centennial Building to find out how to book, where to meet, etc.

Two companies offer bus tours, and if their names seem familiar, it's because they're the same folks who shuttle between town and the ferry terminal and to the airport. **Sitka Tours** (tel. *747–8443*), also known as Prewitt Enterprises, is the main outfit and you'll usually see their yellow buses or blue vans waiting on the docks at Crescent Harbor for lighters to arrive from the cruise ships. (They also have the school bus contract, which means they keep changing the signs on the buses, too!) A fare of around $25 for the three-hour "Sitka Historical Tour" includes entrance fees to museums and the park. The second is **Rusty's Charters** (tel. *747–3598*). Since it has only small vehicles, Rusty's will vary the itinerary to suit the whims of the passengers. A two-hour excursion, without any entrance fees, may cost around $12 in 1990.

Look for two tours on the water, too. We took the 3½-hour "Marine Wildlife Tour" with **Alaska Travel Adventures** (tel. *747–5576*), whose local agent is Alaska Adventures Unlimited. You get to a group of tiny islands on a comfortable 150-passenger catamaran, then switch to a fleet of rubber Zodiacs to flit between the small islets in the bay, searching for birds and animals. We got a little wet, but with a good crew and some interesting wildlife, it's a lot of fun. (Put your camera in a plastic bag if you're going to take it on the rubber boat too.) Figure around $75 for the whole experience in 1990.

The second is a two-hour "Silver Bay" trip with **Allen Marine Tours** (tel. *747–8941*), a somewhat more subdued experience that might be described as a bus tour on the water. The fare may be $25 or so by your visit. It usually leaves Crescent Harbor at 6 p.m., but only on certain days of the week (recheck at the number above or the tourist bureau). We haven't yet climbed aboard ourselves.

Two local bush flying companies occasionally make flightseeing sweeps, although not with the regularity of air operations in other Southeast locations. The last we knew, **Bellair** (tel. *747–8636*), a fixed-wing outfit, featured a Glacier Bay Tour for about $200 per person and also listed local flying at around $50 per person. And **Mountain Air** (tel. *747–2288*), which has both fixed-wing planes and helicopters, offered round trips to Shelikof Beach for around $400. The nearby symmetrically shaped volcano, Mt. Edgecumbe, is usually seen much better from the air.

SPORTS

Of the two dozen or so *charter fishing boats* around, nearly all are represented by **Alaska Adventures Unlimited** (tel. *747–5576*), and you can say hello from us to Chuck Horner there. Sea species are pretty much the same as in other Southeast locations, including salmon, halibut, red snapper, crab, herring, and abalone. Non-resident fishing licenses cost $10. The state Division of Fish and Game (tel. *747–5355* for fishing information, *747–5449* for game information) is at 304 Lake St. *Hunters* like Baranof island for blacktail deer, mountain goats, and brown bears. There are, of course, lots of rules and regs.

The **Sitka Salmon Derby** takes place over several days in late May and sometimes early June.

Don't look for any golf courses in Sitka. There are a few *tennis* courts at Sheldon Jackson University, but getting on them is problematical. *Swimming?* When Sitka swelters and sizzles at 65° or so, you will find a large percentage of the population on a rocky beach out (which they prefer to call Sandy Beach) at Halibut Point. But only mad dogs and children go in the water, which just doesn't warm up enough normally.

As elsewhere in Alaska's Banana Belt, everyone plays or watches *softball* rain, shine, or rain in the summertime and goes equally bananas over *basketball* in the winter.

SHOPPING

If it's Sunday and the cruise ships are in, don't expect to find Sitka stores going full blast just because there's money to be made. This is a fairly conservative, rather religious community, and the advent of modern tourism is not about to change that a heck of a lot. That's one of the charms of the place.

Monday to Saturday until around 6 p.m., most things visitors are interested in are found within a convenient short radius from the corner of Lincoln and Lake streets. Many of the *crafts* created by artisans at the Indian Cultural Center (in the Sitka National Historical Park) end up in Sitka shops.

You'll find an outstanding collection of *things Russian* upstairs at **MacDonald's Bayview Trading Company,** 407 Lincoln St. (next to the small restaurant we mentioned above, neither of which should be confused with McDonald's hamburgers). The items at the boutique, also called the Russian-American Company, include antiques, expensive and delicate painted eggs, lacquered boxes, old icons, samovars, Baltic amber, etc. (Hold on to your kids!) Collectors have been known to shell out thousands for special items. They also have some less pricey objects like those nesting dolls imported direct from the U.S.S.R. On the ground floor, the McDBTC is a conventional clothing and department store.

There's a small but authentic selection of *Indian crafts* at the **Shel-**

don Jackson Museum Shop, in the same building as the museum at 104 College Dr., on the SJC campus.

We would suggest poking along Lincoln St. or Harbor Dr. West of Lake St., but be aware that many of the Native items for sale there may be from other parts of Alaska—or Korea. We particularly liked the great *collection of junque* at the Sitkakwan Gift Shop, 208 Lincoln. *Russian and other antique money* is sold at Mike's Coins, 236 Lincoln St. You'll find three or four serious art galleries in the neighborhood. Free and low-cost Alaska pamphlets and publications are available, along with friendly advice, from the University of Alaska Cooperative Extension Service on the second floor of the old post office building at the west end of Lincoln St. There are at least two good *bookstores* in town: Old Harbor Books, 201 Lincoln, where we bought Michener's *Alaska* the first day it was out. And then, specializing in pre-owned volumes, The Observatory (tel. *747-3033*) is in an historic building at 202 Katlian St. There Dee Longenbaugh also serves as a helpful expert in Alaskana. (She gets telephone orders for books, maps, and prints from all over the world.)

MISCELLANEOUS ADDRESSES AND PHONES

All Sitka phone numbers begin with 747, except for those on Japonski Island which start with 966. (Unlike some other areas, all seven numbers must be dialed in Sitka.) The zip code for all addresses in Sitka is 99835.

- Sitka Convention and Visitors Bureau (tel. *747-5940*), Centennial Building, Harbor Dr.
- City and Borough of Sitka (tel. *747-3294*), 304 Lake St.
- Emergencies of all type (tel. 911).
- Fire department (tel. *747-3233*), 209 Lake St.
- HeadQuarters Hair Salon (tel. *747-8338*), 203 Harbor Dr., inside the Market Place.
- Homestead Laundromat (tel. *747-6995*), 619 Katlian St. (Thomsen Harbor).
- Hospital, Sitka Community (tel. *747-3241*), 209 Moller Dr.
- Police department (tel. *747-3245*), Lake St.
- Sea Mart Supermarket (tel. *747-6266*), 1867 Halibut Point Rd.
- Time of day (tel. *747-8633*).
- U.S. Forest Service (tel. *747-6671*), 204 Siginaka Way.

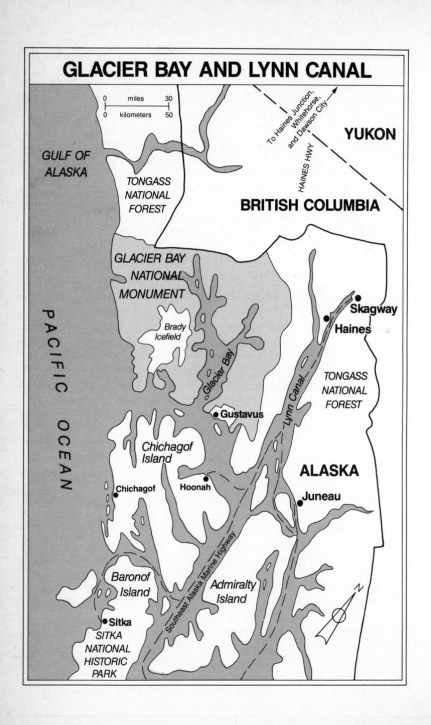

GLACIER BAY AND LYNN CANAL

0 miles 30
0 kilometers 50

YUKON

GULF OF ALASKA

TONGASS NATIONAL FOREST

To Haines Junction, Whitehorse, and Dawson City

HAINES HWY

BRITISH COLUMBIA

GLACIER BAY NATIONAL MONUMENT

Brady Icefield

Glacier Bay

PACIFIC OCEAN

Skagway

Haines

TONGASS NATIONAL FOREST

Lynn Canal

• Gustavus

Chichagof Island

• Chichagof

Hoonah

ALASKA

• Juneau

Southeast Alaska Marine Highway

Baronof Island

Admiralty Island

• Sitka

SITKA NATIONAL HISTORIC PARK

N

DIVIDED TWINS OF THE LYNN CANAL — HAINES AND SKAGWAY

The deep blue slash of water that cuts the green and rugged landscape for nearly 100 miles north of Juneau is called the Lynn Canal. At the far end it is split into two main inlets. To the left, the dignified small city of Haines straddles a narrow peninsula. To the right, seemingly just around the bend, is the gold rush city of Skagway. As ravens and eagles fly, the two settlements are 13 miles away from each other. Naturally enough, they are rivals—in baseball, basketball, and tourism. Unlike other major centers of human habitation in the panhandle, the two towns are connected to the continental road system. Yet they remain very separated, physically and philosophically.

Haines and Skagway are also the last two stops on the Southeast ferry system, and the trip by water between them takes less than an hour against the tide. Many have occasion to fly between the two, about a 10-minute hop. But the rivers, glaciers, and mountains between the communities prohibit any easy access by land. You can indeed drive between Haines and Skagway. But instead of 13 miles, you'll travel 360 scenic but not-too-easy miles of highway, which local promoters like to call the Golden Circle Route. Stopping for lunch at Whitehorse in Canada's Yukon Territory, it's at least an all-day trip each way. Without exception, the basketball teams, their fans, the bands, and the cheerleaders all take the ferry.

HAINES

Like Skagway, Haines owes its continued existence to the discovery of gold, albeit more indirectly. When the precious metal was found on nearby Porcupine Creek early in this century, Canada began making noises about redrawing the national boundaries in the area. President Teddy Roosevelt, speaking softly but carrying his proverbial big stick, decided to set up a permanent military post in the area. Fort William Seward was established at Haines at 1904 as a successful show of strength.

Prior to the gold rush, Haines was a trading center for the Chilkats, a subtribe of Tlingits who won wealth and power while trading fish oil and other coastal products for the furs and skins produced by the Athabascans and Eskimos of the north. After 1881 the area was a Presbyterian missionary center, founded by the Rev. S. Hall Young and John Muir, the naturalist.

Then the gold stampeders arrived, and Haines became the terminus of the Jack Dalton Trail which led up the Chilkat Valley and eventually to the fabled Klondike. The missionaries and Indians no sooner were rid of the prospectors when the soldiers marched in, thus assuring the continuance of a street of bawdy houses that continued for decades— ironically much longer than the brief rambunctiousness of Skagway, a town which today boasts of its 19th-century high jinks.

The fort was deactivated following World War II and later sold to a group of veterans. Today Haines and its immediate surroundings number about 2000 people, most of whom make their living in either fishing or tourism. A few at least are active members of the local art colony.

Yet to many visitors, it is best known as the home of thousands of bald eagles, plus the talented Chilkat dancers who perform often in the area. Haines is also considered one of the driest areas in the panhandle, relatively speaking. It usually totals under 60 inches of rain a year—as compared to about 90 inches in Juneau and 160 or more in Ketchikan.

TRANSPORTATION

The all-weather **Haines Highway** (AK Route 7, BC Route 4, and Yukon Route 3) connects Haines to the Alaska Highway 150 miles north

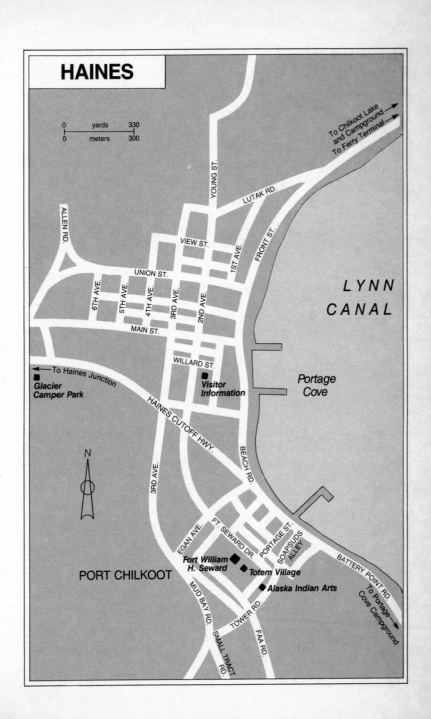

HAINES

0 yards 330
0 meters 300

ALLEN RD.

YOUNG ST.

LUTAK RD.

FRONT ST.

VIEW ST.

1ST AVE.

UNION ST.

6TH AVE.

5TH AVE.

4TH AVE.

3RD AVE.

2ND AVE.

MAIN ST.

WILLARD ST.

To Haines Junction

Glacier Camper Park

Visitor Information

HAINES CUTOFF HWY.

BEACH RD.

3RD AVE.

N

EGAN AVE.

FT. SEWARD DR.

PORTAGE ST.

SOAPSUDS ALLEY

Fort William H. Seward

Totem Village

Alaska Indian Arts

PORT CHILKOOT

MUD BAY RD.

SMALL TRACT RD.

TOWER RD.

FAA RD.

BATTERY POINT RD.

To Portage Cove Campground

Portage Cove

LYNN CANAL

To Chilkoot Lake and Campground
To Ferry Terminal

at the crossroads Canadian settlement called Haines Junction, following much of the original Dalton Trail. (During the gold rush it was a toll road maintained and controlled by one Jack Dalton.) All together, Haines is about 800 miles by road from Anchorage, 650 miles from Fairbanks, 250 from Whitehorse, and 40 miles south of the Canada-U.S. border. (Customs is usually open 7 a.m. to 11 p.m., Alaska time, but it would be a good idea to recheck if you're planning to cross close to those times.)

Bus service from Haines east to Whitehorse and Skagway (perhaps $150 to Skagway) or west to Fairbanks or Anchorage (maybe $200 to Anchorage) is available on the **Alaskon Express** (tel. *766–2030*), formerly White Pass & Yukon Motorcoaches, a common carrier now owned by Gray Line of Alaska (inquire at Wings of Alaska on Second Ave.). A smaller outfit, **Alaska Denali Transit** (tel. *766–2435*) covers similar routes for a little less money. The last we heard, the single van took two days to Anchorage with a stop to sleep along the way. Passengers take care of their own overnight expenses.

State ferries to and from Skagway or Juneau and ports south come into the terminal for the **Alaska Marine Highway** (tel. *766–2111*), about four miles east of town on Lutak Rd. The boat takes about 4½ hours from Juneau. (Be sure to have solid ferry and hotel reservations in late August when Haines hosts the five-day Southeast State Fair.) A shuttle service between the ferry and the hotels is operated in a bus (which sometimes flies the Norwegian flag) called the **Haines Street Car** (tel. *766–2819*), and costs about $4.50. That's about a dollar a mile; the owner blames the high cost of his liability insurance. The same company (and same phone number) also runs a **taxi** service, along with **Haines Taxi** (tel. *776–3138*), the competition.

Not all cruise ships get to Haines, although many cruisers fly over for the day when their liner calls at Skagway. The few cruise ships that do come in tie up at the **Port Chilkoot Dock** just downhill from the fort.

Haines Airport is about three miles west along the main highway. There are scheduled flights on Piper Navajos and similar aircraft between Haines and Skagway (around $25) or Juneau (around $50) on **Haines Airways** (tel. *766–2646*) and on **L.A.B. Airlines** (tel. *766–2222*), both of which are headquartered in Haines, or on Juneau-based **Wings of Alaska** (tel. *766–2030*). All three airlines provide complimentary transportation between the airport, their ticket offices, and any address in town.

There are three automobile rental agencies around, each handled by a different hotel/motel. **Avis** (tel. *766–2733*) cars are rented from the Halsingland and **Hertz** (tel. *766–2131*) vehicles are signed out from the Thunderbird. An independent operation is **Eagle's Nest** (tel. *766–2352*) at the motel of the same name, about two miles out from the center on the Haines Highway. Eagle's Nest also rents **RVs** (motor homes).

HOTELS AND MOTELS

All the addresses in Haines may be written to at zip code 99827. At this writing, Haines does not have a hotel bed tax—just a straight city sales tax of 5%.

The top place to stay, and to some the unofficial center of tourism in Haines, is the family-operated **Hotel Halsingland** (tel. *766–2000*). Installed in two joined-together rambling buildings, one of which was the commanding officer's house and the other the bachelor officers quarters of historic Ford Seward, it is not quite within easy marching distance of the business district. Cozy, creaky lobby with old-fashioned radiators, etc., left over from the military period; small gift shop; popular bar to one side; Commander's Room restaurant beyond that (see "Restaurants and Dining"); upstairs to a host of hodgepodgy rooms, each a little different from the other and perhaps none equipped with furniture that really fits; front rooms with view to the old parade grounds; 50 of the 60 accommodations with private plumbing, others shared; TVs but no private phones; best rooms in the $80 range; substantial discounts off season and for the bathless models any time; plenty of parking across the street. It's not exactly top-to-bottom spit and polish, but as long as Arnie and Joyce Olsson are still the top brass around here, this one usually passes inspection for everyone. (Reservations from the hotel at P.O. Box 1589, or toll-free *(800) 542–6363*.)

Most other accommodations in or near town fall into more conventional categories. Of the motels, many choose the **Captain's Choice** (tel. *766–3111*), conveniently on Second Ave. and high on a bluff overlooking the boat harbor. A long, low building fronted by bright boxes of zinnias, pansies, and daisies; naturally nautical reception area, with lots of paperback books; once-popular restaurant now closed; 40 pine-paneled rooms in two structures, many with panoramas over Portage Cove and the Lynn Canal; generally excellent motel facilities including TV-HBO, direct-dial phones, small refrigerators, free coffee, and quilted bedspreads; some with queen-size beds; some double-doubles; most twin rates about $80 in 1990. Keep your fingers crossed that co-Captains Dalton and Gale Hay have not decided to jump ship by the date of your arrival. (Reservations from P.O. Box 392, or call toll free *(800) 247–7153*.)

Across the street, the **Thunderbird Motel** (tel. *766–2131*) is another possibility for no nonsense, no views, occasional thunder from the nearby power plant—and less money. The lobby is a veritable museum, reflecting the owner's ability at taxidermy. Rooms are well-equipped if unspecial. Most units perhaps renting for $70 by 1990. We'd choose one at the back. (Reservations from P.O. Box 589, or toll free *(800) 327-2556.*)

Meanwhile, back at the fort (or near it, anyway), Arnie Olsson's brother and his partner, Shari, have opened the **Mountain View Motel** (tel. *766-2900*). There is, indeed, a mountain view—the snow-capped Cathedral Peaks on the other side of the Chilkat River. There are only six rooms, but each has a kitchenette. Doubles may be $60, a bargain if you want to rattle your own pots and pans. (Reservations from P.O. Box 62.)

The nearby **Fort Seward Lodge** (tel. *766-2009*) has a good reputation as a dining room, and has also been known as a dormitory. When we were there, the owners were also building a few private rooms, but it was too early to tell much about them. This should not be confused with the **Fort Seward Condos** (tel. *766-2425*), which has a three-day minimum stay for its full housekeeping units, or the **Fort Seward Bed & Breakfast** (tel. *766-2856*), also on the perimeter of the parade ground. (We haven't been through the latter two.)

A couple of miles on the Haines Highway, the **Eagle's Nest Motel** (tel. *766-2352*) also has decent if somewhat forgettable facilities, with TVs and coffee makers in all rooms. Doubles should rent for around $75. A cozy fireplace in the lobby is fired up in cold weather. It's better if you have a car, but if you don't have one, the Eagle's Nest will also rent you one.

RVs are accommodated at the **Eagle Camper Park** (tel. *766-2335*), at 751 Union St., on the west end of town; at **Port Chilkoot Camper Park** (tel. *766-2755*), on Second Ave. near Fort Seward; the **Oceanside** (tel. *766-2444*), overlooking the water at Front and Main; and the **Haines Hitch-Up** (tel. *766-2882*), at Haines Highway and Main.

A youth hostel called **Bear Creek Camp** (tel. *766-2259*) is located past the fort on Small Tract Rd. on the way to the state park. Figure about $15 per pillow. A state-operated campground is at **Chilkat State Park,** seven miles south of town on Mud Bay Rd.

If none of the above will do, check with the Visitor Information Center on Second Ave. They have a list of a few more places with fewer rooms.

RESTAURANTS AND DINING

Haines is especially known for its alder-wood salmon bake at the **Port Chilkoot Potlatch** (tel. *766-2000*), usually held in connection with a performance of the Chilkat Dancers (see "Entertainment") in the Totem Village on the old parade grounds. We enjoyed it, to be sure. Tickets for both are generally available at the Hotel Halsingland, which runs the food portion of the experience.

The best conventional restaurant in Haines is probably still the **Commander's Room** (tel. *766–2000*) in the Hotel Halsingland out at the fort, and if you're not staying there or don't have a car they'll come pick you up. With its tall windows, the dining area looks rather like the CO's former sun porch. Open daily for all three meals, seafood and steak are the specialties. It offers a salad bar *and* potato bar (something new for us) with its evening meals. I liked my steak dijon, Sara enjoyed the dungeness crab. The Captain's Platter (scallops, prawns, halibut, and salmon) ran over $20. There's a buffet-style champagne brunch on Sunday.

That said, the most intriguing restaurant in Haines is surely the tiny **Catalyst** (tel. *766–2670*), 336 Main St. at Third Ave. Seafood is the specialty, but there are wide-ranging possibilities, including soup and sandwiches or even a full German menu. If things are not busy and you are a World War II in Europe buff, or even a former Southeast Asian spook, try to warm up to irascible Erich. If that doesn't work (and it might not), talk to his wife, Fuzzy, instead.

In the former basketball court and PX for the turn-of-the-century American army, the **Fort Seward Lodge** (tel. *766–2009*) has set up an attractive full-service restaurant, which is popular with locals at least as a change from the Halsingland. Sit upstairs for the view. There is money pasted to the ceiling and a felt-lined swing, left over from some previous activity. We haven't managed to swing into here at meal time, yet. If you go, let us know.

After these, things start getting more conventional. The **Lighthouse** (tel. *766–2670*), on the harbor side of the Harbor Bar, sometimes seems to cater to fishermen who don't want to go home to eat. A pretty view, but the efficiency furnishings and our own meal were pretty ordinary. Some praise the buttermilk pie, though. (Usually open until 11 p.m.)

You can't see the harbor from the **Chilkat Restaurant and Bakery** (tel. *766–2920*), on Fifth near Main, but the quality of the baked goods may make up for that. Our lunch was fine but our bear's claw was better. Mexican food featured Fridays. No alcohol. Doors are locked here usually by 8 p.m. (closed Sunday).

The **Bamboo Restaurant,** a no-nonsense adjunct to the Pioneer Bar on Second Ave., has things like barbecue beef on a bun for around $8. Try the apple pie, too. Then there's the **Pizzacutter,** in the Fogcutter Bar on Main St., which cuts up some pretty fair *paisano* pies, along with sandwiches and other things. Popular for lunch. **Porcupine Pete's** is the local teen town, with cheaper pizzas, sandwiches, etc., along with a video game accompaniment. On the edge of town you'll find **Dan's**

& Barb's Drive In, specializing in shakes and bakes. Ten miles up the Haines Highway is the **Ten Mile Steakhouse** (tel. *766–2800*), where we didn't stop, although we probably should have checked it out. Much farther, at the 33-mile marker is the (surprise!) **33-Mile Roadhouse** (tel. *767–5510*), an historic structure which is still a popular stop for burgers, beers, and gas. The next car fuel and carbohydrates will be found after another 100 miles into Canada.

ENTERTAINMENT AND NIGHT LIFE

Some of the best Native entertainment in Alaska is provided by the elaborately costumed **Chilkat Dancers,** who perform frequently during the summer either at the Totem Village on the Parade Ground at old Fort Seward or the nearby Chilkat Center for the Arts (behind the Alaska Indian Arts at 23 Seward Dr.). If you see a non-Indian with a patch on his eye (or one dark eyeglass), remember that the dance group was formed during the 1960s by Carl Heinmiller as a way of recapturing part of the Tlingit culture and as a community youth project, and Carl is also one of the performers. The dance production is often sold in combination with the Port Chilkoot Potlatch salmon bake; get tickets at the Hotel Halsingland. (Save your printed program to help when you show your slides or video later.)

The **Chilkat Center** is also the occasional venue for a community old-time melodrama, **Lust for Dust,** usually launched two or three times a week during the summer months by a local amateur theater group. We've caught similar performances in Skagway, Dawson, and especially the championship one in Whitehorse, but have so far missed Haines' thespian efforts.

A quartet of bars dominate the nighttime scene in Haines. The bar at the **Hotel Halsingland** is generally frequented by the tourist interests. Downtown, the **Harbor Bar** is the fishermen's hangout, and the talk is usually more nautical than salty. Your yuppies, Haines variety, are usually found at the **Fogcutter** on Main St. Our own favorite watering hole is the historic **Pioneer Bar,** on Second Ave., an old-fashioned friendly sort of a tavern where we hit it off well with the bartendress and the other patrons one afternoon. It dates back to about nineteen-ought-seven. (Be careful not to ring the 100-year-old bell, unless the place is empty or you really do want to buy a drink for everyone in the house.)

SIGHTS AND SITES

You'll never tell your Chilkats from your Chilkoots if you don't make two important stops very early in your visit to Haines. The first is the **Visitor Information Center** (tel. *766–2234*) run by the Chamber of Commerce at Second and Willard streets, and the friendly folks there will tell you how and where to find anything you can think of. It would be a good idea to pick up a map and walking tour brochure there. You can write in advance to P.O. Box 1049.

The second is the **Sheldon Museum** (tel. *766–2366*), nearby, almost at the bottom end of Main St. This collection of nature, Indian, gold rush, and other miscellaneous memorabilia is amazingly well displayed for a town of this size. Free Russian tea is often poured by the daughter of the museum's founder or other ladies. Don't miss the movie on the eagles, either. Admission $2.

The **Small Boat Harbor** east of the museum is the haven for the fleet of gill-net fishing vessels which is the chief economic support of the area. At various times of the year, these boats return with shrimp, crab, halibut, salmon, and other local *fruits de mer*.

Visible from the harbor, but about two miles away, are the remaining buildings of old **Fort William H. Seward** (later renamed Port Chilkoot), which was the only military post in Alaska prior to the Second World War. The substantial structures surrounding the parade ground are now all privately owned, but they are all still painted white to give the military post approximately the same look it has had since the early years of the century. Some of the buildings have been converted into art galleries, etc. (see ''Shopping''). The visitors' center publishes a separate walking guide of the fort.

Chilkat State Park, about six miles west of town, should not be confused with the famous eagle preserve to the north (see below). Nevertheless, during the warmer months you are just as likely to see eagles in the park as anywhere else. In the summer the park is especially known for its many species of wildflowers along the hiking trails—the more delicate blooms in early summer and bolder colors in July and August. (If you're lucky, you can sometimes even rent a lone cabin there from the Alaska State Park system, not the USFS as in most other areas of Southeast.) The park also provides good views of two hanging glaciers, the Rainbow Glacier and the Davidson Glacier.

The above also should not be confused with **Chilkoot Lake** in the opposite direction, 10 miles out at the end of Lutak Road. There's a picnic area, and fishing is popular.

About 20 miles north of Haines, on the Haines Highway, the **Chilkat Bald Eagle Preserve** (also called the Valley of the Eagles or the Eagle Council Grounds). It is the winter home to somewhere between 3500 and 4000 individual examples of the American national bird, attracted here by the late salmon runs on an ice-free section of river— some from as far away as Washington State. Unfortunately, they usually don't begin returning to the 48,000-acre site until October, and the very best viewing is in late November. This means that summer travelers visit Haines without catching sight of the eagles in such impressive numbers.

Nevertheless, some eagles will be seen in and around town at any time of year. Look in the tallest trees or perhaps on the banks of the river for a black blob, with smaller white blobs at their tops and bottoms. On closer inspection, these turn into the characteristic white head and tail feathers of these magnificent creatures.

Of course anywhere in the Chilkat Valley you may also see other examples of other bird and animal wildlife including, at times, bear, moose, wolf, lynx, etc. We once sped by a brown bear cub only about two or three miles up the Haines Highway. By the time we turned the car around and came back to get a better look, though, Mom had apparently ushered the little one back into the woods.

SIDE TRIPS

North of the eagle preserve, the **Haines Highway** is a sometimes rough but always scenically spectacular route. At the 21-mile marker a short gravel road leads to **Klukwan,** which is what's left of an old Indian village (not much). At Mile 35, you may be able to see across the river what remains of the ghost town of **Porcupine,** which was the center of mining hereabouts at the turn of the century.

At the top end of the Haines Highway, at Haines Junction, Yukon, is the headquarters for **Kluane National Park** (tel. *(403) 634–2251)*, which is administered by Parks Canada. Drop into the information center, which is open til 9 p.m. (Kluane is adjacent to Wrangell-St. Elias National Park on the Alaskan side of the border in Southcentral.) Featuring glaciers as large as 6 by 60 miles, these parks are the type you have to have some degree of daring to enjoy. There are no roads into Kluane—only hiking trails through the valleys or along the mountain ridges. Flightseeing tours take off from Haines Junction. Information in general is available from the Superintendent, Kluane National Park, Haines Junction, Yukon Y0B 1L0.

North of the junction, past Destruction Bay on Kluane Lake, is the privately owned **Burwash Landing Resort.** Sorry, but we haven't had time for an inspection of these facilities yet, but this area in general is certainly among the most scenic on the Alaska Highway. If you go, please do let us know. We did stop overnight once at the **Kluane Wilderness Village,** and if you've ever wanted to find out all about burls, this is the place to do it. (Check out the burl bar.)

Haines is also a popular take-off point for flightseeing tours or just flights to **Glacier Bay,** covered in detail in the previous chapter. Gustavus is actually closer to Haines than it is to Juneau, as a matter of fact, and you can fly there on Haines Airways or Wings of Alaska. Both L.A.B. and Haines have tours (see below).

TOURS AND CRUISES

Popular flightseeing over the best parts of Glacier Bay, including some parts of the park you won't see from the water, are offered from Haines by **L.A.B. Flying Service** (tel. *766–2222*), **Wings of Alaska** (tel. *766–2030*) and, for perhaps a little less money, by **Haines Airways** (tel. *766–2646*). Both tours take about one hour, but they do not land on their circular route. It might be a little under, but figure on about $100 per person. L.A.B. also offers several other trips, including a half-hour flight over some nearby glaciers, perhaps at around $75 in 1990.

Back down to earth, now, the aforementioned **Haines Street Car Company** (tel. *766–2891*) has a couple of bus tours—the three-hour city tour for around $20 and a one-hour version designed for ongoing ferry passengers at $10 or so.

Bird-watching bus/hiking excursions into the Valley of the Eagles are offered by **Alaska Nature Tours** (tel. *766–2876*). Figure on $50 or so by now for a three-hour experience. It's not cheap, but they do throw in a bottle of jam. We haven't been; if you go, let us know.

Four-hour rubber raft float trips on the quiet, glacier-fed Chilkat River through the eagle preserve are launched daily in the summer by **Chilkat Guides** (tel. *766–2409*), P.O. Box 1049. This includes a look at the Indian village of Klukwan and travel through wild and scenic areas not accessible by road. There's no whitewater travel, but it's considered by some to be one of the nicest trips of its type in Alaska. The fare may be up to $60 or $65 by now for the 4½-hour experience. This one is on our "must do" list. The same company also offers a two-day fly-in, raft-out adventure deep into the mountains and glaciers for around $250. Recheck for details or write to Box 170 in Haines.

Longer rafting and hiking expeditions—from 3 to 10 days—have been set up by **Alaska Cross Country** (tel. *766–2040*). Call or write in advance for details to Box 124.

Some of the above experiences plus a few of their own are offered by the **Travel Connection** (tel. *766–2585*), which is headquartered across from the Visitor Information Center. A two-hour cruise along the shores of Chilkoot Lake will cost perhaps $30.

SPORTS

If your shoes were made for *walking,* be sure to pick up the pamphlet entitled *Haines Is for Hikers* from the visitors' center. *The* big hike in Haines up nearby Mt. Ripinsky (nearly 4000 feet), and the trail begins at the end of Second Ave. But there are some suggestions in the brochure for less challenging treks, too. Don't forget to take noisemakers to warn any bears that might be on your same itinerary!

Fishing, both ocean and freshwater, is generally good out of Haines. Fly fishing for dolly varden and perhaps cutthroat trout is popular in both Chilkat Lake and Chilkoot Lake. The former is in the eagle preserve. The latter is at the end of the road north of town. The atmosphere is unsurpassed at either location. Ocean fishing for halibut is usually excellent throughout the summer. For fishing guides and charter boats, check for a list at the visitors' center. Fees may run about $125 a day.

Hunting? There's a lottery for moose permits, and they all go to the local residents. Try goats, maybe, in the fall.

As in other Southeast cities, the whole town goes nuts over *basketball* in the winter and *baseball* in the summer. Guest cheerers are always welcome.

SHOPPING

After eagles and dancers, Haines also enjoys a current reputation as an artists' colony, and more than 30 are now in residence. Native and non-Native works in several media can be purchased all over town.

Several galleries and workshops have been installed in the old military buildings at Fort Seward. The **Sea Wolf,** in the Totem Village (on the parade ground next to the salmon bake), features *Indian-inspired woodwork, jewelry, and prints* by Treshem Gregg, who grew up in Haines and returned in later years. Genuine *Native crafts* are featured at **Alaska Indian Arts** in the former post hospital at 23 Fort Seward

Dr. (You can even buy a whole totem pole if you want.) The nonprofit shop was set up by Carl Heinmiller, of Chilkat Dancers fame, to revive lost Indian carving talent. In a back room of the same building, Fred and Madeleine Shields sell their own *jewelry, prints, etc.,* at **The Wild Iris.** And woodworker Lowell Knutson, a retired logger, runs **Knute's Shop** at No. 5 Officers' Row. The **Art Shop,** a former military telegraph office, is on Beach Rd., just downhill from the parade ground. Several local artists are represented there.

In downtown Haines, at **Chilkat Valley Arts,** at 307 Willard St., Tlingit artist Sue Folletti shows her *silver and wood carvings* along with the works of others. **Northern Arts Gallery,** featuring *silk screens* by Pete Andriesen, is another worth looking into across Second Ave. from the Visitor Information Center. Nearby, **The Trading Post** sells *furs and Indian crafts.* **Helen's Shop,** on Main Street between Second and Third avenues, has some *Alaskan-made jewelry.*

Tlingit artifacts are sold in the shop at the **Sheldon Museum,** at the foot of Main Street. You'll also find plenty of *gimcrack and bric-a-brac* at **Bell's Store** on Second Ave., across from the Pioneer Bar (overnight film developing, too). *Antiques* and other old stuff are fun to poke through at the **Moose Horn** at Third Ave. and Main St.

Gasoline? When we were last in Haines, the best gas prices (cash only) were at **Totem Oil,** on the way out of town at the corner of Main St. and the Haines Highway. Since then, **Second Avenue Auto Service,** 355 Second Ave., has been running Friday afternoon "happy hours" with 10 cents per gallon off! The last gas in the U.S. before crossing the Canadian border is at the **33-Mile Roadhouse,** 33 miles north on the Haines Highway.

Groceries? Try **Howsers Supermarket** on Main St., between Second and Third avenues.

Bookstores? An intellectual publishing, sales, and rental establishment is the **Gutenberg Dump** a block or two north of the center on Second Ave. "We try to salvage a few good books from the tons of trash published annually," they explain. So do we all. (Irregular hours.)

MISCELLANEOUS ADDRESSES AND PHONES

The Haines zip code in 99827, and probably all of the places mentioned above can be written to with that, even if you forget the box number or street address. All telephone numbers in Haines itself begin with 776.

- Alaska Laundry and Dry Cleaners (tel. *766–2030*), c/o Wings of Alaska, Second Ave.
- Alaska State Fish & Wildlife (tel. *766–2533*), Main St. above Howsers Supermarket.
- Alaska State Parks (tel. *766–2292*), between Second and Third on Main St., above Helen's Gift Shop.
- Canada Customs (tel. *767–5540*), Mile 42, Haines Highway.
- Chilkat Center for the Arts (tel. *766–2160*), P.O. Box 288.
- Emergencies of all types (tel. 911).
- Fire department (tel. *766–2115*).
- First National Bank of Anchorage (tel. *766–2321*), Main St.
- Haines Visitor Association (tel. *766–2234*), Second Ave. and Willard St., P.O. Box 518.
- Hair Bender Beauty & Tanning Salon ("Styling for Men and Women," tel. *766–2969*), above Harbor Bar, foot of Main St.
- Medical Center, Dr. Stan Jones (tel. *766–2121*).
- Police (tel. *766–2121*).
- Post Office (tel. *766–2930*), Haines Highway near City Hall.
- State Troopers (tel. *766–2552*).
- Susie Q's Laundromat, Main St. across from the museum.
- U.S. Customs (tel. *767–5511*), Mile 42, Haines Highway.
- Visitor Information Center (tel. *766–2234*), Second Ave. near Willard St.

SKAGWAY

Once they called it "Hell on earth," but today Skagway is just plain fun. In 1898, of course, it was the largest town in Alaska and one of the wildest and woolliest towns in the world. It was ruled with an iron hand by Jefferson "Soapy" Smith and his gang of professional con men and crooks. They preyed on the hopes and dreams of thousands of prospectors who landed first in Skagway to begin their struggle to reach the gold fields of the Klondike.

You'll read and hear again and again of the final shootout between Soapy and town surveyor Frank Reid, a relatively upstanding citizen who finally had stood enough. Both men died—one a villain, the other a hero—and you can compare their graves in the local boot hill.

Probably the most intriguing aspect of Skagway is that virtually all of the buildings in its center date from just before and just after the turn

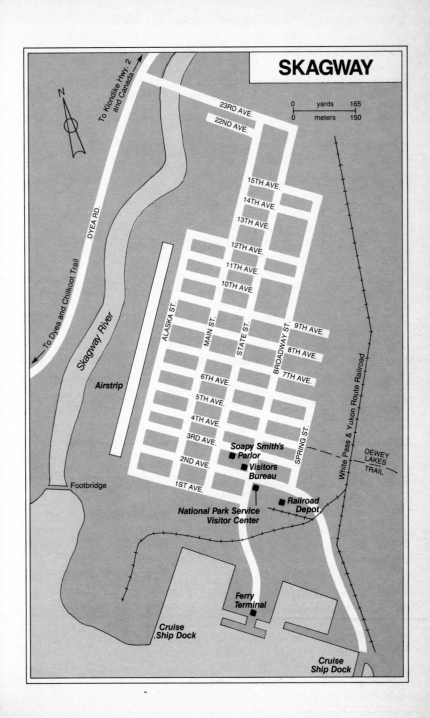

SKAGWAY

yards 0 — 165
meters 0 — 150

To Klondike Hwy. 2 and Canada

23RD AVE.
22ND AVE.

DYEA RD.

To Dyea and Chilkoot Trail

Skagway River

15TH AVE.
14TH AVE.
13TH AVE.
12TH AVE.
11TH AVE.
10TH AVE.
9TH AVE.
8TH AVE.
7TH AVE.
6TH AVE.
5TH AVE.
4TH AVE.
3RD AVE.
2ND AVE.
1ST AVE.

ALASKA ST.
MAIN ST.
STATE ST.
BROADWAY ST.
SPRING ST.

Airstrip

Footbridge

White Pass & Yukon Route Railroad

DEWEY LAKES TRAIL

Soapy Smith's Parlor

Visitors Bureau

National Park Service Visitor Center

Railroad Depot

Ferry Terminal

Cruise Ship Dock

Cruise Ship Dock

of the century. If Soapy were to come alive today, he would have no trouble getting his bearings. There is the hotel, the theater, the railroad station, and other structures which formed "his" town; even Soapy's old bar is still around, although perhaps in much better condition than he ever knew it to be.

One of the reasons for all this is that much of the town itself is an integral part of the Klondike Gold Rush National Historical Park. Here rangers do not take out nature hikes and speak of bears, birds, rocks, and trees. Instead, they lead historical walks, pointing out taverns and hardware stores and explaining their significance in the history of Alaska and the Yukon. The buildings controlled by the National Park Service have been authentically restored, right down to the color of the paint they wore nearly a century ago.

With Frank Reid's strict grid pattern of avenues from First through Twenty-second, and streets with dignified, urban-sounding names like State and Broadway, Skagway addresses sound like locations in an early Chicago or New York. But the city, which held 20,000 or more a century ago, now numbers a permanent population of less than 750, and in winter it truly becomes a community more of ghosts than of living residents.

Skagway today is simply an American small town, where most folks know one another, and on a one-to-one basis, it's one of the friendliest places in Alaska. Outside of the few involved in fishing and the shipping business, most are concerned primarily with tourism, spending nine months of the year preparing for what we will spend during the other three. In June, July, and August it successfully recaptures some of the excitement, although without the danger, of the "Days of '98."

TRANSPORTATION

The town is the most northern port on the state ferry system, and all boats tie up to the terminal of the **Alaska Marine Highway** (tel. *983–2941*) right at the end of Broadway. It is the ideal place to leave your ferry tour of Southeast before heading up into the Yukon and thence to Central Alaska. (If you are considering joining the ferry system here, be sure to see our remarks on the Marine Highway in general in "Coming Into the Country.") In summer, try to arrive in Skagway on a Friday or Saturday, when there are seldom any cruise ships in town and things are less crowded.

Most cruise ships, like Princess Cruises or Regency Cruises, disembark at the special **Cruise Ship Dock** just southeast of town. Incidentally, large ships of the Holland America Line do not come to

Skagway, avoiding a schedule that would find them sailing up the scenic Lynn Canal in the dark. Most of their passengers who want to continue on to Skagway stay overnight in Juneau first and then travel aboard the day boat called the *Fairweather* run by **Westours** (tel. *983–2241*), a Holland America subsidiary. Cruisers joining Holland America ships in Juneau, of course, take the *Fairweather* in the opposite direction from Skagway.

Independent travelers can make the 4½-hour cruise in either direction, too, for around $125. The *Fairweather* ties up at the Small Boat Harbor. Another dock, normally used by ore boats, is at the end of State Street, to the west of the ferry terminal. The *Stardancer,* the cruise ship that carries cars and motor homes, usually ties up there.

Long considered fairly isolated, Skagway has marked the southern end of the **Klondike Highway** (Route 2) since the road was completed in 1978. The highway travels about 110 scenic miles to Whitehorse in the Yukon Territory, and it's now open year round. (Don't forget to gas up in Skagway where it's cheaper than in Canada.) As noted earlier, road travelers can now make a 360-mile "Golden Circle" route between Skagway and Haines, two towns that are less than one hour or 15 miles apart on the ferry—or 10 minutes by air.

Drivers on the Skagway-Whitehorse route should watch out for the many heavy trucks that travel this route, most of them 85-footers carting ore from Yukon lead, zinc, and silver mines to be shipped out from Skagway. These somewhat frightening bright-yellow vehicles, some with about 30 wheels, and each of which carry four round brobdingnagian jars, are usually operated by excellent drivers who pull over at specially constructed points on the highway to let individual automobile traffic go by. Drive with your lights on along this highway, even during the day.

Bus service between Skagway, Whitehorse, Haines, Fairbanks, Anchorage, Denali, and points in between is available via a Gray Line subsidiary now called **Alaskon Express** (tel. *983–2241*), formerly White Pass & Yukon Motorcoaches, headquartered in the Westmark Hotel. Fares for 1990 are uncertain at this writing, but figure somewhere around $60 for Skagway-Whitehorse or $200 for Skagway-Anchorage.

Airports? Well, an air strip runs almost the full length of the community on the west side of town next to the Skagway River. No jets are permitted in this mountainous terrain, but there is scheduled prop service to or from Juneau non-stop on **Skagway Air Service** (tel. *983–2218*), and via Haines and/or Gustavus on **L.A.B. Flying Service** (tel. *983–2472*) or **Haines Airways** (Haines tel. *766–2646*), both headquartered in Haines, along with **Gustavus Air Service** (from Gustavus), and the well-known **Wings of Alaska** (tel. *983–2442*), out of Juneau. A tiny terminal beside the runway at Alaska St. and 11th Ave.

As for getting around town, the place is too small for a bus service.

Taxis come and go, but at present you can try **Goldie's** (tel. *983–2321*) or **Sourdough** (tel. *983–2521*). Sourdough will also take you as far as Whitehorse in about eight hours, at rates competitive with the bus. (A couple of other outfits in town act as taxis when they're not busy taking out tours.) And a horse-and-buggy operation (we mean that literally) is run by **Skagway Hack** (tel. *983–2472*).

All hotels offer courtesy transportation from the ferry and the airport. You can get around the immediate central area without a car, but if you're going to stay in Skagway two days (two or three is a good idea), you probably would like to have a car for at least one of those, for tripping out to the cemetery, over to Dyea, etc. There were a couple of car companies at last report. **Avis** (tel. *983–2550*) parked at the Westmark, and the independent **Services Unlimited** (tel. *983–2595*), at the Second Street Chevron Station. It is affiliated with Eagle Car Rentals in Haines, so one-way trips may be arranged over the "Golden Circle." Motor scooters and bicycles can be rented from **STS** (tel. *983–2519*). Hourly rates may seem expensive. You'll get the best deal, of course, with all-day rates.

What about Skagway's famous railroad? The train is mainly an excursion only, although at this writing it is just about to be possible to travel between Skagway and Whitehorse by a train/bus combination. Full details are full speed ahead in "Tours and Cruises."

HOTELS AND MOTELS

Better have your reservations nailed down solid for July—and it's a darn good idea in June and August, too. Sales tax in Skagway is 4%, except for hotel rooms which are taxed at 6%. Many stay in Skagway only one night; we recommend at least two, possibly three. All hotels may be written to at zip code 99840.

The nicest rooms at the best price are at an unlikely motel operation run by a former brakeman out by the railroad yards. The **Wind Valley Lodge** (tel. *983–2236*), 22nd and State St., is almost the first place you see after driving into town. Large, high-ceilinged lobby, with a ticking clock and lots of railroad pictures; fireplace and TV in the lounge; new landscaping outdoors; guest laundry; spread-out layout of 30 large, well-kept, well-equipped rooms; room telephones and TVs (both fairly unusual in Skagway); table and chairs; good lighting and storage space; comfortable twin or queen beds; free transportation to and from ferries, trains, and planes; easy-on-the-pocket rates, probably still around $65 for two. This place started out as a retirement project by Les Fairbanks and his wife Judy, and when we were there last it was by far the fairest deal in town. (Reservations from the hotel at P.O. Box 354.)

Some other establishments admittedly are a little more conveniently located for carless travelers. For airplane buffs (and tobacco abstainers) this goes double for the **Gold Rush Lodge** (tel. *983–2831*) open from June through August right next to the Skagway runway. (In fact some plane tie-downs are right outside the back door.) There are only a dozen rooms, but all are neat, clean, and feature twin beds, color TVs mounted on the walls, clean showers, etc. There are no room phones, but a convenient pay phone is available. Ask Vicki to show you the hole in the wall to keep your milk cold. This one is for nonsmokers only, and be aware that some planes may start taking off earlier than you do. Double rates at perhaps $75 or so for 1990. (Reservations from P.O. Box 514 in Skagway or address winter correspondence to P.O. Box 924, Alturas, CA 96101.)

Unfortunately you won't find his famous husky, Yukon King, living at **Sergeant Preston's Lodge** (tel. *983–2521*), on Sixth Ave., just a half-block from Broadway. But the comfortable lobby is occupied by a nameless bear and mountain goat (who I guess aren't really *living* there either, come to think of it). Spread out from that point are a grassy lawn and picnic table, a large flag, and 24 generally comfortable rooms with twin beds (many with TVs). Most doubles have private bath at around $70 or so. A few share some common plumbing at rates of around $60. Fresh popcorn is available in the lobby after 5 p.m. for a dollar, but continental breakfasts are included in the room rates. Housekeeping can be a little erratic at times. (It's hard to keep your staff when the *Columbia* sails in from Seattle and outbids everyone for every maid in town for the day.) All in all, we call it pretty good for the price. (Reservations from P.O. Box 538.) By the by, Sergeant Preston's has been affiliated with the nearby and much smaller **Irene's Inn** (tel. *983–2520*), which now has gotten its own phone number. Sorry, we haven't inspected Irene's separately, but we will next time.

Certainly the most interesting accommodations in Skagway are at the venerable **Golden North** (tel. *983–2451*), which stakes a claim to being the oldest hotel in Alaska, tracing its framework back to 1898. You'll see their ad in reproductions of the same issue of the paper that reports the death of Soapy Smith (at an address before it was towed, in 1908, to its present site at Third Avenue and Broadway and then enlarged). This is also home of "Mary," a benevolent apparition who usually floats around Room 13 or Room 24 (accounts vary) in her wedding dress. There are 33 rooms, each dedicated to a local family who contributed the old-fashioned furnishings in it. The place is a bit creaky and antiquey, but there's a dining room/bar, and it's certainly authentic—ideal for the more adventurous spirit. Choose the third floor for more light and less noise. Doubles are around $75 with private bath, maybe $10 less than that with plumbing "down the hall." (Open year round; reservations from P.O. Box 431.)

In a similar vein (historic, although not haunted), the **Skagway Inn** (tel. *983–2289*), at Broadway and Seventh Ave., is a former bordello. A piano gracing the old-fashioned parlor; dining room to one side (with excellent meals); most rooms up the creaky stairs; all with names of former occupants instead of numbers; Alice, a front room with brass bed and sun porch, our own favorite; Hattie also light and airy; no units with their own bathroom, unfortunately; doubles should be in the $50 range. Fun for some, anyway. (Reservations from Suzanne Mullen at P.O. Box 13.)

Some might put the expensive **Westmark Skagway** (tel. *983–2291*), formerly the Sheffield Klondike, at Third and Spring, near the top of the category. However we found it inefficient in nearly every way. Among our criticisms: no phone, no TV, no closet, no drawers, no full-length mirror, frequently no bellhop, cheap, banged-up furnishings, small rooms, and almost no light—and all that for plenty of money—in excess of $125 a night, amounts that almost seem to be calculated to discourage FITs. The restaurant is all right, except perhaps for the loudspeaker announcements. The lobby is often crowded to excess. All in all we found naivete at almost every turn in an operation geared almost exclusively to mass—rather than class—tourism. (Open summer only.)

We know of two tiny bed-and-breakfasts in town. **Mary's** (tel. *983–2875*), at 10th Ave. and State St., has only three rooms. **Gramma's** (tel. *983–2312*), has only four. Sorry, we haven't seen either; both are often hopelessly booked.

There are three RV parks—**Pullen Creek Park** (City RV Park), on the waterfront, is the most attractive. **Hoover's Chevron,** at Fourth Ave. and State St. is more convenient, within easy walking distance of most sightseeing targets; and **Hanousek Park,** at 13th Avenue and Broadway, is an area that doesn't show us much. All these are under the same management and can be phoned at *983–2454* or written at P.O. Box 304.

RESTAURANTS AND DINING

Probably still the best restaurant in town is **Miss Suzanne's Tea Room** (tel. *983–2289*), in the creaky old dining room of the creaky old Skagway Inn. Surrounded by flowered wallpaper and an undisciplined philodendron, we enjoyed some gourmet presentations (try the chicken breast in puff pastry). It's unpretentious, and with the acoustics that prevail you may overhear some occasional disagreement between the waiters and the cook. Nevertheless, it's obvious that somebody in charge really cares about food. No alcohol.

When things were not crowded, we were satisfied with the **Chilkoot Dining Room** (tel. *983–2291*) in the Westmark, for standard hotel fare. Decor of *fin de siecle* blowups of Skagway, overhead fans, and wooden walls; willing if amateurish service; tables too close together; good sour mash stew. Be warned that it has a habit of broadcasting to tour groups over the p.a. And like some other Skagway chuck wagons, it also closes promptly at 9 p.m.

There are two or three popular local hangouts for small-town honest, fair-and-square meals. The **Northern Lights Cafe** (tel. *983–2225*) features one of those black-felt paintings you see all over Alaska—a lonely cabin huddled in the snow under the shimmering protection of the Aurora Borealis. (Sometimes these are painted on gold pans or saw blades.) Outside is a signboard featuring Soapy Smith: "Soapy says, 'You always get a square deal at the Northern Lights Cafe,' " a dubious recommendation since S.S. was Skagway's most notorious crook. Anyway, the soup, roast beef, mashed potatoes, etc., were fine on our evening under the Northern Lights. We know a discerning local gourmet who goes there especially for halibut burgers.

Another old standby is **Prospector's Sourdough** (tel. *983–2865*), on Broadway at Fourth Ave. Pink walls, linoleum floor, black booths, bright fluorescent lights—that kind of place. Our evening grub was okay, although service was somewhat harried (pork chops or fried chicken for around $10). Breakfast is better known for things like sourdough waffles with reindeer sausage. Some report better luck at the **Sweet Tooth Saloon** (tel. *983–2405*), at least for homemade soups and hamburgers, and one of the largest breakfasts in town. The doughnuts are fresh, too, It's also on Broadway, nearer to Third Avenue. And on Second Avenue, between Broadway and Spring, across from the depot, **Jo-Dees** is a usually dependable choice for salmon, steak, or burgers.

Sweet stuff? For ice cream, fudge, and all that, try the **Kone Kompany** at the corner of Broadway and Fifth Ave.

Pizza? Take out and delivery orders are handled at **Kountry Kitchen** (tel. *983–2440*), at Fourth Ave. and State St.

ENTERTAINMENT AND NIGHT LIFE

Skagway's big summer show for summer visitors is the production of *Skagway in the Days of '98* (tel. *983–2234*), a full-scale live musical melodrama. Based generally on the true story of Soapy Smith and the gold rush, the performance is in the Eagles Dance Hall at Broadway and Sixth. If you skipped similar productions in Ketchikan, Juneau, and Haines (or even if you didn't), this may be the one you've been waiting for. It also includes an hour of mock gambling at blackjack and roulette tables first. Fare for all the fun is around $15. We had a great time. Don't miss it.

A half-hour movie, "White Pass & Yukon" is sometimes shown throughout the day at the **Arctic Brotherhood Hall** (tel. *983–2908*). Originally a 1963 CBC documentary, it costs $2.50. Another film, "Days of Adventure, Dreams of Gold," narrated by Hal Holbrook, is shown free several times daily in the N.P.S. Visitor Center.

Skagway's favorite bar for young and old alike is the **Red Onion Saloon** at the corner of Broadway and Second Ave., housed in a former house of ill repute. It's decorated with an appropriate assortment of moose antlers, life preservers, snow shoes, 1890s-style pinups, and other flotsam and jetsam. Music runs the full range in here, from rock to reggae to ragtime, depending on the crowd. This is the place where the shipboard entertainers often whoop it up on their own time, doing all the stuff that's forbidden on the more stuffy cruises. Sometimes the Onion gets a little crowded, and couples find themselves dancing outside on the boardwalk.

Lots of locals hang out at the rough-looking **Moe's Frontier Bar,** which claims to be the oldest tavern continuously under one name in Alaska (and it has been advertising on the side of the cliff for almost a century, too). It's on Broadway, between Fourth and Fifth avenues. If you see any frightening people in Moe's, they're probably only tourists.

SIGHTS AND SITES

First, head for the headquarters of the **Klondike Gold Rush National Historical Park** (tel. *983–2921*) in the old railroad station which has become the park visitor center. (Open 'til 8 p.m. in summer, 6 in winter) it's catercorner from the Red Onion Saloon at Broadway and Second Avenue. Be sure to pick up at least two free pamphlets, the full-color park service brochure and either the N.P.S.'s "Skagway: Some Steps on the Gold Rush Trail" or "Skagway Alaska Walking Tour: Footsteps Into the Land of Gold," produced by the Skagway Convention and Visitors Bureau.

Check out the photo displays and 30-minute movies, and make arrangements to tag along with the lone ranger on one of the hour-long walking tours through the old town, perhaps still leaving at 11 a.m. and 3 p.m. (Incidentally, the sidewalks are still wooden in Skagway, but they draw the authenticity line at dirt streets; thankfully, they're all paved.)

Among the places you will see on your town walk are the **Arctic Brotherhood Hall** (called the A. B., locally), faced with thousands of pieces of driftwood, and which is probably the most photographed structure in the state; **Jeff Smith's Parlor,** the bar/headquarters owned by Soapy Smith, the old-time "boss" of Skagway; the **Golden North Hotel,** with its golden dome, and **Captain Moore's Cabin,** dating from 1887, the very first building in Skagway. There are many more.

We were fascinated, too, with the sad ruins of the **Pullen House** and its grounds, all of which is private property and dangerously run-down (don't enter the building). It was once *the* grand hotel of Skagway. President Warren Harding stayed there as the guest of Harriet "Ma" Pullen, who operated it for 50 years. Nearby is the **Trail of '98 Museum** upstairs in the former court room over the City Hall/Police Station at the end of Seventh Ave. Check out the blanket made entirely from the skin of duck necks. Admission $2.

You'll need a car or a taxi, but don't forget to head out to the **Gold Rush Cemetery** beyond the railroad yards north of town (follow State Street, then the train tracks). You'll see the contrasting graves of Soapy Smith and Frank Reid, the man who shot him. Many other markers also tell sad tales of life on the northern frontier.

SIDE TRIPS

As in Haines and Juneau, you can take flying trips to the previously described **Glacier Bay.** Most flightseeing excursions run about 90 minutes. (See "Tours and Cruises.")

With a car, you can drive 10 miles of twists and turns to the site of Skagway's rival city, **Dyea** (pronounced "die-yee"), which became a ghost town in 1903 and now has almost totally disappeared. (Some Dyea buildings were floated to Şkagway where a few survive. Skagway itself was kept alive by the railroad.) Before you reach Dyea, keep an eye out for the ranger's cabin where you can pick up a Xeroxed map of the areas, pointing out the few ruins which remain.

Also near here is the trailhead for the famous, or infamous, **Chilkoot Trail,** one of the passages into Canada to the Klondike goldfields. Those who plan to backpack over the 33-mile trail should get a copy of the special map/folder produced jointly by the U.S. National Park Service and Parks Canada (the Canadian equivalent). We also recommend buying a 200-page handbook, *Chilkoot Pass* by Archie Satterfield, if you can find it. At a minimum, you should have a lightweight tent, camp stove, food, warm clothing, and rain gear, even in summer. So many artifacts are scattered along this trail it has been called the longest outdoor museum in America, and about 2000 hike the trail annually. Some change their minds after seeing the steep portion once dubbed the "Golden Stairs," but the brochure is interesting even to those who forego the hike. (You can now return on the train—see "Tours and Cruises.")

If you're driving the Klondike Highway to Whitehorse, you'll find the 24-hour Canadian customs station after about 20 generally steep miles at **Fraser.** (The WP&YR Railroad will probably be operating to here again by the time you read these words.) Most travelers pause at **Carcross,** 65 miles from Skagway on the shores of Lake Bennett. There's an old stern wheeler now permanently beached, and some other outdoor museum pieces around. The former WP&YR railroad station has been made into a souvenir shop. We had a hamburger in the old hotel. (We graded it B for the burger; A for authentic rural atmosphere.) The sand dunes a mile north are considered to be the smallest desert in the world.

TOURS AND CRUISES

In the early 1900s, shortly after the Klondike gold rush had run its course, someone suggested to the president of the railroad that ran between Skagway and Whitehorse that his company might be able to pick up some change by catering to tourists. "Tourists!" the man exclaimed. "What in hell would a tourist want to come to this God-forsaken country for?"

For the past two years, Skagway's best tour and its premier attraction of all kinds has been the recently rejuvenated **White Pass & Yukon Route Railroad** (tel. *983–2214*). This summer-only excursion represents a labor of love for many who worked for years to bring the narrow-gauge train back to life. Built during the height of the gold rush, the railroad ran a regular schedule for the 100 miles between Skagway and Whitehorse from 1900 to 1982, when it was closed down after losing its freight business to the highway. In 1988 the railroad was reopened for 20 scenic and historic miles as a tourist attraction, following the scenic and historic Trail of '98 at least as far as White Pass itself. A 3½-hour, 40-mile round trip on the line cost around $70, and normally there are two trips a day, at 9 a.m. and 1:30 p.m. This schedule may be amended, however, since the railroad now has permission to travel as far as the Canadian Customs station at Fraser, and there are also active plans to take it eventually at least to the town of Carcross.

As things stand now, you can buy a special combination ticket which will take you as far as Fraser, a little beyond the Canadian border, on the train. There you change to a bus operated by **Atlas Motor Coaches** out of Whitehorse. The whole trip, in either direction, takes about 3½ hours and tickets are around $100.

Sore-footed hikers who have spent three or four days on the Chilkoot Trail to Lake Bennett can now catch the train and travel back to Skagway for around $70, the same price as a round-trip excursion ticket from Skagway. Other refinements that may be in effect soon include a train/plane excursion with **Temsco Helicopters** (see below). Passengers would travel one way by train, the other through the pass back to Skagway by helicopter.

The exact picture on all this could be different in the summer of 1990, although it will be a long time, if ever, before the train is put clear through to Whitehorse itself again. For the very latest before arriving in Skagway, you can call the WP&YR's own toll-free number, *(800) 347–7373*.

By the way, today's WP&YR station is the more modern building next to the old depot which was commandeered by the N.P.S. The atmospheric old steam engine is only used on the flat areas; for the trip up to the pass, they switch to a more modern diesel. We recommend riding the last car, especially for photographers. However you do it, by all means, don't miss the train.

A 2½-hour bus excursion known as the *Skagway Historical Tour* is run daily in the afternoon by **Gray Line of Alaska** (tel. *983–2241*), leaving from its headquarters in the Westmark. Besides the tour through the streets, it includes stops at the museum and the cemetery for a total price of around $20. There's a similar tour, with perhaps more personality, given by uniformed drivers of the **Skagway Streetcar Co.** (tel. *983–2908*). The SSC piles everyone into buses that date back to about 1936 and were once used at Yellowstone. We're going to try them next time. Also **Frontier Excursions** (tel. *983–2512*), a taxi operation, will set up some personalized tours to the areas we've been talking about.

Gray Line (tel. *983–2241*) also offers a casual two-hour "Trail Head Cruise" aboard the 65-foot *Glacier Queen I* along the headwaters of the Lynn Canal as far as Dyea, and a stop at a fish hatchery. We'll guess the fare in 1990 at about $32, including some smoked salmon munchies.

Alaska Yukon Gold Rush Camping Tours (tel. *983–2289*) may still have a 3-hour trip to Dyea which includes some goldpanning experiences for a fare of $35 or so. This may be a better deal for cruisers than for individual travelers who will have many more opportunities for gold panning throughout Alaska and the Yukon. Cruise ships also sell a *"Tent City" tour,* in which visitors are taken to a re-creation of an 1890s mining camp for food and entertainment. We haven't been able to run this one down by press time, and it may not even be available to FITs. If you go, let us know.

Three or four helicopter tours may be available this year on **Temsco Helicopters** (tel. *983–2909*) from their headquarters in the little cabin between the town and the ferry dock. The "Chilkoot Trail and Glacier" tour is 45 minutes over the famous trail and includes a landing on an alpine glacier for around $125. The "Trails of '98" tour includes all that plus a flight over the White Pass Trail, for 1¼ hours for around $175. A half-hour "Valley of the Glaciers" tour also has a brief glacier landing for around $85. And, as indicated above, a new trip may involve a combination with a trip on the WP&YR railroad. (We haven't taken these, but were happy with our Temsco trip in Juneau.)

There are several *flightseeing tours* in fixed-wing aircraft, too. Figure about $125 for a one-hour trip, of $75 for a half-hour. **Skagway Air Service** (tel. *983–2218*) offers a 45-minute "Gold Rush Tour" over the Chilkoot Pass and a 1½-hour "Glacier Bay Scenic Flight." **L.A.B. Flying Service** (tel. *983–2471*) has a one-hour Glacier Bay tour and a 30-minute Skagway Trail of '98 tour. Some similar trips may also be available on **Wings of Alaska** (tel. *983–2442*).

SPORTS

Forget hunting in this area; it just isn't practical if you don't live here. Dedicated *anglers* who don't give a hoot for history might check with **Seatonic Charters** (tel. *983–2834*), which has a 45-footer that can be had for around $500 a half-day or an 18-foot aluminum tri-hull which goes for around $15 per hour per person.

Hikers will find plenty of trails to follow, but first be sure to see the U.S.N.P.S. program on local hiking at the Visitor Center. (In 1988, it was given daily at 4 p.m.) You can head for the Dewey Lake Trail straight out of Third Ave. in Skagway, and fish for lake trout when you get there. The infamous gold rush Chilkoot Trail begins at Dyea and extends for 33 miles. Now that the WP&YR has reopened its spur to Lake Bennett, you no longer have to trudge back, as long as you've got $70 or so in your poke. Hikers will also appreciate the fact that Skagway is probably the driest city in the panhandle—less than 30 inches of rain most years.

Like others in Southeast Alaska, Skagway folk follow *basketball* in the winter and *softball* in the summer, playing until it gets dark— usually at around 11 p.m. at the ballpark at 13th Ave. and Main St. You'll find a tournament most weekends throughout the summer.

Running has become an avid avocation for many in Skagway in the 1980s. There are several events, of which the most arduous must be the Klondike Trail of '98 Road Relay. Teams from all over the U.S. and Canada compete in the race which runs, walks, or staggers the 110 miles between Skagway and Whitehorse. Much more fun, surely, is the Hugs and Kisses Run in August. The winners—and even the losers—are rewarded by (you guessed it), given of course by members of the runner's opposite sex.

SHOPPING

The work of Alaskan *artists and artisans,* some of them from the Skagway area, is for sale at shops up and down Broadway. Among popular items are *gold nugget jewelry, carved walrus ivory, jade wood, or soapstone carvings,* and, of course, *paintings, silk screens,* etc.

For *ivory* products, we'd normally head first to **Corrington's** in the green-and-yellow structure with a turret at Fifth and Broadway. In addition to items for sale, Dennis Corrington (from St. Louis) now has opened an attractive museum on the premises with more than 1000 artifacts and 32 exhibits. You may also find that Tlingit totem pole carver at work there, and it's worth the $2 or so extra to go through.

Another interesting and historic store is **Kirmse's,** for *jewelry and handicraft,* across Broadway from Corrington's. See the big watch up on the side of the cliff east of town? Kirmse's has been advertising there since it first opened its doors in 1897. You'll also find gold nugget jewelry at **Taiya River** at 252 Broadway, across from the A. B. Hall between Second and Third avenues. Casey McBride is the resident goldsmith.

One of Alaska's best-known *ivory sculptors* is represented at the **David Present Gallery** at Broadway and Third, across from the Golden North. Several other Alaskan artists are also exhibited. And for *Pacific Northwest Indian art,* try **Inside Passage Arts,** Broadway and Fourth, which carries some of the best *Native masks* and other crafts in the Panhandle. Also, there is **Native Carvings & Gifts,** at Second and Broadway, where owner/artist Richard Dick exhibits some of his own work.

If you're interested in learning more about the railroad and its role in the gold rush, look for a small blue book entitled *Doing the White Pass* by Howard Clifford. The period is also covered well in *Chilkoot Pass* by Archie Satterfield.

Groceries? You'll find most of the necessities of life at the **Fairway Market** at Fourth Ave. and State St.

MISCELLANEOUS ADDRESSES AND PHONES

A telephone often seems to be a rare animal in Skagway. Almost never do you get one in a hotel room, and even coin-operated phones are hard to find. We searched out six public phone locations, but we hope there are more by now: outdoors (often in the rain) on the wall of the Sweet Tooth Saloon; at the ferry terminal (when it is open); at the City (Pullen Creek) RV Park near the waterfront; at the cruise ship dock; at Hoover's Chevron Station, Fourth and Main; and at the Gold Rush Lodge. Since we were last in town, new phones were also installed in the 1900s Building on Sixth Avenue, next to the Molly Walsh Park.

Telephone numbers in Skagway all begin with 983, and you have to dial all seven numbers these days. The zip code is 99840.

- Dahl Memorial Medical Clinic (tel. *983–2255*), 11th Ave. and Broadway.
- Emergencies, miscellaneous. Telephone police number below.
- Fire Department (tel. *983–2300*), Fifth Ave. and State St.
- Klothes Rush Laundry (tel. *983–2370*), corner of Fifth Ave. and Broadway.
- National Bank of Alaska (tel. *983–2264*), Broadway and Sixth Ave.
- National Park Service (tel. *983–2921*), Broadway and Second Ave., P.O. Box 517.
- Police department (tel. *983–2301*), Broadway and Spring streets.
- Post Office (tel. *983–2330*), Broadway near Sixth Ave.
- Principal Barber (tel. *983–2547*), Broadway between Fifth and Sixth avenues.
- Public library (tel. *983–2665*), Eighth Ave. and State St.
- U.S. Customs Service (tel. *983–2325*).
- Visitors Bureau (tel. *983–2854*), City Hall, P.O. Box 415.

THE CALL OF THE YUKON—WHITEHORSE AND DAWSON

It has a magical sound to it still. In the 1890s, gold stampeders headed for "The Yukon," or sometimes "The Klondike," with only a vague idea of its meaning or location. It was up north somewhere and it possessed gold available just for the scraping. It might as well have been "Valhalla."

A half-century later, radio listeners thrilled to the adventures of Yukon King, a magnificent malamute and noble friend of "Sergeant Preston of the Yukon," an officer in the North West Mounted Police. The exploits of this red-coated Mountie and his faithful canine companion were almost the only thing I knew about Canada in the 1940s. (Years later, I discovered the sergeant and his dog were the creations of a Detroit radio station—the same folks who gave the world the Lone Ranger.)

Today the Yukon is an official territory whose boundaries make it larger than California. Its capital is Whitehorse, a small city near the beginning of the Yukon River. Most road travelers pass through Whitehorse en route to Central Alaska, whether they come up the Alaska or Cassiar highways from southern Canada or over the Klondike Highway from the ferry terminus at Skagway. Only passengers disembarking at Haines skip Whitehorse, although they must still cut through a corner of the Yukon Territory on their way to Tok and thence to Fairbanks or Anchorage.

Dawson, the former seat of government, is often called Dawson City today in order to avoid confusion with Dawson Creek, at the beginning of the Alaska Highway in the province of British Columbia. In the old days, both were called simply Dawson—not much of a problem then, since virtually no one dared try a land route from the Canadian provinces to the Yukon.

It was this community, at the confluence of the Yukon and Klondike rivers, that sprang up to service the miners and would-be millionaires. These were the men who moiled for gold, as Robert Service put it, in and around nearby Bonanza Creek. Today the town is a living museum, much of it designated as heritage sites by the Canada Parks Service (formerly called Parks Canada). Truthfully, if you liked Skagway, you'll love Dawson City. It's like Skagway—only more so.

WHITEHORSE

Prior to World War II, Whitehorse was a sleepy village of a few hundred souls, many living in log cabins. Like Skagway, the town was kept alive by the WP&YR railroad. It was a transfer point for passengers and goods to continue by paddle wheel vessels on the Yukon River up to Dawson and thence to the interior of Alaska. It was the home of Robert Service, a bank teller who wrote some of his most well-loved poems there, including "The Shooting of Dan McGrew" and "The Cremation of Sam McGee." (Later, the bank transferred him to Dawson City.)

In the summer of 1942, almost overnight, Whitehorse became a boom town as soldiers, contractors, and road workers poured in to build the Alaska (ALCAN) Highway. The railroad and the sternwheelers are now gone, but because of the highway and government activities, Whitehorse remains a lively transportation center. It has settled into a comfortable population of about 20,000 although its sophisticated facilities make it seem like a much larger community. In 1953 the seat of government was officially transferred from Dawson to Whitehorse, and today it is the political and cultural center of the territory.

During gold rush days, stampeders described Whitehorse as "just a place to wash your socks." Today civic boosters try hard to coax travelers to stay a week, but with little success. With its good restaurants, shopping, etc., the city is a civilized oasis and a wonderful place to recharge your batteries. Nevertheless, most find that one or two overnights will do the trick before they push out into the bush again on their way north to Dawson or west to Fairbanks.

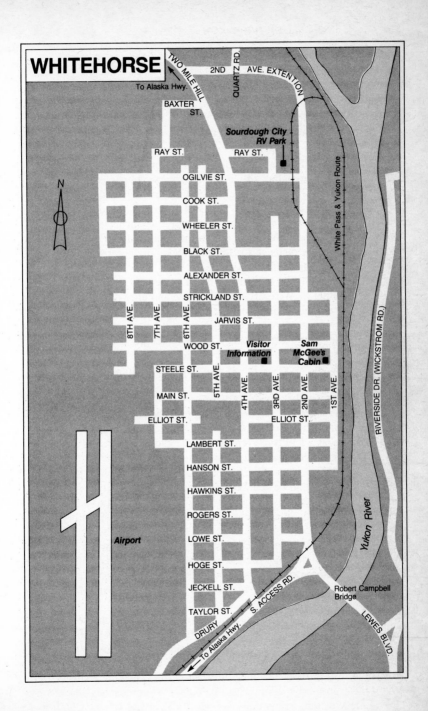

TRANSPORTATION

The Alaska Highway (Yukon Route 1) provides the life blood to Whitehorse, although the city itself is actually bypassed west of the downtown area. (Those ore trucks don't have to slow down much on their run between the lead-zinc mines at Faro and the docks at Skagway.) At 285 miles, it is a good day's drive (with an early start) between Whitehorse and Watson Lake to the southeast. To the northwest, it's about the same distance to Beaver Creek, just before the U.S. border and the Alaskan Interior.

Whitehorse is 110 road miles north of Skagway on the Klondike Highway (Route 2). Wise drivers will allow an entire day for that route, too, leaving plenty of time for difficult traffic, road construction, and some sightseeing at Carcross and other points en route. Whitehorse is also 333 miles south of Dawson City, another good day's drive on a highway that is paved at least most of the way, but remember that you have to share the road as far as Carmacks with those monstrous ore trucks (see "Divided Twins of the Lynn Canal—Haines and Skagway"). Warm-weather travelers who go up to Dawson can then enter Alaska via the unpaved, summer-only Top of the World Highway (Route 9). By the way, the law of the Yukon requires you to drive with your headlights on at all times, even during the day (some say it's because of dust problems in some areas).

In contrast to situations in Alaska, all communities in the Yukon except Old Crow can be reached from one another by road. Of course there are few settlements in the Territory by comparison to Alaska. For up-to-date road condition reports all over the Yukon Territory, telephone *(403) 667–5644.*

There are real parking meters in Whitehorse—perhaps the only ones in the Territory—although the last time we let one run out, instead of a ticket, our Washington-licensed car received only a friendly note under the windshield informing us of the free lot at the end of Main Street beyond Sixth Avenue.

Believe it or not, you can travel to or from Whitehorse over the Alaska Highway by bus, at least during the summer. **Greyhound Lines of Canada** (tel. *667–2223*) arrives six times a week from Vancouver, Edmonton, and other southern points. Details at their Whitehorse office at 3211-A Third Ave. In other directions, the **Alaskon Express** (tel. *667–4494*), formerly White Pass & Yukon Motorcoaches, owned by Gray Line/Westours, runs daily service to Skagway (about C$60) and less frequently to Haines (about C$75) or to Fairbanks (about C$135) or to Anchorage (maybe C$150).

Gray Line (tel. *668–3225*) offers a five-day, four-night "Klondike Explorer" bus excursion between Whitehorse and Fairbanks, via Dawson, Eagle, and Tok, for around C$1000, including accommodation and meals. It also includes the *Yukon Queen* boat trip between Dawson and Eagle, described in the Dawson portion of this chapter. **Norline Coaches** (tel. *668–3355*), 3211A Third Ave., is a local bus service between Whitehorse and Dawson via several other towns.

Railroad/bus combo: You can no longer take the train all the way between Whitehorse and Skagway, but **Atlas Tours** (tel. *668–3161*) will set up a combination bus/train ticket in which you travel by bus (or motorcoach, as the Canadians prefer to say) as far as the U.S. border at Fraser and then take the White Pass & Yukon Route Railroad the rest of the way into Skagway. (Be sure to see details on this historic railroad in "Divided Twins of the Lynn Canal—Haines and Skagway.")

River routes: Just as in the days of '98, travel on the Yukon River between Whitehorse and Dawson City may again be feasible. See the description of the M.V. *Anna Maria* in "Tours and Cruises."

Air travel: Whitehorse's modern airport is on a plateau about 300 feet higher than the town. When fog rolls in over the city itself, the runways remain clear. Check out the permanently mounted Canadian Pacific DC-3 there; if breezes blow at least 10 miles an hour it pivots like a weather vane to show the wind direction! The ultra-modern flagstone terminal is set up with arrivals on the left, departures on the right. A restaurant/bar is upstairs overlooking the tarmac.

Jet service between Whitehorse and other southern Canadian cities is provided by two airlines. **Canadian Airlines International** (tel. *668–3535*), formerly Canadian Pacific Airways, formerly CP Air, flies from Whitehorse to Watson Lake and points farther south, including Edmonton and Vancouver. **Air BC** (tel. *668–4223*) jets nonstop to its Vancouver hub and then has backtrack connections to several British Columbian points, including Prince Rupert and Prince George. It also flies to Victoria and Seattle (its only U.S. airport).

Scheduled regional air services include those relatively low-altitude DC-3 flights on **Air North** (tel. *668–2228*) south to Juneau and Watson Lake and north to Dawson and Fairbanks. They sometimes seem to be flying between the peaks. Then **Alkan Air** (tel. *668–6616*) has scheduled one-hour flights between Whitehorse and Dawson along with some other small airports, including Inuvik. Despite the name, its only flights into Alaska are on charters.

Taxis: Several companies cruise Whitehorse. The largest is **Yellow Cab** (tel. *668–4811*), 106 Main St., which offers radio-dispatched, 24-hour service. Not only that, it takes Visa and MasterCard. (Airport service is also provided by the folks at Yellow.)

Municipal bus: Whitehorse is big enough to have a genuine public bus service, daily except Sunday. The **Whitehorse Transit Commission** (tel. *668–2831*) charges C$1 a ride, at last report.

Rental vehicles: **Hertz** (tel. *667–2505*) is parked both downtown at Fourth Ave. and Black St. and at the airport. You might get better rates at **Tilden** (tel. *668–2521*) or at **Economy** (tel. *668–2355*), at Fourth and Strickland streets (credit card only). You can rent motor homes (RVs) from **Klondike** (tel. *668–2200*), 108 Industrial Rd. Bicycles and motorbikes are available at the **Bike Shop** (tel. *667–6051*) in the alley beyond the Yukon Inn, just off Baxter Street. And if you'd like to canoe your way up to Dawson on the Yukon River, you can rent 17-foot canoes from **Rainbow Tours** (tel. *668–5598*), Third Ave. and Lambert St. A fare of around C$175 for a week includes paddles, life jackets, and a free canoe drop-off in Dawson City.

If you lose your way in the core area of Whitehorse, look for a student (male or female) dressed in a bright red coat and a blue-and-yellow cap, either sometimes rather ill-fitting. These are young folks in authentic mountie-style uniforms of the 1890s, and their summer job is to be generally helpful, to direct strangers around town, and to pose for pictures with you if you want. (As you can see, the NWMP did not wear wide-brimmed hats in those days.) Also, drivers with an FM radio may want to tune to CKYN, the visitor radio station at 96.1 megahertz, as they approach Whitehorse.

HOTELS AND MOTELS

Whitehorse has almost a bewildering number of accommodations for its modest size, many of them catering to truckers and commercial traffic, and some devoted almost entirely to the mass tour trade. We didn't have time to check out all the Bates Motels around town, unfortunately. If you find a bargain, we'd like to hear about it. Unlike many hotels at Skagway, however, nearly all we did see have television, telephones, private baths, clothes closets, and other standard amenities. All rates, estimated for 1990, are of course in Canadian dollars and so will seem cheaper when converted to U.S. currency, depending on the exchange rate in effect during your visit.

Most would agree that the two Westmarks are the leading hostelries. Of those the **Westmark Whitehorse** (tel. *668–4700*), formerly the Sheffield, at Second Ave. and Wood St., is more convenient. Midcity location with 180 units; some with two doors, one on the hallway and the other curbside for convenient parking right outside; generally good furnishings; some units on the small side; popular bar, coffee shop, and restaurant; theater on premises for "Frantic Follies"; usually helpful staff; most doubles in the C$135 range.

Do not confuse the above with the **Westmark Klondike Inn** (tel. *668–4747*), which is also on Second Ave., but much farther north out of the downtown area (after Second is bent to connect with Fourth). For some reason, this Westmark seems to be the more highly advertised. With a car, of course, location is no problem. Small lobby, often crowded with tour groups; well-regarded Charlie's restaurant to one side; popular bar (Sternwheeler) and night club (Trappers) adjoining; spread-out corridors leading to 100 rooms, some average, some really ample in size; most rates around C$130 for two; generally friendly folks on duty. (Reservations for either through the Westmark organization in the U.S., toll-free tel. *(800)544–0970* or in Canada, call toll-free *Zenith 06003*.)

Almost in the same price range, the **Yukon Inn** (tel. *667–2527*), at 4220 Fourth Ave., is not far from the previous entry. New lobby under construction during our visit; popular McGrew Restaurant with Old West theme; 100 rooms, some brand new; generally warm tones; good lighting and furnishings; patterned black-out curtains; most of the comforts of home; double rates of C$100 or so. Your hostess is a personality-full lady who calls herself Colleen the Ice Queen. (Reservations from the hotel at Whitehorse, Yukon Y1A 1K1, Canada.)

The **Taku Hotel** (tel. *668–4545*), downtown at 4109 Fourth Ave., is also a decent possibility. Tiny lobby with loud radio; new dining room on the street side; a bar named Cheers, complete with a brass rail and small wooden tables (but without Sam and the gang); squeaky corridors; 53 rooms, at least clean if not too well designed and decorated; double rates in the C$90 range. (Reservations from P.O. Box 4308, Whitehorse, Yukon Y1A 3T3, Canada.)

Across the street the **Town and Mountain,** also known as the T and M, and where they wouldn't let us inspect any accommodations, is not recommended—at least not by us.

The modest **Edgewater** (tel. *667–2572*), at 101 Main St., known as the Edge, cuts a sharp bargain for some travelers. Known as the location of one of the city's best restaurants, the old-style hotel also has about 15 comfortable if somewhat dark and creaky rooms, all with private bath and TV, and all one flight up. Most will probably rent for around C$75 or so by your visit.

Out by the airport the **Airline Inn Hotel** (tel. *668–4400*) is officially at Mile 916.8 or Kilometer 1475 on the Alaska Highway, and is the home of Rudy's German Restaurant and a convenience store as well as a 30-room hotel. Some units with a fridge are large and bright (we liked #206). Figure on double rates of around C$75 or C$80 by now, but have a look at the room before signing in. A Jacuzzi and sauna on the premises could make the difference, too.

The similarly priced **Stratford Motel** (tel. *667–4243*), back in town

at the corner of Fourth and Jarvis, is a definite maybe if you want to
have a kitchenette, although other facilities seem less inspiring. (We
can never really recommend a hotel with virtually no bathroom shelf
space.) Other hotels we took a peek at include the **Whitehorse Centre,**
known more for its live country music and general weekend revelry,
and the traffic-side **Chilkoot Trail Inn,** which we felt were not to our
minimum standards. If you disagree, or if things have changed, please
drop us a line.

There are two or three small bed-and-breakfasts around. See the
Visitor Reception Centre at 302 Steele St. for the latest. RV parks include **Pioneer** (tel. *668–5944*), five miles south of town; **MacKenzie's**
(tel. *633–2337*), about six miles north, and the **Sourdough** (tel. *668–
7938*) behind the Second Avenue Chevron Station downtown (reservations required).

RESTAURANTS AND DINING

There are a lot of restaurants in Whitehorse, most of them in the
budget or fast-food category, and owners and chefs change over quickly
from season to season. As in many Canadian restaurants, you'll have a
hard time finding a "no smoking" section. As in Alaska—but not in
the rest of Canada—portions tend to be large.

At the moment, the town's most delicious dining room is the viewless, basement premises called **The Cellar** (tel. *667–2572*), under the
Edgewater Hotel at First Ave. and Main St. It's an anomaly in a way,
since it seemed at first that the budget-conscious guests in the rooms
upstairs might be the least likely to take advantage of the house cuisine.
Subdued music; elegant settings with pink tablecloths, quilted chintz,
and antique light fixtures; paper place mats are a surprise. Prime rib is
the house specialty, but we had some steak and seafood selections which
were just about perfect. (Sockeye salmon steak was about C$16.) Ser-
vice was also efficient and especially speedy when we explained that
we had to cut our dining time short to get to the theater. Figure about
C$40 for two, with two glasses of wine, a very fair price for this neck
of the woods.

Also a snappy choice for dinner is the **Golden Garter** (tel. *667–
2626*), at 212 Main St. The place is nicely decorated, the cuisine is
French, the beef is Alberta, and it is generally well presented. Specialties include beef stroganoff, frog's legs, and steak tartare. After that,
several Whitehorsemen and Whitehorsewomen ride over to **Charlie's**
(tel. *668–4747*) in the Westmark Klondike, at 2288 Second Ave. (almost the end of the street). You'll find turn-of-the-century decor with

red velvet booths, hanging oil lamps, and steaks in the C$20 range. We missed that personally, more's the pity; we did try the **Village Garden** in the other Westmark and were disappointed. (Tiny tables, too close together, with a mediocre smorgasbord.)

If you're going to go Italian, search out the suburban branch of **Christie's** (tel. *633–6060*) at 1901 Sycamore St. in the Porter Creek Mall. There's another one downtown at 209 Main St., where the food is okay and not expensive, but we rated it zilch for atmosphere—particularly after the ragamuffins began drifting in about 9 p.m. Locals like the "Chinese truck stop" called **McCrae's** (tel. *668–4177*), whose official address is at Mile 910, Alaska Highway (near the turnoff for Miles Canyon). Mexican gastronomes head for **Sam 'N' Andy's** (tel. *668–6994*), open daily for lunch and dinner at 506 Main St. Authentic German food is available at **Rudy's** (tel. *668–4400*) in the Airline Inn, 16 Burns Rd. A good, standard American-Canadian restaurant that's open 24 hours? We know of one—maybe. **McGrew's** (tel. *667–2527*) in the Yukon Inn at 4220 Fourth Ave. is at least open all night Fridays and Saturdays; but you'd better recheck for the latest on other nights of the week.

For lunch, you might look into the **Potbelly,** a tiny place hidden between the shops in the Horwood Building at the bottom of Main Street. You'll get goulash for about C$5, meat pie for C$7.50, or a pierogi for C$7 or so, all including a salad. Soup's usually great, too. For more midday munching, try the **No Pop Sandwich Shop,** 312 Steel St., corner of Fourth Ave., under a ceiling of whirling fans. You'll find food fans at the tables, too, for that matter. Yes, indeed, they have no (soda) pop for sale—but you can buy espresso coffee and lots of imported beers to go with your soup and sandwiches. The **Gallery Lounge,** the bar at the Edgewater Hotel, has some creative sandwiches and small steaks in addition to a daily lunch special. The **Bench and Gavel** at 2141 Second Ave. is your basic Yukon yuppie pub, decorated in legal paraphernalia. Here you'll find quiche, croissants, and all that. And submarine sandwiches, hoagies, or whatever you like to call them, are sold at **Yukon Sub** (tel. *668–3292*) at Fourth Ave. and Alexander St. They bake muffins too.

Fast food? Sure; this is civilization, after all. **McDonald's** is at 4227 Fourth, more or less behind the Westmark Klondike; you can hope for a finger-lickin' day at **Kentucky Fried Chicken** (tel. *667–7755*), at Second Ave. and Rogers St. (We include the phone number because the colonel delivers in Whitehorse.)

ENTERTAINMENT AND NIGHT LIFE

Almost reason enough to go to Whitehorse during the summer is to catch a performance of its famous **Frantic Follies** (tel. *668–3161*). A dozen highly professional young actors and musicians recreate a zestful gold rush vaudeville revue, and for our money it is the best of several similar efforts we have seen in both Alaska and the Yukon. You'll meet Sam McGee, Dan McGrew, Klondike Kate, the Lady known as Lou, and other characters, real and imagined, all apparently orchestrated by a man named Lyall Murdoch, with help from lots of his relatives. We haven't met the Murdochs, but we think all should be commended in print for producing a fresh, entertaining show season after season. Tickets will probably run C$16 or C$17 by the summer of 1990. The box office is near the theater right in the Westmark Whitehorse. In high season, there are usually two performances a night, and they're often sold out. Get reservations and tickets as soon as you arrive in town; better yet, write in advance to Atlas Tours, P.O. Box 4340 (postal code Y1A 3T5).

A second live gold rush show, which we haven't been able to get to yet, is named **Eldorado!!** (tel. *668–6472*), complete with two exclamation points, given nightly except Monday at the Pioneer Trailer Park five miles south of Whitehorse on the Alaska Highway. Those who have seen both shows claim they like them both (if you go, let us know). These shows are seasonal, of course, but if you happen to come to Whitehorse in February, try to make it the last week in that month, which is devoted to the Yukon Sourdough Rendezvous.

Check at the Whitehorse Public Library (tel. *667–5239*) to see if they are going to repeat the **Sour Dough Summer Cinema** this summer. Any of several local-interest films may be shown from Tuesday through Saturday at 2 p.m.

Whitehorse has a tradition of active night life. The **Kopper King,** on the Alaska Highway, is considered one of the best country-and-western bars in Canada. At the **Roadhouse Saloon,** 2163 Second Ave., you might find Hank Carr and his guitar. He's an artist who has given up city life to perform where he likes to live.

The **Boiler Room,** next to the Yukon Inn, 4220 Fourth Ave., is popular with all over the age of consent. Bop-'til-you-drop music and dancing is on tap in **Trappers** in the Westmark Klondike Inn, 2288 Second Ave. You'll find a more subdued and sophisticated drinking den at the **90 Below Tavern,** which is warmer than it sounds. It's underneath the New Whitehorse Hotel catercorner from the Westmark Whitehorse. Bill English has run the bar for a number of years now. It should not be confused with the **98 Hotel**, where some patrons overdo things a bit.

SIGHTS AND SITES

If you were a stampeder and returned to Whitehorse, you would want to have a look at **Miles Canyon,** whose Yukon River rapids took the lives of many who tried to negotiate the raging waters in homemade boats. Jack London was one of the river pilots who worked the canyon. Today the water has been raised and calmed by a new dam and Miles Canyon is in an attractive park just off the Alaska Highway, about five miles south of town. Several hiking trails parallel the river canyon.

A scenic site at the south end of Second Avenue is now occupied by the beached **S.S. Klondike,** an old sternwheeler authentically restored to the 1930s era by the Canada Parks Service and operated as a National Historic Site. It was one of a fleet of hundreds of similar vessels that once traveled the river between Whitehorse and Dawson, and it looks much like the captain and crew just walked off the boat before you walked on. You can see it on guided tours only, several times a day during the summer. Admission is free. Don't miss it.

At First Ave. and Steele St., drop in to the **McBride Museum** (tel. *667–2709*), an old log structure which displays lots of gold rush memorabilia. (Open daily; admission about C$3.) There are several old log buildings in Whitehorse, including the **Old Log Church,** built in 1900 and now a missionary museum, at the corner of Third Ave. and Elliot St. (Donations accepted; we suggest C$2.) Nearby, on Lambert St., a favorite photographic subject is one of the last remaining **Log Skyscrapers,** three- and four-story structures which were put up during the construction of the Alaska Highway in 1942. Log buildings are still popular and often built in the Yukon and Alaska in modern times. One is the **Visitor Reception Centre** (tel. *667–2915*), at 302 Steele St., open until 8 p.m. during the summer months.

A couple of sleepers often missed by travelers to the Whitehorse area: the **Yukon Gardens** (tel. *668–7972*), a privately owned, 22-acre botanical display just opposite the beginning of the city's South Access Road off the Alaska Highway. Northern flowers, fruit, and vegetables are growing and on display from June 1 to Sept. 15. (Admission about C$5.) The other is the **Northern Splendor Reindeer Farm** (tel. *633–2996*), about 30 minutes' drive north on the Klondike Highway, virtually on the marge of Lake Lebarge, if you will (turn east on Shallow

Bay Road). You can help feed the reindeer, if you want—and you can be sure at least one of them is named Rudolph. (Open daily until 9 p.m.; admission C$2.)

If you don't believe salmon will swim upstream for 2000 miles, you can see for yourself during August at the **Whitehorse Rapids Dam and Fish Ladder** (tel. *667–2235*), at the end of Nisutlin Drive in suburban Riverdale. A glass window will allow you to spy on these hearty chinooks as they make their way against the current. It is said they represent the longest salmon migration anywhere in the world.

SIDE TRIPS

North of Whitehorse, about 100 miles on the Klondike Highway on the way to Dawson, the village of **Carmacks** is near Five Finger Rapids, the notorious stretch of the Yukon which was a navigational hazard to river steamers running from Whitehorse to the goldfields. Most of them had to be winched through the narrow channel. Watch for the scenic lookout north of town.

A good day's drive south of Whitehorse along the Alaska Highway is the community of **Watson Lake** (pop. 1600 or so). Considered the Gateway to the Yukon, it is more famous for what one local told us was "the world's largest collection of stolen property," the forest of signs that have been put up there, originating from all parts of the U.S. and many from foreign countries. (Sara even found one from her home town of Gisborne, New Zealand!) Stop in to the Alaska Highway Interpretive Centre next to the signposts. We tucked ourselves in at the modern *Belvedere Hotel,* preferring it to the cramped quarters we saw in the more atmospheric *Watson Lake Hotel* near the signboards, the visitors center, and the museum. In a tent in the same complex is a 1940s-style "Canteen Show," based on military construction days of the Alaska Highway (although they had canceled the performance the night we showed up to review it).

Farther south on the Alaska Highway in British Columbia, you might spend a night at **Fort Nelson.** The *Coachman* is the traditional leader in accommodations. The best restaurant in town may still be *Peter's Place,* which offers a surprising gourmet meal. At the beginning of the Alaska Highway in **Dawson Creek,** one of the most interesting restaurants around is the *Alaska Cafe.*

TOURS AND CRUISES

Free *walking tours* of the downtown area are sponsored daily by the **Yukon Historical and Museums Association** (tel. *667–4704*). They leave daily from the Donnenworth House, 3126 Third Ave., and sometimes include readings from the diaries of early Yukoners. Free *nature walks* are led Monday through Friday by the **Yukon Conservation Society** (tel. *668–5678*), 302 Hawkins St. Morning and afternoon *hikes* are conducted up Grey Mountain or the trails of Miles Canyon and elsewhere. Call for details.

What might be called your standard city sightseeing *bus tour* is offered by the ubiquitous **Gray Line** (tel. *668–3225*), headquartered in the Regina Hotel, as well as by **Atlas Tours** (tel. *668–3161*), in the Westmark Whitehorse. We opted for the two-hour Gray Line tour once, and called it just adequate for C$15. (The regular driver/guide was sick, and the substitute at least was a little rusty.) Atlas handles lots of visitor activities in Whitehorse in general.

On a bright sunny day, nothing kills two hours more delightfully than the *Yukon River Cruise* aboard the M.V. *Schwatka,* sold by **Atlas Tours** (tel. *668–3161*). The 10-mile cruise, with Captain Rachael at the helm, chugs through Miles Canyon and alongside other historic areas on the once-wild river, now tamed by the dam. Fare is about C$15 if you show up at the dock yourself—C$5 more if you get picked up at your hotel. We opted to join the group at the gangplank and enjoyed the people and the ride.

Since we were last in Whitehorse, two separate and distinct cruise operations have begun to ply the traditional 460-mile gold rush route between Whitehorse and Dawson. We know a little more about the four- or five-day trip launched by **Karpes and Pugh** (tel. *667–2873*), a well-established firm previously concerned only with fishing charters and canoe rentals. Staterooms and deck passage are available on the 65-foot M.V. *Anna Maria,* the first on-board-accommodations vessel to sail the river since the last paddle-wheel steamer was retired 40 years ago.

Don't hold us to these prices, but based on the fares announced previously for '88 and '89, the 1990 berth passage will probably run around C$1200 for the longer cruise upriver (south) or around C$1100, for the shorter downriver cruise (north), including all meals. Deck passage will probably run around C$400 or so in either direction, and you may need to carry a tent. The boat does not travel after dark. Overnight stops will be made at three or four destinations en route, and deck passengers must make shore arrangements. This is a trip we would like to make, and we hope they do a good job. Better get full details in advance by calling the above phone, or direct from Gus Karpes and Irene Pugh, P.O. Box 4220, Whitehorse, Yukon Y1A 3T3, Canada.

A second, somewhat similar excursion but for smaller groups has been announced by **Youcon Voyage, Inc.** (tel. *668–2927*). It is using a 28-foot catamaran named the *Youcon Kat* for a week-long round-trip experience that includes five days on the boat, a one-day visit to Dawson, and a one-day return to Whitehorse by road. The fare will run around C$1200 or so. Details by phone or from the company at 1 Morley Rd. in Whitehorse, Yukon Y1A 3L2, Canada. If you have had some personal experience with either of these two cruises, please drop us a line.

Guided *canoe trips* in the summer or *dog-sled trips* in the winter are offered by **Wanderlust Wilderness Adventures** out of Lake Laberge. Sorry, we know little about this outfit. Write for details to Ned Cather, Wanderlust, Box 5076, Whitehorse, Yukon Y1A 4S3, Canada. And if you go, let us know. Also **Sky High Wilderness Ranches** (tel. *667–4321*) has guided *horseback trips* in the summer and *dog-sled excursions* in the winter. It's 15 miles west of town on the Fish Lake Road. Write for details at P.O. Box 4482, Whitehorse, Yukon Y1A 2R8, Canada.

Some *flightseeing* tours out of Whitehorse are offered in the float-planes of **Glacier Air Tours** (tel. *668–7323*), some of them to Destruction Bay or as far as Kluane National Park. The airline also has its own wilderness cabin and will set up a fly-in camping adventure centered on it. You'll also find **Tagish Air Service** (tel. *668–7268*) interested in taking you flightseeing in a float-equipped Cessna 185 based at Schwatka Lake.

SPORTS

Fishing for lake trout is popular in several southwestern Yukon lakes from mid-June to mid-Sept. Catches average 5 to 10 pounds but can run up to 45 pounds. Northern pike can be caught in many roadside lakes. Arctic grayling are available in most good-sized streams, and some Yukon fishermen swear they put a pan on the fire and butter in the pan before they drop a fly in the water! A nonresident license costs C$20 and can be bought from most sporting goods shops in the territory. "Fly-in" fishing trips are relatively inexpensive compared to Alaska (25% to 50% less), and certainly are less crowded too.

Persons interested in *hunting* should write the **Yukon Department of Renewable Resources**, P.O. Box 2703, Whitehorse, Yukon Y1A

2C6, Canada or contact the **Yukon Outfitters Association** (tel. *667–2755*) for details on the complicated seasons and other regulations. Dall sheep are popular game.

Believe it or not, Whitehorse has a genuine *golf* course. The **Mountainview Golf Course** (tel. *633–6020*), off Range Rd. north of town, was recently enlarged to 18 holes. Green fees run around C$10. Not fast enough for you? The **Whitehorse Racquet Club** (tel. *668–4171*) has *squash* and *racketball* courts available at 38 Lewes Blvd. *Bowlers* head for the five-pin alleys at **Riverdale Lanes** (tel. *668–4277*) at 95 Lewes Blvd.

Cross-country skiers head for the **Mount McIntyre Recreation Center** (tel. *667–2500*). Take Hamilton Boulevard off the Alaska Highway at Valleyview and turn right on Sumanik Drive. These are world-class facilities for nordic skiing. *Downhill skiers* are out of luck in Whitehorse, although there is a community ski area in Watson Lake, 285 miles south (T-bar lifts only).

As far as spectator sports are concerned, Whitehorse is not as big on basketball as the neighboring communities in Alaska. *Softball,* however, is as big here as anywhere else, and games are regularly played with Alaskan teams.

SHOPPING

Some of the best *handicraft* and *cottage industry items* are found at **Yukon Native Products** (tel. *668–5935*), at 4230 Fourth Ave., across from McDonald's. The double-shelled "Yukon Parkas" made and sold there are wool duffel with a nylon lining, plus an outer windbreaker with fur trim. Other items include caribou hide slippers, moosehair brooches, porcupine quill crafts, etc. A good wooden mask will run at least C$500. The store is an outlet for a coop operation to produce *Inuit and Indian arts and crafts*. You might want to ask for a mail order catalog and order form. **Northern Images,** at Fourth Ave. and Jarvis St., also has a good selection of Indian and Inuit arts and crafts.

A nearby store specializing in the mineral for which this part of the world is most famous is called, naturally enough, **Pot O' Gold.** You can buy loose nuggets, if you want, plus other items made from *gold*. A well-stocked sporting goods store is **Kluhanni Sports,** at 4143 Fourth Ave. And some unusual historic photographs are for sale to the general public from the **Yukon Archives,** Second Ave. and Hawkins St., next to the library.

There are two districts for general shopping, the downtown core area, centered mainly along **Main Street,** and the **Qwanlin Mall,** at

Fourth Ave. and Ogilvie St. Downtown stores include the **Yukon Gallery** (tel. *667–2391*), which displays several local contemporary artists in its shop at the Westmark Whitehorse, **Murdoch's Gem Shop,** 207 Main St., with *gold nugget jewelry* and *bone china carvings;* **Jim's Toy & Gift,** 208 Main St., with topographic *maps* and other interesting items; two *bookstores,* **Books on Main,** 203 Main St., and the well-known **Mac's Fireweed,** 305B Main St., carry several books and magazines devoted to Yukon and Alaskan subjects (for a good look at the romantic riverboat period on the Yukon, try to find the book *Lifeline to the Yukon* by Barry C. Anderson); and **Hougen's,** next door to Mac's, has lots of specialty items plus a pretty well stocked photo department.

Back at the Qwanlin Mall, which has an interior rock wall made entirely of ore samples, there are 14 stores. Most are of more interest to local residents. You'll find *film and camera supplies* at **Photo Vision;** *books* at the **Book Shelf;** and *gourmet coffee,* along with *postage stamps,* at **Coffee, Tea & Spice;** and *nugget jewelry, etc.,* at **Designers North.** The big *food market* at the mall is named **SuperValu** (closed Sunday). Whitehorse's main *department store,* **the Bay** (Hudson's Bay Company), is at 4201 Fourth Ave., across Ogilvie from the Qwanlin Mall.

In the summer, most stores are open until 6 p.m. daily, except Thursday and Friday to 9 p.m. If that's not good enough, the **Riverside Grocery,** 201 Lowe St., is open 24 hours, 7 days a week, across from the S.S. *Klondike.* So is the **Expressway,** 407 Steele St. (We told you Whitehorse was not a one-horse town!)

MISCELLANEOUS ADDRESSES AND PHONES

The telephone area code for all of the Yukon is 403. Phone numbers in Whitehorse begin with 667, 668, or 663. Sorry, there are several six-digit postal codes; all begin with Y1A, however. Remember to allow extra time for mail to or from anywhere in Canada to or from the U.S.:

- Ambulance (tel. *668–9333*).
- Artsline Cultural Information Service Recording (tel. *667–ARTS*).
- Body Fitness Centre (tel. *668–4628*), 38 Lewes Blvd.
- Fire emergency (tel. *667–2222*).
- Medical emergency (tel. *668–9444*).
- Northwestel Long Distance Calling Booth (tel. *668–3434*), 211 Elliott St., corner of Third Ave.

- Parks and Recreation Dept., City of Whitehorse (tel. *667–6401*), Municipal Services Building, 4210 Fourth Ave.
- Police emergency (tel. *667–5555*).
- Royal Bank of Canada (tel. *667–6416*), 4110 Fourth Ave.
- Royal Canadian Legion (tel. *667–2800*), 306 Alexander St.
- Shoppers Drug Mart (tel. *667–2485*), 211 Main St., and also in the Qwanlin Mall.
- Tourism Yukon (tel. *667–5340*), Box 2703, Whitehorse, Yukon Y1A 2C6.
- Victoria Faulkner Women's Centre (tel. *667–2693*), 204 Main St.
- Visitor Reception Centre, Whitehorse Chamber of Commerce (tel. *667–2915*), 302 Steele St., at Third Ave., Whitehorse, Yukon Y1A 2C5.
- Yukon Conservation Society (tel. *668–5678*), Box 4163, Whitehorse, Yukon Y1A 3T3.
- Yukon Dry Cleaners (tel. *667–6828*), Qwanlin Mall.

DAWSON CITY

It would be wrong to think of Dawson as a ghost town, although it's impossible to believe that those dusty streets and empty buildings can be entirely devoid of the dynamic spirits who dwelled here less than a century ago. Dawson is not dead. It is, in fact, a kind of municipal museum and those who live there are, by and large, its curators. During the summer at least, it is certainly one of the liveliest communities for its size in Canada. (You'll find most things closed in the winter.)

Dawson was created by the Klondike Gold Rush of 1897–98, built almost overnight on the nearest piece of flat land to Bonanza Creek, the site of the first discovery. At its peak, the population is estimated to have been more than 30,000, by far the largest city in western Canada. Most of its residents in those days were United States citizens, men who headed for the area they called The Klondike to seek their fortune. Very few were successful.

Times were lusty, but the Yukoners would have you remember that theirs was not a lawless city like Skagway or Nome. The Mounties kept a tight rein on Dawson, and there are no sad tales of large-scale graft and corruption like those told of many parts of Alaska during the same period. Two famous literary figures who lived in Dawson are Robert W. Service, perhaps known better by Canadians but recognized by all

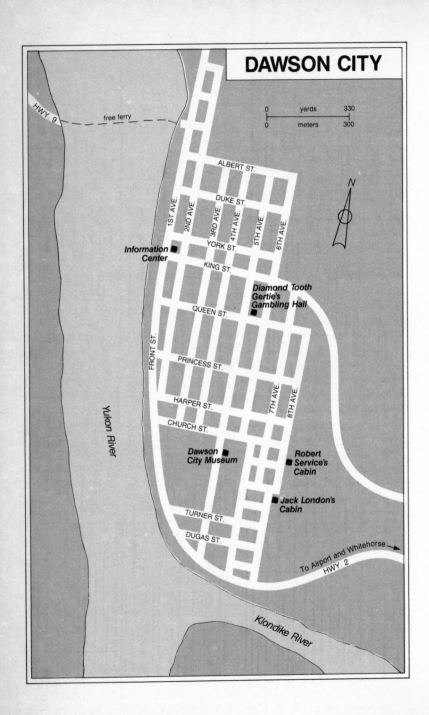

through his poetic rhymes like "The Shooting of Dan McGrew," and Jack London, his name recognized more by Americans and remembered everywhere for "The Call of the Wild" and other stories set in the Klondike.

The population of Dawson began to peter out after the turn of the century and dropped to only a few hundred in the 1940s. Today it has increased to around 1800. Many of its original buildings remain, however. Some have been restored by the Canada Parks Service and a few private owners. Many more have continued to deteriorate into authentic and picturesque ruins.

TRANSPORTATION

By road there are two ways into or out of Dawson. From Whitehorse, 330 miles south, stretches the all-season Klondike Highway (Route 3), which is paved most of the way. The other route is via the 70-mile-long Top of the World Highway, the high-altitude and highly scenic Route 9. It's a good gravel thoroughfare (watch out for flying stones from opposing traffic) which leads from the Taylor Highway (Route 5 between Tok and Eagle). In the winter Route 9 is kept open only on the Canadian side of the border. At the very end of Route 9 is the Yukon River. To get over the River to Dawson, you can cross by 24-hour territorial ferry in the summer or via an "ice bridge" built every winter. (There is a period of a few weeks every fall and spring when crossing the river by vehicle is absolutely impossible.)

Scheduled bus service is available all year via **Norline Coaches** (tel. *993–5331*) between Dawson and Whitehorse, although of course several all-inclusive-package guided tours also make the run as part of their circuit through the territory.

Can you float into Dawson on the Yukon River? You can, indeed, on at least three different cruises. The trip between Dawson and Eagle via Westours/Gray Line is described in "Tours and Cruises." From the other direction, the four- or five-day trip on the M.V. *Anna Maria* should have been launched by the time you read these words. And the catamaran *Youcon Kat* also moves down the river from Whitehorse during the summer. Both have been covered in detail above in "Tours and Cruises" under Whitehorse. You can also rent canoes from Rainbow Tours and other companies, as described in Whitehorse "Transportation."

Dawson Airport, about 12 miles south of town, is served by no less than three separate airlines, two of them on international routes. **Fortymile Air** (tel. *993–5200*) runs commuter-plane schedules between

Dawson and Eagle, AK, and thence to Fairbanks and several other Interior Alaska airports. Dawson is also a stop for **Air North** (tel. *993–
5119*), sometimes called Air North Canada, on its DC-3 or DC-4 service
between Fairbanks and Whitehorse. And **Alkan Air** (tel. *993–5440*) has
scheduled one-hour hops between Dawson and Whitehorse (and to other
Yukon destinations out of Whitehorse).

Dawson is simply too small to have a municipal bus service. Even
a normal taxi is generally too much of a luxury, although a service does
start up every now and then. You can hail a horse-and-surrey on occasion, however. We have not yet found a single rental car company in
Dawson. If you think a pickup truck or a four-wheel-drive will do,
however, try **Visa Truck Rental** (tel. *993–5624*). It's also known as
Van Every Inc. or Klondike U-Drive. Most hotels offer free transportation to and from the airport.

HOTELS AND MOTELS

You'll find five major hotels in Dawson (which don't vary a lot in
overall quality), a couple of motels on the outskirts of town, and three
or four bed-and-breakfast operations scattered here and there. The only
two hotels open year round (i.e., in the winter too) are the Downtown and the Eldorado, and that seems to give them an edge on general
maintenance and facilities. (They also have winter plug-ins for your car
heater, of course.) All were built in recent years, although all maintain
the architectural style and atmosphere of gold rush days. When business
is slow, you might talk any Dawson hotel into a good discount if you
have any excuse for one at all. (Some modestly dressed guests manage
to get a ''miner's rate'' in May or August, but don't say we said that!)
Again, everything in this chapter is our estimate expressed in Canadian
dollars, and in our order of preference.

A winner on location, especially, the **Downtown** (tel. *993–5346*),
at the corner of Second Ave. and Queen St., replaces an earlier model
of that name which burned down awhile back. Red-and-white exterior;
locally popular (and often crowded) saloon and Jack London Grill; outdoor Jacuzzi on tap; 60 clean, cheerful rooms equipped with double-
double beds; good baths; cable TVs and phones; clothes racks instead
of closets (not really unusual at these latitudes); good housekeeping on
our inspection; double rates probably around C$115 in 1990; sometimes
filled with Princess Tours groups. (Reservations from the hotel at P.O.
Box 780 in Dawson.)

The **Eldorado** (tel. *993–5451*), owned by the town mayor, is situated at Third Ave. and Princess St., across from the historic Harrington's Store. A slate-blue building with a white verandah; popular Bonanza Dining Room and Sluice Box Lounge ("gold dust accepted") equipped with TV and pool table; long, dark hallways through the rambling structure; clean though not large rooms decorated in brocade and velvet; TVs and telephones; tiny, doorless closets; mixture of new and old furnishings; double rates officially in the C$100–110 range; good discounts sometimes available. You'll often find the Maupintour mob in residence here. (Reservations from P.O. Box 338.)

The **Triple J** (tel. 993–5111), at Fourth and Queen, is only a whoop and a holler past famed Diamond Tooth Gertie's Gambling Hall, and this kind of convenience to the action may be enough to recommend it to some. Green-and-cream wooden building with verandahs on lower and upper stories; Sourdough Steak House on the premises; neat-looking lobby with overhead fan; coin laundry for guests; 10 hotel rooms and one suite in the main building (#201 a nice corner double); 18 units in the adjacent motel building; 18 rather charming log cabinettes, each with fully equipped kitchenette; all with phones and TVs; most prices set at around C$100 or so. We might try out those cabins ourselves next time. Open May–Oct. (Reservations from the hotel at P.O. Box 359.)

Another entry in the chain of Alaska-Yukon hotels owned by Holland America/Westours/Gray Line, etc., is the **Westmark Inn** (tel. 993–5542). Red-and-white facade built in a kind of U-shape; interior courtyard where Sunday barbecues are often served; lively bar on the second floor; acceptable restaurant on the ground floor; 52 rooms with Victorian decorations; comfortable furniture; good baths; some units with TVs and phones; often filled with their own tour groups; FIT rates probably at around C$135 or more for two, higher than competitive establishments; friendly staff; better units in the front (main) building on Fifth Ave. Open May 15–September 15. There's only one Westmark in Dawson to date, so you'll avoid the confusion present in Whitehorse and other cities which have more than one. (Reservations from the hotel at P.O. Box 420 or through the Westmark organization in the U.S., toll-free tel. (800)544–0970 or in Canada, call toll-free Zenith 06003.)

The **Midnight Sun** (tel. 993–5495) shines brightest, perhaps, from its busy bar at the corner of Third Ave. and Queen St. Tiny, old-fashioned lobby with an interesting intaglio ceiling; popular Chinese restaurant; about 40 rooms spread into three or four nearby buildings; all with TV, phones, patterned bedspreads, and traditional furnishings; nicest and brightest rooms in the main building; unfortunately, as long as the bar is open they're also the noisiest; rates at around C$110. Open May–September. (Reservations from the hotel, when open, at P.O. Box 840.)

We don't really recommend the **Westminster** (tel. 993–5463), although it does have a few rooms to rent because you can't have a public bar in the Yukon without having a few rooms to rent. No private bathrooms either.

On Seventh Ave. near Church St., a block from the Bard's real cabin, the **Robert Service Motel** is now administered by the Westmark. There are only a few rooms, with tubs but no showers—and no Lady Known as Lou. Sorry, we haven't seen it. Ditto for the **Gold Nugget Motel** (tel. *993–5445*). There are 10 units for double rates at around C$60 or C$70. And the same goes for **Mary's Rooms,** which has no phones. Doubles run around C$50 or C$60. Prices are similar at the year-round **Dawson City Bed & Breakfast** (tel. *993–5649*) at 451 Craig St.

RVs and tent campers can stay at the **Gold Rush Campground** (tel. *993–5247*), at Fifth and York, which offers hook-ups and all facilities. Rates around C$20 if you want the full enchilada. Rates are a little cheaper south of Dawson at **Guggieville** (tel. *993–5008*), almost directly on historic Bonanza Creek.

RESTAURANTS AND DINING

Most restaurants are located in the hotels, but one of the best dining places in town is not. That's the **Claims Cafe** (tel. *993–5762*), staked in an old private home at 833 Third Ave., and which succeeds at a European or ethnic menu with some excellent sauces. I had a fine chicken satay, and Sara was very happy with the pork schnitzel. Dessert was some kind of ambrosial Moroccan pastry, I think, called Tiramasu. This kind of cordon bleu cuisine may only continue as long as Jeffrey Cook is still the cook, however—and he was thinking of selling out the last we heard. Better recheck when reserving. Open May–August.

For dinner in a hotel restaurant, we would take a chance on the Call of the Wild salmon and White Fang steaks (or whatever) served at the **Jack London Grill** (tel. *993–5346*) in the Downtown Hotel (you can order from the same menu in the bar, incidentally). We had a bully lunch there ourselves. Good prospects at the **Bonanza Dining Room** (tel. *993–5451*) in the Eldorado Hotel are salmon or special Chinese dishes.

We thought our meal at **Mulrooney's** in the Westmark was just okay. Sorry, we haven't yet sat down at the tables in the other two hotels, although we understand there are some good things done at the **Midnight Sun** in their Oriental restaurant.

We enjoyed lunching al fresco at **Nancy's,** which dishes out soup, sandwiches, and sometimes pizza next to the bakery at the corner of

Front and Princess. You might have to stand in line for a breakfast of sourdough pancakes. For more modest offerings, the **98 Drive In** on Front St. opposite the Steamer Keno is the closest that Dawson comes to a fast food outlet—featuring Big MacGrews, Red Hot Malamutes, Gold McNuggets, or perhaps their more prosaic equivalents.

ENTERTAINMENT AND NIGHT LIFE

For some Yukoners and neighboring Alaskans, whooping it up in Dawson is the be-all and end-all of the whole place. Much of the action centers on **Diamond Tooth Gertie's,** a gambling casino and dance hall that sounds rough, but Gertie's is actually a tame Jane created and tightly run by the Klondike Visitors Association. In the spirit of the days of '98, you can, indeed, gamble there every night (black jack, poker, roulette, and a couple of "money wheels") during the summer—the only place in Canada where that is so. There are three shows a night (9 p.m., 11 p.m., and 1 a.m.), and tickets for all the fun cost C$4 for as long as you want to stay. (Tickets sold at the door, and we'd advise getting in line early.) You'll find no sharpies and high-rollers here, and it's probably safe to say that most of the patrons are fellow first-timers at the tables. (If you're just learning, there's even a "beginners' table" that uses phony money.)

Almost as big a draw as Gertie's is the gold rush musical melodrama called the **Gaslight Follies,** with a cast of a half-dozen young people, held at 8 p.m. nightly at the restored Palace Grand Theatre (admission C$10). We enjoyed the show despite the uncomfortable chairs—but that's authenticity for you. Gaslight tickets can be purchased in advance at the Visitor Information Centre.

All the hotels manage to fill their bars with chatty folk, and several will hire live contemporary (non–Gay '90s) musical entertainment from time to time. One of the most famous gathering spots is the **Sluice Box Lounge** at the Eldorado Hotel. That's the one that serves, on demand, the Sour Toe Cocktail—a champagne cocktail embellished with a genuine pickled phalanx (reusable). Another popular year-round watering hole is the **Sourdough Saloon** at the Downtown Hotel. There are similar lounges in the Triple J and the Westmark. We were less fond of the bars at the Midnight Sun and at the Westminster, the latter of which especially caters to less inhibited members of the community.

Valid, too, as entertainment (but not night life) are the hour-long poetry reading and lectures given twice daily at the **Robert Service Cabin,** at 10 a.m. and 4 p.m. (recheck at the Visitor Information Centre).

Finally, be aware that Dawson numbers a succession of special celebrations, holidays, and festivals, most of them during the summer, which mean a lot of special entertainment of one kind of another which just might be in progress during your visit. Most are on the weekends.

SIGHTS AND SITES

History and an appreciation for the "last great American adventure" is the thing in Dawson. If you don't dig that stuff, you picked the wrong town. Make your first stop at the two-story log-walled **Visitor Reception Centre** (tel. *993–5566*) run by Tourism Yukon on Front St., corner of King St., and they'll help you make plans on what to do and see. Don't forget to pick up interesting free brochures produced by the Canada Parks Service, like the one on the life of Robert Service. (They are not just advertising publications.) Also ask for a map of the town. If you have only a short time, don't miss one of the free *walking tours* taken out several times daily by interpretative officers of the Canada Parks Service. All leave from this building. More than 35 of the historic buildings are part of the Klondike National Historic Site and have been authentically restored by the national park system.

Among the sites to see, whether they are on the walking tour or not, and not necessarily in this order: The **Steamer Keno** a beached sternwheel freighter on the river bank near the Visitor Centre. Separate special tours are given daily. The **Canadian Imperial Bank of Commerce** on Front at the end of Queen, the building where Robert Service worked as a teller when his first royalty checks began coming in. (He soon quit and began devoting himself full time to iambic pentameter.) The building continued to serve as the town bank until this year. Precise plans for the structure are now undecided. In any case, be sure to see the *Gold Room museum,* on the second floor.

The **Palace Grand Theatre** on King between Second and Third. Originally built by "Arizona Charlie" Meadows in 1899, it has been restored to its former elegance. Charlie used to have wrestling bears or horses leaping into vats of water on the stage, which were a bit too flamboyant for the Canada Parks Service or the KVA to duplicate. Today it's used for the Gaslight Follies, a vaudeville revue (see "Entertainment and Night Life"). The **Old Post Office** across the street, now available for stamp sales and mail drops only. (The real post office is on Fifth Ave., between Queen and Princess streets.) **Ruby's Place** on Second near Princess, another place that is no longer what it once was. Ruby was one of the most popular gals in old Dawson, but she has long been out of business.

The following are a little too far afield to be included in the walking tour: **Strait's Auction House** at the corner of Harper and Third, which has not been restored, and may not last until the ink is dry on these words. If this 1901 structure is still standing, it is probably still "the most photographed building in Dawson." The **Dawson City Museum** on Fifth near Church, was the Territorial capitol from 1901 to 1953. (Open to 6 p.m.; admission about C$3.) **Jack London's Cabin** on Eighth Ave. near Fifth St., is actually only half his cabin, and originally didn't stand on this site, either, although it's closer than the other piece. Believe it or not, it was moved to Oakland, California. A second cabin was brought in to serve as an interpretive center.

Robert W. Service's Cabin on Eighth near Church, is totally authentic, however, and hasn't been lived in or hardly changed since Service moved out in 1912, and if you knew the number, you just might be able to ring his 1909-model telephone. It was here that he wrote the novel *The Trail of Ninety-Eight* and several poems. Partly because we share the same first names, and partly because of our mutual addiction to travel, your obedient servant has always had an affectionate regard for this man. On his cabin wall is a sign he posted to help him fight writer's block: "Don't worry. Just work!" In a modern equivalent, those words now come up on my computer when it's turned on at the beginning of the day.

SIDE TRIPS

With a car you should be sure to head for the summit of **Midnight Dome** (on June 21, you can see plenty of daylight at midnight). It overlooks Dawson and the three rivers—the Yukon, the Klondike, and far-distant Bonanza Creek. Then drive out toward Bonanza to see what's left of **Guggieville,** named after New York's famous Guggenheim family, who eventually bought and consolidated many of the claims. On Bonanza Road, which parallels the creek, you'll find a few fairly benevolent tourist traps. Stop to see **Gold Dredge No. 4,** a behemoth now maintained as an attraction by the Canada Parks Service. (It's hard to believe that thing once floated on its own pond.) It was the discovery of gold on Bonanza Creek on August 16, 1896, that started the gold rush—but only after ships arrived in Seattle and San Francisco with the proof nearly a year later. (Incidentally, don't try to do any gold panning yourself except under supervision at designated areas, or you could be accused of claim jumping!)

Something more than a side trip, perhaps, is the 1000-mile round trip to the village of **Inuvik,** which at least a few make each year simply because it is there. The gravel-surfaced Dempster Highway (Route 5) connects with the Klondike Highway a few miles east of Dawson. It then heads north through the mountains and into the Northwest Territories to end at the little Inuit village on the Mackenzie River Delta next to the Beaufort Sea. It is the farthest north you can drive yourself anywhere in North America, and it is a trip that should not be made without considerable thought and preparation. We haven't done it, although it's on our wish list for a future edition of this volume. You can get details about the Dempster from the Visitor Centre in Dawson. Or for advance information contact the Western Arctic Visitors Association. (tel. *(403)979–3756)*, P.O. Box 1525, Inuvik, NWT X0E 0T0, Canada.

Another destination we have been fortunate enough to reach—although not yet in the most interesting way—is the little Alaskan wilderness outpost on the Yukon River named **Eagle.** We drove there from Tok via Chicken over the sometimes-difficult Taylor Highway, and thence backtracked a ways to take the Top of the World Highway into Dawson. You can certainly do that trip in reverse too. A much more intriguing alternative, though, would be to take the boat from Dawson to Eagle (see "Tours and Cruises").

If you stay in Eagle, one of the most untouristy towns reached by road in Alaska, we recommend the *Eagle Trading Company* (tel. *(907) 547–2220)* for both food and lodging, and make sure they teach you how to light the kerosene stove in your room. Take the *Museum Tour* in town, or you'll miss the moose-blood map and other delights (and if your guide is Yvonne or Miriam, please say hello for us). Check out the crafts for sale in the *Village Store,* along with things for sale upstairs at the museum and at the *Artist's Co-op.* Eagle is one of the featured locales in John McPhee's book *Coming Into the Country,* but he warned that not everybody thinks it's worth navigating the Taylor Highway for. Personally, we loved it and will go back again.

TOURS AND CRUISES

We've already mentioned the free *walking tours* under "Sights and Sites." For those who would rather ride and travel farther afield than they can walk, we'd check first with itineraries set up by **Gold City Tours** (tel. *993–5175)*, headquartered on Front St. across from the Steamer Keno. Prices run from under C$10 for short trips on up to around C$40 for all-day experiences through the goldfields, a gold mine, and some practice at gold-panning yourself. We know less about **Cheechako Trail Tours** (tel. *993–5460)*, a competing operation with some similar experiences. It's headquartered in the lobby of the Eldorado Hotel. The ubiquitous **Gray Line** (tel. *993–5542*) has a three-hour Dawson and Goldfields Tour for around C$20 and a Midnight Dome Tour for around C$10. **Atlas Tours** (tel. *993–5467*), set up at Third Ave. and King St., also has some competing tours or will arrange step-on guides for their coaches coming up from Whitehorse.

If you want to get out *on the river* for a short time, consider the **Yukon River Cruise** (tel. *993–5482*), aboard the *Yukon Lou*, a sort of miniature sternwheeler built and operated by diamond-toothed Captain Dick Stevenson. The 1 p.m. departure ("precisely") cruise takes about an hour and a half and may run around C$10 in 1990. We were glad we opted for the evening Smoked Salmon Barbecue cruise (departure times vary), which stops for a meal on Pleasure Island, a small dollop of land in the river. Check in at the Birch Cabin, on Front St., near the boat landing. The bearded captain, incidentally, is the inventor of the aforementioned Sour Toe Cocktail. Thankfully, it is not available on the cruise.

But to many, the *real* cruise out of Dawson on the Yukon is the trip on the M.V. *Yukon Queen IV* operated by **Gray Line** (tel. *993–5542*). The 49-passenger vessel takes about four hours to travel 108 miles downriver to the Alaskan hamlet of Eagle, and then another six hours to come back. The boat is often booked far in advance, especially for the downriver trip. If you can cadge a ticket, figure around C$100 each way, or significantly less if you're a stand-by. (The exact structure of the excursion may change before the first date you can cast off; check to see if you can pick up one of Gray Line's *tour buses* in Eagle, whether to return to Dawson or to continue on to Tok, Fairbanks, etc. A five-day, four-night excursion between Whitehorse and Fairbanks by bus, boat, and bus, with two overnights in Dawson, and one each in Tok and Fairbanks will run around C$1000.)

Two companies provide *helicopter sightseeing* from helipads just south of Dawson. **Trans North Air** (tel. *993–5494*) offers 20 minutes over the goldfields for around C$70. **Capital Helicopters** (tel. *993–5700*) we know less about; sorry. *Fixed-wing tours* in a nine-passenger aircraft are sometimes given by **Top of the World Flying Service** (tel. *993–5383*). These planes usually wander farther afield than the chopper operations, including at least one tour that will give you an aerial preview of the Dempster Highway over the Ogilvie and Richardson mountain ranges.

SPORTS

It seems that most folk's interest in sports doesn't go much beyond the card-and-chip exercises and elbow-bending routines at Diamond Tooth Gertie's.

Swimming? Sure. The **Dawson City Pool** is open to the weather and to the public—along with scores of the local small fry at the same time. It's in Minto Park, next to the museum. You may be able to pick up a game of horseshoes in the park too.

There is the **Trail of '98** *miniature golf* course just out of town near Bonanza Road. Nine holes are gussied up in a historical mining motif. As in other northern areas, residents of Dawson go batty about *slow-pitch softball* during the summer months. You're welcome to watch the games, which are often played after dinner. *Fastball* tournaments are occasionally held as part of Dawson's many festivals and celebrations, however. Other than that, there are a few races held on special occasions. Besides some winter dog-sled races, the Midnight Dome Marathon pits runners against the 3000-foot mountain behind the town, and the Klondike International Outhouse Race on the Sunday of Labor Day weekend. (You might have to see it to believe it.)

SHOPPING

It's a little confusing to shop in Dawson because a building may be prominently labeled what it once was, so it's hard to tell a real store from what is nothing more than a museum piece with nothing really for sale. The **Dawson City General Store,** for example, is real; **Harrington's Store** is not (at least not in the present time frame).

The town is not known for any particular bargains, although confirmed browsers will have plenty to poke through. There are *gold flakes* and *nuggets,* of course, and a couple of *semi-precious stones* found in the Yukon, lazulite and rhodonite.

Authentic *handicrafts* will be found at **Yukon Native Products,** a branch of the same company in Whitehorse, here at the Chief Isaac Memorial Centre on Front St., next to the Visitor Centre. (The day we tried the door, it was locked for no discernible reason.) We found some interesting *non-Native crafts* at the **Cabin Gift Shop,** across Fifth Ave. from the Westmark.

We were impressed by **Wild 'n' Wolly,** at the Third and Princess. It sells sweaters and other *handknit wool products* produced by Romy Jansen, a delightful Swiss lady (who told us about how she and her husband once floated down the entire 2000-mile length of the Yukon). The **Klondike Nugget & Ivory Shop,** at the corner of Front and Queen, makes *gold nugget jewelry* right on the premises. It also sells mail order. Next door is **Maximillian's Gold Rush Emporium,** with books, film, souvenirs, and the like. The **Raven's Nook** at Second Ave. and Queen St. also has *nuggets* and *ivory,* along with other kinds of knick-knacks on the ground floor with *ladies' wear* sold upstairs.

MISCELLANEOUS ADDRESSES AND PHONES

All addresses in Dawson have the same postal code, Y0B 1G0. Phone numbers all begin with 993, and, like Whitehorse and the rest of the Yukon, they are in area code 403.

- Arctic Drug Store (tel. *993–5331*), Front St. near King.
- Canadian Imperial Bank of Commerce (tel. *993–5447*), corner of Third Ave. and Queen St.
- Dawson Hardware Store (tel. *993–5433*), Second Ave near King.
- Emergencies in general. Ask telephone operator for *Zenith 50,000* (toll-free), or call R.C.M.P (below).
- Fire department (tel. *993–5555* to report a fire).
- Government Liquor Store, corner of Third Ave. and Queen St.
- Hair Cabaret (tel. *993–5222*), Queen St., between Second and Third avenues.
- Hospital—Father Judge Nursing Station (tel. *993–5333*), Sixth Ave. near Church St.
- Post office (the real one; tel. *993–5342*), Federal Building, Fifth Ave. between Queen and Princess streets.
- Public library, in the Robert Service School, Fifth Ave. and Queen St.
- R.C.M.P. (tel. *993–5444*), Front St. near Turner.
- Visitor Information Centre (Klondike Visitors Association, tel. *993–5575*), Front and King streets.

THE ALASKAN INTERIOR—FAIRBANKS AND DENALI

FAIRBANKS

They like to call Fairbanks the "Golden Heart City." It is a wonderful sobriquet, implying at least three things at once. It is a gold rush town that, unlike hundreds of others, managed to survive and grow to maturity. It also appears to be in the heart of Interior Alaska. And if friendliness and generosity of spirit are meant by a heart of gold, Fairbanks generally qualifies on that score, too. It might also be called a city of extremes. Here you will find some of the hottest and the coldest temperatures in Alaska. Summer readings can get close to 100°, although there are usually only a few days like that. In winter 40° and 50° below zero are not uncommon.

These numbers sound worse than they are. The air is fairly dry in Fairbanks, reducing the effect of both high and low temperatures. You'll see few air conditioners in the summer; Fairbanks folk believe an electric fan does the job well enough. In the winter youngsters usually find the snow too flimsy to build snowmen. Their parents seldom do any shoveling, either; mostly they simply sweep the snow to one side— sometimes a futile exercise, of course, since it just blows back again.

Fairbanks may hold a lesson about being ready for anything in Alaska. We had a lot to get done one July afternoon during which the temperatures reached the mid-90s, so we were taking care of our er-

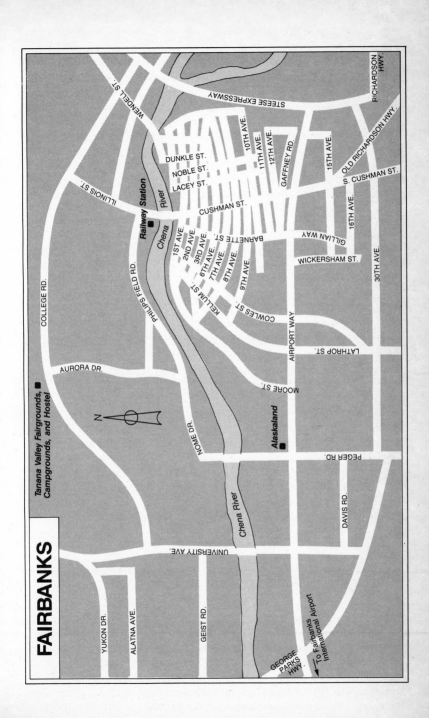

rands with the automobile air conditioner on. After a late dinner, we found the evening a little nippy, so we drove back to our hotel with the heater turned on just enough to keep us toasty. It is the only time we can remember using an air conditioner and a heater in the same 12-hour period.

The town was founded in 1902 on both sides of the winding Chena River, not far from its confluence with the Tanana. In the early years, there was a solid connection between the two halves only during the winter when a crude bridge was built across the thick ice. Every April the bridge was demolished by the forces of nature. The name of the town had nothing to do with the fair banks of the Chena, by the way; it was named after a senator from Indiana who became Vice President of the U.S.

You still find log cabins nestled among the taller and more modern structures in downtown Fairbanks. You'll also find a large number of shopping centers spread out over a wide area of the countryside, serving a resident borough population of around 76,000 plus many more who come in from the bush to enjoy the state's second largest city. The economy of Fairbanks is based now on tourism, the University of Alaska, two important military bases, and the trans–Alaska Pipeline. North of the city, however, among the huge piles of tailings left by four score and seven years' worth of dredging, the past is faintly echoed by at least a modicum of gold mining that still continues today.

Probably the best time to visit Fairbanks is from mid- to late July. "Golden Days," the largest summertime event in the state, will probably run from around July 13 to 22. On the heels of that will be the four-day world Eskimo-Indian Olympics and then the Fairbanks Summer Arts Festival.

Fairbanks is not a political capital, but it does serve as the unofficial fulcrum for villages scattered over the vast Interior and even those like Barrow and Deadhorse on the North Slope. It is also the closest population center to Mount McKinley and Denali National Park.

TRANSPORTATION

Fairbanks is the traditional terminus of the Alaska Highway, although technically it ends at Delta Junction, 100 miles south of the city. In any case, motorists who have worked their way along that historic route for 1500 miles from Dawson Creek are sometimes surprised to find themselves virtually flying into Fairbanks on a four-lane freeway (Route 2, the Richardson Highway). If you notice that you're crossing the river, you've probably missed the turnoff and gone farther than you intended. You are instead on your way north of town, now on the Steese Highway (still Route 2). Another divided thoroughfare, known as Airport Way, bisects central Fairbanks and approximately parallels the Chena on its way out to **Fairbanks International Airport,** just west of the metropolitan area.

As in other Alaska airports, a collection of majestic dead bears and other animals will greet you inside the terminal. There's also a terrific panoramic painting of walruses riding an ice floe. Entering the building, the ticket lobby for major airlines is on the right (west). Upstairs is the entrance to Gates 3 through 8, along with a bar, restaurant, and gift shop. Baggage Claim is downstairs in the center of the terminal, sharing the space with moose, bear, caribou, buffalo, goats, and sheep—or rather only the heads thereof. There's an old plane suspended from the ceiling above the rental car desks (the first Jenny flown in Alaska) and, on the left, there are check-in counters for commuter airlines, along with Gates 1 and 2. On the floor above that is a runway observation area. On the way out of the airport, you'll ride under the iridescent sculpture "Solar Borealis" by Robert Behrens. Its colors are created by refracted sunlight or (after dark) automobile headlights.

The airport serves three *major jet trunk carriers.* At this writing, **Alaska Airlines** (tel. *452–1661*) flies between Fairbanks and Seattle and the Lower 48 via Anchorage and Juneau. **United Airlines** (tel. *(800)241–6522*) stops only at Anchorage on its way south to Seattle and Denver. (Fairbanks and Anchorage are a little less than one hour's jet time apart.) And **Delta Airlines** (tel. *(800)221–1212*) has nonstops between Fairbanks and Juneau (in 1½ hours) that continue on to Seattle and then connect with their other flights farther down the line. Other major intrastate jet service to Fairbanks is provided by both Alaska Airlines and **MarkAir** (tel. *452–7577*). One or the other will provide flights not only to Anchorage but to major destinations like Prudhoe Bay, Barrow, Nome, Kotzebue, King Salmon, Valdez, Seward, Homer, Kodiak, and others.

Scheduled *commuter lines* (prop planes) at the airport include **Air North** (tel. *452–5555*), the Canadian DC-3 outfit that flies to Dawson, Whitehorse, and Juneau; **Fortymile Air** (tel. *474–0518*) to Central, Circle, Eagle, and Dawson; **Frontier Flying Service** (tel. *474–0014*), which will take you clear to Nome via lots of gravel and grass strips along the way; **Larry's Flying Service** (tel. *474–9169*), another with a milk run to more than a dozen towns and villages; and **Tanana Air Service** (tel. *474–0301*) to Tanana, Rampart, Nenana, and Lake Minchumina, among others.

If you arrive in Fairbanks without wheels, and you are at all inclined to rent a car anywhere in Alaska, we would suggest you do it in Fairbanks. As in Anchorage, things to see and do are so spread out from one another that you'll have trouble making maximum use of your time with bus and taxi. If you're considering renting a car for long-distance travel, however, remember that drop-off fees in Alaska can be huge—typically $100 to $200.

Five *car rental agencies* still had counters at the airport at last report: **Avis** (tel. *474–0900*), **Budget** (tel. *474–0855*), **Hertz** (tel. *452–4444*), **National** (tel. *474–0151*), and **Payless** (tel. *474–0177*). Others parked in town will be a little cheaper, and will also probably pick you up at the airport. (If they don't, please let us know.) These include **Arctic** (tel. *451–0111*), 1408 Turner St.; **Rainbow** (tel. *457–5900*), 310 Birch Hill Rd.; **Rent-A-Dent** (tel. *452–3368*), 4870 Old Airport Way; and **Rent-A-Wreck** (tel. *452–1606*), 2105 Cushman St. (The latter two rent both used and new cars.)

Bus service? Long-distance bus travel is via the summer-only **Alaskon Express** (tel. *456–7741*), formerly White Pass & Yukon Motorcoaches, with an office in the Westmark Inn. They travel between Fairbanks and Haines, Dawson, and Skagway, and will pick up and drop passengers anywhere along the road. **Atlas Tours** (tel. *452–7373*), headquartered at the Captain Bartlett, has bus trips to and from Dawson City. The **Alaska Sightseeing Tours** (tel. *452–8518*) offers bus rides to and from Valdez and to and from Anchorage (11 hours each way to either), and **Gray Line/Westours** (tel. *452–2843*), also has trips to Anchorage. This picture may change by 1990; check with the tourist office to be sure. Local bus service in Fairbanks is handled by **MACS** (tel. *456–EASY*), daily except Sunday. Regular fare is $1.50, and a one-day pass is $3. MAC's Red Line (Route 10) goes to Bentley Mall, College Road, South Cushman, and Memorial Hospital. MACS's Blue Line (Route 20) goes to Yak Estates, University West, University of Alaska, the University Museum, Alaskaland, and the Noel Wien Library. Better get some local advice if you're planning to use the line extensively.

Taxi? You can get a cab by calling the **Checker Cab** (tel. *452–3535*) or the **Independent Cab Company** (tel. *452–3375*). There are also several more.

Going to Anchorage or Denali? Consider taking the **Alaska Railroad** (tel. *456–4155*), the passenger depot for which is at 280 North Cushman, a couple of blocks north of the bridge across the Chena. One of North America's most scenic routes, the modern passenger train leaves Fairbanks at 8:30 a.m. ADT daily during the summer, travels to Denali National Park in less than 4 hours, and then on to Anchorage where it arrives at 8 p.m. Full meal service is available during the summer. Figure a basic one-way fare of around $90 city-to-city, which allows one stopover at the national park. (There's only one train a week in the winter, meals are confined to what's available from vending machines, fares are a little cheaper, and the schedule will be different; so recheck everything if you're traveling between Sept. 17 and May 20.) We have more on this train in the following chapter, but if you want to phone the railroad for last-minute details from out of state, you can call this number toll free: *(800) 544–0552*.

HOTELS AND MOTELS

Among conventional accommodations, we found two or three hotels we liked very much, certainly as compared with the offerings in any other Alaska/Yukon city except Anchorage, which also has some excellent accommodations. The four following our first trio are certainly acceptable too. (All but the Wedgewood offer free pickup from the airport, and perhaps, by arrangement, the train.) Rates tend to be expensive. There may be some other good deals in Fairbanks, and if you find any, please tell us. Meanwhile, we suggest that Fielding travelers limit their advance Fairbanks reservations to those below.

Here are our lucky seven, in our order of preference (unless otherwise noted, all are open year-round; the city bed tax is currently running 8%).

Luckily we pulled in on time to **Sophie Station** (tel. *479–3650*), which is stationed at 1717 University Ave., about midway between downtown and the airport. Set way back from the street, and behind a carpet of greenery and flowers, the L-shaped building seemed more like an elegant three-story apartment complex than a hotel. Plenty of parking space; pleasant reception in a split-level, green-and-gold lobby; small sundries shop adjoining; well-respected Zach's Restaurant and Express Room bar on the upper story; room service from the same place; quiet, carpeted corridors; good guest laundry; 221 attractive units, each one at least a junior suite with fully equipped kitchen and separate bedroom; all with complete luxury amenities including cable color TV, direct-dial phone (free local calls), desk, small balcony, plenty of storage space, twin doubles or queen-size bed; no air conditioning (fan available on request); excellent baths; rack rates perhaps up to $150 for two in the summer of 1990; often populated with groups from Princess/Royal Hyway Tours; discounts available off season. Having a car is preferable, but it is within walking distance of the small University Mall shopping center on Airport Way. For the comfort and value received, we judged Sophie Station easily one of the best hotels in Alaska. (Reservations from the hotel at Fairbanks 99709.)

If you don't have your own set of wheels, or even if you do, you may enjoy the **Regency Fairbanks** (tel. *452–3200*), at 95 Tenth Ave. Bright, attractive exterior with flowers; just off Noble Street near the city center; pattern-carpeted lobby with chandelier and lots of sink-down-in chairs and couches; pleasant though viewless restaurant and bar in the basement; guest laundry; 128 warm-toned rooms, about half with kitchenette (including microwaves and stoves); reverse-cycle air conditioners (for individual heating or cooling); good furnishings, if sometimes too large or too much for the room size; satellite TV; free local phone calls; third-floor units with two-person Jacuzzis; excellent maintenance and housekeeping; rates similar to Sophie's. Altogether a comfortable choice. (Reservations from the hotel at Fairbanks 99701.)

Some would rank one of the Westmarks third, but we prefer to slide in an entry that seems to have more Alaskan character than any other place in town. The **Captain Bartlett Inn** (tel. *452–1888*), at 1411 Airport Way evokes the gold rush period with its woodsy public areas. Log-and-flagstone porte cochere; friendly reception form a red-spruce front desk and gold-pan lamps; large, high-roofed lobby with barrels for ash trays; gift shop to one side; rustic Captain's Table restaurant, lit by wagon-wheel lamps and warmed by the ''largest fireplace in Alaska''; atmospheric sled-dog saloon a sort of cabin-within-a-cabin (entertainment often on tap, darts and other games available when it isn't); 197 well-maintained bedrooms, although not decorated in the same prospector theme; all with color TVs, phones, quilted bedspreads, and matching curtains; clothes racks instead of closets; no air conditioners; all baths with showers but no tubs; summer rates around $125, double or single. (Reservations from the hotel at Fairbanks 99701, or national toll-free tel. *(800)544–7528,* or Alaska toll-free tel. *(800)478–7900.*)

Now bear with us, because the two similarly named Westmarks are often confused with each other by Fairbanks travelers, travel agents and, goodness knows, by travel writers. FITs should be warned that either are often filled to the gunwales with Holland America/Westours/ Gray Line groups. First, the **Westmark Fairbanks** (tel. *456–7722*), known for years as the Travelers Inn, has been crafted in a traditional U-shaped motel court arrangement at 813 Noble St., at Ninth Ave. Spread-out, two-story building, not far from downtown; lots of birch trees, flower beds, and mining memorabilia on the grounds; small lobby with artificial flowers on the front desk; beauty salon and gift shop; two restaurants including a coffee shop and the elegant and super-expensive Bear 'N' Seal dining room; popular piano bar to one side; 238 rooms in this large campus; one wing closed in winter; the nicest year-round units on the fourth floor, some with views of the park; generally good furnishings with slate-blue rugs, orange-wood furniture, easy chairs, etc.; cable TVs and push-button phones; black-out curtains; rack rates around $145 for two persons. (Reservations for this or the following through the Westmark organization, toll-free tel. *(800)544–0970,* or inside Alaska, except Anchorage, at *(800)544–0970.*)

The **Westmark Inn Fairbanks** (tel. *456–6602*)—in some listings ''Fairbanks'' is left off just to confuse things a little more—is the former Fairbanks Inn, at 1521 South Cushman St., a little farther away from the action. This place is *open in summer only,* which means some-what less polished facilities on the one hand, but that most rooms are air-conditioned on the other hand. Attractive entrance with a dolphin fountain in an unattractive neighborhood; high-ceilinged lobby with a TV showing an Alaska travel video tape over and over again; two mis-matched chandeliers, an oil painting and dark walls; Felix's Barbecue Restaurant with dark-wood paneling off the lobby; clean, well-main-tained, fully equipped but thoroughly undistinguished bedrooms with rabbit-ear TV, etc,; no shelves in some bathrooms (my, how we hate to see that); a few nice suites available; official rates in the $140 range for twin pillows. It's far from our first choice, but certainly a decent choice.

At least the **Super 8 Motel** (tel. *451–8888*) seems to have an ap-propriate phone number even if it doesn't have a restaurant, bar, gift shop, or other froufrou or falderal. This northern link in the stainless steel motel chain is right next to Denny's, the northernmost in the world, for whatever that's worth. Gray-shingled building on the busy highway to the airport; small, split-level lobby with high ceiling; three floors (but no elevator); 77 (not 88) units, including some for nonsmokers; guest laundry a definite plus; acceptable if somewhat sparse furnishings (few chests of drawers, some with a table but those without a lamp over it, only one lamp between two beds, etc.); TV taking up most of the built-in desk. If we were running things, we'd be tempted to rename it an easier-to-remember "Super 9." It's address on Airport Way is No. 1909, and, as a guess, double rates will hover between $90 to $99 by 1990. (Reservations at toll-free tel. *(800)-843–1991,* or the hotel itself at Fair-banks 99701.)

Finally, **Wedgewood Manor** (tel. *452–1442*), in a residential apartment complex, is the only one of our group with a genuine (indoor) swimming pool. Unusual location at 212 Wedgewood Dr., off College Rd., next to the bird sanctuary; good-size reception area with a fire-place; large, modern pool in the same building; also a Jacuzzi, Ping-Pong, pool table, and a rather institutional-looking cafe; a laundromat in each building; total of three buildings with 86 small apartments in the transient rental program; all with separate living room, bedroom, and fully equipped kitchen; walk-in closet (in a part of the world where motel rooms often have no closets at all!); efficiency furnishings with clock radio/TV; plenty of storage space; unattractive bright green and rough carpeting; small balcony or sun porch; rates in the $90 range for two, very fair for what you get. A car would be desirable, but the place is close to the No. 10 Route on MACS. (Reservations from the manor at Fairbanks 99701.)

Less expensive places? Yes, but watch out. Generally speaking we avoid hotels down by the river, between First and about Fourth avenues. These areas are fine in the daytime, but we don't enjoy any place where a drunk may come lurching into the lobby, where loud arguments break out, where bottles break on the street below our window. And for the time being, anyway, we would avoid any hotels out near the airport other than those mentioned. Some bargain-basement accommodations may be found at the following, but ask to see the room before signing in: the **Tamarac Inn** (tel. *456–6406*), at 252 Minnie St., north of the Chena, or the **Alaska Motel** (tel. *456–6393*), 1546 South Cushman St., in the busy commercial area south of Airport Way. To date, neither has been personally inspected by us. Rates may still run in the $50 to $75 range.

If you strike out on all the above, you may have to throw yourself on the mercy of the FCVB in the Visitor Information Center (see ''Miscellaneous Addresses and Phones''), who have a wider list of hotels. It may also be helpful to know that there are a score or more of bed-and-breakfast operations regularly going into and out of business in and around Fairbanks, most offering only one or two rooms. We know of only one centralized referral service, which represents itself and about eight of the other operations. That's **Fairbanks Bed & Breakfast** (tel. *452–4967*), or you can write Greg and Barbara Newbauer in advance at P.O. Box 99707, Fairbanks, AK 99707. Figure at least $40 for one person and $50 for a double (those with private bath will be more like $75). The Visitor Information Center will also give names of more current B&Bs. Incidentally, the Newbauers are weekend gold miners, and they often teach their guests how to pan for gold, letting them keep any flakes they find.

Campgrounds for RVs? The only ones we could find with full facilities (hookups, etc.) at a reasonably central location in Fairbanks are **Norlite** (tel. *474–0206*), at 1660 Peger Rd., a few blocks south of Alaskaland; and **Pioneer** (tel. *452–8788*), 2201 South Cushman St. Figure about $18–20 a day for these two. The CVB tourist information center may have an up-to-date list with more, including tent camping.

Lastly, the **Fairbanks Youth Hostel** is in a genuine quonset hut at College Rd. and Aurora Blvd. Open June through mid-Sept., it can be written to anytime at P.O. Box 2196, Fairbanks, AK 99707. You can join the Alaska Youth Hostel Association on the premises.

RESTAURANTS AND DINING

We've counted well over 100 places to dine out in Fairbanks, more than we ever thought we would find at what is almost the last outpost south of the Arctic Circle. Before we forget, you'll find in Fairbanks at least one branch of every kind of American national franchise fast food you've ever heard of, probably stumbling across them without any help or hindrance from us. Now, here is what's new and different:

The most elegant, and most expensive, establishment in the borough is probably the **Bear 'N' Seal** (tel. *456–7722*) in the Westmark Hotel at 813 Noble St. In windowless surroundings of red-brick walls, wood-beam ceilings, leather chairs, and starched white tablecloths, Fairbanks gourmets (sometimes dressed in their best flannel shirts) enjoy classic continental cooking delivered by waiters in tuxedos. The cuisine is haute enough, to be sure, although we thought the tables a little too close together. Some diners manage to consume $50 worth of cordon bleu, without half trying. (Dinner only; reserve always; closed Sunday and Monday.)

Much more entertaining, for *cheechakos* as well as the locals, is the **Pump House** (tel. *479–8452*), a riverside celebration of Alaskana you reach by driving a mile or so down the Chena Pump Road (about 20 minutes from downtown). The place began a utilitarian existence in 1933, pumping river water uphill as part of the massive gold mining operations in the area. Its heavy wooden construction serves as an atmospheric background for the restaurant, decorated in "Alaska chic"— with attic and antique trappings like mining instruments scattered here and there. There are several delicious steak and seafood specialties, including halibut steak and baby back ribs. The salad is crisp, and you might enjoy the Silk Pie or Chocolate Pizza for dessert. The Pump House is always busy and noisy, and you're really supposed to reserve, at least for dinner. We didn't, and were lucky. Our bill for two came to around $40, with drinks. Warm-weather lunches out on the riverside deck are also fun.

For those who want to escape to merrie olde England, or a northland approximation of same, there is always (take a deep breath) **Clinkerdagger Bickerstaff & Petts** (tel. *452–2756*), which many shorten to Clinks. You'll find its baronical premises at 24 College Rd., on the fringe of the Bentley Mall. Inside you'll find mahogany Tudoresque furnishings, with Holgarthian paintings and mounted flintlocks, plus friendly wenches to take your order. Roast beef is a specialty, but you'll generally find some of the freshest baked or broiled fish in town too.

A quick roundup of some other dinner choices would include **Cafe de Paris** (tel. *456–1669*), once a good lunch-only soup-and-quiche place in an old house at 801 Pioneer Rd., near the RR station, which has become popular enough to also begin turning out dinners. (Closed Sunday.) New York–style Italian specialties are featured at **Gambaradella's** (tel. *456–3417*), sometimes called Pasta Bella's. It's at 706 Second Ave., not far from the CVB. Delicious hotel dining is possible at **Zach's** (tel. *479–3650*), on the second floor of Sophie Station Hotel. Service can be slow, and we have found the tablecloths not changed when soiled.

Go on a warm day and sit on the terrace. The **Regency Dining Room** (tel. *452–3200*) in the windowless cellar of the Regency Hotel is also popular, although you'll never know what the weather outside is like. The **Alaska Salmon Bake** (tel. *452–7274*) is in open-sided pavilions during the summer inside the gates of Alaskaland. We've had salmon bakes elsewhere, but not here. Others have told us they enjoyed it, however.

Mexican food? *Si si!* Three places stand out. Believe it or not, one is called **Flannigan's** (tel. *451–6100*), at 354 Old Steese Highway, where the food tastes better than it looks like it would. Another is the more authentically titled **Don Diego's** (tel. *479–7999*), a small, inexpensive place at Old Steese Highway and College Rd. (behind Clink's), and *muy popular* with the *estudiantes*. (Closed Sunday.) And some Fairbanks regulars swear by the venerable **Los Amigos** (tel. *452–3684*), which has been holding the fort for several years at 636 28th Ave., near Cushman St., and which stays open until midnight.

There are very few Oriental choices around. One is the **Tiki Cove** (tel. *452–1484*) on the top floor of the Polaris Hotel at 427 First Ave. Some tables have a good view when the windows are clean. The menu lists Chinese, Japanese, Indonesian, Polynesian, and other Asian specialties all together. However the **Hunan Garden** (tel. *456–8847*), not far away at 513 Fourth Ave., is at least 100% Chinese, and probably spends more on its food than on its decor. The **Peking Garden** (tel. *456–1172*), which recently moved to 11th Ave. and Noble St., is also good, and you'll find the traditional gilded dragons gazing hungrily over your shoulder. Strangely enough, the P.G. also features some Japanese food and a sushi bar.

Lunches and lighter meals: For maximum midday munching, many downtown workers head for the healthy-like premises of **A Moveable Feast,** in North Gate Square, a little strip mall at 338 Old Steese Highway. They're not much on decorations—a mounted quilt, a few; Wedgwood plates, etc. We enjoyed our soup, salad, and sandwiches, and found out that on a warm July day the Moveable Feast moves to tables outdoors. (Closed Sunday.)

The **Bakery Restaurant** has just moved to more prosaic premises at 69 College Rd., in a sort of plastic place that a burger joint moved out of. The sandwiches, muffins, pancakes, etc., are just as good, however. Back downtown, the **Co-op Restaurant and Fountain,** 535 Second Ave., is an unassuming place in the Rexall Drug Store where you can get good milkshakes and a cheap and dependable grilled cheese sandwich and fries. "It's the kind of place where all the waitresses call you 'hon,' " says a local fan. "I love it!"

Pizza? You can get it any way you want it all over town. A particular local favorite, however, is the **Klondike Lounge,** 1347 Bedrock St., near the University Center Mall.

The Northern Suburbs: Here are a couple of dinner or lunch establishments in Fox, just north of central Fairbanks. The **Fox Roadhouse** (tel. *457–7461*), at Mile 11, Old Steese Highway, is known for good burgers and steaks; the **Turtle Club** (tel. *457–3883*), just a mile before that on the same road, is another funky-looking place big on the steak and roast beef circuit, but which also serves some delicious giant prawns—five for about $25. (Everything includes salad bar.)

ENTERTAINMENT AND NIGHT LIFE

It is de rigueur that every town in Alaska and the Yukon with any tourists at all offer a history-based revue. Fairbanks is no exception, and you'll probably find "Good as Gold" still whooping it up at 7:30 and 9 p.m. at the **Palace Saloon** (tel. *456–5960*) in Alaskaland. Tickets are around $7, or maybe $5 for the more risque 10:30 p.m. "after hours" show, starring local entertainer Jim Bell.

At the Fairbanks Center of Entertainment, which locals usually abbreviate to just "The Center," look for *Center Stage,* a sort of Comedy Store–type production on Friday and Saturday nights. Chances are it will be staged at **The Roof** (tel. *479–3800*) nightly at 8:30 p.m., with tickets around $5. The Center (and The Roof) are on Market Street, just south of Airport Way.

A popular demonstration that may be continued again this coming summer is Northern INUA, a nightly demonstration of Eskimo and Indian games that are normally part of the annual World Eskimo-Indian Olympics held each July in Fairbanks. The hour-long program has been held at the **Alaskaland Theater** (tel. *456–8131*) at 8 p.m. in the Alaskaland Pioneer Park at Airport Way and Peger Rd. You might learn something about the ear-pulling competition or the muktuk eating contest. Admission at the door is around $5 or $6.

Fairbanks folk often head for Fox on the weekends. The **Howling Dog** (tel. *457–8780*) is a rock-n-roll institution at Mile 11 on the Steese. You'll see all types in here—from legislators to guys in from the bush wearing knives in their back pockets.

In the other direction, there is almost always some fun going on at the **Cripple Creek Resort** (tel. *479–2500*) at Ester, eight miles out the Parks Highway. This year you might find *The Crown of Light,* a multimedia production about the Aurora Borealis, in the early evening (admission about $5), and *Service With A Smile,* an old-time music and comedy production following that (admission perhaps $6 or $7). Recheck the exact time, and fares, though; and while you're at it, better get exact driving instructions too.

Meanwhile, closer to town the antique-filled bar called the Senator's Saloon at the aforementioned **Pump House Restaurant** is usually fun. There is live folk music at least on the weekends. Recently the restaurant also put up a tent to house some weekend rock parties too. Some of the hotels offer live music when things are busy. The **Kobuk Room** in the Westmark Hotel has live bands Friday and Saturday, and it's a good place to sip and chat on other nights. There's generally some kind of action, at least a singer and pianist, at the **Captain's Lounge** in the Captain Bartlett Inn at 1411 Airport Way.

We would avoid the seedier bars right in the old downtown section of Fairbanks, including those along First, Second (especially), and Third avenues between Cushman and Noble streets, and the unpleasant encounters that often occur there.

In case you think you might be missing anything special that's going on at the moment, you can get a recorded phone announcement of all the latest activities by dialing *456–INFO*. The message is changed daily by the Fairbanks CVB.

For stay-at-homes, the Fairbanks TV stations include KTVF, Channel 11; KATN, Channel 2; and KUAC, Channel 9.

SITES AND SIGHTS

Make your very first stop at the FCVB's **Visitor Information Center** (tel. *456–5774*), a sod-roofed log cabin at 550 First Ave., just at the southeast end of the Cushman Street Bridge, where you can load up on published information and last-minute advice. You'll learn a heck of a lot more about Fairbanks than your average *cheechako* if you pick up the pamphlet *Fairbanks Walking Tour: Past and Present* and then follow it for the next hour or two. You'll also see things everyone else misses—like a fence made entirely out of war surplus skis, for example. There is also a *Fairbanks Driving Tour* pamphlet, which takes in many more of the sights the city is known for. Among places not to miss in the area are the following (approximately clockwise): **Golden Heart Park,** along the river just outside the Visitors Center, with its statue of the Unknown First Family. The **Alaska Public Lands Information Center** (tel. *451–7352*), at Third and Cushman, will answer all your "ology" questions about Alaska—geology, geography, sociology, etc. Documentary films are also shown here throughout the day. **Alaskaland** (tel. *452–4244*), the sourdough's answer to Disneyland, was created in 1967 after a severe flood threatened some of Fairbanks' oldest and most historic buildings. These structures were moved here, where they are now on display along with old railroad engines, mining equipment, the sternwheeler *Nenana,* and other historical objects. Two museums are part of Alaskaland: the **Pioneer Museum** and the **Alaska Native Museum.** The admission is free to the 44-acre site at Airport Way and Peger Rd., next to several city parks.

The **University of Alaska Museum,** whose inside entrance is guarded by "Otto," one of the biggest teddies in the world, is one of Fairbanks' proudest sights. Seek out the wildlife exhibits and the collection of gold nuggets. After Otto, you'll want to meet "Effie" and "Blue Babe" too. It's at the UAF campus, at the corner of Yukon and Sheenjek drives. (Open daily, 9 a.m. to perhaps 7 p.m. during the summer.) Guided walking tours of the UAF campus leave from the museum at 10 a.m. Monday through Friday. Often missed is the **University of Alaska Geophysical Institute** (tel. *474–7581*), near the corner of Farmers Loop Rd. and Army Rd. It studies the atmosphere, the Northern Lights, earthquakes, etc., and guided tours are given free by the Office of University Relations. Not far away, on Yankovich Rd., check out the University's **Large Animal Research Station,** also known as the Musk Ox Farm (but not to be confused with the more well-known farm in Palmer). Researchers also study reindeer, caribou, and moose, and all the animals can be seen from an outdoor viewing platform. Guided tours are available during the summer. Farther east on Farmers Loop Rd., the **Alaska Dog Mushers Museum** (tel. *457–MUSH*) is the center of a large complex dedicated to dog sledding. (Admission $3.)

Of course the **trans–Alaska Pipeline** can be seen at several places along its 800-mile length, but one of the best is at a pulloff (or turnout, as they say up north) on the Steese Highway (Route 2) a little north of Hagelbarger Road, at about milepost 8.5. You can see a display explaining it all, and sometimes a couple of busloads of people all trying to do just that.

About a mile farther north, follow Goldstream Road and various signs in order to search out **Gold Dredge No. 8** (tel. *457–6058*), now a privately owned tourist attraction and the center of a rustic restaurant/ hotel operation. Nevertheless, this monstrous gold-mining machine, built in 1928, is on the National Register of Historic Buildings, and the guided tour through it is one of the best for learning how these things really operated. Admission tickets, which include the tour and a gold-panning experience, are around $5.

SIDE TRIPS

As the northernmost city of any population, Fairbanks is, naturally enough, the base for several trips into the Interior and also Arctic Alaska, including Prudhoe Bay and Barrow. (Other popular bush destinations in Western Alaska, like Nome and Kotzebue, are more easily reached from Anchorage, and they are covered in "Southcentral Alaska.")

NORTH OF FAIRBANKS   When Fairbanksans head north by road they often toss a towel and bathing trunks into the car and set out for one of three volcanic hot spots. The closest and most popular is the resort at **Chena Hot Springs,** about 60 miles away in the Chena River State Park. You can get detailed park information in Fairbanks from the Alaska State Division of Parks (tel. *479–4114*), 4420 Airport Way.

It's a beautiful drive, winter or summer, along the fully paved Chena Hot Springs Road. If you don't see any animals en route, stop at the **Pleasant Valley Animal Park** (tel. *488–3967*). Also, there is **Tack's General Store** for some great pies and great old-time atmosphere. The state park is a popular place for hiking in the summer and Nordic skiing in the winter. At the end of the road, the **Chena Hot Springs Resort** (tel. *452–7867*) is not exactly the Ritz, but most who make the trip enjoy the pool, Jacuzzis, hot tubs, etc., where water temperatures reach a high of about 160° (although most are kept lower than that). Overnight lodging in the lodge is fairly expensive; rustic cabins are cheaper. One of the owners is occasionally bidden to recite a Robert Service poem or two. And between about September and April, there may no place better to see the Northern Lights.

More of a real excursion, and a somewhat rougher trip, is the Steese Highway (Route 6) some 150 miles (each way, of course, and mostly on gravel) to **Circle Hot Springs.** This is a spectacular drive through the White Mountains and into the high tundra. The **Arctic Circle Hot Springs Resort** (tel. *520–5113*), at the end of a spur off the main road, has a good reputation, but we haven't yet seen it. If you want to dip your toes into the (much colder) Yukon River, continue another 30 miles on the Steese to **Circle.** Stop in to see the **Circle District Museum.** There is at least one motel in town, but we've lost the name—sorry!

The third place you can get into hot water north of Fairbanks is **Manley Hot Springs.** This means a trip of about 150 miles up the Elliott Highway (Route 2). The road is rough, but those who have driven it (not us, to date) say the view is worth all the shakes, rattles, and rolls. At the end of the road is the **Manley Hot Springs Resort** (tel. *672–3611*). In the village itself, the **Manley Roadhouse** has reportedly made the best hamburgers on the tundra since 1906. There's also a side spur to the old Indian village of **Minto.**

Real gluttons for a springs, shocks, and axle workout can indeed now drive during the summer alongside the **trans–Alaska Pipeline** on the gravel-only Dalton Highway. You'll bridge the Yukon River (there's a truck stop and motel units just on the other side), and then actually cross the Arctic Circle (marked by a huge sign) to continue as far as the group of buildings called **Coldfoot,** about 250 miles north of Fairbanks. A restaurant and hotel rooms are available at the **Arctic Acres Inn** (tel. *678–9301*), and this is the first place we ever saw *triple* glazed windows. Rooms average around $100, and you'd better have a paid reservation, since it is often filled with bus tours during the summer. Coldfoot is also considered the gateway to the **Gates of the Arctic National Park,** which you can only enjoy by hiking into or flying over. (We chose the latter, taking off with the sightseeing plane stationed on the strip alongside the Inn.) This is about as far north as the law allows you to drive. They'll turn you around for sure at Disaster Creek, about 35 miles from Coldfoot, since there are no more road services available for the last 200 miles to Prudhoe Bay. Those who continue on must show that they have a permit to do so.

The options for northern exploration open up considerably for those who fly from Fairbanks, however. One popular destination, to which there are no roads at all, is **Fort Yukon,** the old Hudson Bay Company headquarters almost precisely on the Arctic Circle, and at the point where the Porcupine River enters the Yukon River. Basically an Athabascan community, the village is served from Fairbanks by **Larry's Flying Service.** Fort Yukon does have a guided tour for those who arrange it in advance through the airlines. Indian beadwork items are good buys. Overnighters can stay at the **New Sourdough Hotel** (tel. *662–2402*) or at the **Gwitchyaa Zhee Lodge** (tel. *662–2468*). The town is completely "dry," meaning no alcoholic beverages are allowed at all.

THE NORTH SLOPE Although you're not allowed to drive up the northern portion of the Dalton Highway, you can at least fly to **Prudhoe Bay,** or rather to its service community of **Deadhorse.** Be warned, however, that this is entirely a no-nonsense work community for the vast oil fields that feed the trans–Atlantic Pipeline. There is virtually no evidence of civic pride or any kind of aesthetic effort, other than to keep things neat and clean in an attempt to forestall criticism from environmentalists and others who fear ecological damage to the North Slope, its herds of caribou, etc. All buildings are prefabricated—ATCO containers and similar boxy constructions—and many of them stand on stilts to avoid melting the permafrost. There are no permanent residents, and someday, when the oil runs out, man and all things manmade are supposed to be completely removed.

ARCO and Sohio, the two main oil companies, reportedly have some excellent indoor facilities strictly for their employees (theater, gym, swimming pool, etc.), but others are not permitted there and these are not even shown on the tours. In truth, most workers at Prudhoe Bay seem to have very little understanding or sympathy for visitors to the area. No alcohol is allowed at Prudhoe, and if you get on the same plane to "town" with these guys, you'll find out that's the first thing they want plenty of and fast.

You'll find nothing in Deadhorse/Prudhoe to make it seem like a normal town—no children, pets, parks, museums, art galleries, shopping malls, taxis, gourmet restaurants, frontier days celebrations, or anything to give any spirit to this community beyond simply doing the job. There are also very few women. We found it depressing, on a social level, and yet technologically fascinating at the same time. Wildflower appreciation and birdwatching for rare species which appear among the pipes, pumps, and ponds are considered excellent.

In any case, unless you have a business reason for going there, we believe Prudhoe Bay should be visited only as part of a guided tour. Hotels and cafeterias arranged by the packagers could best be described as "clean and functional," and are run with militarylike precision. If you don't get out of the dining room on time, somebody just might kick you out. Take mosquito repellent and prepare for summertime temperatures that are usually in the 50s—but sometimes lower or higher than that. Both **Princess Tours** (Royal Hyway) and **Holland America** (Gray Line) have good excursions from Fairbanks in which you are bused one way, flown the other. **MarkAir** also offers tours in connection with its flights to Deadhorse, and any of these would be a good way to see and learn something of this unique facility at the top of the world.

The northernmost community in North America, easily reached winter and summer by regular air service, is the Eskimo community of **Barrow,** which was most recently in the public eye during the efforts to save three California gray whales trapped under the ice there. Generally Barrow Eskimos are known for harvesting whales themselves, although a different kind (the bowhead) and during a very short season (April-May). Barrow is also remembered as the place where Wiley Post and Will Rogers were killed in a 1935 air crash, and a memorial marks the scene.

MarkAir jets to Barrow (via Prudhoe Bay) from Fairbanks (or Anchorage), and you can fly up in the morning, take a tour during the day, and then fly back in the evening. (MarkAir's tour fare from Fairbanks, including everything except meals, may run around $325 by your visit or perhaps $400 with overnight accommodation.) You can get around town by taxi, tour bus, community bus, or even rental car. (But look out; gas costs nearly $3 a gallon.) Sightseeing is mainly an appreciation for how a 20th-century version of a largely Eskimo community of 3000 survives on the tundra, in a location where the sun doesn't come up from Nov. 18 until Jan. 24, and doesn't go down between May 10 and Aug. 2.

Barrow's warmest month is July, by the way, when temperatures usually soar to the mid-40s. It often seems as if the wind will never stop blowing, so dress warmly. The treeless town is a strange conglomeration of wooden shanties leaning crazily among modern and expensive structures of glass and chrome—a reflection of modern profits from the oil fields. Front yards are decorated with dogs, truck parts, snow machines, sleds, and racks of drying skins.

Most travelers stay in the *Top of the World Hotel* (tel. *852–3900*), owned by the same Native corporation which owns *Tundra Tours,* the principal sightseeing operation. You can also stay at the *Barrow Airport Inn* (tel. *852–2525*). FIT rack rates for two at either will run around $125–150. Restaurants include *Pepe's North of the Border,* in modern Mexican motif; and *Mattie's Cafe,* where reindeer soup is a specialty.

EAST OF FAIRBANKS   Believe it or not, you can drive east of Fairbanks about 14 miles to get to **North Pole.** Between you and me while the kids are out of the room, that's North Pole, AK, not *the* North Pole. Nevertheless, as you drive along the Richardson Highway, you'll know it by the colossal red-and-white bearded statue of You Know Who. Next to that brobdingnagian Saint Nick is the famous **Santa Claus House,** a large, kitschy retail store where Christmas never ends. And lest you think that this area represents only the commercialization of Christmas and all that, North Pole also happens to be the location of a curiosity called **Jesus Town,** a large mission project which is housed in a group of log cabins with sod roofs.

Technically, the portion of Route 2 between Fairbanks and **Delta Junction** is part of the Richardson Highway (which continues down to Valdez), although many drivers (and even some books) consider it the last 100 miles of the Alaska Highway. You'll see occasional sections of the trans–Alaska Pipeline along this route. Near there, too, you'll find the **Big Delta State Historical Park,** just a half-mile off the road. The restored **Rica's Roadhouse** is the center of activity in the park. You sometimes see buffalo in this area.

Two hundred miles east of Fairbanks, the town of **Tok** is the first real community that Alaska Highway drivers see after entering Alaska from Canada, and it is there where you choose either to continue on to Fairbanks or take Route 1 (the Glenn Highway) to Anchorage. We inspected several accommodations in Tok, determining that the two Westmarks were the best places to stay, when they're not filled with bus people. (The **Westmark Tok** has the better facilities; the **Westmark Inn** has the better restaurant and it runs the KOA campground.) **Fast Eddy's** is also a popular restaurant. There are several other motels in the immediate vicinity. At the **Golden Bear Motel** you can ride Bucky, a stuffed moose (and have your picture taken). Don't miss the summer evening sled-dog demonstration sponsored by the **Burnt Paw,** a gift shop near the post office. There's also an excellent Alaska Public Lands Information Center and new visitors center right on the highway, just east of the junction.

WEST OF FAIRBANKS   The well-maintained all-weather George Parks Highway (Route 3) heads first west and then south out of the Golden Heart City, and it is the major route from Fairbanks for about 360 miles to Anchorage. On the way it passes Denali National Park and then the fertile Matanuska Valley (Wasilla and Palmer). About four miles out of Fairbanks the old village of **Ester** is known for nearby **Cripple Creek,** a rustic resort with perhaps more appeal to Alaskans than travelers from Outside. All the drinking, dancing, and drama may be fun for an evening, but the overnight accommodations we saw were not up to our minimum standards.

Another 50 miles or so along the highway, **Nenana** is most famous for its spring Ice Classic, for which bets are taken all over Alaska as to the exact date, hour, minute, and second the **Tanana River** will break up in the spring. Stop at the log cabin visitors center next to the highway. (For $2, you can cast a ballot there, too, but remember that if gambling is illegal in your home state, you will have to travel to Alaska again to collect your winnings.) Another 70 miles along the highway will bring you to *Denali National Park,* which is covered in detail in the second part of this chapter.

TOURS AND CRUISES

Fairbanks' premier tour for the past 30 years or so is aboard the paddle-wheeled riverboat *Discovery,* which is launched every morning during the summer by Captain Jim Binkley's **Discovery Riverboat Cruises** (tel. *479–6673*). Binkley himself is semi-retired now, but his family carries on, hiring knowledgeable young people, and buying still bigger and bigger boats to carry all who sign up for Fairbanks' most popular visitor attraction.

The boat leaves from his dock, off Dale Road, out by the airport, probably still at 8:45 a.m. and 2 p.m. and spends the next three hours cruising the Chena and Tanana rivers, passing some of the most interesting homes and other sites in the area. There are two stops, at an Athabascan village and at a dog mushers' training kennel; the operation makes the most of both, demonstrating the life and skills of the Indians and the care and training of sled dogs. If you can judge a tour by how much you learn and how much fun you had at the same time, this one wins on both counts. (We thought we had had enough Indian lore and dog stuff elsewhere in Alaska before the cruise, but this one turned out to be the best.) Of course the mid-season large crowds can make things difficult, but on balance it was worth the crush. If you make your own way to the dock, fares for either the morning or afternoon cruise may be around $30 by 1990, and it would be a darn good idea to reserve in advance. (It will cost you more in combination with a bus tour, of course.)

As for *bus tours* around the area, there are four or five sightseeing companies operating in Fairbanks. Three of them are headquartered out of state: **Gray Line of Alaska** (tel. *452–2843*), owned by Holland America/Westours; **Royal Hyway Tours** (tel. *452–8801*), also sometimes called Tour Alaska, and owned by Princess Cruises; and **Alaska Sightseeing** (tel. *452–8518*), also called TravAlaska, and headquartered in Seattle. All three have had many years of experience in Alaska. The local firms, who may reply with a brochure if you call or write them in advance, are **Red Hat Tours** (tel. *457–3000*), P.O. Box 10622, Fairbanks, AK 99710; and possibly **Gold Rush Tours** (tel. *455–6208*), 1170 Propwash Dr., Fairbanks, AK 99709. Much is sometimes made over their local spirit and special knowledge imparted by longtime Fairbanks residents and all that stuff. That's as may be, but we have found that the big boys from out of town are often smart enough to hire good local guides and drivers, too. Perhaps a more legitimate reason for choosing Red Hat or any local sightseeing firm anywhere is that they are less likely to be chock-full already with large and gregarious cruise and tour groups. FITs (individual travelers) like us sometimes feel a little like the new kid in class.

Any of these outfits will probably offer a three-hour morning or afternoon tour of Fairbanks for around $25, an all-day tour of Greater Fairbanks for around $45, including lunch, plus various combination deals at higher rates, which include the *Discovery* cruise, the salmon bake, the Good as Gold evening show, etc. Some will also have two-day (overnight) tours to Denali National Park which either return you to Fairbanks or take you on to Anchorage. Figure roughly $250 per person for one of these.

One different kind of tour of downtown Fairbanks is **Helgeson's Livestock** (tel. *452–2843*), if it is still available. This looks sort of like an old-time trolley car, except on rubber tires and pulled by two "Registered Belgian" draft horses. The one-hour trot may cost around $7 or $8.

One of the best long-distance tours we have made anywhere was the three-day, two-night excursion out of Fairbanks for 500 miles up the Dalton Highway, alongside the trans–Alaska Pipeline to **Prudhoe Bay,** the oil well complex at the top edge of Alaska on the shores of the Beaufort Sea. Our tour, operated by **Royal Hyway Tours** (tel. *456– 8131*), the land facility for Princess Cruises, began in Fairbanks, stopped overnight in Coldfoot, just north of the Arctic Circle, continued across the Brooks Range and down the North Slope to Deadhorse, the support town for the oil fields. After another night there and a tour through the facilities we flew back to Fairbanks on MarkAir. You can take this tour in reverse, but we preferred the way we did it, and if you get as good a guide as we did (his name was Paul, by the way), you'll see and learn about the Alaskan bush, particularly the seldom-seen tundra and caribou country above Coldfoot where private vehicles are generally not allowed.

Princess/Royal Hyway pioneered this unusual trip, although a very similar tour is now offered by its principal rival, **Gray Line** (tel. *452– 2843*). Its tour is called the *North Slope Explorer,* and we have heard no complaints about their operation, either. Fares for 1990 for either one are not available at this writing, but figure in the neighborhood of $600 or $700, including transportation, accommodations, and some meals. The trips are only available approximately between June and August, and try to reserve as far in advance as possible, particularly for the busy July departures. (If you are reading this before your Alaska trip, check with a travel agent or the addresses and/or toll-free numbers listed in "Coming Into the Country"; if you are in Fairbanks at the moment, you could get lucky if you call the above numbers.)

Both Princess Cruises (Tour Alaska) and Holland America (Gray Line) also offer competing excursions in their own special *dome cars of the Alaska Railroad* to Denali National Park, and these can be taken either from Fairbanks or Anchorage (see details in "Southcentral Alaska"). Gray Line also lists a four-day, three-night bus trip out of Fairbanks called the Alaska Highway Explorer, which will take you via Whitehorse to Skagway. Full fare is in the $500–600 neighborhood for that one. (Of course, from Skagway you can take a boat for Juneau or Seattle.)

If you would like to experience something of the Dalton Highway at least as far north as the Arctic Circle, you might check out the *one-day excursion* from Fairbanks offered by the **Northern Alaska Tour Company** (tel. *479–3402*). On the way back these buses stop for dinner at the truck stop just beside the Yukon River. Cost for the journey should run around $75 by your visit.

Some *wilderness experiences* on the Yukon River are taken out by the **Yukon Explorer** (tel. *479–8817*), a one-man operation headquartered in Fairbanks. Alfred "Bear" Ketzler, Jr., tailors his itinerary largely to the interests of his passengers. All are vanned up to Circle City first, where they board his 21-foot Gregor, licensed for seven passengers. A weekend camping and exploring the river in the Circle area will run around $300 per person. Longer trips up the Yukon to Eagle and Dawson City, one-way or round-trip, will run appreciably more. Plan this trip a long time in advance, and write Captain Bear at 201 First Ave., Fairbanks, AK 99701. We haven't gone, but it sounds like it could be a lot of fun.

Another *river excursion* into the bush is offered by trapper Bob Harte under the name **Porcupine River Voyages** (tel. *488–0436*). Harte follows an old fur-trading route, taking his people from Circle City on canoes (for more experienced travelers) or riverboat (for us tenderfeet) on the Yukon River to Fort Yukon then up the Porcupine River to Old Crow in the Yukon, or the reverse. Usually Harte also makes a side trip up the Coleen River into the Arctic National Wildlife Refuge (ANWR), currently the center of an oil-versus-caribou controversy. Trips run from one to two weeks. Prices vary widely depending on exact arrangements, but figure on something between $500 and $1300, plus air fares. If you go, let us know. You can write Trapper Bob at 240 Skye-Lee Way, Fairbanks, AK 99712.

A little less complex, perhaps, are the new **Spell of the Yukon Tours** (tel. *455–6128*). The two-day, one-night tour is a *bus tour* to Circle, which also includes a *riverboat tour* on the Yukon, as well as dog mushing and gold-panning experiences. Perhaps $300, including meals. (Recheck this by phone or with the folks at the FCVB.)

Aerial tours: Jet air excursions to the Eskimo village of **Barrow** and on to the oil fields at **Prudhoe Bay** are flown from Fairbanks or Anchorage by **MarkAir** (tel. *452–7577*). These Top of the World Tours come in several configurations depending on whether you stay overnight in Barrow, in Prudhoe Bay, or both. Figure a total outlay of about $325 to $450 round-trip from Fairbanks. These same tours are also sold by **Alaska Sightseeing** (tel. *452–8518*) in Fairbanks.

Several of the commuter airlines mentioned in "Transportation" will offer aerial tours or flightseeing into the Alaskan wilderness from Fairbanks, although you should ask each about landings and the availability of ground tours at each one. More well-established ones include the following: **Larry's Flying Service** (tel. *474–9169*) has flights to the Arctic National Wildlife Refuge (ANWR) at Kaktovik, to Fort Yukon, to Arctic Village and to Deadhorse (Prudhoe Bay). **Wright Air Service** (tel. *474–0502*) has tours to Anaktuvuk Pass (around $230) and Denali (about $150). **Midnight Sun Aviation** (tel. *452–7039*) has flights running from 30 to 90 minutes over Fairbanks and vicinity, running for around $75 to $175. **Frontier Flying Service** (tel. *474–0014*) is less structured; you go along with the mail plane to whatever bush villages are on the schedule for the day.

Helicopter? **Era Aviation** (tel. *474–0838*), well known in several places around the state, has one popular chopper tour out of Fairbanks that we know about: Tour F-1, The Great Interior, a flight around greater Fairbanks that lasts about 25 minutes and costs about $85, as last report. Era also has sightseeing flights at Prudhoe Bay (P-1, 30 minutes for around $130).

Winter visitors should be sure to check with the CVB log cabin Visitors Center to see what is available off season. One we have heard of and which sounds interesting is **Alaskan Treks** (tel. *455–6326*). They set up some special dog-mushing experiences in the bush, and perhaps some other things like guided cross-country skiing.

SPORTS

Fishermen will find some of the state's best grayling and pike fishing in streams around the Fairbanks-North Star Borough. You can even catch some salmon in the Tanana River, but not much; the water is clouded with so much glacial silt the fish can't see the lures! *Hunting* is excellent, with trophy-size kills of moose, caribou, bear, Dall sheep, and various water fowl possible. Full information on guides, licenses, etc., is available at the Alaska Public Lands Information Center (tel. *451–7352*) at Third Ave. and Cushman St.

Believe it or not, you can play 18 holes of *golf* at the **Fairbanks Golf and Country Club** (tel. *479–6555*) for three or four months out of the year. You'll find it at 1820 Yankovich Rd., near the Musk Ox Farm. Green fees are around $12, and the greens are constructed of Astroturf. For military duffers, there's another set of links on the post at Fort Wainwright. As we recall, both claim to be the northernmost course of their type in the world. The fairways are difficult to keep in good condition during the short growing season, of course.

Tennis is not a very popular sport in Fairbanks, although you will see a court here and there around town. A couple of local athletic clubs offer indoor tennis. *Bowlers* can exercise their talents at **AlaskaLanes** (tel. *479–3800*). *Hiking* and *biking* is big in this flat countryside, along, of course, with their winter equivalents, *snow-shoeing* and *cross-country skiing*. All this is particularly popular in the **Birch Hill Ski Area** off the Steese Highway and the **Skarland Trails** behind the UAF campus. (Ask the visitor center for a list.) You can rent *bicycles* or *canoes* at the **Lucky Sourdough Tourist Trap** (tel. *456–2522*) at Third Ave.

and Barnett St. Canoe rentals are also possible at **Riverfront Rentals** (tel. *479–8968*), which may even teach you to canoe, too.

As far as spectator sports are concerned, *hockey* is wildly popular in Fairbanks. The Alaska Gold Kings, a semipro team, has a loyal following. The summer equivalent is *baseball,* and the Fairbanks Goldpanners have often been ABL champions. Its most famous contest, of course, is the midnight baseball game that is played at Growden Field on a weekend day closest to the summer solstice—without benefit of artificial lighting!

SHOPPING

Fairbanks has at least seven—count 'em, seven—shopping malls, which seems surprising for a city of this size, until you begin figuring it out. For one thing, malls (most of them enclosed) are an important part of social life throughout the cold and dark winter. For another, Fairbanks serves as a mecca for an extremely large rural community. When folks living in villages or isolated cabins hundreds of miles away talk of going "to town," they mean Fairbanks.

Largest of the type is the **Bentley Mall** at the corner of Old Steese Highway and College Rd., north of the river. Others include the **University Center Mall** at University Ave. and Airport Way; **North Gate Square** at 338 Old Steese Highway; **Gavora Mall,** Third St. (not Third Ave.) near the Steese Highway; **West Valley Plaza,** near the University; **Shopper's Forum** at Airport Way and Wickersham St.; and **Washington Plaza** at 3417 Airport Way, corner of Washington St. Not all department stores are in the suburbs, however. Downtown firms include **J. C. Penney** at 610 Cushman St. and **Nordstrom's** at 610 Second Ave.

Local products to buy in Fairbanks include, of course, all those *Eskimo carvings* of ivory and soapstone sold all over the state. We also saw some of the best Eskimo-made caribou-hide *masks* in Fairbanks. But beyond that, look for locally made *Athabascan handicraft* like birch bark baskets, fine bead work, and gloves and other products made from moose and caribou hide, perhaps trimmed with beaver fur. Athabascan earrings made of porcupine quills are attractive and not expensive. They're also known for beaver skin hats, although these are becoming a little hard to find, except at bazaars and other special fairs. Products made of qiviut (musk ox underfur) are wonderful—but expensive—anywhere you see them. (One of the nicest things about qiviut, as far as we are concerned, is the knowledge that the animal is not sacrificed nor harmed in any way in order to collect this supersoft material.)

More conventional *furs* are sold at **Gerald Victor** (tel. *456–6890*), a long-time Fairbanks family firm at 212 Lacey St., between Second and Third avenues. Some of their goods are imported. Another, with more local furs, is the **Fur Factory** (tel. *452–6240*) at 121 Dunkel St., corner of Wendell. If you don't know furs, take someone with you who does into any fur store. Always question terms like "Alaskan sable" (there is no genuine sable in Alaska, and the animal was probably a marten).

In downtown Fairbanks there are two or three high-quality *souvenir, crafts, and art stores*. The **Arctic Travelers Gift Shop** (tel. *456–7080*), at Second and Cushman, has a large selection. The clerks wear kuspuks, and sometimes artisans are at work on the premises. (Postcards, at 10 cents are a loss leader.) **Beds and Things** (tel. *456–2323*), formerly known as the Alaska Native Artists and Crafts Center, on Second Ave. east of Cushman, is a co-op operation owned by several Native groups. More possibilities include the **Craft Market** on the corner of Fifth Ave. and Noble St.; the **House of Wood,** an art gallery in an historic building at 411 Sixth Ave.; and **New Horizons Gallery,** at 815 Second Ave., which specializes in *Alaskan art.*

Meanwhile, out in Alaskaland, you may want to peek into the **Pick-N-Poke** shop in Cabin 57. Also **Alaskan Apparel,** which sells *parkas, mukluks, etc.,* in Cabin 31. *Crafts* and *paintings* are also featured at **The Art Works** (tel. *479–2563*) at Campus Corner, College Rd. and University Ave. There are also some authentic items sold at the aforementioned **University of Alaska Museum** on the UAF campus.

Remember to look for the "Made in Alaska' sticker of two bears, or the oval shape with the silver hand, which signifies handmade Native goods; or the Alaska map logo, which means genuine Alaskan handicraft.

Gold nugget jewelry is sold at some of the above plus some addresses that specialize in jewelry. Sorry, but we didn't dig far enough into this to recommend any place over any other. Some of the better shops appear to include **A Touch of Gold** at the Bentley Mall; **Perdue's Jewelry,** at the Shoppers Forum Mall; **Gold Mine Jewelers,** at 402 Fifth Ave. (between Lacey and Noble streets); and **Matrix/Oxford Assaying,** at 208 Wendell Ave. The later company also mints its own silver souvenir, a one-troy-ounce Alaska medallion, which sells for around $10 (depending on the silver market).

Book stores? You'll find these major outlets in Fairbanks. A branch of the famous **Book Cache** (tel. *479–6727*) is installed in the University Mall; **Martin's Books** (tel. *456–2240*), especially for rare Alaskana, is upstairs at 455 Third Ave.; and **Waldenbooks** (tel. *456–8088*) does a good business in the Bentley Mall.

MISCELLANEOUS ADDRESSES AND PHONES

Fairbanks' address idiosyncrasy is that it has mainly numbered avenues, but at least a few numbered streets, too (e.g., Fourth Avenue is quite different from Fourth Street). As in virtually all of Alaska, the telephone area code is 907. Most phone numbers begin with 45, but a few begin 47. Zip codes all start with 997, running between 99701 and 99775.

- Alaska State Department of Fish and Game (tel. *452–1531*), 1300 College Rd.
- Alaska State Parks and Recreation Division (tel. *479–4114*), 4418 Airport Way.
- Crimestoppers (tel. *456–CLUE*).
- Denali National Park, recorded information (tel. *452–PARK*).
- Diet Center (tel. *452–SLIM*), 1028 Aurora Dr.
- Emergency calls of any kind (tel. 911).
- Fairbanks Memorial Hospital (tel. *452–8181*) 1650 Cowles St.
- Fairbanks Clinic (tel. *452–1761*), 1867 Airport Way.
- Fairbanks Police (non-emergency, tel. *452–1527*), 656 Seventh Ave.
- Fire and ambulance service. (tel. *452–1527*).
- Northern Lights Council of Dancers (round and square) (tel. *452–5699*).
- Northward Barber Shop (tel. *452–2480*), Northward Building, Fifth Ave. and Lacy St.
- Plaza Cleaners and Laundry (tel. *479–0791*). Washington Plaza, 3417 Airport Way.
- Poison Control Center (tel. *474–0137*).
- State police (tel. *452–1313*), 1979 Peger Rd.
- Thrifty Truck and Car Wash (tel. *479–4961*), 175 University Ave.
- U.S. Post Office (tel. *452–3203*), Downtown Station, 315 Barnette St.
- Visitor Information Center (CVB) (tel. *456–5774*), 550 First Ave. (Toll-free from out of state *(800) 327–5774*).

DENALI NATIONAL PARK

Any first-time visitor to Fairbanks or Anchorage who does not set aside some quality time for Denali is probably missing the main point of an Alaskan vacation. While Denali is not the only wilderness experience in the state, it is one that nearly every *cheechako* can have, no matter how tender his feet.

The park is named after Mount McKinley, the peak the Indians called Denali—the high one. At 20,320 feet, the majestic mountain in the Alaska Range is the tallest in North America—and reputedly the highest mountain on earth compared with its surrounding terrain. No less astute an observer than Captain George Vancouver, who first saw Denali from the deck of a ship more than 200 miles away, called it "stupendous." Conversation at the park, on the train or on the highway often revolves around whether or not "the mountain is out." Indeed, Denali is obscured by clouds about 60% to 70% of the time; when it is out, however, it is an impressive sight.

But the 6-million-acre park has a second claim to fame, and one which is much more dependable than a clear, unobstructed view of the famous mountain. It is the home of more than 30 species of mammals and an incredible 150 kinds of birds, not to mention a botanist's dream, full of floral and plant species—and all this on virtually treeless alpine tundra. If you didn't see grizzly bears, moose, caribou, and wild sheep elsewhere in Alaska, you'll see them in Denali. You may also be lucky enough to get a close-up view of wolf, wolverine, red fox, lynx, snowshoe hare, and more.

TRANSPORTATION

The park entrance is about 120 miles south of Fairbanks or 240 miles north of Anchorage, easily reached from either city by the George Parks Highway, the Alaska Railroad, or by air. Via any of these routes, when the weather is good, the scenery is stunning. There are no taxis or rental cars available locally. Still, you don't need a private car to get

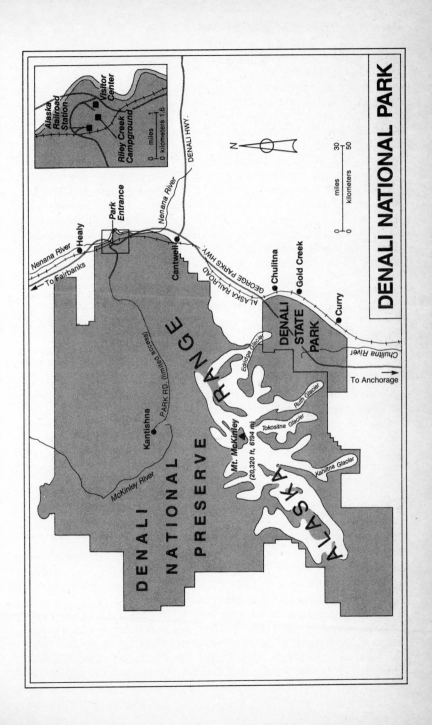

DENALI NATIONAL PARK

around in the immediate vicinity, and with various parking problems, a car might be a liability anyway.

The most popular way to come to the park, and usually the most convenient, too, is via the **Alaska Railroad** (see Fairbanks and Anchorage listings for telephone numbers). The train to the park takes about four hours from Fairbanks or about seven hours from Anchorage. One stopover is allowed on a trip between the two cities, and that is typically made at Denali. The train runs daily during the summer, weekly during the winter; the fare is around $90 between the two cities in the railroad's own Vistadome car, where the 24 good seats up top have to be shared by trading seats from time to time with the 36 passengers on the lower level. Of course, some folks come to Denali on the super-luxurious dome cars of either *Tour Alaska's* Midnight Sun Express (Princess Cruises) or *Westours'* McKinley Explorer (Holland-America), attached to the same trains (see Anchorage "Tours and Cruises" for details).

Long-distance bus service is provided by **Alaska-Denali Transit** (tel. *683–2798*) to and from Haines via Anchorage; **Alaska Sightseeing Tours** to and from Fairbanks and Anchorage; **Gray Line of Alaska,** which is run by Westours, to and from Fairbanks and Anchorage; and **Royal Hyway Tours** (tel. *683–2282*), also called Tour Alaska, also to and from Fairbanks and Anchorage.

The national park has its own airstrip, which is within walking distance of the hotel and the information center. **Era Aviation** schedules flights from and to Anchorage only. Flight time is one hour and 15 minutes in Era's DeHavilland Twin Otters. (With their reversible prop pitch, these planes can land in less than 100 yards, if they want to.) The one-way fare between Denali-Anchorage is around $100. The only flights between Denali and other areas, including Fairbanks, are via air taxis.

HOTELS AND MOTELS

We saw a half-dozen places to stay in the National Park area, and all will do, at least as far as basic facilities are concerned. You will want one with a dining room that opens by at least 5 a.m. so you can have something to eat before leaving on a park tour. You can make advance reservations at some of the area resorts, along with several tours and other activities, from Denali National Park Central Reservations (tel. *274–5366*), P.O. Box 200984, Anchorage, AK 99520. Or ask them for an up-to-date brochure and rate sheet. None of these are open in the winter; the closest cold-weather accommodations are in Healy, 12 miles north.

On convenience alone, the winner has to be the **Denali National Park Hotel** (tel. *683–2215*), owned by the Federal government but operated by ARA Outdoor World, the official national park concessionaire. If the facility has a sort of temporary look and feel, that's because it is. The original hotel burned down a few years back. First they put everyone up in some old railway cars, and when that was finally judged unsafe they put offices in them instead and then hooked together several modular prefabricated buildings. A new hotel will not be built from the ground up until at least 1992.

Rambling structures spreading out from a large but often crowded lobby; Whistle Stop Snack Shop and Denali Dining Room to one side; Gold Spike Saloon installed in one of the railroad cars; 300-seat auditorium for park presentations; McKinley Gift Shop also on the premises; about 100 no-nonsense bedrooms with double or twin beds, an easy chair, desk, lamp, and that's about it; no televisions or telephones; all well-maintained if unspectacular; double rates perhaps $110 or $120 by 1990 (but check for a possible two nights for the price of one between mid-May and mid-June). This is the only hotel located near the airport, railroad station, information center, etc., and still within the park itself. (Reservations from the hotel or in winter from ARA headquarters, tel. *(907) 276–7234,* or write to 825 W. Eighth Ave., Anchorage, AK 99501.)

Although there is no real town connected with the park, there is quite a lot of commercial activity along the highway just north and south of the park entrance, and there are frequent shuttle buses to the park from some hotels. The nicest lodge overall for miles around is the recently enlarged **Harper Lodge** (tel. *683–2282*), operated by the Princess Cruises/Tour Alaska/Royal Hyway interests on the west side of the road. Comfortable, colorful log lobby with wood-burning fireplace; tasteful gift shop; friendly bar/lounge; popular Summit dining room with river view; cheerful staff; open Jacuzzis out back on the picnic deck; 187 bedrooms in several configurations; a few with private Jacuzzis; all fully equipped with phones and TVs (unusual in the area); some smaller models with two single beds, used often for tour groups; excellent maintenance and housekeeping throughout; units in the building above the lobby with panoramas of the Nenana River; high-season rack rates from around $135; good discounts in the shoulder season (about May 26–June 16 and Sept. 6–18, closed about Sept. 19–May 25). This was our own headquarters recently, and we certainly weren't sorry. (Reservations through Princess Cruises, tel. *(800) 426–0442.)*

Another deservedly popular choice outside the park is the **Mc-Kinley Chalet Resort** (tel. *683–2215*), a rambling set of cedar log buildings on a wide campus a little north of Harper Lodge, run by ARA

Services, and often populated with the overflow from the Denali Park Hotel. Active, wood-paneled lobby, often punctuated by loudspeaker announcements; non-stop videotape on Alaskan wildlife; Johnny Johnson nature photographs everywhere (except in the living units where walls are generally bare); good bar and attractive dining room with terrific river view; health club, small swimming pool and activity center in a separate building; popular and fun Cabin Night wilderness dinner show on the premises; 220 rooms in 14 buildings; many a long huff-puff down the hill from the lobby; a shuttle from them usually available; most living units unspectacular but neat enough with two single beds; no closets; double room rates about $130 or so; two-for-one deals perhaps mid-May through mid-June. (Reservations from the hotel or as above under the Denali National Park Hotel.)

Other establishments on the highway outside the park include **Mt. McKinley Village** (tel. *683–2265),* seven miles south and also run by ARA. Fairly basic double rooms will run around $100 there. (Some guests told us that they couldn't get an early breakfast, though.) Then there's next-door **Denali Cabins** (tel. *683–2643*), where private-bath units run around $100, share-bath units perhaps $80. Similar rates and facilities are available at **Denali Crows Nest Cabins** (tel. *683–6723*), which also has some hot tubs. And all rooms at the **McKinley Wilderness Cabins** (tel. *683–2277*) are with shared bath, at rates of around $80, including breakfast. If you're a family of four, these last three are a pretty good deal.

Three other interesting places to stay are over 90 miles inside the park and are on private property which is protected by a grandfather clause. **Camp Denali** (tel. *683–2290*) and the nearby **North Face Lodge** are both under the same management, and reservations must be made in advance for specific arrival and departure dates between mid-June and early-Sept. Both have some excellent views of the mountain. Camp Denali has 17 individual cabins with outside running water and no electricity, and is famous both for its food and for naturalist tours in the park. North Face Lodge has 15 rooms, all with indoor plumbing and electricity. Figure a little over $200 per person per night at either, with all meals and several activities included. (For information off season, call *(603) 675–2248* and ask for a brochure.)

We also saw the cabins five miles farther at the **Kantishna Roadhouse** (tel. *733–2535*), on the site of a 1905 mining camp. Today Kantishna even has its own air strip, and guests can and do fly in to stay, even in the winter. The living facilities seem fairly primitive and are not cheap, although each cabin does have electricity and gas heat. The meals are good, and for the right people the lifestyle can't be beat. Rates vary widely with different package arrangements. Write for details to the Kantishna Roadhouse at P.O. Box 130, Denali National Park, Kantishna, AK 99755.

Campgrounds: The National Park Service operates seven campgrounds within the park, some for both RVs and tents. Most campsites are around $10. You can register for up to 14 days or, if all sites are full, book a site no more than 24 hours in advance at the park's Riley Creek Information Center (see "Sights and Sites"). For complete information, write the Superintendent, Denali National Park, AK 99755 or tel. *(907) 683–2294.* The closest place with full RV hook-ups (dump and electricity) is the **McKinley KOA Campground** (tel. *683–2379*), 12 miles up the road in Healy.

RESTAURANTS AND DINING

You'll find no truly gourmet restaurants in or near Denali, but a few are worth noting. One of the best is the **Summit** (tel. *683–2282*), in the Harper Lodge. Knotty pine interior with green accents; a high, beamed ceiling; most entrees in the $17–20 range; carafe wine available. Sara had reindeer Estouffade and I ordered chicken breast pecan, and both were excellent. Be aware, however, that the burnt cream dessert is served warm. (Not our cup of *brulee.*)

The river view is unsurpassed in some reaches of the blue-and-white dining room just up the road a piece at the **McKinley Chalet Resort** (tel. *683–2215*). Unfortunately for us reformed tobaccoholics, the grandest vistas are in the smoking section. Specialties include the Salmon Wellington with Pernod, about $18.75, and the Veal Saltimbocca, about $20. A different location at the McKinley Chalet is also the site of the Cabin Night dinner theater (See "Entertainment and Night Life"). Unfortunately, both the Summit and the Chalet Resort seem to have a water source that contains enough calcium and other natural minerals to alter the taste of the water—and the coffee. (You may get used to it after a couple of days, but few visitors hang around that long.)

The **Denali Dining Room** (tel. *683–2215*) in the Park Hotel, is unfancy but serviceable. Cream-colored walls with walnut wainscotting; globe wall sconces; isolated ivy pots; oaken tables with high-backed chairs; overhead fans. You can get a special lunch buffet for around $9.95. The fettucine Alfredo is a specialty—perhaps $6.95 at lunch, $9.95 at dinner.

You'll find a raft of snack bars all around the place. At the park hotel, next to the dining room, the **Whistle Stop Snack Shop** offers faster food up to midnight. You'll find pretty good pizza and some Mexican specialties at **Lynx Creek,** next to Harper Lodge. See if the jukebox still has on it the Johnny Horton number that goes: "When it's springtime in Alaska, it's forty below . . .''

ENTERTAINMENT AND NIGHT LIFE

The wisdom around here is that wildlife and night life don't mix very well. That is, since most folks look forward to getting up at 4 a.m. and leaving an hour later so they can be entertained by bears, moose, and such, they're not much interested in any late-night carousing.

One entertaining exception is "Alaska Cabin Night," a rollicking good time in the special dinner-theater cabin at the **McKinley Chalet Resort** (tel. *683–2215*). For a one-price ticket—probably still under $20—they get a family-style meal of salmon, ribs, beans, corn, potatoes, salad, dessert, and more. Before some folks are finished chowing down, the waiters and waitresses turn into actors and actresses and put on a show based on gold rush days in the Interior. This one is a little different than some other north country revues. We liked meeting the other folks at the table and then enjoying the performance together. If you choose the early show, you can still be in bed by 9 p.m.

If we expand "entertainment" to include things interesting and educational (and try to forget the night life angle for a while), there are several activities to consider.

Three times a day rangers give a **Sled Dog Demonstration** to show how they use dogs during the winter. There's a free bus from the hotel and other places to the kennels.

In the auditorium at the Park Hotel, evening programs are usually given at 7 p.m. and 9 p.m. by the park rangers. These are **narrated slide shows, movies,** and other subjects related to the national park itself. Check the hotel and park bulletin boards for details.

Park rangers generally led **off-road hikes** from time to time, going for as long as three or four hours in the taiga or on the tundra. Some get to the starting point by a bus ride. For the less energetic, they also do an **evening walk and talk** for an hour or so through the spruce and aspen forest near the park hotel probably beginning at 8 p.m. There's still plenty of light, of course.

Beyond that, most of the hotels in the vicinity have a bar attached for die-hard stay-uppers. A few will offer some live entertainment on the weekends.

SIGHTS AND SITES

The biggest mistake that anyone can make at Denali National Park is to come in and leave on the same day. Our strong advice is to spend at least one night in the area, preferably two. And those who hang around even longer than that can have still more experiences that they would otherwise miss.

Schedule yourself to arrive no later than the early afternoon, and save the rest of that day to become oriented and to make arrangements on precisely what to do the following day. This is particularly important if you show up during the busiest time between late June and early August, when the park is most popular—and most crowded. Keep an eye out for *Denali Alpenglow,* the free tabloid-size newspaper put out once each summer by the National Park Service. It is chock full of essential information on the best way to enjoy the park and surrounding area, as well as such important advice as how to avoid too-close en-counters with grizzly bears.

The first stop in the park should be at either the original **Riley Creek Information Center** or the brand-new **Visitor Access Center,** which is due to open nearby in 1990. At this writing, it is not precisely clear which facility will handle what activities. At one or the other you will pay your park entrance fee ($3 at this writing; seniors and young-sters free), register for any campground space (and check out your bear-proof food containers), and pick up any free shuttle bus tickets to go farther into the park. (More on this in a minute.) Neither of these cen-ters should be confused with Park Headquarters, which is in still another location. It is strictly for administrative activities and generally not for public use.

There is really only one two-lane road in Denali, and it extends for more than 90 miles. If you bring in a private car, you will only be allowed to drive along the paved portion for the first 12 miles west, and if you're lucky, you can see **Mount McKinley,** albeit still 80 miles away at this point. Sighting wildlife along this short stretch is also prob-lematical, although you could spot a few moose, caribou, and Dall sheep in May and early June during the calving season (and perhaps a grizzly too). As the weather gets warmer, though, the wildlife generally moves farther west.

There are four ways to get farther into the park yourself, and two of them we cover in the our section on "Tours and Cruises." A third way is to ask for a back-country camping permit from the Park Service. (Only a limited number are available.) The easiest method and the one chosen by most Denali visitors is to take the free shuttle buses, which are nothing more than yellow school buses diverted to park use during the summer. A certain number of tickets are set aside for each shuttle bus departure, and you might have to wait two or three hours before your bus leaves. (Show up 10 minutes before departure time, too, or they may give your seat away to someone on a line of standbys.) Be aware that during the busiest periods, the park service even runs out of tokens for that day. (Except for perhaps the first bus of the day, they don't give out one token for each seat, either, since the bus must save room to pick up passengers who have left other buses along the way.) The only way to be sure of getting on one of these departures, and perhaps on the bus you want, is to show up the previous day since they may be reserved 24 hours in advance (another good reason for over-nighting at the park).

Once you have begun your bus trip, however, you can get off and on these buses wherever you want (except near a bear, of course) and as often as you like, picking up another bus that may be going in the same or the opposite direction. If you stay on one single bus, however, note that the shortest round trip is 5½ hours and goes as far as **Poly-chrome Pass,** 46 miles into the park. A second route goes farther, 66 miles to the **Eielson Visitor Center,** for a total of eight hours round trip. The center is a terrific place to photograph the Mountain if it is out. It is also only a half-mile from the massive Muldrow Glacier on the lower slopes of the famous peak.

The longest trip is the 86-mile one to **Wonder Lake,** which uses up 11 hours all told. *These trips are not guided tours.* The drivers are school bus drivers, and they do not have any kind of lecture responsi-bility. They'll stop for a while whenever any passenger asks them to do so—a request that's usually as simple as shouting "Moose! Moose!" (or whatever the creature may be). Or they'll stop for a moment if you want to get a good picture of Mount McKinley or just a panoramic view of the alpine tundra. Rest room stops are routinely scheduled about every hour and a quarter.

If the shuttle schedule continues as it has been, the first bus leaves at 6 a.m. and then another comes along every half-hour until 1 p.m. Then they run on the hour until 5 p.m. The late bus leaves at 7 p.m., returning around midnight, and very few tickets are given out for that one since it must be able to pick up stragglers who are already in the park. On any bus, take something along to eat and drink, although water is available from time to time, and there are a few vending machines at the Eielson Visitor Center, if you're going that far into the park.

If all this sounds complicated, it will become clear to you after you arrive at the park. Try to be patient with the system; the use of the shuttle buses has been a successful alternative to allowing the public to drive lots of private cars into the park, which tends to frighten away the wildlife. (During short slow periods at the very beginning and end of the season, cars are sometimes allowed past the checkpoint.) Don't forget to take food, warm clothes, insect repellent, binoculars, camera, and lots of film. (For other ways to get farther into the park, see "Tours and Cruises.")

SIDE TRIPS

About 40 miles south on the Parks Highway and then about 14 miles back on a side road, sits the strange and rather rustic town of **Talkeetna,** which seems not to have changed a whole heck of a lot in the last 50 or 75 years. This sleepy backwater community, once a main stop on the Alaska railroad, now plays a distinctive role in connection with Denali National Park. It serves as the principal staging area for climbers of Mount McKinley (Denali). This is partly because Talkeetna is also the traditional headquarters for several air taxi companies, and climbers employ these bush pilots in order to reach the area on the lower slopes of the mountain where the climbs normally begin.

Persons interested in climbing or learning something about mountaineering in the Alaska Range should check with the NPS Ranger Station (tel. *733–2231*), P.O. Box 327, Talkeetna, AK 99676. Air taxi operations, all of which are fully qualified to operate flightseeing tours of the park, include **Doug Geeting Aviation** (tel. *733–2366*), **K2 Aviation** (tel. *733–2291*), and **Talkeetna Air Taxi** (tel. *733–2218*), which is the one run by Lowell Thomas, Jr., the former lieutenant governor and son of the famous travel writer. You'll see all their offices on the main street (the only one that's paved). Figure an average of about $100 per person for an hour-long flight over Denali and the Alaska Range.

Persons tarrying in Talkeetna a little longer can eat and sleep at the historic *Fairview Inn* (tel. *733–2423*), which serves as an unofficial community center, or at the *Talkeetna Roadhouse* (tel. *733–2341*), where we had a meatloaf sandwich for around $5. Double rooms at either run around $35–40. (There are also a couple of motels in the immediate area.) The *Talkeetna Museum* has an interesting display and serves as an unofficial information center for the village. Many Alaskans know Talkeetna as the site of the annual Moose Dropping Festival the second Saturday in July.

TOURS AND CRUISES

Back at the park itself, a more comfortable and more enlightening alternative to the yellow shuttle buses is to take the six- to eight-hour experience offered by **Tundra Wildlife Tours** (tel. *683–2215*). This is the same as the hotel phone number since both operations are owned by ARA Outdoor World, the official park concessionaire. There are at least four big advantages to these tours over the shuttle buses: (1) they include the services of a combination driver-guide who gives a good running commentary, (2) they provide a box lunch and coffee, (3) they're a heck of a lot more comfortable to ride in, and (4) they pick people up at most nearby hotels.

These tours go into the park as far as Wonder Lake before turning around again, and at this writing the cost for the trip is still less than $40, certainly a very fair fare. (Children about half price.) They leave two or three times in the morning (probably at 6, 6:30, and 7 a.m.) and once in the afternoon (perhaps 3 p.m.), and again, reservations are essential. Always choose as early a trip as possible in order to have the best chance at seeing more wildlife. (You'll also need an early bus if you need to return in time to catch the evening train to Anchorage.)

A trip you'll hear less about is the all-day *Wilderness Trails Tour* offered by the **Kantishna Roadhouse** (tel. *683–2710*). This is a privately owned operation at the end of the road, 90 miles deep into the center of the park, on one of the few plots of private property left at the old mining camp there. Since it is not the official camp concessionaire, you won't find its brochures at any of the ARA affiliated businesses. The 12-hour tour leaves your hotel around 6 a.m. and travels the entire park road, stopping for any wildlife or scenic views, and then provides a hot lunch at the Roadhouse itself.

After lunch, a horse-drawn wagon takes you to a nearby creek for gold panning. (Everybody in our group came up with a few flakes.) The cost for this tour in 1990 hasn't been set, but we'll guess it at around $85 per person. A strange note in our trip was that our guide was a trapper in the winter, so what we like to refer to as "wildlife," he preferred calling "game (!)" Our only real caveat is to try not to be picked up last so you won't have to sit in the back seat of the van. There you can't see out the window well, the ride is rougher, and you can't hear the guide. (A different van would be less of a problem.)

The Roadhouse, which rents out a few cabins, also offers a spring dog-mushing adventure and some other packages for which you have to fly in to the Kantishna air strip. Make reservations for any of these at the phone number above or by writing the Roadhouse at P.O. Box 397, Denali National Park, Kantishna, AK 99755.

Outside the park itself, **Princess Tours** (tel. *683–2282*), which is also Royal Hyway tours, sometimes offers an unusual *Burning Hills Tour.* Leaving from Harper Lodge, these 1½-hour excursions travel to the former coal towns and hills of coal that have been ignited by spontaneous combustion. We had to save this one for next time ourselves.

Now, whether these come in the category of "cruises" or not is debatable, but there are several *raft tours* on the Nenana River alongside the park. Most leave from somewhere near the park entrance, and some coast clear to the town of Healy, about 22 winding miles downstream. All range between $35 and $50, depending mainly on the length of the trip. **Owl Rafting** (tel. *683–2215*), associated with ARA, is about the best-known of these operations. It offers either a Canyon Run white-water float or a Scenic Float in calmer waters. There is also a package price for floating to the McKinley Chalets' Cabin Night. **McKinley Raft Tours** (tel. *683–2392*) has three different tours: Tour A is 2½ hours on calm water; Tour B is a 4-hour extension on a somewhat more exciting stretch; and Tour C is 10 miles of pure whitewater rapids. **Denali Raft Adventures** (tel. *683–2234*) offers four different tours, the fourth being a combination of two of the others. This one seems to have been in business the longest, and it also offers rafting tours in other parts of the state. All these outfits offer wet-weather gear, life vests, etc. Tip: While it may be more exciting up front, you'll stay much drier if your seat is in the back of the raft.

Something similar, but in wooden boats instead of rubber rafts, may still be launched by **Sundog Dories** (tel. *683–2399*). For around $50, Sundog offers morning or evening excursions. This new trip was just getting under way when we talked to the operators, so we don't know if the business is still afloat or not.

Flightseeing? In addition to the bush pilot outfits we mentioned out of Talkeetna, **Denali Air** (tel. *683–2261*), formerly Denali Wilderness Air, launches hour-long aerial tours from the park's own air strip in Cessna 207s taking you over peaks and glaciers and around the Mountain itself, weather permitting. Per-person fares may be around $125 by your visit. We opted for the helicopter tour with **Era Aviation** (tel. *683–2574*), which often provides a closer view of wildlife on the ground (although the pilot was careful not to harass any animals). We enjoyed the experience, although clouds kept us from approaching McKinley too closely. Figure a fare of around $140 for an hour tour.

SPORTS

There are few sports, in the conventional sense of the word, in the area. Since it is federal land, you don't need a permit to fish in the park. However fishing isn't considered very good. Of course hunting is out within the park itself, although some hunting is allowed in the federal preserve adjoining the park.

We've already covered *river rafting*. *Hiking* or *backpacking* within the park is popular, of course, but there are lots of rules and regulations. All who want to head into the back country need to have a consultation with the National Park Service first. Check with the rangers in the Riley Creek Information Center or the new Visitor Access Center. And *mountain climbing?* As we said, all that is controlled from the NPS station in Talkeetna—and only the most serious mountaineers should apply.

SHOPPING

Locals claim that the **Denali National Park Gift Shop** is the most popular of the species in the state. Attached to the hotel, the shop has a wide selection of *Native handicraft* including carvings of walrus ivory, whalebone, soapstone, etc., along with other Eskimo and Indian arts and crafts.

Outside the park entrance, too, nearly every hotel has a shop attached. We really like the *mounted nature photographs* by Tony and Kathy Dawson sold at the **Harper Lodge Gift Shop,** and were later sorry that we didn't buy one particularly dramatic one with a moose standing in a lake and silhouetted against a sunlit Denali.

In the Riley Creek Information Center (or perhaps now at the new Visitor Access Center), the **Alaska Natural History Association** has a good collection of *maps, books,* and other *local lore* for sale. For a dollar we picked up a good pamphlet on finding wildlife in Denali.

MISCELLANEOUS ADDRESSES AND PHONES

It may be worth remembering that there are no telephones west of park headquarters until you come to Kantishna.

- Administration Office, Denali National Park (tel. *683–2294*), P.O. Box 9, Denali National Park, AK 99755.
- Alaska-Denali Guiding, Inc., P.O. Box 566, Talkeetna, AK 99676.
- Alaska Natural History Association, P.O. Box 230, Denali National Park, AK 99755.
- Chevron Gas Station, 100 yards from National Park Hotel.
- Emergencies of any kind within the park (tel. *683–2295* or 911).
- Emergencies outside the park (tel. 911).
- General information, Denali National Park (tel. *683–2686*).
- Healy Clinic. (tel. *683–2211*).
- Talkeetna Ranger Station (tel. *733–2231*), P.O. Box 588, Talkeetna, AK 99676.
- Tri-Valley Volunteer Fire Department (tel. *683–2222*).
- U.S. Post Office, near the park hotel.

SOUTHCENTRAL ALASKA

ANCHORAGE

The way Anchorage hits you psychologically has a lot to do with how you hit it physically. If you've been traveling out in the bush or are suffering from cabin fever, those little-town blues, or whatever, Alaska's largest city appears to be a glittering, civilized metropolis, promising sophisticated rewards of cultural and physical satisfaction. On the other hand, if you fly in direct from London, Amsterdam, Zurich, or New York, it's a pretentious if well-intentioned backwater community. As someone in Anchorage once put it, the traditional municipal aesthetic since World War II has been American Quonset Hut. In recent years there has been some excellent construction and other valiant attempts at urban design and landscaping along with a warm-weather trend to produce masses of colorful flowers in public areas. But to some all those bright blooms in June and July doth protest too much, and in the final analysis its sprawling streets, empty lots, neon lights, and suburban shopping centers are effectively ameliorated only by the glorious natural surroundings of sea and mountains.

Its overall aspect reminds some of Athens and others of downtown Denver of a decade or two ago, suffering from too many cars and too few trees. Even Anchorage residents are prone to put down their city. It's a local cliche that "the best thing about Anchorage is that it's only a half-hour from Alaska."

We enjoy Anchorage a lot, although we must admit that is partly due to its convenience as a launching pad to other places in the state. From Anchorage you can easily drive north to the Matanuska Valley,

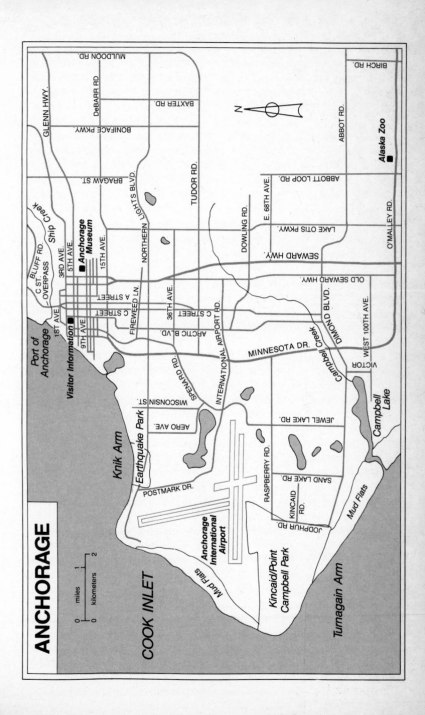

east into the Chugach Mountains, or south to the Kenai Peninsula. You can fly in a short time to almost any place of interest in the state. And you can still be back in time for a superb dinner and a comfortable night in a truly deluxe hotel—a combination you would be hard put to find elsewhere in Alaska.

Transportation has always been an important feature of Anchorage. It was founded on Cook Inlet in 1914 as the main construction camp for the Alaska Railroad, and as the point where goods were transshipped from sea routes to land routes. Since World War II, air routes have proved important to Anchorage, and for many years the city was promoted as the Air Crossroads of the World. This was due to its ideal position for refueling over-the-pole or Great Circle flights from major European cities and the U.S. East Coast on their way to Japan and elsewhere in the Far East. But for European or Asian flight crews, Anchorage means little more than a temporary limbo in which they can catch a few hours' sleep. With the confusion of time zone and dateline changes, most have little knowledge of or interest in the attractions of Alaska. Their biological clock is completely out of whack, and they usually don't even know what time it is during their short stay. Many believe that the sun never goes down in the summer and never comes up in the winter.

The Anchorage Chamber of Commerce has finally dropped the Air Crossroads catch phrase. For the past couple of years, Anchorage and all of Alaska have been stoked with the idea that with *glasnost,* Alaska and Russia can enjoy a renewal of mutual interests, and Alaskans and Siberians have begun warmly visiting and trading with each other again. Ironically, the world's airlines also have been looking at a more open Soviet Union, wondering whether an airport in Siberia might soon make a more convenient and more economical world air crossroads—if one is needed at all. A few of the new long-range passenger jets have begun bypassing Anchorage entirely since they have no need to refuel there, saving about five hours by flying over Soviet Siberian territory instead, a matter of some concern to city fathers.

Meanwhile, the Chamber has been updating Anchorage's image, now calling it the Star of the North. Campaigns to increase public awareness of Anchorage's attractions have involved a spirited song and slogan called "I'm just wild about Anchorage" plus a dancer in a moose suit who is unabashedly named Seymour of Anchorage. (In Juneau and Fairbanks, they sometimes like to joke that they are "mild about Anchorage," and all in all they might prefer a dancing bear named Seeless.) In any case, you can hardly say that Anchorage is not a representative part of today's Alaska. With a population of somewhere around 220,000, Anchorage accounts for nearly half the state's population.

Perhaps the most significant single event in Anchorage's history was the Good Friday Earthquake which began to violently shake South-central Alaska at 5:36 in the afternoon on March 27, 1964. The destructive tremor continued relentlessly for more than four minutes, and it was measured as high as 8.7 on the Richter scale, by far the strongest recorded earthquake in North America. A total of 131 persons were killed, but only nine of these were in Anchorage, an amazingly low number because schools were out and many businesses had closed early for the holiday. Electric and gas services were cut immediately, so there was no fire. Property damage was extremely heavy, notably among those structures that were built on bluffs on a section of Fourth Avenue in downtown Anchorage and also a few miles away in an expensive residential subdivision overlooking Cook Inlet. Under both the earth seemed to simply crumble away.

Partly because of the earthquake, the city today has an unusual look about it, with parking lots and small-frame and log buildings next to larger and more modern structures. Fearing the unstable land in downtown Anchorage, many have put up major businesses and high-rise office buildings much farther inland. Others have stubbornly built and rebuilt in the traditional commercial center, an area underlined with soft clay and which scientists say is sure to be badly damaged by another major earthquake some day.

Warmed by the Japan Current and other elements in the Gulf of Alaska, and protected from the north winds by the Alaska Range, Anchorage and surrounding areas enjoy a much more moderate climate than Fairbanks and the Interior. Under normal circumstances temperatures seldom drop to below 10° or 20° in the winter or rise above about 75° in the summer. Winter is not severe, but it is long; summers are mild but relatively short.

Anchorage's cultural and climatic predominance is felt to the south throughout the Alaska Peninsula and the Kenai Peninsula to Kodiak Island, key elements of the area called Southcentral. To the north, the Matanuska and Susitna valleys also fall within its sphere of influence, whether the Mat-Su folks like it or not. And every now and then, Anchorageites are reminded that they really *are* part of Alaska. Despite the advent of Seymour of Anchorage, or maybe because of it, a traffic jam can still develop after a major thoroughfare is blocked by a temporary visitor. Some insouciant moose from out of town has simply refused to keep right except when passing and then trotted confidently through every red light in sight.

TRANSPORTATION

Motorists from the Lower 48 typically drive into the Anchorage area either on Route 3 (the Parks Highway) from Fairbanks and Denali, or on Route 1 (the Glenn Highway), which shoots down from the Alaska Highway at Tok. South of Anchorage, the Seward Highway heads onto the Kenai Peninsula leading to Seward. It's called Route 1 and then Route 9. The Sterling Highway branches off of that to become the continuation of Route 1 to the end of the road in Homer. (The numbers don't match too well with the highway names.) All these are well-maintained, paved roads. The Glenn and Seward highways even have four lanes and a medial strip for a few miles in and out of Anchorage. Tip: In Anchorage, be aware that one taxi company and automobiles in the Anchorage police fleet have approximately the same color scheme— blue and white. (The taxi's blue is slightly darker whereas the cop car is more of a powder blue.)

Anchorage by *bus:* Not many visitors arrive at or leave Anchorage by common carrier (as opposed to tour or charter buses) but there are a few. Check with **Alaskon Express** (tel. *279–0761*), in the Gray Line office at 547 West Fourth St. Formerly named White Pass & Yukon Motorcoaches, the line still travels from Anchorage via Tok either to Haines or to Whitehorse and Skagway (and reverse). Figure a fare of around $200 between Anchorage and Skagway. Of course, **Gray Line** (tel. *277–5581*) itself also has several trips, although these are generally guided tours. That is also true for the **Alaska Sightseeing Company** (tel. *276–1305*), which has summertime trips via Denali between Anchorage and Fairbanks for a fare of $100 or so. A smaller operation, **Alaska-Denali Transit** (tel. *273–3234*), 1505 West 13th Ave. offers van trips to and from Denali in one direction (for around $40) and to and from Haines (around $125) or Skagway (around $150) in the other direction. Bus trips between Anchorage and Haines or Skagway are designed to connect with the ferries in the Southeast System of the Alaska Marine Highway. There's also a small van service called the **Seward Bus Lines** (tel. *278–0800*), parked in Anchorage at 720 Gambell Blvd., which offers service to Seward and back again, and the **Valdez Anchorage Bus Lines** (tel. *337–3425*), at 208 Muldoon Rd., with similar runs to Valdez.

The *state ferry* system: The Big Blue Canoes of the Southwest System of the **Alaska Marine Highway** (tel. *272–7116*) ply the waters of Southwest and Southcentral, although they don't dock at Anchorage. (They also do not tie up with the Southeast System.) The ferries connect landlocked Cordova with Valdez and Whittier, but notice that Whittier itself is also locked out of the road system. Its only land connection is via the spur on the Alaska Railroad, which goes through a series of mountain tunnels to Portage. The ferries continue to Seward, Seldovia, and Homer, and then across the opening of Cook Inlet to Kodiak Island. A few sailings go on to the Aleutian Islands as far as wind-swept Dutch Harbor. Service is generally on the ocean-going M.V. *Tustumena,* affectionately known as the Trusty Tusty, or sometimes the smaller M.V. *Bartlett.* Both vessels have a dining room with bar service as well as an upper-deck solarium. The *Tustumena* has two- and four-berth cabins. (For reservations and information, call the Anchorage number above or toll free to *(800) 642–0066.* And be sure to see our remarks on the ferries in "Coming Into the Country."

Cruise ships: To date, Anchorage is not a major cruise-ship destination, although it hopes to be such and is even building a new and more attractive dock that may be in operation by the summer of 1990. Today those that do sail in find themselves pulling up to a pier designed for container ships in the railroad switching yard. Cruise ships calling at Anchorage may include the *Royal Viking Star,* the *Sagafjord,* and the *Sea Venture.* The *Europa* usually calls once a year as part of her round-the-world cruise. Most others either confine their routes to Southeast Alaska or off-load their passengers at Whittier and Seward, where they catch a bus or train for Anchorage.

Taking the *train:* Beginning at the port of Seward, the famous **Alaska Railroad** (tel. *265–2494*) runs via Anchorage and Denali National Park to Fairbanks, and it is perhaps the most scenic train route in North America. The one-way Anchorage-Fairbanks fare in 1990 may be around $90, allowing for a stopover at the national park. At this writing the summer express schedule calls for a train to leave both Anchorage and Fairbanks at 8:30 a.m. ADT, arriving in the opposite city at 8 p.m. (The railroad has been considering whether or not to add a second daily express during summer peak periods, especially since the trains have been running with too many cars to fit the terminal facilities in Denali.)

Each car carries a hostess, and a full lunch service is available at an extra cost. Note that the railroad's observation cars have 36 seats downstairs plus 24 upstairs in the Vistadome. When necessary, passengers are asked to exchange places from time to time so that everyone gets a good view. (Winter service consists only of a single no-dome diesel car once a week, and you should recheck the schedule on the scene. There's also a summer whistle-stop run two or three days a week.) Keep your fingers crossed, and you might meet Harry Ross, the singing conductor.

You're more likely to meet the locals in the train's own cars, and everyone usually rides facing forward. But for more comfort and extra service on the summer run and a transparent dome that extends the full length of the cars, there are also the more luxurious—and more expensive—options offered by Tour Alaska or Holland America-Westours (see "Tours and Cruises" for details).

You don't hear as much about it, but during the summer you can also ride the train between Anchorage and Seward. The last schedule we saw called for the moose-gooser to leave Anchorage at 7 a.m. arriving in Seward at 11. Then it leaves Seward at 6 p.m. to arrive back in Anchorage at 10. Figure a round-trip fare of around $75, unless it's already packaged with a cruise deal. It also traverses some spectacular scenery en route.

In the summer time, if you want to take the train to Whittier (the Whittier Shuttle), you have to take a bus or drive to Portage first. (They'll arrange the bus as part of the ticket—about $40 round-trip total.) For about $60, you can also put your own car on the train and take it to Whittier, but few visitors do that. Unless you're continuing on the ferry, there's virtually no place to drive to in Whittier. You can also drive to the Portage terminal, park your car, and then take the train for around $15 round trip. (In the winter you can take the train all the way from Anchorage to Whittier on Saturdays.) In 1988, one Alaskan was so angry at missing the train at Portage that he tried to drive his pickup truck along the tracks to Whittier. He was arrested and jailed.

Some combination deals may be available this summer. Call the above number in Anchorage for information on all these train subjects, or drop into the wonderful 1939-style station on First Ave. Outside of Alaska, phone toll-free *(800) 544–0552.*

Air service: In some ways it is more convenient to fly to Anchorage from a foreign gateway than it is from cities in the Lower 48. It's about the same distance from Anchorage to Tokyo as it is from Anchorage to New York. There are nonstop flights to Anchorage from London or Tokyo and other Asian or European cities, but the only nonstop from the eastern U.S. is from New York City on China Airlines. And you can't buy a ticket to Anchorage on that because of that same old cabotage law that forbids travel between two American ports on a foreign carrier. However, you may be able to stop over in Anchorage on a ticket between New York and Taipei.

There are nonstop jet flights between Anchorage and Juneau (1½ hours) or Seattle (3 hours) or San Francisco (4½ hours) on **Alaska Airlines** (tel. *243–3300*). Other Anchorage nonstops are offered by **Northwest Airlines** (tel. *243–1123*) from its headquarters in Minneapolis (5¾ hours) and from Seattle; by **United Airlines** (tel. *563–2771*) from its hubs in Chicago (6½ hours), Denver (4½ hours), or Seattle; by **Morris Air Service** (tel. *258–2323*), a cut-rate charter outfit (usually using Braniff jets), from Salt Lake City and from Seattle; and by **Hawaiian Airlines** (tel. *243–1010*) from Honolulu (5½ hours). **Delta Airlines** (tel. *243–1311*) is also prominent in Alaska, although its only

Anchorage nonstops are from Salt Lake City (4¾ hours), Seattle, or Fairbanks. Some of these major carriers do have direct flights (same plane service) between Anchorage and several other cities in the contiguous U.S. (See "Coming Into the Country" for their toll-free phone numbers.) As a general guide, coach flights between Anchorage and Seattle run between $300 and $500 round-trip.

Among the local (intrastate) airlines are **Era Airlines** (tel. *248–4422*), **MarkAir** (tel. *243–1414*), **Peninsula Airways** (tel. *249–2295*), **Reeve Aleutian Airways** (tel. *243–4700*), **SouthCentral Air** (tel. *561–8733*), and **Wilbur's Flight Operations** (tel. *277–0511*).

Anchorage International Airport: Logically enough, the airport is at the end of International Airport Rd., just west of the metropolitan area. Unless you're on one of those exotic Asia-Europe runs, you probably won't see the small **North Terminal** for international flights. It's across a parking lot and on the other side of the control tower from the main (domestic) terminal. (A free shuttle bus runs between them as well as to the nearby Alaska Aviation Heritage Museum.) Just for the record, under a panoply of national flags, and in the presence of an army of display cases full of stuffed wildlife, you'll find the ticket counters for KLM, China Airlines, Korean Air, Air France, S.A.S., Lufthansa, British Airways, Sabena, Swissair, and Japan Air Lines. Departure gates N1 through N8 and a cafeteria are up the escalator. Arriving passengers exit Customs downstairs from doors behind the escalator. There are direct flights available between Anchorage and London, Copenhagen, Amsterdam, Zurich, Stockholm, Madrid, Tokyo, Taipei, Seoul, and Hong Kong.

The main terminal, which seems to have a lot more life to it, has been crafted in a sort of semicircle, tied by an underground walkway to the nearby parking garage. Baggage claim and rental car counters are on the lower level. Ticketing is on the upper level, in a large lobby intelligently designed so that persons who need to get from one end to the other can easily do so by walking *behind* the airline counters and not coming into conflict with lines of passengers waiting to check in. These lines often extend to the outside wall, but don't look for any of those speedy curb-side check-ins. In the winter it would be too cold for the skycaps who would have to remain outdoors. Also, plans call for the lobby to be expanded outward by about four feet, and that will narrow the sidewalk quite a bit.

Airlines represented in the main lobby at last look were (left to right from the front) SouthCentral, MarkAir, Delta, Reeve, Alaska, Hawaiian, Northwest, and United. In a separate area on the extreme right were Wilbur's, PenAir (Peninsula), and Era.

On the runways side of the structure, A gates are on the left, B gates are out on a separate concourse in the middle, and C gates are in a one-story wing on the right. Gates A1 through A8 and all the B gates

(B1 through B11) are for larger aircraft and are reached from the upper level. Gates A9 through A11, for smaller planes, are on the lower level to the left. All C gates (C1 through C5) are on the lower level to the right, and these are also generally for smaller airlines, air taxis, etc.

Be careful about asking someone to meet you in an airport bar or restaurant without being awfully specific. On the upper level are the Upper One Lounge, the Upper One Dining Room, the Cheechako Snack Bar, the Greatland Cafeteria, and the Greatland Lounge. On Concourse B you'll find the Sourdough Snack Shop.

A *bus* to and from downtown hotels is run by the Airport-City Express, better known as the **ACE Airporter** (tel. *248–5114*), and it takes about 15 or 20 minutes from its last pickup to the airport or from the airport to the first hotel on the list. It *takes reservations for trips from your hotel to the airport,* so it's a good idea to call first. Fare in 1989 was $5.

Rental car counters at the airport are staffed by **Avis** (tel. *243–2377*), also downtown at Fifth Ave. and B St. (tel. *277–4567*); **Hertz** (tel. *243–3308*); **National** (tel. *243–3406*), also downtown at Third Ave. and E St. (tel. *274–3695*); and **Budget** (tel. *243–0150*); also downtown at 521 West Third Ave. (tel. *276–2100*). Some firms parked in areas outside offer free pickup and delivery, but you'd better confirm that by phone. Other firms include: **Thrifty** (tel. *276–2844*), 3730 Spenard Rd. (near the airport); **Rent-A-Dent** (tel. *561–0350*), 512 West International Airport Rd. (also not far away); **Rent-A-Wreck** (tel. *561–2218*), 1313 Laona Circle; **Holiday Payless** (tel. *243–3616*), at 5000 West International Airport Rd.; **Practical** (tel. *276–1230*), at 1209 Gambell Blvd.; **Continental** (tel. *562–2722*), at 4940 Old Seward Highway, which specializes in four-wheel drive vehicles; and **Cal Worthington** (tel. *276–5300*), 1950 Gambell Blvd., a car dealer who rents Fords only. (Try not to listen to his "Go see Cal" TV commercial or you may never get that jingle out of your mind!)

Motorhome and RV Rentals: There are several in Anchorage, including **Number One** (tel. *277–7575*), at 322 Concrete St., Anchorage, AK 99501 (perhaps the largest); **Sweet Retreat** (tel. *561–4772*), at 3605 Arctic Blvd., Anchorage, AK 99503; **Clippership** (tel. *276–6491*), 3200 Mountain View Dr., Anchorage, AK 99511; and **Murphy's** (tel. *276–0688*), P.O. Box 202063, Anchorage, AK 99520. We believe you should take insurance against loss or damage to equipment, and don't rent from someone who will not be around to answer the phone if you have a problem. We believe these four, at least, will respond to a request with brochures, but we have had no personal experience with such firms. If you have, we'd like to hear from you.

A *taxi* from the airport to downtown will run around $12 or so. Taxis include **Alaska Cab** (tel. *563–5353*). (That's the blue-and-white one we mentioned earlier, so be careful not to hail a police car by mistake.) Strangely, **Checker Cab** (tel. *276–1234*) doesn't seem to drive checker cars. There's no mistaking **Yellow Cab** (tel. *272–2422*), however.

Local buses: Anchorage has a public transit system that calls itself, modestly enough, the **People Mover** (tel. *343–6543*), headquartered at the Transit Center at 6th Ave. and G St. It's 80 cents a ride (exact change only), and you can buy a system map for 60 cents. (Route 6 goes to the airport, but it takes forever. Route 2 goes from downtown to the zoo, but also at a slothful pace.) There is also a free, red, London-style, double-decker bus, sponsored by a group of local businesses, that travels between some hotels and shopping centers, but the exact routes and even its continued existence are subject to change from year to year. (Usually daily during the summer, except on Sunday.)

HOTELS AND MOTELS

We've stayed in a half-dozen hotels in Anchorage, and inspected a dozen more, and our findings are here. Please write us if you agree or disagree; we would like especially to have room-service reports from readers. Unlike other chapters in this guide, we have divided our listings in two. First, there are expensive hotels—those with double rooms generally renting for upwards of $100 a day. Second, we list several more economical hotels—those whose rooms generally go from something less than $100 for two travelers. There's no sales tax in Anchorage, but there is an 8% municipal hotel tax. (In the winter you should call around to find rates that may be considerably lower than the summer rates.)

EXPENSIVE ACCOMMODATIONS:

In terms of facilities, the first few establishments are fairly even—with cable TVs, adequate closets, good storage and shelf space, phone service, adequate lighting, blackout curtains, enough desk and table surfaces, well-equipped baths, and all that—so location may prove to be particularly important, especially for carless travelers. Note that the Clarion and the International are both near the airport, not downtown. Most in this group will offer free transportation between hotel and airport, but perhaps not in the wee hours.

The hands-down winner is the venerable **Captain Cook** (tel. *276–6000*), which runs between Fourth and Fifth avenues and between I and K streets (there is no J) in downtown Anchorage. Three gold-colored towers covering an entire city block near the Cook Inlet shoreline; large, tiled lobby often clicking and clacking from high-fashion high heels;

requisite stuffed bear ready to pounce at one entrance; sumptuous though darkish public areas done in men's-club mahogany, teak, leather, oil paintings, and brass; 18th-century nautical air everywhere reflecting the owner's interest in the great British explorer; a score or more shops tying the structures together; four restaurants including the viewful 20th-floor Crow's Nest, the publike Fletcher's (named for the *Bounty* mutineer)—a pizza and pasta place, the 24-hour Pantry and the exclusive Quarter Deck (for athletic club members and hotel guests); several bars, including the Whale's Tail for dancing; two well-equipped athletic clubs (men's and women's) encompassing a common racquetball court, Jacuzzi, and 17-meter swimming pool in the basement ($10 extra); large parking garage. Total of 600 bedrooms, the best generally in the 20-story (1978) Tower III, or in the 18-story (1972) Tower II; one level an entire floor of suites ranging from about $350 to $500 or so, another level a complete non-smoking floor; original (1965) Tower I usually saved for airline crews and some groups; several non-smoking rooms available on request; standard doubles in about the $150 range; others much higher than that; most units in warm tones with orange, yellow, and brown predominating; excellent furnishings including hotel features you've almost forgotten existed if you've been traveling in the bush; corner rooms particularly bright and sunny; all with sea or mountain views; very good maintenance and housekeeping throughout the house. At one time you could ask the staff to wake you when the Northern Lights were worth seeing, and perhaps you still can. The Captain Cook is one of a vanishing breed of independent, family-owned, luxury hotels. It may be the most expensive hotel in Alaska, but it's probably the best too. (Reservations from the hotel or by calling *(800) 843–1950* from outside the state, or *(800) 478–3100* within Alaska except Anchorage.)

Once known as the old Westward, the now-stylish **Anchorage Hilton** (tel. *272-7411*) commands the corner of Third Ave. and E St. downtown. Two structures, the newer, round Anchorage Tower dwarfing the boxish building of the 1940s; large, well-lighted lobby with several distinct areas; mirrored pillars and crystal chandeliers; front desk clocks with time in Tokyo, Honolulu, Anchorage, New York, and London; excellent Hilton city map available; health club and small swimming pool (no extra charge); three bars including the Lanai Deck next to the pool and health spa, Sydney's (after Sydney Lawrence, the father of Alaska painting whose oils are on the walls), and the Signature Room disco; two dining areas including the contemporary Berry Patch and the panoramic Top of the World, one of the city's best (and terrific at sunset); perhaps still a little short on parking space. Total of 640 full-featured accommodations with comfortable if relatively no-nonsense furnishings; green colors predominating (in the ones we saw); suites with more decorative originality; many units with excellent views of Cook Inlet or the Chugach Mountains; unusual air conditioning (which may be important between 1 and 3 some Thursday afternoon in July); some no-smoking models; standard rates around $150 for two. Owned by one of the Native regional corporations, the Hilton has been out mainly for the year-round business traveler, and has consequently suffered with the depressed state economy in the late 1980s. Though there's talk of a sale, it nevertheless has so far remained one of the more handsome choices in Anchorage. (Reservations from the hotel or the Hilton toll-free number, *800-HILTONS.*)

Some would jump over to the giant Sheraton or out to the rambling Clarion from here, but we prefer to slide in the recently upgraded and vastly improved 14-story **Westmark Anchorage** (tel. *272–7561*), which has been our own home away from home on two occasions thus far. Very central location at 720 West Fifth Ave. (between G and H streets); small but winsome lobby reached either from the street or the parking lot; grandfather clock and concierge cheerfully on duty; green-and-white Manor House coffee shop adjoining; down a long winding corridor to a small shop and the dark House of Lords bar and intimate French restaurant on the G Street side; up the elevator to the top floor for the attractive bar and Penthouse restaurant (where you often see the same Denali view that the Captain Cook and the Hilton folks enjoy). Total of about 100 rooms, all good sized, some in unusual shapes; many with bars and refrigerators; all with private balconies, a highly unusual feature in Alaska (we kept our milk cold out there one winter); plenty of artificial house plants, too; good decorations in powdery pinks, blues, greens, and grays; busy Fifth Avenue side rooms for better views; rear units quieter during the day; three floors of non-smoking rooms; double rates beginning at around $135. You may notice a lot of daytime "do-not-disturb" signs here, reflecting the needs of airline crews who use the Westmark to mark time on their Great Circle layovers. The Westmark Anchorage has come a long way since its old Sheffield days, and it's now an excellent human-size city hotel, probably the Cinderella of the Westmark family. About the only danger we can think of is that when it's full they may point you toward their "ugly stepsister," TraveLodge, which (though not really ugly) will never get invited to the ball. (Reservations from the hotel or through the Westmark chain, *(800) 544–0970* outside Alaska, or *(800) 478–1111* within Alaska except Anchorage.)

Out by the airport, the only hotel around that seems to approach the atmosphere of a genuine resort is the **Clarion** (tel. *243–2300*) at 4800 Spenard Rd. Two- to four-story structure, spread out along Lake Spenard, a busy float-plane harbor; ideal for fishermen and others with immediate bush-flying plans; outdoors a parklike setting with jogging paths, etc.; free shuttle to airport and to town; parking sometimes difficult on weekends when local folks come to call; high-ceilinged lobby and public areas in turn-of-the-century Alaskan decor; marble reception desk backdropped by giant old photomural; rugs over a polished stone floor; leather chairs in front of a stone fireplace; requisite moose head above it; popular, sometimes noisy Fancy Moose bar, with oriental paddle fans (great for watching planes, ducks, and geese on the lake); adjoining Flying Machine restaurant in aerial motif (outside deck also used in good weather); third floor with health club and meeting rooms; fish-cleaning and -freezing available; 248 well-decorated rooms, most a l-o-n-g hike from the lobby; many accommodations with built-in fridges, double sinks, and pull-out couches; creamy walls with gray rugs and patterned quilts; very nice tiled baths; air conditioning; 24-hour room service with full menu; minimum summer double rates perhaps $130 by your visit; most more like $150; some reductions off season. All in all, a very good choice for anyone with a car or a need to be near the airport or float-plane facilities. (Reservations from the hotel toll free at *(800) 544–0784* outside Alaska, and *(800) 478–2100* within Alaska except Anchorage.)

Just to finish things up out in the airport area, the **Anchorage International Airport Inn** (tel. *243–2233*), 3333 International Airport Rd., is about five minutes from the main terminal, also on Lake Spenard, not far from the Clarion. Elongated two-story buildings, a little hard to reach now that the new roadway has opened; 24-hour airport shuttle service; plenty of parking; fish freezer available; large lobby/lounge with fireplace; Trophy Room bar/restaurant with large-screen TV popular with local crowd; daily buffet special; wide hallways; good bedrooms with queen- or king-size beds; air conditioners; patterned wallpaper; TV with HBO; baths with liquid-soap dispenser. There may be a few standard rooms barely under $100 here, but the better deals are the miniature suites for about $10 or $15 more, which include a refrigerator, complimentary coffee, daily newspapers, and other special amenities. (Reservations from the hotel or phone toll-free at *(800) 544–0986* from Outside or *(800) 478–2233* within Alaska except Anchorage.)

Jumping back toward the traffic mainstream, the imposing **Sheraton** (tel. *276–8700*), next to a cemetery on Calista Square at 401 East Sixth Ave., seeks to compete with the Captain Cook, the Hilton, and any other big boys who may sail into town. A massive plant that appears lonely in the low-rise to no-rise neighborhood; V-shaped floor plan; skylit, three-story atrium featuring tropical trees, a startling (and pleasing) sight in the depths of winter; polished stone floor accentuating the outdoorsy look; numerous Indian and Eskimo artworks and decorations; brass-railed "million-dollar" floating stairway of Alaskan jade to the mezzanine; pinkish Calista Cafe coffee shop off the lobby; colorful Paimuit cocktail lounge; elegant Josephine's restaurant on the top (15th) floor; 24-hour room service; second-floor health club with sauna and Jacuzzi; 410 generally ample rooms in dark wood and bold colors; adequate furniture for the category; full-length mirrors a plus; one bed lamp between two beds a minus; some units with king-size beds; doubles beginning at around $150; lovely, fan-shaped suites starting at $300; express video checkout system. The Sheraton was planned and built when this neighborhood was thought to be up and coming, but commercial expansion moved in another direction. Popular with some business and government folk, but somewhat on a sidetrack for shoppers, for whom stores are a little too far away. (Reservations from the hotel or through Sheraton's national toll-free number, *(800) 325–3535.*)

Not far away, lots of business folk spend their nights at the **Days Inn** (tel. *276–7226*), formerly the Plaza Inn, but now a well-polished link in the D.I. chain at 321 East Fifth Ave. Three-story structure around an interior courtyard, a little east of the center; limo to and from the airport; narrow lobby lit by about 50 light bulbs in a steel ceiling; small, neat 24-hour restaurant; athletic workout room with a tanning booth; 116 well-cared-for units; mauve carpet, cream walls, and patterned bedspreads; phone desk cleverly doubling as a bedside table; hanging rack in lieu of closet (as in many Alaska hotels); rates probably a little over $100 for the summer of 1990. If there's not a lot of personality here, it's not a lot of money, either, by today's standards. (Reservations through the Days Inn number, toll-free at *(800) 325–2525.*)

The local **Holiday Inn** (tel. *279–8671*) has been installed on the side of a hill along a somewhat seedy block at 239 West Fourth Ave. No-nonsense, strung-out, three-story, cinder-block building, with a floor plan shaped rather like a monkey wrench; many rooms down the handle are a very long way from the lobby and the restaurant (where our meals were mediocre and service was poor); no room service between 10 p.m. and 6 a.m.; good indoor swimming pool; guest laundry; about 150 hard-used rooms (ours seemed to be falling apart); heavily utilized by groups; rack rates for FITs set at around $125, a little too much for the limp rewards. If this place were priced lower, we might give it serious consideration in our second bunch below. But for the individual traveler paying full rates, we think several less-expensive places are better in several ways. Please tell us if you disagree.

We liked even less the local **TraveLodge** (tel. *274–6631*), at 115 East Third Ave. Surprisingly, it is administered by the same Westmark organization that has one of the best hotels in town. (The Westmark name was not displayed prominently at this hotel during our visit.) The restaurant looks nice enough, but the hallways and bedrooms we saw were dank and musty, and the location isn't all that great, either.

Last on our list of higher-priced models is the **Mush Inn** (tel. *277–4554*), in an industrial area east of town, although a few of its rooms may still be in the under-$100 category. There's no restaurant, bar, or room service. In any case, the woman at the front desk told us she was interested in "Alaskans," not in "tourists," and refused to let us see any rooms. The Mush Inn has reportedly gained some local notice for the heart-shaped water beds and other frills in some specialty rooms.

Anyway, the lady told us she had never heard of the Fielding guide series; and we told her that we can't recommend what we can't see; and she said that was all right by her. So as far as we are concerned the Mush Inn has mushed out.

We have so far had to miss the **Northern Lights Inn** (tel. *561–5200*), a 145-room hotel at 598 West Northern Lights Blvd., somewhat away from the downtown area. Popular for business meetings, etc., it's now on our must-see list for an upcoming business trip of our own. We also plan future reviews of the **Barratt Inn** on Spenard Rd. and the **Golden Lion** on 36th Ave., both of which are operated by Best Western.

BUDGET ACCOMMODATIONS:

By "budget," of course, we don't mean any real cheapies. But here are a few choices for hotels or motels where two travelers may still find a decent place to stay for an outlay of something less than $100 a day.

The real sleeper this year is an address where Will Rogers reportedly stayed, an architectural antique called simply the **Anchorage Hotel** (tel. *272–4553*). Still doing business conveniently at the corner of Fourth Ave. and E St., the Anchorage has taken a new lease on life. Unlike 50 years ago, it is no longer the only hotel in town, and unlike five years ago, it is no longer a leaky fleabag with a seamy reputation. Three-story 1930s building with stucco minarets, next to the Hilton; most of downstairs taken up by a Fourth Ave. gift shop; unprepossessing entrance off Fourth on E; attractive, old-fashioned lobby with a rose-colored carpet and large painting of Mt. McKinley; artificial flowers here and there; friendly reception (ask for the complete story on how the hotel was bought and changed); no elevator; no bar or restaurant (but a plethora are nearby); up the stairs to the 31 rooms, all now with bath; generally successful mixtures of prewar fixtures and modern pastel colors; blond-wood furnishings; color TVs; free local phone calls; morning newspaper delivery; complimentary breakfast coffee and rolls in the lobby; normal rooms hopefully still around $95; a few minisuites made from two rooms, $120 or so, also a good price for the facilities; good discounts off season. If double rates go above $100, we would have to rank this place on about the same level as the Sheraton. (It's much less fancy but much better located.) You won't find noisy groups here, and the Anchorage is an encouraging demonstration that new life can and should be breathed into old institutions. (Reservations toll-free from Outside at *(800) 544–0988* or by mail from the hotel at 330 E St., Anchorage, AK 99501.)

A similar project was accomplished a few years back at the **Voyager** (tel. *227–9501*), another place with a past at 501 K St., a block from I Street. (Local legend has it that there is no J Street in Anchorage

because the town was surveyed by a party of Swedes who did not recognize and could not pronounce the letter—by yumpin' yimminy.). Four-
story, 1950-ish building just across Fifth Avenue from the Captain Cook;
blue-awning entrance to an attractive, low-ceilinged lobby with a world
clock; owner/manager's office adjoining; bar and locally respected Corsair restaurant in the basement; upstairs to 38 well-designed and well-
maintained bedchambers, all with one queen and one double daybed;
modern table lamps; cable TV on the chest of drawers; some units with
desks; free local phone calls; full-length mirror; refrigerator; Pullman
kitchen (and equipment on request); a whole floor of no-smoking rooms;
discounts for seniors. At rates of around $90 double, $80 single at last
report, the Voyager is often filled to the gunwales, so you'd better reserve in advance. (Call toll-free *(800) 247–9070* from Outside or *(800)
478–9501* within Alaska except Anchorage.)

If you're staying in Anchorage more than just two or three days,
you might consider the **Inlet Towers** (tel. *276–0110*), in an old but
nice residential neighborhood at 1200 L St., about 10 blocks from
downtown. (At the outset, this should not be confused with a similarly
named but cheap hotel, the Inlet Inn.) The Inlet Towers calls itself a
condo-style hotel: massive, green-and-cream apartment-style building
convenient to park and jogging trails; parking no problem; tiny split-
level lobby with stone pillars; no bar or restaurant; guest laundry; sauna
and exercise equipment available; two elevators to 14 living stories;
high floors with great view of Cook Inlet (actually Knik Arm); all units
with living rooms, separate bedrooms, and complete kitchens; rather
heavy, motelish furnishings in the units we saw; all reasonably well
cared for; corner units a little more cheery; satellite TVs; one-bedroom
units still under $100 at last report; two-bedroom units over that amount.
(Reservations from the hotel or toll-free *(800) 544–0786*.)

The **Eighth Avenue Hotel** (tel. *279–4148*), at 630 W. 8th Ave.,
is another possibility. Four-story apartment building between F and G
streets; parking lot adjoining; no restaurant or public areas; laundry facilities available; one apartment turned into a reception area; about 40
no-nonsense flats in one-and two-bedroom configurations; efficiency
furnishings with TV, separate kitchen area, etc.; lots of kitchen equipment (including a coffee pot and ground coffee); altogether a reasonable
bargain at around $80 or so for a pair of penny-pinchers. We tried it
for a night and could have stayed longer.

We also had one day's accommodation at its sister operation, the
Sourdough Motel (tel. *279–4148*), at 801 Erickson St. Location across
the tracks from Anchorage but convenient to Elmendorf Air Force Base;
standard motel U-shape in two stories; laundry facilities; convenient
parking; about two dozen units with all the necessary furnishings; full
kitchen; separate bedroom and living room; TVs and phones; rates probably also around $80 by now; discounts announced for seniors, military,

school teachers, and government employees. The Sourdough is neither sour nor overly sweet, and it might save you some dough.

One of the most unusual motels we've seen in a long time is the **Alaskan Samovar Inn** (tel. *277–1511*), in an equally far-out location at Seventh Ave. and Gambell St. Traditional U-shaped motel; restaurant with stained glass windows; bedrooms a weird collection that seem to have been imported from a pasha's palace, with oriental themes, Gay Nineties themes, and others; padded headboards; florid floral wallpaper; velvet, felt, and fringe trimmings everywhere; lots of mirrors; one unit with a bathtub snuggled right up to the bed; conversely another with a chaise lounging in the bathroom; double rates around $75 up. There are lots of amenities for the price, but the Samovar just doesn't make our cup of tea. Perhaps you'll disagree.

Of all the hotels and motels we've inspected in Anchorage, the one we like positively the least, so far, is the **Kobuk** (tel. *274–1650*) at Fifth Ave. and Karluk St. a long way east. There's a man behind a pane of bullet-proof glass, and you pay him $60 or $70 in advance through a hole—plus $3 for a key deposit. The walls are covered with lists of do's and don'ts. And the rooms we saw seemed more like cells sorely in need of cleaning and airing than hotel units to our way of thinking.

Bed and breakfasts: These operations open and close all the time in Anchorage. Several are registered with a few booking agencies, who will try to steer you to just the right B&B. These include **Accommodations in Alaska** (tel. *345–4671*), P.O. Box 110624, Anchorage 99511, which has received some especially favorable publicity; **Blackberry Gardens** (tel. *248–2052*); and **Sourdough Bed and Breakfast Association** (tel. *563–6244*), 889 Cardigan Circle, Anchorage 99503. We suggest writing in advance, or better yet phoning when long-distance rates are cheapest in order to set yourselves up in an affordable room. If you arrive in Anchorage without a reservation, the latest information and brochures on current B&Bs will be at the log-cabin visitors center downtown.

Youth hostels: The 60-bed **Anchorage International Hostel** (tel. *276–3635*) has a terrific downtown location at 700 H St., corner of Seventh Ave., just across from the bus station, and you can get there via People Mover Route No. 6 from the airport. Open all year, the cost was about $10 for members and $15 for nonmembers the last we looked. You don't have to be young, either. (Ask for a brochure from the above address at Anchorage, AK 99501.) And near the Alyeska Ski Resort, in Girdwood, is the **Alyeska International Youth Hostel** (tel. *277–7388*). Write them at P.O. Box 10-4099, Anchorage, AK 99510.

RV Parks: We know of only three places to park your rig reasonably near the center of things. **Golden Nugget** (tel. *333–2012*), at 4100 DeBarr Ave., Anchorage 99508 and **Highlander** (tel. *227–2407*), at

2704 Fairbanks St., Anchorage 99503 are both open year around. **Hillside** (tel. *258–6006*), 2150 Gambell St., Anchorage 99503, may be in operation only in the summer.

RESTAURANTS AND DINING

As elsewhere in Alaska, Anchorage revels in things that were swimming just this morning, particularly salmon (king, silver, and pink), trout, and halibut. Crab, including king and dungeness, along with shrimp, are also deservedly popular. That said, restaurants are equally adept at specialties you'd expect to find in any other modern American city. Steaks, roast beef, veal, and vegetables are cooked with domestic and foreign accents, along with a few local variations such as reindeer sausage and mooseburgers. Men might feel like wearing a jacket or tie in the big hotel restaurants, perhaps; nevertheless casual but neat dress is acceptable virtually everywhere. As one Anchorage bon vivant put it: "Restaurants here operate with a behavior code more than they do a dress code." If you're staying on one of Anchorage's top hotels, be reassured that their main dining rooms are also considered tops by the local gentry. In the case of three vigorously competing establishments, we mean that quite literally. The **Crow's Nest** (tel. *276–6000*), capping the Captain Cook; the **Top of the World** (tel. *272–7411*), at the summit of the Anchorage Hilton; and **Josephine's** (tel. *276–0320*), crowning the Sheraton, are all on their respective highest floors, providing some terrific panoramas of cityscapes and mountainscapes. The Crow's Nest is deservedly famous for its Sunday brunch. The Top of the World regularly flies in tuna and other specialties from the South Pacific.

The **House of Lords** (tel. *272–2313*) in the Westmark, 720 West Fifth Ave., is also a pretty good hotel restaurant, but it's on the ground floor, and a notch or two below the above three in some other ways. Instead of a view, it offers a more intimate atmosphere in a sort of British baronial motif. Chicken Chanterelle will run around $18. At lunch, a halibut burger will run around $7. Also in the Westmark, the **Penthouse** (tel. *272–2313*) on its top floor, has a relatively modest kitchen serving prime rib, hot sandwiches, and a delicious view.

At least three other gourmet choices are near the Captain Cook. **Simon and Seafort's** (tel. *274–3502*), at 420 L St., seems to be Anchorage's most well-known restaurant among non-residents, and it is indeed worthy of fame. In a noisy room decorated more or less a la turn-of-the-century New York, patrons enjoy the view of Cook Inlet while feasting mainly on seafood. The prime rib, steaks, and chicken are also consistently good. Try the halibut in cucumber sour cream sauce or the steamed clams. Just up the street, on the ground floor of an office building, the **Kayak Seafood Grill** (tel. *274–7617*), at 510 L St., is still known by many in Anchorage as the Kayak Club. We floated into its elegant interior one winter night when super-busy Simon's said no way and were happy with our halibut and delighted with the chicken Dijon. It has the same view too. Around the corner at 944 West Fifth Ave. is the **Corsair** (tel. *278–4502*), where the owner/chef specializes in French and German cuisine. Duckling nivermais (duck in port wine) is a house specialty. So is skoblianka (veal and mushroom baked with sour cream and glazed with cheese sauces). The dark interior and high-backed chairs give a feeling of intimacy and privacy, and it has perhaps the best wine cellar in the state.

Continuing our restaurant ramble downtown, some of the most inventive dishes are turned out at the **Marx Brothers Cafe** (tel. *278–2133*), in a 1916-model frame house at 627 West Third Ave. Surrounded by stained glass windows, you might enjoy roast duck with Malay chutney or veal stuffed with king crab, for $25 or $30. (Bring plenty of lettuce—the spendable kind.) Other downtown possibilities for lunch, although they also serve dinner, include the viewful **Elevation 92** (tel. *279–1578*), in a commercial building perhaps 92 feet above sea level at 1007 West Third Ave. The Express Plate for midday munchers is a nonstop bargain at perhaps $6.95. We had the Seafood Chalupa Salad (shrimp, salmon, crab, tomatoes, avocados, and onions served in a tortilla shell) for around $10.95. The extensive hors d'oeuvre menu attracts a lot of people into the bar. (The 92 was in Chapter 11 when we were last in town; we hope things are still okay.) The other lunch place is the somewhat yuppish Sack's Fifth Avenue (tel. *276–3546*) at 625 West Fifth Ave. The Sack family had to change the name officially to **Sack's Cafe** after high-powered attorneys for a giant New York department store which shall remain nameless began to lean on them. You might lean on the Alaskan reindeer Polish sausage sandwich (with cheese, red onions, sauerkraut, etc.). The Russian cream dessert is almost as good as Sara's own recipe.

A little more modest, but just as good in its own way is the **Downtown Deli and Cafe,** at 525 West Fourth Ave. It's the closest thing to a New York deli in Anchorage. Somehow I managed to leave my notes in the natural-wood booth, but I remember we had some good roast beef sandwiches there.

Two other dining areas should be considered on the downtown, hotel-walking-distance list. Some of the best steaks in town are served at the unprepossessing **Club Paris** (tel. *277–6332*), in the back of a nondescript pub at 417 West Fifth Ave. Few *cheechakos* are aware of this place, but here is where many sourdoughs scarf up their beefsteaks, while keeping one ear on the sound of the TV set over the nearby bar. You say there should be something French about the Club Paris? Okay, you can order the steak stuffed with bleu cheese. The other nearby choice is the outdoorsy **Old Anchorage Salmon Bake** (tel. *279–8790*), at 251 K St., just over the bluff along Third Avenue. If you go at lunchtime you can try a salmon burger for around $7. Locals call this touristy but tasty.

If you have a car or take a taxi, of course, a considerable number of additional restaurants are within easy striking distance. We had an Edenistic experience on a cold winter's eve at the **Garden of Eatin'** (tel. *248–FOOD*). It's a rather hard-to-find address—2502 McRae Rd., which spins off Spenard Rd. near the Woodland Park School (corner of Arkansas St.), but relatively convenient to the airport hotels. This place is installed in an honest-to-Adam, war-surplus Quonset hut, and has some good, standard fare at good, standard prices. You can have your halibut baked, or tempura, or something called Olympia (I forget what it means, but oysters are involved and the flavor is great). Be sure to read the tongue-in-cheek calorie-conscious back page of the menu.

Folks from the Deep South who have a hankering for some real Creole from the bayou country have been searching out the new **Dossman's Cajun Restaurant** (tel. *274–5315*) at 4119 Mountain View Dr., corner of Klevin. It may be strictly a paper-plate-and-oil-cloth establishment, but the owner/chef knows what to do with onions, garlic, cayenne pepper, gumbo file, sassafras leaves, and that kind of thing. This is the place for jambalaya (choice of shrimp, crawfish, or chicken), along with potato salad and gold ol' pinto beans.

Authentic Cajun food is also featured (but not exclusively) at the **Double Musky Inn** (tel. *783–2822*) in Girdwood, near the Alyeska Ski Resort. If you get out that way, try the shrimp with remoulade sauce. The steaks are also great. Be aware, though, that there are no reservations taken and this is one of the most popular restaurants in the state. You can spend your waiting time in the bar studying the Mardi Gras masks and other Mississippi mud memorabilia on the walls. Nearby is the well-known **Turnagain House** (tel. *653–7763*) at Mile 102 on the Seward Highway. Our steaks were okay, but we were disappointed in the general lack of atmosphere, especially at tables far from the bar. It remains a local favorite, however, so you may have to make up your own mind on this one.

Every time we spend more than a few days in a town, we develop a favorite coffee shop—some place that we end up going back to, even though we really should be checking out some new places. In Anchorage that has turned out to be **Harry's** (tel. *561–5317*), in the Key Bank of Alaska building at 101 West Benson Blvd. The restaurant pays tribute to the West Coast Harry Truman, the mountain man who would not be moved from the slopes of Mount St. Helens a decade ago—he was never seen again following the eruption. (Harry wasn't an Alaskan, but many think he was in spirit.) Anyway, Harry's spirit is alive here with a wide selection of spicy meals, sandwiches, and gourmet microbeers. Try the outstanding barbecued baby back ribs for around $15, or perhaps the Eiffel burger for $7.

The way we feel about Harry's is the way some longtime Anchorage folk feel about two or three other places. Many crow over **Wings 'n' Things,** at 529 I St., between Fifth and Sixth avenues. Westernstyle spicy chicken wings and submarine sandwiches (hoagies) are the thing here, but there's one specialty called the Philadelphia Cheese Steak. Another chicken palace is the **Lucky Wishbone,** especially the one at 1033 East Fifth Ave., at Kobuk St. The atmosphere is zilch, the menu is limited, but plenty of satisfied pan-fried chicken chompers don't care. The burgers are pretty good too.

A long-time local favorite, with plenty of Alaskan personality, is **Gwennie's Old Alaska** (tel. *243–2090*) not far from the airport at 4333 Spenard Rd. (west of Minnesota near Forest Road on the south side of Spenard). There are two dining floors, each surrounding you with antlers, bear skins, Iditarod posters, and other cornball trappings. We enjoyed the barbecued beef, but that sauce is hot, hot, hot. A fun place anyway. Sorry, we haven't yet dug in for a meal at the **Sourdough Mining Company** (tel. *563–2272*), at the corner of Juneau St. and International Airport Rd. (between the Old and New Seward Highways). Inspired by an old gold mine, it specializes in barbecued ribs and the like. (If you go, let us know.)

Nothing seems to fire up a debate faster than a question about the best burgers in town. Anchorage folk often pooh-pooh our Harry's suggestion. One that consistently comes out on top we also tried and concur with: the **Arctic Roadrunner,** perhaps also called the Local Burgerman, 5300 Old Seward Highway, on the bank of Campbell Creek just south of International Airport Rd. Sometimes described as an Alaskan McDonald's, it dates back more than 25 years, long before McDonald's was even a gleam in an Eskimo's eye. Amid totem poles, dog sleds, and other local accoutrements, you'll find at least a dozen types of relatively inexpensive hamburgers listed on the yellow board, including a Lord Baranof burger, and the like. If the weather is warm, take your meal all the way through the building and sit out on the banks of the stream below.

Other good burger choices include the **Red Robin Burger and Spirits Emporium** in the Northway Shopping Mall on Penland Parkway (the kind of place you can take your kids to and still get a drink), open until about 1 a.m., the economical **Burger Jim,** 704 East Fourth Ave. (and Ingra St.), and the **White Spot,** a tiny spot, to be sure, at 109 West Fourth Ave., near the Holiday Inn, where you might make your own french fries. Anchorage folks sometimes spot former Gov. Jay Hammond in here. Another popular non-chain, fast- (not to say junk-) food establishment is true blue, red-and-white-and-red **California**

Roll, at 2960 C St. The atmosphere may be rather plastic, but the food is more than palatable and relatively cheap—maybe $8 for a burger and beer. Tables are put outside in good weather. We took a peek through the window at the **Hogg Brothers Cafe,** at 2421 Spenard Rd., and decided that it indeed looked like the little pig's house that the wolf blew down, and so we didn't go in. Later we learned it has a reputation for serving the best omelets in town. (Some recommend entering via the next-door **Fireside Cafe** and ordering from there.) So maybe we made a mistake, and will be back for another huff and a puff.

Something unusual that doesn't quite fit elsewhere is **Cyrano's** (tel. *274–2599*), a combination creperie and bookstore at 413 D St. A guitarist may accompany your browse and your dessert. (Closed Sunday.)

Italian restaurants: Several pasta palaces dot the cityscape. Notable among them is **Fletchers,** an informal pesto and pizza pub at the Captain Cook Hotel. You'll find a much wider choice, however, at **Romano's** (tel. *276–0888*), at 2415 C St., corner of Firewood Lane. Romano's has patrician standards—in fact, there's a sign asking their more plebeian patrons to take off their hats while dining. Lots of polished brass and etched glass; booths and tables a little close together; good, standard Roman dishes like veal scallopine piccata around $13; no complaints from us. We also once enjoyed a lunch at **Armen's Mazzi's** (tel. *279–9547,* at 2052 East Northern Lights Blvd., although it's open until 2 a.m. Scampi is a specialty. (The double-possessive name is because some other Mazzi's in another city threatened to sue.) Locals also like the **Villa Nova** (tel. *561–1660*) at 5121 Arctic Blvd. Owned by a Greek, it offers somewhat heavier, creamier dishes. The decorations are Italian, but Greek specialties are often offered, too. Sorry, we haven't yet tried **One Guy from Italy** (tel. *277–6823*) at 3020 Minnesota Dr., which features several vegetable specialties—and is allegedly owned by one guy from Japan. Often judged one of the better pizza places (besides Fletcher's) is **Legal Pizza** at 1034 West Fourth Ave. (Funny name; we guess you can order yours with pepperoni but not pot.) But some swear by **Sorrento's** (tel. *278–3439*), at 610 East Fireweed Lane, near the Fireweed Cinemas.

Mexican dining: One of the best Tex-Mex restaurants north of the 60th parallel is **La Mex** (tel. 274–7678), at 900 West Sixth Ave., which is a short *paseo* from many downtown hotels. Amid a mixture of modern pinlights and Aztec renderings, the standard *platos picantes* are served on *platos calientes.* The margaritas are *grande,* and the music *gracias a Dios,* is not always Mariachi. (If you and your dining companion don't agree on the love of jalapeno and guacamole, they also serve a fine prime rib for *gringos.*) Two other good south of the border choices are **Mexico in Alaska** (tel. *349–1528*) at 7305 Old Seward Highway, where the food is considered *mucho mas autentico,* and which offers the much wider variety of choices you might find in Ciudad Mexico.

(Try the delicious meatball soup.) This is where members of Anchorage's substantial Mexican community often find themselves. Last on the list is **Garcia's of Scottsdale** (tel. *561–4476*), at 4140 B St., which represents a lighter, perhaps somewhat AZ-Mex style of cooking.

Oriental flavors: You get a lot of debate about this, too, depending on the diner's background and experience. Some of the Japanese restaurants bow especially to Japanese visitors, and this includes the **Tempura Kitchen** (tel. *277–2747*), at 3826 Spenard Rd., and **Kumagoro** (tel. *272–9905*) at 533 West Fourth Ave. (You can get a genuine Japanese breakfast there.) Those not that much into authentic Rising Sun exotica may be better off picking up chopsticks at **Daruma** (tel. *561–6622*), 550 West Tudor Rd.; or the large **Oriental Gardens** (tel. *344–2756*), rather far out at 11321 Old Seward Highway; or the delicately decorated **Akai Hana** (tel. *276–2215*), formerly the Tokyo Gardens, at 930 West Fifth Ave. (not far from the Captain Cook), which specializes in succulent sushi. Take a crack at the soft shell crab tempura style, too.

Northern China (tel. *377–1912*) at 353 Muldoon Rd., just might be the best in town for hot and sour soup and other spicy Szechuan cooking today, but it's not cheap. For the same kind of thing, the highly decorated (but not Chinesey) **Tea Leaf** (tel. *276–5970*) is preferred by some. If you want, you can dine in high-backed chairs at the bar and while watching all the action in the exhibition kitchen. It's at 313 E St. **Ah Sa Wan** (tel. *562–7788,* a more conventionally fancy entry at 560 West Tudor Rd., has some of the best moo goo gai pan. Owned by another branch of the same family, **Fu-Do** (tel. *561–6611*), at 2600 East Tudor Rd., has a reputation for large portions and good service. (Your bill may come buried in jelly beans.) Lunch specials average around $6. Some have praised the **Peking Palace** (tel. *277–5027*), at 500 E. Benson Blvd., but to date we haven't peeked in. Another palatial possibility is the **Imperial Palace** (tel. *274–9167*), at 400 Sitka St., near Merrill Field. It features both Cantonese and Mandarin cooking.

As we were ready to leave Anchorage last time, we heard of the new **Thai Cuisine** (tel. *277–8424*) at 444 H St., downtown near the Anchorage *Times*. You can choose how hot you want your main course. Initial reports by peanut sauce gourmets have been favorable. Also, the **Thai Kitchen** (tel. *561–0082*) at 3405 East Tudor Rd., is near the Capri Cinema and is suitable for pre- or post-movie munching. Try the Pad Thai (rice noodles, chicken, scrambled egg, and peanuts). Lastly, a new Indian restaurant, the **Maharajah** (tel. *272–2233*), has begun awakening Anchorage taste buds to the joys of curries and chutneys. Look for it near the Captain Cook on Fourth Ave. at about K St. It's also on our taste-test list for next trip.

Eskimo and Alaskan Indian dining? The cafeteria-style **Tundra Club** (tel. *278–4716*), at 250 Gambell St. (corner of Third Ave.) offers some of the stuff you've only heard of. You'll also hear plenty of Inupiat, Yupik, and Athabascan spoken by fellow customers as they lap up things like Eskimo ice cream, Indian fry bread, fish pie, etc. This modest establishment may be designed mainly for Natives, but they welcome anyone who dares to experiment (and they serve some more familiar dishes, too).

Late night dining? You know you've reached a toddlin' town when you can get meals after midnight. First of all, the coffee shops in the Captain Cook, the Westmark, and the Hilton are usually open all night during the summer. Then try **Annie's Cafe,** 312 West Fourth Ave., which has home-cooked meals early and late, closing only to wash the floors between 4 and 6 a.m. **China Garden,** at 204 East Firewood Lane, serves a full Oriental menu until 5 a.m. The **Fancy Moose** in the Clarion Hotel, 4800 Spenard Rd., usually continues to browse (yes, that's what moose do) until 2 a.m. The **Day Break Coffee Shop,** 321 East Fifth Ave., will break eggs for 24 hours. **Leroy's,** at 2420 C St., is another place that never pulls the shutters closed. The **Peanut Farm,** in a log cabin at Old Seward Highway and International Airport Rd. (locals usually just say "Old Seward and International"), turns out burgers, pizzas, etc., until about 1:30 a.m. **Phillip's International Inn,** at 3801 DeBarr Rd., is open 24 hours with full international dinners. And the **Village Inn Pancake House,** 1130 East Northern Lights Blvd. or 740 West Dimond Blvd., keeps on flipping at any hour.

Chain restaurants? Anchorage has one or more links in just about any Lower 48 chain you can think of, including Arby's, Burger King, Chi-Chi's, Church's, Dairy Queen, Denny's, Domino's, Kentucky Fried Chicken, McDonald's, Pizza Hut, Popeye's, Shakey's, Sizzler, Stuart Anderson's, Taco Bell, Tony Roma's, and more. You'll stumble onto them all without our help.

Final dining tip: Perhaps the best and most complete salad bar in town, as well as a heck of a good delicatessen, isn't even at a restaurant. We found that at **Carrs,** a super supermarket with branches all over town. We particularly liked the one at the corner of Minnesota and Northern Lights Blvd. On a nice warm day, we once loaded up on salad and soup at under $3 a pound and then took it to some picnic tables beside Lake Hood for a terrific (and cheap) outdoor lunch.

ENTERTAINMENT AND NIGHT LIFE

Anchorage has more bars than you can shake a cocktail at. Some of those along Fourth Ave. near the Holiday Inn are still rough, although nothing compares to the general mayhem during pipeline days, when there was a shooting or a knifing almost every night.

Spenard Road, a street that wanders like a drunken sailor through the more regular patterns of the map between downtown and the airport, represents the nighttime action central in Anchorage. Over the years the name has become almost synonymous with drugs, prostitution, adult book stores, strip bars, topless-bottomless dancers, and the like. But there are now good hotels and restaurants in the Spenard area, and in general the neighborhood is less seamy and steamy than a few years ago. It is also well patroled by police. Today some of the city's most interesting, safe, and legal night life manages to coexist with what's left of all the vice. Some places are open until 2:30 or 3 a.m.

Perhaps the most famous entertainment palace in town is **Chilkoot Charlie's** (tel. *272–1010*) at 2435 Spenard. Koots is actually four bars in one. The disco is upstairs; downstairs there's a rock-and-roll bar, a more quiet bar, and yet another room for special concerts. During nice weather, some like to sit in the courtyard, perhaps joining in a game of horseshoes. It's particularly popular on those Sundays when a free barbecue is served with your drinks. By the way, Charlie's bartenders have instructions to cut off anyone they think has had enough.

There's often some action at the **Midnight Express** (tel. *279–1861*), almost just across the road at 2610 Spenard. It's usually thumping with live country-and-western music—except when Vickie and the Mustangs are in residence and belting out their 1950s and 1960s numbers. It purports to have the largest dance floor in Spenard. C&W is also the mainstay at the **Buckaroo Club** (tel. *561–9251*), at 2811 Spenard Rd., which claims to be the oldest of the genre in Anchorage. A third country possibility is the **Sawmill Club** (tel. *562–2135*), at the corner of Old Seward Highway and Dowling Rd.

Another Anchorage institution is the **Fly By Night Club** (tel. *279–SPAM*) at 3300 Spenard. The owner, known as Mister Whitekeys, is identified particularly with Spam. As we've heard the story, he has observed that the Hormel company sells millions of pounds of Spam each year, yet almost no one admits to eating it. So he serves Spam hors d'oeuvres at his club, and fronts a musical group called the Spamtones. (Reportedly the Hormel company has not been amused and has asked him unsuccessfully to cease and desist some of these Spamanigans.) On some nights he also produces the two-hour Whale Fat Follies, which he says is ''the Alaskan show the state Division of Tourism does not want you to see,'' featuring musical production numbers like ''Humpies from Hell,'' a tap-dancing outhouse, and the like. You'll recognize the Fly by Night by its airplane tail.

Anchorage's most famous burlesque show is the **Great Alaska Bush Company,** which has two branches: at 531 East Fifth Ave. and out on

International Airport Rd. The bumps and grinds usually begin at 4 p.m. and continue well past midnight.

Musicals, melodramas, or mysteries might be on the boards presented by any of several amateur theater companies, including the **Anchorage Community Theater** (tel. *344–4713*), the **Theatre Guild** (tel. *561–4423*), and the **Alaska Light Opera Theatre** (tel. *561–7515*). In the past they have used the historic Fourth Avenue Theater, but now all seem to have embraced the new performing arts center (see below).

Anchorage's best known tourist production is the non-alcoholic **Larry Beck's Alaska Show** (tel. *278–3831*), a one-man gold rush performance perhaps still at the glass-walled William A. Egan Convention Center, 555 West Fifth Ave., between E and F streets. With quick costume changes, Beck sings, recites, and reenacts such Robert Service poems as the "Cremation of Sam McGee" and the "Ballad of Bessie's Boil." It's about $15 for a 90-minute show, but recheck that price and the exact location. This may also be promoted as the Alaska Heritage Review or Larry Beck Tonight.

Native dancers often perform in the auditorium at the **Anchorage Museum of History and Art** (tel. *343–4326*) during June, July, and August. Several different groups are usually on stage Monday through Saturday for about a week at a time. Admission $3 or so.

Be sure to check on what's in production at the **Alaska Center for the Performing Arts** (tel. *277–1988*), the snazzy new structure that has finally opened in the block bounded by Fifth and Sixth avenues and F and G streets. (The $45 million civic project eventually costs $70 million because of design and construction problems.) It includes three theaters, the 350-seat Sydney Lawrence Theater, the 800-seat Discovery Drama Theater, and the 2100-seat Evangeline Atwood Concert Hall. The long-delayed center cut the ribbons after our last Anchorage visit. Classical music possibilities include performances of the **Anchorage Symphony Orchestra** (tel. *274–8668*), which sometimes works some Native numbers into the act; the **Anchorage Concert Association** (tel. *272–1471*), which routinely flies in some top-flight guest musicians; the **Anchorage Opera** (tel. *279–2557*), which also sometimes invites some big names in the field; and the **Alaska Light Opera Theatre** (tel. *561–7515*), which is bustin' out all over in June and July with Broadway-style extravaganzas. Some popular crowd-pleasers also manage to fill Anchorage's **George M. Sullivan Sports Arena** (tel. *279–2596* for recorded information).

Anchorage has literally dozens of movies playing at any one time. You'll find about 10 each at the **Fireweed Cinemas** (tel. *277–3825*), at Fireweed Lane and Gambell St.; **University Cinemas** (tel. *562–1250*), at 3901 Old Seward Highway; **Totem Cinemas** (tel. *333–8222*), at 3101 Muldoon Rd.; or four at the **Polar-Tri Cinemas** (tel. *563–3466*), at

Dowling Rd. and New Seward Highway. A movie house with an unusual twist is the 100-seat **Capri Cinema** (tel. *561–0064*) at 3425 East
Tudor Rd., which devotes itself almost exclusively to the old classics,
foreign films, and other non-first-run selections.

Pleasant bars for sipping and chatting? Those at the five big hotels
are usually mentioned first—**Fletcher's** or the **Whale's Tail** at the Captain Cook, **Sydney's** at the Hilton, the **Penthouse** at the top of the
Westmark, the **Paimuit** at the Sheraton, and the **Fancy Moose** out at
the Clarion. The bar at **Simon and Seafort's** is deservedly popular,
even if you don't end up eating there. And it also seems to have any
Scotch you have ever heard of. Also popular for tippling is the aforementioned **La Mex,** especially for its magnum margaritas. An attractive
bar just down the street from the log-cabin visitor center is the **F Street
Station,** at 325 F St.

Television: For stay-in-the-rooms, Anchorage has five local TV
stations—KTUU, Channel 2 (NBC); KTBY, Channel 4 (Fox); KAKM,
Channel 7 (PBS); KTVA, Channel 11 (CBS); and KIMO, Channel 13
(ABC). In many hotels these are augmented by a raft of cable stations
which bring the commercials, programs, and civic concerns of such
unlikely centers as Detroit, New York, and Atlanta onto the tubes of
Anchorage.

Newspapers: Anchorage has two excellent papers, the lively morning *Daily News,* which has won two Pulitzer Prizes, and the *Times,* the
long-established evening paper. Both are sold all over the state.

SIGHTS AND SITES

You'll develop a list of sightseeing targets based on your own interests. Meanwhile, here are a few that are either well known or ones
we found, plus some of our own comments.

If you've been with us throughout the rest of Alaska and the Yukon, you will correctly surmise that you should head first to the local
log-cabin **Visitor Information Center** (tel. *274–2531*). Sponsored by
the Anchorage Convention and Visitors Bureau, it's on the southeast
corner of Fourth Ave. and F St.; in summer the sod roof is usually
green and colorful with living grass and flowers. Often supervised by a
cheerful Massachusetts maven named Donna, the log cabin always has
a staff of helpful folk ready with sheaves of solid information on Anchorage and the surrounding area. (If you want to listen to a recording,
though, call the All About Anchorage line at *276–3200*.) The panoply
of blossoms outside make this cabin a colorful photo subject itself. You'll

also notice baskets of blooms hanging from lamp posts up and down Fourth Ave. during the summer.

Just catercorner from the cabin, in the old post office at 603 West Fourth Ave., be sure to stop in at the **Alaska Public Lands Information Center** (tel. *271–2737*) too. The stop is essential if you're going to do any real wilderness walking, fishing, or hunting, but the displays are attractive and informative in any case. (Psst: Clean rest rooms are there, too.) Across the street, check out the **Fourth Avenue Theater,** sentimentally restored a few years ago.

A one-block stroll via F or G street to Fifth Avenue will take you to the flower-filled **Town Square** and the next-door Performing Arts Center (see "Entertainment and Night Life"). At the corner of G and Sixth is the highly touted **Alaska Experience Center.** It consists of two parts: a 40-minute Alaska travelogue film on one of those wraparound cinemaxiscreens, and an earthquake exhibit (and another short film) based on the Alaska tremor of 1964. If you get this as part of a tour, okay. We didn't think too much of the main film, and thought the shaking seats in the earthquake portion corny and unrealistic. Considering the inconvenient wait on busy days, and a whopping walk-in fare of $10, it is highly overpriced in our humble opinion.

Also in the immediate neighborhood, at 725 West Fifth Ave. (across from the Westmark) is the **Imaginarium.** Not everyone will appreciate it, but the attraction for us is watching kids get one on one with this hands-on science center, building a soap bubble around themselves, learning about oil wells, etc. Of course, if you've seen the Exploratorium in San Francisco. . . . Admission for adults $4, youngsters $2.

Okay, maybe you understandably passed over the last two points of interest, but don't skip the storefront **Alaska Wilderness Museum** (tel. *274–1600*). (This should not be confused with the now-defunct Alaska Wildlife Museum.) There are lifelike displays of bears and other animals in realistic settings. We saw this museum when owner/sculptor/ taxidermist Ron Nason was building it early in 1988, and although we have been in and out of Anchorage a few times since, we somehow never got back to review the completed project. Nevertheless, we were impressed with the dedication to realism and accuracy and feel it's well worth its admission fare of $5.

You can get an idea on what some of the first permanent houses in town looked like by visiting the **Oscar Anderson House** (tel. *274– 2336*) at 420 M St., two blocks west of the Captain Cook Hotel on Fifth Ave. Anderson, one of a group of pioneer Swedes in town, built his modest house in 1915, which is ancient history by Anchorage standards. (Wednesday–Sunday, 1–4 p.m. Admission $2.) The house is just across the street from **Elderberry Park,** a quiet place to view Cook Inlet. It's also a short walk down L Street to **Resolution Park,** named after Captain Cook's ship. The statue of the good captain there seems to turn his back on Anchorage. Wooden stair steps from the park lead down to the **Coastal Trail,** part of the 120 miles of hiking, biking, jogging, and skiing trails that wind through the Anchorage area.

It would be a long hike, but this trail eventually leads about three miles west to **Earthquake Park.** Prior to March 27, 1964, this was an expensive subdivision called Turnagain by the Sea, perched on a bluff over Cook Inlet, and the home for many of the city's movers and shakers—until the earth began moving and shaking. It was virtually destroyed by the Good Friday Earthquake, however, and now there's not much left but the crumbled earth and hundreds of new trees that have begun growing up in the middle of it all. An easier way to get there would be to drive west on Northern Lights Blvd. (And if you do that, consider continuing even further to the little park at **Point Woronzof.** It's approximately underneath the takeoff path from Anchorage International, providing some unusually close and dramatic views of jumbo jets as they launch themselves to some of the farthest frontiers of the earth.) On the way back, if you turn off Northern Lights onto Aircraft Dr., you may search out the **Alaska Aviation Heritage Museum** (tel. *248–5325*) at No. 4721, on the south shore of Lake Hood. You can look over 15 old planes plus various models, exhibits, etc. (Open daily; admission about $5.) Out back, the **Lake Hood Air Harbor** is a busy take-off point for many float- or ski-equipped planes for fishing or other trips into the Alaskan bush.

At the corner of Seventh Ave. and A St. is the city's absolute don't-miss, the **Anchorage Museum of History and Art** (tel. *343–4326*). It's an attractive enough art museum, with permanent and traveling exhibits, and one worthy of any modern American city on the ground floor. (Many early Alaskan artists are represented, including the famous ''Mount McKinley'' by Sydney Laurence.) On the top floor, however, is the 15,000-square-foot Alaska Gallery, an essential display of dioramas and other exhibits of Alaskana covering accurately and interestingly almost every aspect of Alaskan history and culture. You can go through yourself, although there are occasional guided tours that will bring it all together even better. There's also a cafe and gift shop on the ground floor. (Admission $2; open daily until 5 or 6 p.m., except closed Monday during winter.)

Anchorage has a goodly share of park land within the city. One with somewhat of an unusual shape, however, is the **Delaney Park Strip,** which is one block deep (between Ninth and Tenth avenues) by 14 blocks long (from A Street to P Street). It was converted years ago from a former airplane grass-and-dirt landing strip.

Out past the shopping districts of Midtown (which is what Anchorage folks call anything between 15th St. and International Airport Rd. and between the Seward Highway and Minnesota Dr.), is another museum collection housed at the new **Z. J. Loussac Public Library** (tel. *261–2846*) at the corner of 36th Ave. and Denali St. The Loussac Collection has paintings by Sydney Laurence and Eustace Ziegler, plus the Alaska Collection in a separate three-level wing. (Monday–Thursday noon to 9 p.m., Friday and Saturday 10 a.m. to 6 p.m., and Sunday noon to 6 p.m. There's no admission charge, but they would be happy if you looked through their gift shop. You can also get there on People Mover No. 60 or No. 2.

You say you haven't gotten close enough to some animals? You wanted to see a polar bear? Well, despite our own Alaska animal experiences, we still enjoy a visit to the compact **Alaska Zoo** (tel. *346–2133*), which is a bit out in the sticks at 4731 O'Malley Rd. There are about 50 different species of Alaskan birds and animals plus a few exotic creatures, like an elephant here, a hyena there. Drive out the Seward Highway, take the O'Malley Road exit to the east for about four miles. (Open from 10 a.m. to about dusk; admission $4.)

NORTH ANCHORAGE   If you have a car, you'll find out how quickly you can get into the wilderness if you drive out the supermodern Glenn Highway about 13 miles to **Eagle River** and thence another 13 miles to the visitor center for **Chugach State Park** (tel. *694–2108*). There are short and long trails through the boreal forest and wild flowers to the river. Afraid of bears? Go on the weekend, when you'll see plenty of folks from Anchorage out there—but no grizzlies. We'd go on a weekday—when you probably still won't see a bear.

If you continue on the Glenn Highway another 13 miles from Eagle River you can take the overpass across to the little Indian community of **Eklutna.** The principal attractions are the **Russian Orthodox Church,** built about 1850, and the colorful little spirit houses covering graves in the cemetery adjoining. The highway continues to **Palmer** (see the Mat-Su Valley in "Side Trips").

SOUTH ANCHORAGE   The **Seward Highway** is almost a destination in itself as it travels alongside the scenic Turnagain Arm of Cook Inlet. (As you may hear over and over again, that was named by Captain Cook when he had to turn again when he found it was not the opening to the long-sought Northwest Passage.) Keep an eye out for Dall sheep on the hills beside the road. Turnagain is often the place to watch the bore tide, a three- to six-foot wall of water that speeds in from the ocean at between 10 and 15 m.p.h. If you stop, don't be tempted to walk out on the mud flats, which are as dangerous as quicksand—more so since the surface first appears to be solid. You could get stuck and then drown as the bore tide bears down on you. (All kidding aside, it regularly happens to moose and has happened several times to people.)

About 10 miles south of central Anchorage, there's a parking space at the beginning of the boardwalk to **Potter Marsh Bird Sanctuary** (officially Potter Point State Game Refuge). You may spot eagles, geese, swans, and several other examples of the winged creatures illustrated on the signs. After another couple of miles, stop at the **Potter Section House** (tel. *345–2631*), a former 1929 railroad station and engineers' headquarters which is now a state museum. Check out the old rotary snowplow and other railroad equipment there. A little past the former Indian village called Indian, a local landmark is a half-sunken tavern called the **Bird House.** You'll see the big bird protruding from it; inside, the bar has slanted at an impossible angle and the walls have been covered with everything from business cards to dirty underwear. (Sara says she felt claustrophobic and will never go in again.)

About 35 miles out of Anchorage, a paved side road heads inland first to the village of Girdwood. About 3½ miles down an unpaved side road to the side road is the historic **Crow Creek Mine** (no phone), a functioning family gold mine now also operating as a family tourist attraction. For about $5, they'll give you a pan and some instructions and you can keep any gold you can find. At the end of the paved road is the **Alyeska Resort** (tel. *783–2222*), Alaska's premier ski resort and winter sports center, around which Anchorage has been hoping some day to center the winter Olympics (see "Sports"). During the summer, you can take the 20-minute, mile-long chairlift ride to the top of Mt. Alyeska for around $10. There's a soup-and-sandwich bar at the 4000-foot summit.

The last area considered part of greater Anchorage, about 48 miles from the center of town, is the former village of Portage, which was all but wiped out by the sea wave which followed the 1964 earthquake. (You'll see a few ruins of buildings among the trees killed by saltwater.) Turn left onto the Portage Glacier Road and drive five more miles to reach **Portage Lake** and **Portage Glacier.** The glacier itself has been retreating up the lake in recent years so it's no longer a particularly good view from land. However, the **Begich-Boggs Visitor Center** (tel. *783–2326*) there is a wonderful state-run facility for explaining about glaciers and nearby nature subjects. Pay the extra dollar or so to see the excellent film *Voices from the Ice,* which puts that super expensive superwide-screen movie back in Anchorage to shame. Also in operation by the time our ink is dry will be the new hour-long Portage Glacier summer cruise (about $20) through the icebergs on the M.V. *Ptarmigan* (continue across the Byron Creek Bridge to the end of the road to the new boat dock and orientation center).

Back on the Seward Highway, if you continue south you will be headed to Seward or Homer on the Kenai Peninsula (see "Side Trips").

SIDE TRIPS

As we said, Anchorage makes a great launching platform for driving or flying trips to several other areas in Alaska. We have eight favorite destinations to cover, in a little more depth than is usual in our "Side Trips" sections—Matanuska-Susitna, Valdez, Kenai Peninsula (Seward and Homer), and the Pribilof Islands. (The last five are aerial destinations, usually taken on all-inclusive one- or two-day tours from Anchorage.) If you're not going to travel outside of Anchorage and the immediate area, you could skip over the next several pages and continue with "Tours and Cruises."

MATANUSKA-SUSITNA   When folks in Anchorage talk about "the Valley," they historically have meant the fertile Matanuska Valley about 45 miles north, by train or car, and centered generally around the town of **Palmer,** on the Glenn Highway. Today, however, the definition has been broadened to include also the Susitna Valley, whose headquarters is the town of **Wasilla,** on the Parks Highway. The term also includes all within the official boundaries of the Matanuska-Susitna Borough, which extends generally from the edge of Denali National Park to the town of Glennallen far to the west. Talkeetna, described in "The Alaskan Interior", is also officially part of the area. Today there is talk about renaming the borough "Denali" to give it a more definite identity and also apparently to make it easier for foreign investors and visitors to pronounce. Meanwhile, it is often referred to simply as Mat-Su.

To an Outsider, Mat-Su seems to be an uneasy alliance between the folks in Palmer, largely representative of the hard-working, generally religious midwestern farm folk that were resettled there in 1935 during the Great Depression; and the more laid-back population of Wasilla, whose pioneer settlers predated those families who became part of the Colony near Palmer. A few years ago the borough was the fastest-growing county in the nation. But with the recent oil glut, unemployment has been high and at least a third of the residents now commute to Anchorage.

To most visitors, Mat-Su represents 75-pound cabbages (an image locals have largely tired of) and that funny, furry animal called the musk ox, who occasionally decide to play rugby with each other. The **Palmer Musk Ox Farm** (tel. *745–4151*), the only such in the world, gives interesting guided tours for $3 or $4. Take the Glenn Highway a couple miles northeast of Palmer and watch for the signs (officially at Milepost 50.1).

On the big cabbage file, if you do want to see one of those Mean Green Mothers from Outer Space (remember the film *Little Shop of Horrors*?), you'll find Audrey II, along with other dramatic vegetables and brilliant flowers in the special garden in Palmer at the log-cabin **Visitors Center** (tel. *745–2880*). It's across the railroad tracks on South Valley Way, just south of Evergreen Ave. The phenomenal growth of these specimens of course is due to the long hours of sunlight available during the short growing season. Samples of other *experimental veggies* (such as softball-sized radishes) can be seen not far from the log cabin at the University of Alaska **Agricultural Research Center** at the east end of East Fireweed Ave. in Palmer.

After the musk oxen, we enjoyed the drive up above the tree line to scenic **Hatcher Pass** and the old **Independence Gold Mine** buildings there now maintained as a state historical park (take the Fishhook Willow Road west from Palmer or the Fishhook Wasilla Road north from Wasilla). Near the park, you might drop in at the strictly smoke-free **Hatcher Pass Lodge** (tel. *745–5897*), a good place for lunch or dinner. (Sara said her rhubarb pie was the best pie she'd ever had in Alaska.) It also rents out a few cabins for urban folks with mountain fever. Look for what the locals call low-bush grizzlies (tiny, almost tame, Arctic ground squirrels).

Other popular sites and sights in Mat-Su include the **Knik Glacier,** which can't be reached from the road. At least three companies offer three-hour *nature tours* via *airboat* to it for around $75. (You'll need instructions from the visitor center on exactly where to meet the boat on the Old Palmer Highway.) There are also some exciting rubber-raft trips on nearby rivers.

On the Wasilla (Susitna) end of things, the **Museum and Visitor Center** (tel. *376–2005*) is at the corner of Main St. and Swanson Ave. Ask your way to the new location for the **Museum of Alaska Transportation,** which may have moved from Palmer to the Jacobsen Lake area by now. Anchorage folks like to vacation in and around the 180 or so lakes in the area, including **Big Lake** and **Nancy Lake.** All offer lots of fishing, boating, and swimming in the summer, and snowmobiling, Nordic skiing, and madcap sports like snowshoe baseball and a lake-ice golf course in the winter. The real (non-ceremonial) start of the annual Iditarod sled dog race is in Wasilla, and there's an interesting mushing museum at the **Iditarod Trail Headquarters** two miles down the Knik-Goosebay Road.

Good places to stay in the area include the rustic **Mat-Su Resort** (tel. *376–3228*) on Wasilla Lake. (Sadly the Lake Lucille Lodge, a former favorite, seems to have closed for good.) The Mat-Su Resort also has a popular restaurant, but a good summer 24-hour coffee shop is the **Alaska Pantry Cafe** in the Carrs Mall.

VALDEZ Sometimes known as Alaska's Little Switzerland, the town and port of Valdez (pronounced "val-DEEZ"), is known as the northernmost ice-free harbor in the world. Of course it is also famous as the southern terminus for the 800-mile trans–Alaska Pipeline. (It was a few miles out of Valdez's harbor in Prince William Sound where America's largest oil spill tragically took place after a tanker ran aground in March 1989.)

Valdez is a 300-mile drive from Anchorage, approximately two-thirds of which is along the Glenn Highway (Route 1) through the Matanuska Valley (keep an eye out for the **Matanuska Glacier** in the distance at about Milepost 102) to Glennallen. Then you drive down the southern portion of the Richardson Highway (Route 4) through the area known as the **Copper River Basin,** often paralleling the pipeline. (There is also a side road called the Edgerton Highway that leads, after about 90 often-difficult miles, to the former copper-mining center of **McCarthy** far inside the boundaries of the Wrangell-Saint Elias National Park, the largest in the U.S.)

The dramatic entrance to Valdez by road is over the Chugach Mountains via Thompson Pass (about 2700 feet) and beside several waterfalls and the **Worthington Glacier,** an unusually approachable hanging glacier. Three warnings: Watch out for fog, walking on that glacier is dangerous at any time, and note that in the winter the road can be closed for days in this area.

Bus service to Valdez is via *Valdez Anchorage Bus Lines* (fare about $60). Scheduled air service from Anchorage to Valdez is operated by **Era** and **Wilbur's.** Valdez is also a port on the Southwest System of the Alaska Marine Highway (tel. *835–4436*), so you can ferry from there to Whittier, Cordova, Seward, Homer, Kodiak, etc. Several cruise ships come into Valdez during the summer, most of them tying up to the world's largest floating dock.

In Valdez, the principal sight today is surely the 1000-acre **trans–Alaska Pipeline Marine Terminal,** which you're only allowed to see on a carefully supervised guided tour. It's about $15 for a two-hour trip with Gray Line (tel. *835–2357*), from the Westmark Hotel. Town tours are also offered by **Valdez Sightseeing** (tel. *835–4776*). On the way into town you pass the deserted site of **Old Valdez,** which was virtually wiped out by the 1964 earthquake and several resulting tsunamis (33 persons were killed).

The CVB **Visitors Center** (tel. *835–2984*), on Fairbanks St., includes a small museum and an interesting film on the earthquake (movie admission a dollar or two). For free, however, they'll point you to places to see, eat, and sleep. Be sure to go through the **Valdez Heritage Center** (tel. *835–2764*), a museum in the Centennial Building on Egan Dr.

and Chenega St. (suggested donation $1). And have a look in the waters of the **Valdez Small Boat Harbor** for harbor seals and especially sea otters. Those are those furry fellows doing the back stroke while simultaneously opening clams with a rock on their tummy, or perhaps carrying their young ones that way. (Prince William Sound is generally known for its large seal and otter populations.)

Besides the Pipeline terminal tour, the other important excursion is the cruise to the famous 4½-mile wide **Columbia Glacier** and throughout Prince William Sound run by **Stan Stephens Charters** (tel. *835–4731*), also headquartered at the Westmark (9-hour trip, including a salmon bake, for about $75; 5½-hour trip for about $50). Stephens also has a toll-free phone number, *(800) 478–1297*. A second local company with short cruises only is **Glacier Charter Service** (tel. *835–5141*), on Kobuk Dr. Helicopter tours over the sound are launched by **Era** (tel. *835–2595*) and **Soloy** (tel. *835–4999*). Figure about $125 per person for a one-hour experience. If the weather is good, Valdez has some terrific hiking trails, notably the mile-long trek from the end of the road up **Mineral Creek Canyon** to the old gold-stamping mill there.

Places to stay include two well-polished links in the Westmark chain, the **Westmark Valdez** (tel. *835–4391*), which also has an attractive restaurant; and the summer-only **Westmark Inn** (tel. *835–4485*). Other good hotels include the **Village Inn** (tel. *835–4445*), and possibly the **Totem Inn** (tel. *835–4443*). (Doubles in any of these will average around $100, plus 6% tax.) RVers will find convenient hook-ups at the **Bear Paw Park** in downtown Valdez. There is not a lot of serious shopping for visitors in Valdez, although we enjoyed poking around the **Last Frontier Gallery,** across the street from the city museum. If you're writing to Valdez, the zip code for everyone is 99686.

THE KENAI PENINSULA—SEWARD AND HOMER Try not to drive south from Anchorage on a weekend. Then you won't be competing for road, hotel, and restaurant space with Anchorage folks who also head for the peninsula for fishing, picnicking, or other relief from the urban Alaska version of cabin fever.

The 125-mile-long Seward Highway first climbs through the dramatic country in the **Chugach National Forest** to cross over Moose Pass in the Kenai Mountains. On the way, the traditional lunch and gas stop is at **Summit Lake Lodge,** one of those peculiarly Alaskan sort of places with lots of signs warning you, among other things, that they don't deal with Outside nonsense like credit cards or checks.

At the end of the highway, and at the foot of Mount Marathon and other snow-capped peaks, the port town of **Seward** (population 3000 or so) has yet to see its first traffic light. It also departs from Alaskan tradition in that its **Visitor Information Cache** (tel. *224–3094*) is not in a log cabin but an old railroad car more or less permanently parked at Third and Jefferson streets. Seward was founded in 1903 by railroad surveyors who saw that it was a good, ice-free port that could be connected by railroad with the Interior. The **Alaska Railroad** (tel. *224–5550*) is still a wonderfully scenic way for cruise-ship travelers who disembark in Seward to continue their Alaskan experience on land. Or you can take the train to Seward from Anchorage several days a week during the summer season. Many trips are in single self-propelled RDCs (rail diesel cars). We don't know the 1990 rates yet, but we estimate about $35 or $40 each way.

Unlike Cordova, Valdez, and Whittier, Seward is not on Prince William Sound. It is at the head of **Resurrection Bay,** west of the famous sound but still, of course, on the Gulf of Alaska. Seward's principal claim to touristic fame is as a launching point for cruises to **Kenai Fjords National Park,** which has 580,000 acres of mountains, waterfalls, sea mammals, glaciers, sea birds, and generally spectacular scenery.

If you want to walk up to and touch a glacier, though, you can get to the only portion of the park easily approached by land by taking the 12-mile side road just before entering town to find **Exit Glacier.** The ranger station there will direct you to the face of the icefield. However, the national park headquarters (tel. *224–3175*) is outside the park in the Seward Small Boat Harbor, next to the Harbor Master's office. Be sure to see the displays and pick up a brochure. Two well-known commercial *sightseeing* cruises head out to the fjords daily during the summer: **Quest Charters** (tel. *224–3025*) and **Kenai Fjords Tours, Inc.** (tel. *224–3668*), both located in the Seward Small Boat Harbor, have day-long tours. Including lunch, these will run around $80 or so.

Seward is also famous for being the beginning of the original Iditarod Trail on which many gold rushers began their trek to Nome early in the century. (But it is not a section used on the annual sled-dog race). The town is the location for the annual halibut-fishing tournament throughout the month of July and the week-long silver salmon derby in August. You might also like to see the earthquake and Russian exhibits in the **Historical Society Museum** in the basement of city hall at Fifth and Adams streets. (Admission about $1.)

You can fly between Seward and Anchorage in about 35 minutes via **Harbor Air** (tel. *224–3133*). It also has sightseeing flights over the national park for around $75 per person. Seward is a stop on the Southwest System of the Alaska Marine Highway (tel. *224–5485*), on the Fourth Avenue Dock downtown, homeport of the system's Trusty Tusty. You can ferry east to Whittier, Cordova, and Valdez, or west to Homer, Seldovia, Kodiak, and some of the Aleutian Islands. A few folks travel between Seward and Anchorage on the **Seward Bus Line** (tel. *224–3608*)—about $25 for a three-hour trip.

We checked out some accommodations in Seward and liked the

newer rooms in the **New Seward Hotel** (tel. *224–8001*), downtown at 217 Fifth Ave. (The stuffed creatures in the cluttered lobby won't bite, but we almost got it there from a live dog!) For nonsmokers only, the **Breeze Inn** (tel. *224–5237*) next to the Small Boat Harbor has decent, nicotine-free facilities and a pleasant view. One of the best restaurants in Seward is the **Harbor Dinner Club** (tel. *224–3012*), on Fifth Avenue downtown. A less-expensive family establishment is **Christian's** at the corner of Third and Monroe streets. In the boat harbor area, the **Salmon Cache** has some great (as in HUGE and tasty) ice cream cones for a buck or so. For Alaskan gift browsing, meander through the tiny shops downtown in the tiny A.D. 1903-model **Brown & Hawkins Mall** (which is not really a mall at all). Check especially the **Alaska Gallery** in the rear. Writing to Seward? It's a small town, and just about everyone and everything can be addressed at zip code 99664.

If you bypass Seward (or backtrack about 35 miles to the intersection in the Moose Pass area), you can continue west on Route 1, the Sterling Highway. Traveling the length of the peninsula you pass the cutoff for the oil town of **Kenai** (headquarters for all those Tesoro stations you see in Alaska), go through the village of **Soldotna** (headquarters for the Kenai National Wildlife Refuge), and along Cook Inlet to the end of the road at the particularly picturesque little town of **Homer** on Kachemak Bay, 250 miles (five hours' drive) from Anchorage. Homer usually doesn't get very cold in the winter, but one story that made the Anchorage papers in early '89 was the one about the Homer cat whose fur became frozen to a tree in subzero weather. The hapless feline (that's newspaper talk) was eventually rescued without harm by somebody's Dad who climbed a ladder and then successfully applied a hair dryer attached to a long extension cord.

Geographically, Homer is distinguished by the unusual appendage called the **Homer Spit,** a narrow, low-lying peninsulette that protrudes for about five miles, almost half-way across the bay. The Spit, which features a hotel, a ferry landing, several bars, lots of tent and RV campers, and many charter fishing operations, is pretty much the center of the action in this vacation-oriented community. You can also dig for clams and mussels along the rocky beach. In any case, drop in to the **Chamber of Commerce Visitor Center** (tel. *235–5300*), in a small log cabin about halfway out the Spit on the left. (There's a similar information center downtown.)

Scheduled flights to and from Anchorage are on **SouthCentral Air** (tel. *235–6171*) or **Era Airlines** (tel. *235–5205*) in less than an hour. Both carriers also carry on to Kodiak Island. You can also ship in and out of Homer on the **Alaska Marine Highway** (tel. *235–8449*)—1½ hours to Seldovia or 10 hours to Kodiak (cabins available on the M.V. *Tustumena*).

The town's most interesting hotel, due to its unique location at the

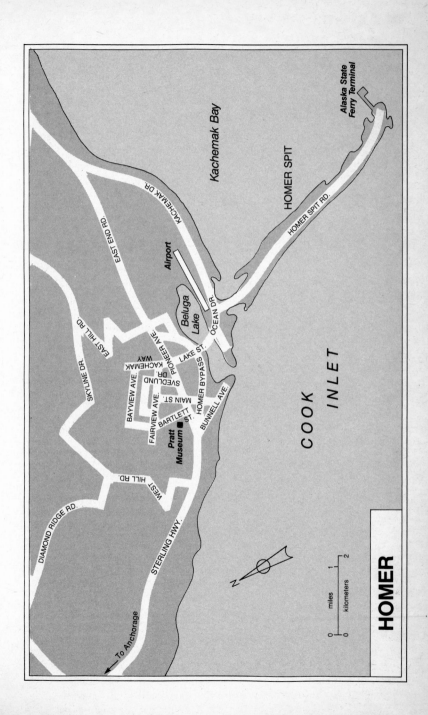

HOMER

very tip of the Spit, is the two-story, not-too-surprisingly named **Land's End Resort** (tel. *235–2500*). (Better that than Last Resort, I guess.) The best rooms are around $100 for two, and seem a little small. But the balconied bayside units have a virtually unparalleled panorama of sea and mountains, and that makes up a lot for a lack of elbow room. Its **Chartroom** restaurant vies with the nearby **Porpoise Room** (tel. *235–7848*), at 874 Fishdock, for the title of the best dining on the Spit. (For either, request a window seat along with your reservation.)

Other Homer accommodations include the **Best Western Bidarka Inn** (tel. *235–8148*), on the edge of town, where our own room was okay except for the skinny towels; and the hillside **Lakewood Inn** (tel. *235–6144*), near the main part of Homer. The visitor center has some information on more hotels and motels plus **Homer Bed and Breakfast** and some other good B&Bs. Other recommended restaurants are the **Fresh Sourdough Express** (tel. *235–7571*), at 1316 Ocean Dr., which we can't help returning to again and again (and it also sells baked goods), and the more modest **Duncan House,** which we've only hit once for lunch. **Don Jose's,** at 127 Pioneer Ave., features both Mexican and Italian specialties. *Viva!*

One of the state's most famous (and generally most crowded) saloons, the **Salty Dawg,** occupies what seems to be a decrepit log-walled light house out on the Spit. Live amateur theater is produced at **Pier One** (tel. *235–7333*) all through the summer, halfway out the Spit. Homer doesn't really have a set of golf links, unless you count the nine-hole miniature course that is set up on the dance floor at **Alice's Champagne Palace** on Pioneer Avenue during the off season. (The artificial turf and tin cans come down on Saturday nights so the patrons can dance, but are back up on Sunday for the Palace Open.)

Homer's **Pratt Museum** (tel. *235–8635*), on Bartlett St., is considered one of the better small museums in the state, combining contemporary art with cultural and natural history in the same building. And maybe they'll let you feed the octopus. (Admission about $3.) Be sure to get a guide sheet to the museum gardens, too, and check out the items in the gift shop. You'll see the museum and several other sights on **Homer Tours** (tel. *235–8996*), usually a four-hour ground excursion for $25 or so. (It's owned by a retired minister and his wife.) A popular cruise is aboard the small passenger ferry called the **Danny J** (tel. *235–8110*), a workboat which leaves Ramp No. 1 (near the Salty Dawg) at noon to visit the bird sanctuary and other bucolic destinations at Halibut Cove, returning to Homer in the late afternoon, for around $30. (That gives you a couple of hours over there to meet the cove's resident artists, admire their work, etc.) **Rainbow Tours** (tel. *235–7272*) also has a cruise to some of the same areas for around the same price. Or you can take Rainbow Tours to Seldovia, the little isolated village across the bay. If you're in a hurry, you can even hydrofoil to Seldovia.

The principal occupation, avocation, and source of admiration on the Spit involves fishing—especially for halibut and sometimes for salmon. Even if you don't go yourself, head out onto the Spit in the early evening and admire the wonderful specimens others have been bringing in. **Icicle Seafoods** in the big turquoise building near the end has a retail shop where you can sometimes taste the goodies.

Back in town, a store with an excellent reputation is **Grandma's Antiques,** at 708 Nielsen Ave., near the Lakeside Mall. You'll also find several art galleries, and about 50 local artists and artisans are exhibited at **Ptarmigan Arts,** a co-op on Pioneer Avenue. Just catercorner from that, you might like to stop in the log-cabin shop run by a man known as the state's Jelly and Jam King. **Alaska Wild Berry Products,** at 528 East Pioneer Ave., is a bit of a tourist trap, but it's still fun, and the grape goop and other sticky stuff is pretty good. Free samples are sometimes available.

KODIAK ISLAND   A long trip from Homer on the ferry, or a short one from Anchorage on a MarkAir jet, brings you to the town of **Kodiak** on Kodiak Island, sometimes known as the Emerald Isle. Be aware at the outset that although the island's claim to fame is as the home of the largest bears in the world (some of these maxed-out brownies are about 10 feet from nose to tail and weigh in at three-quarters of a ton), the chances of your catching a casual peek at any unstuffed Smokies is pretty slim. The Kodiak bears would have you believe they're an *Ursus raris,* making themselves scarce and staying well out in the wilderness.

In the normal day tour around greater Kodiak, a traveler could be forgiven for thinking that wildlife has actually shrunk here. You'll be lucky if you can catch sight of some dog-sized black-tailed deer, and about the only four-footed beasties you can absolutely count on seeing will be some tame miniature horses who live on the little island across the bridge from town. Be sure to look in the harbor for sea lions, often attracted there by the overflow from the canneries. (Be careful not to feed them, however; in their enthusiasm they have a tendency to confuse food and the feeder!) There are plenty of summer wildflowers around the island, and the wild salmon berries you pick along the roads are delicious.

At 3950 square miles, Kodiak is the second largest island in the U.S. (after the Big Island of Hawaii). But unless you're an outback hunter or hiker you won't see much of it. Very few roads thread the eastern end of the island near the town. (If you contract to go along with whatever bush pilot operation is currently serving mail routes to the outlying villages, you might see a bear or two or some other wildlife along the way.)

Kodiak can lay claim to being the first capital of Alaska, since the Russian-America Company was based here from 1784 until the early

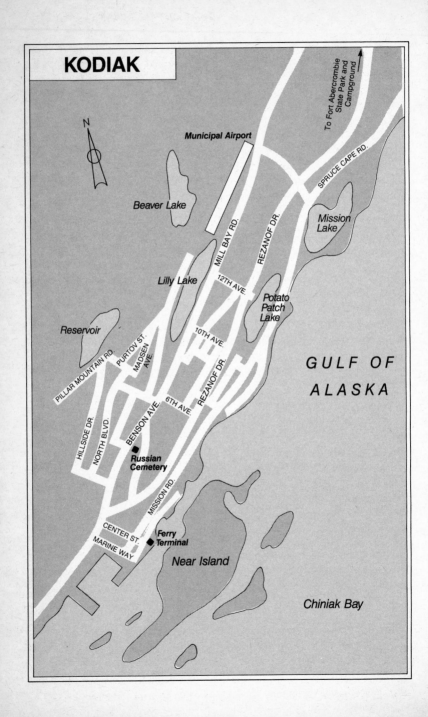

KODIAK

Municipal Airport

Beaver Lake

Lilly Lake

Reservoir

Mission Lake

Potato Patch Lake

MILL BAY RD.

REZANOF DR.

12TH AVE.

10TH AVE.

6TH AVE.

REZANOF DR.

SPRUCE CAPE RD.

To Fort Abercrombie State Park and Campground

PILLAR MOUNTAIN RD.

PURTOV ST.

MADSEN AVE.

HILLSIDE DR.

NORTH BLVD.

BENSON AVE.

MISSION RD.

CENTER ST.

MARINE WAY

Russian Cemetery

Ferry Terminal

Near Island

GULF OF ALASKA

Chiniak Bay

N

1800s when Lord Baranov moved his account books to Sitka. Today this relatively untouristy town serves as the center of a no-nonsense commercial fishing fleet. (The fishy odor you detect right away has a way of becoming unnoticeable after a few hours.) Fishermen go out in all kinds of weather, and the town traditionally has had and still has a high percentage of its men lost at sea.

Two natural disasters also have struck hard at Kodiak: the 1964 Good Friday earthquake and tsunami, which almost wiped out the fishing industry (notice that one cannery, hastily built afterwards out of an old Liberty Ship, is still in operation today); then there was the 1912 eruption of Mount Katmai on the Alaska Peninsula, from which soot fell on Kodiak (for days) until it was a foot and a half deep.

The **Visitor Information Center** (tel. *486–4782*) is down by the ferry dock near the center of town. Be sure to see the **Baranof Museum** (tel. *486–5920*), 101 Marine Way, which has been established in the boss' former headquarters, whose interior walls have been standing since 1808. Nearby, check out the blue-domed **Holy Resurrection Church,** center of the oldest Russian Orthodox parish in America and which celebrates the life of Saint Herman, who did his good works in Kodiak and is now the church's only canonized North American. Other things to see in the immediate area include the visitor center for the **Kodiak National Wildlife Refuge,** out near the airport, and the old coastal military fortifications built when a Japanese invasion was feared during World War II.

There are two tour companies in operation in Kodiak. We took the homegrown one, Lola Harvey's **Island Terrific Tours** (tel. *486–4777*), about $50 for a full day. From other reports, we believe the tour run by **Gray Line** (tel. *486–3332*) for around the same fare is also good. (Gray Line also has an overnight package from Anchorage including air, hotel, and tour for $300 or so.) If you're going to guide yourself, you can get a car at the airport from **Hertz, Avis, Budget,** or **Rent-a-Heap.** Shopping is mostly from small stores near the town square (sometimes known locally as Pass Out Park).

Many travelers save their Kodiak trip until August, because only during that month can you choose among several performance dates for the historical drama, **Cry of the Wild Ram** (tel. *486–5291*) presented rain or shine in the special outdoor amphitheater outside of town. The story recalls Russian days in both Kodiak and Sitka. (Its 24th season will be in August 1990; some of the town's citizens have grown up with the production, starting as children and then playing ever older parts.) Tickets are about $10.

Kodiak's two best hotels are the **Westmark** (tel. *486–5712*), at 234 South Benson St., the site of our own stay; and the **Buskin River Inn** (tel. *487–2700*), out by the airport. Both have good restaurants too. Seafood is the specialty at all dining rooms on the island, except at

Kodiak Pizza, which serves Mexican stuff. And the Chinese restaurant fries some pretty good hamburgers, we're told.

KATMAI NATIONAL PARK   Just across Shelikof Strait from Kodiak Island is Alaska's volcanic area on the Alaska Peninsula. In June 1912, the violent eruption of **Novarupta Volcano** darkened skies and lowered temperatures around the world. A National Geographic explorer coming across the scene of devastation four years later found thousands of smoking fumaroles there, naming it the **Valley of the Ten Thousand Smokes.** Although the Smokes have pretty much ceased, this scene of geological wonder is the center of today's **Katmai** (pronounced "CAT-my") **National Park.**

Most Alaskans think first of grizzly (brown) bears when they think of the park. A rich salmon stream here, easily accessible by both man and bear, provides one of the most reliable settings for the two species to co-exist in close proximity. In other words, the wisdom is that if you really want to see a bear close up, at least while the salmon are running, you can always go to Katmai.

There are no land or sea routes to Katmai. Traveling there involves first an hour-long jet trip out of Anchorage aboard **MarkAir** (or a slower prop trip from Kodiak or Anchorage with **Peninsula Air**) to the village of **King Salmon,** famous enough as a fishing center on the Naknek River, and next door to a small U.S. Air Force base. The best place to stay overnight is the **Quinnat Landing Hotel** (tel. *246–3000*), which also features a good restaurant. You can arrange fishing trips at the activity desk. (Sara caught several silvers there while I poked around musty museums and stuff; she had a much better time.) The hotel will cook your salmon for you, but we were surprised to be charged as much as if the house itself had provided the fish.

Amphibians take off from King Salmon from time to time and fly in 30 minutes to the privately owned **Brooks Lodge** (tel. *246–3079*), a rustic resort operated by an Anchorage company named Katmailand on Naknek Lake in the center of the National Park. (If you see any floating rocks, they're not just in your head; they're air-filled pumice stones left over from old volcanic eruptions.) Make your arrangements carefully so you can be sure to get a seat on the bus for the 23-mile morning tour to the Valley of the Ten Thousand Smokes (about $50). Someone had us down for the wrong day, and no amount of pleading with the folks at Brooks Lodge or the National Park Rangers could get us on a fully booked bus or into any other vehicle (and you thought travel writers had clout!).

The valley from the air is also dramatic. The pilot for **Hermens MarkAir Express** at King Salmon felt sorry for us and gave us a close aerial inspection of the neighborhood for no extra charge. At Brooks Lodge be sure to check in with the rangers (who will probably meet your plane on the beach to give you a speech about dealing diplomatically with bears), and then take part in any nature walks they may set up. All these treks inevitably end up at a special bear-viewing platform at Brooks Falls. Keep your fingers crossed; there are an estimated 1000 grizzlies living in Katmai, including 40 who summer in the Brooks area. On our day, we saw about that many leaping salmon but not bear one—allegedly a very unusual situation. (Later someone said they had seen all the Brooks bears berry-picking on the other side of the nearby mountain.)

Of course you can hang around **Brooks** for longer if they have a cabin available. (Showers and johns in a separate building.) At last report these rented for $110 per person per day—pretty stiff for what you get, we thought, although they are often fully booked. (There are two-day package rates from Anchorage that include air, cabin, and the bus tour for $600 or so.) Cafeteria-style meals ($40 a day for three squares) are not exactly gourmet, but are satisfactory and substantial. (If you're interested, there's a toll-free number for Katmailand *(800) 544–0551*). The National Park is headquartered in King Salmon (which we didn't know until too late). Write for information to the Superintendent, Katmai National Park, P.O. Box 7, King Salmon, AK 99613 (or tel. *(907) 246–3305*) and ask for the colorful map/brochure.

NOME   Just 90 minutes out of Anchorage, you can jet on an Alaska Airlines 737 to the Golden Beaches of Nome on the Seward Peninsula, next to the Bering Sea. (Sit on the right side flying from Anchorage to either Nome or Kotzebue in order to have a chance at seeing Mt. McKinley, about 20 minutes out of Anchorage; and if you miss the mountain, better sit on the left coming back.)

Tens of thousands of prospectors braved considerable hardships to reach Nome in 1899 and 1900, and today a few hardy souls still sift the sands in front of Front St. finding a few flakes and the occasional (very occasional) nugget. And you may see the giant 14-story monster Bima dredge a couple of miles off shore, a commercial operation which continues to scoop gold off the ocean floor at the rate of more than a ton a year (a total of 35,500 ounces in 1988, a drop from the 36,700 ounces in 1987).

Once Nome was the largest town in Alaska, with about 20,000 population, before much of it was wiped out from time to time due to storms, fires, diseases, and economic reasons. Today the number of residents is down to around 3700, about 60 percent of which are Eskimos (speaking three different dialects of Yupik). Remember that things are really popping in Nome in March with events surrounding the finish of the Iditarod Sled Dog Race. Most first-timers arrive in Nome on a short guided tour from Anchorage, usually sold together with a short guided tour of Kotzebue with an overnight in one town or the other (see "Tours and Cruises"). If you come in to Nome independently, however, better stop in soon to the CVB **Visitor Information Center** (tel. *443–5535*) on Front St., opposite the end of Division St. The CVB claims they'll find you a place to sleep no matter how busy things get, and they maintain a list of private homes who take paying guests. Ask them for a walking-tour map. They'll also see if you can find a commercial tour to join, either summer or winter. You might check our remarks on the Gambell Village Tour in "Tours and Cruises." Travelers already in Nome can book onto this tour with the **Northwest Tourism Center** (tel. *443–2700*), at 110 Seppala St.

Other things to see include several old gold dredges within walking distance of the town (but they'll crumble if climbed upon). If you pick up a gold pan from a local store, you're welcome to try your own luck on the beach, but watch out for private claims inland. You can take dogsled rides, any time (with summer sleds on wheels, of course), and you'll probably want to see the **Carrie McLain Museum,** on Front St. near the information center. It has exhibits featuring Eskimo culture and Nome's role in the gold rush. Other things suggested by the CVB include wildflower excursions to Anvil Mountain, watching Eskimo dancing, and even playing bingo (Wow!).

Remember that we said you'd probably never see a wild polar bear in Alaska? Well, you can better your odds somewhat during the fall, winter, or spring with flightseeing trips from Nome. Check with **Bering Air** (tel. *443–5464*), or **Cape Smythe Air** (tel. *443–2414*), or **Evergreen Helicopters** (tel. *443–5334*). If those bleached bruins continue to elude you, you may have to be satisfied with aerial sightings of walrus, seals, reindeer herds, and other creatures.

If you feel like getting out for a drive over the treeless tundra, or are in town for some serious hunting, fishing, berry-picking, or bird watching (e.g., the long-tailed Yaeger or yellow-bellied loon), you can rent a truck from either **Alaska Cab Garage** (tel. *443–2939*) or **Bonanza Rentals** (tel. *443–2221*) for about $80 a day or $15 an hour. It's well known that there are no roads connecting Nome to Anchorage or anyplace else that goes anywhere. However, there are more than 200 miles of gravel roads from Nome to three or four small villages and ghost towns on the peninsula. We wouldn't advise driving in the dark— an utter impossibility anyway in the summer when there are at least 20 hours of sunlight per day (and plenty of twilight for the other four hours).

Checking in for a short stay in Nome, we would reserve in advance at the year-round **Nome Nugget Inn** (tel. *443–2323*), overlooking the ocean on one side and the action on Front Street on the other (doubles about $100). It also features **Fat Freddie's** restaurant (you'll know the owner/cook when you see him) and a nice bar—at least it is when everybody doesn't have their eyes glued to the tube. (They may turn it off when RATNET has a cooking show or something equally inspiring.)

The **Polaris** (tel. *443–2268*) is another hotel possibility, although we haven't inspected the premises personally.

Other places to eat include **Nacho's,** a Mexican place at Front and Federal streets; **Milano's,** next door, where a Korean chef turns out Italian pizza and, as I recall, some Greek specialties; the **Polar Cub Cafe,** across the street has sandwiches and seafood; the **Twin Dragon,** Bering St. and Alley Way, for Chinese; and just a mile outside of town the rustic **Fort Davis Road House.** There you might be able to try reindeer or moose steaks or a few other *specialites de la maison* you won't find at Maxim's.

Many interior communities in Alaska are dry, but that's not the case in Nome, which is after all the Nome of poems, novels, and motion pictures. Today there are only 10 bars, the hundreds of frontier taverns run by the likes of Wyatt Earp having finally bitten the permafrost. For nightlife, the **Polaris Bar** has live music and is particularly popular with the locals. The **Board of Trade Saloon** is the traditional informal old-Alaska bar, and has been since 1899. If you're so inclined, you'll find a few others. Be aware that any of these can get a little rough late on a Friday or Saturday when the noise and the blood alcohol levels begin to rise proportionately in some of the regular patrons.

Nome might be the place to buy your Eskimo skins and ivory carvings at prices generally below what you'd pay in Anchorage or Fairbanks. (We were even approached by a billiken sculptor on the street, but his products were pretty crude.) Stores with some interesting and sometimes classy items for sale include the **Arctic Trading Post,** across from the Nugget Inn, and the **Board of Trade Ivory Shop,** next door to the famous saloon of the same name.

Lastly, be prepared to run across lots of bad puns: Nome is where the heart is—no roads lead to Nome—the gnomes of Nome—friends, Nomans, etc. (No man can accuse us of anything like that. No matter how tempted. No ma'am.)

KOTZEBUE Whereas Nome is considered a Gold-Rush-and-Sourdough town, the equally lively and friendly community of **Kotzebue** (pop. 3700) is almost thoroughly Eskimo. It is the headquarters of one of the more profitable Native corporations known as NANA—the Northwest Alaska Native Association. Before modern hunting restrictions were imposed, the town was also proudly known as the Polar Bear Capital of the World. Today it is beginning to be known as the jumping off place for the new Red Dog silver, zinc, and lead mine (also owned by NANA), about 100 miles north. Take some warm clothes; Kotzebue varies from cold to chilly, even in July.

Kotzebue was founded several centuries ago on a narrow spit of land extending from a narrow peninsula. It seems less isolated in the winter when the waters of the inlet freeze, providing easy access via snow machine or dogsled to the mainland. The town is also about 25 miles above the Arctic Circle, and in June or July at midnight you might still use 1/250th of a second at f/8 to photograph fishermen on the beach working on their nets (or balloon-tired ATVs tearing around town piloted by amazingly untired young people).

You can fly in on your own hook (and on one of **Alaska Airlines'** Double Arctic flights) twice daily. To or from Kotzebue you sometimes have to share your Boeing 737 with unusual cargo like dogs or fish, both of which usually make their presence known in their own way to other passengers. Air service to a dozen small villages in the region is provided by **Bering Air** (tel. *442–3187*) or **Cape Smythe Air** (tel. *443–3020*).

Be sure to have your reservation pre-booked at the surprisingly comfortable **Nullaġvik Hotel** (tel. *442–3331*), corner of Front St. and Tundra Way, the only hotel we've ever stayed in which is properly spelled with a dot over the "g." (The word means "overnight place.") It is also an establishment which is often filled to the roof with guided tours. It has a pretty good restaurant for uncomplicated dishes, but ask your waitress how to pronounce "We hope you enjoyed your meal; please come see us again soon" in Inupiat (it's spelled out in only three words on your place mat). A second restaurant down the street, called the **Arctic Dragon** is Chinese. The nearby **Hamburger Hut** is open until midnight. Time was when Kotzebue was known as the home of the northernmost Dairy Queen in the world, but no more; the franchise was lost and today it's known as the **Arctic Queen** (closed only from 2 a.m. to 4 a.m., believe it or not).

There's no bar at the hotel—Kotzebue is as dry as a beached whalebone. Or at least it was, because this kind of thing can be voted in and out from time to time in rural Alaska. There is at least one locked-up place in town bearing a Budweiser sign that looks like it could spring to life at the drop of an antler. (Technically, Kotzebue is only "damp"; i.e., it is not illegal to possess and use alcohol, only to sell it.)

The principal tourist stop in Kotzebue is at the impressive, super-sophisticated **NANA Museum of the Arctic** (tel. *442–3304*), which also serves as the Visitor Information Center, and one of the best souvenir shops in town. The two-hour special program at the museum is also interesting, but disappointing when the dancers perform and the blanket toss is demonstrated indoors where it is difficult to photograph, even with a flash. Admission about $20.

Our advice is that if you did not fly in with a group, stop in and see if you can join one of the buses for the village tour. You should drop in and see the modern senior citizens' center and the demonstration fish camp run by high school students on the edge of town. Huge jade boulders are barged to Kotzebue from Jade Mountain, also owned by NANA, and you can watch the gem being cut and processed at a jade factory near the museum. Renting a car is problematic, and unless you can talk some kid into packing you aboard his three- or four-wheeled Suzuki, you could be out of luck. There are, however, a couple of taxis in town.

There's a second smaller and often-overlooked museum called **Ootukahkuktuvik** (translation: "Place Having Old Things") in the former Episcopal parsonage, which is open erratically. You can't miss it; a statue of a polar bear appears to have been quick frozen while trying to leap off the roof.

Kotzebue is also the headquarters for several national parks, preserves, and monuments throughout the Brooks Range and other nearby mountains, and rangers sometimes give lectures at the Nullaġvik Hotel. However, the parks and protected areas themselves remain effectively unreachable to the casual traveler. Backpackers, kayakers, and other intrepid types should write for information to the Superintendent, Northwest Alaska Areas, National Park Service, P.O. Box 1029, Kotzebue, AK 99752 (or tel. *(907) 442–3760*). Commercial tours along the Kobuk River and other bush areas in this part of Alaska are offered by **Sourdough Outfitters** (tel. *(907) 692–5252*), P.O. Box 90, Bettles, AK 99726.

THE PRIBILOF ISLANDS There are two main islands, **St. George** and **St. Paul,** but when most folks talk about going to visit the Pribilofs, or the Pribs, they usually mean to St. Paul, the larger island. Shaped rather like a free-form pork chop, St. Paul and its neighboring islands are isolated by about 300 miles from Mainland Alaska out into the Bering Sea (technically, they are even farther west than Hawaii). The ideal time to visit is from mid-June to mid-August, and don't forget to bring some warm clothes along with your camera and binoculars.

The island receives two or three flights a week during the summer from **Reeve Aleutian Airlines** (tel. *546–2238* on St. Paul), which flies from Anchorage usually via Cold Bay in the Aleutians. Their dependable Lockheed Electra turboprops date back to the 1950s. (Would that modern jets had so much leg room.) **Peninsula Airway** flies a slower version of the route, via Dutch Harbor, sometimes stopping at St. George along the way. (Compare all the air fares carefully, because you might come up with an all-inclusive tour rate for not much more than the round-trip fare alone.)

The history and culture of the isolated, treeless volcanic islands is interesting in itself, with a population of about 600 Aleuts, most of whom are also descendants of Russian colonists and are now devout members of the Russian Orthodox Church. But the principal attraction is the wildlife—as many as a million noisy fur seals in five separate rookeries on St. Paul, plus the arctic fox, reindeer, more than 200 species of pelagic birds, and many different kinds of wildflowers. (There are no dogs and no mosquitoes on the island.) Photographers are delighted with how near they can get to the seals and rare birds. The latter often rest on ledges just below the top of grassy, 200-foot-tall sea cliffs where you can edge your way on your stomach as close as you dare.

St. Paul, which is also the name of the town as well as the largest island, has only one rather basic hotel, called the **King Eider** (tel. *546–2312*), P.O. Box 88, St. Paul, AK 99660, named after a much more magnificent duck. (Don't land without having your living arrangements nailed down first.) There's also a choice of one or two restaurants, and absolutely no nightclubs at all. There are no cars available, although you might be able to rent a four-wheel ATV or a two-wheel mini-bike, if you feel comfortable on one of those. There are also lots of Federal rules and regulations designed to protect you and the seals from one another. And if you show up in St. Paul without any specific plans, our strong advice is to join one of the tours in progress. Most folks come out on previously arranged excursions, which is the only way we've done it ourselves.

In any case, be sure to see **Saints Peter and Paul Church,** built in 1907, with some of its precious Russian icons (although Father George won't let you take pictures inside). Stop in next door at **City Hall** (tel. *546–2331*). For a really good wrapup on the Pribilofs then and now, look for *The Pribilof Islands,* a 50-page book by Susan Hackley Johnson, which may be for sale at the city hall or in the hotel for about $5.

In St. Paul, a lot depends on your tour guide. We had two excellent ones, both full of knowledge and with a terrific sense of humor at the same time; they almost managed to convert us to avid birders. Unfortunately, after we left the island, their company was shot out from under them, and we have no idea if they are still around. Take some recent magazines to leave with whomever you meet on the island, and if you see Barbara or Jeannie, give them our best and ask them to write us because we never even got their last names.

TOURS AND CRUISES

Tour and cruise businesses start up and then go belly up every year in Anchorage as in most parts of the world. Here are a few that we believe will continue on solid ground for awhile. Be aware that the same experiences are often sold not only by the operating company but by other agencies too. The price is usually the same no matter where you buy the ticket. Many tour and cruise companies have storefront locations along Fourth Avenue.

City bus tours around Anchorage (three or four hours for around $20 or $25), and other tours including areas as far afield as Portage Glacier and Eklutna are offered by at least four companies. Check with **Alaska Sightseeing Tours** (tel. *276–1305*), 543 West Fourth Ave.; or **Gray Line** (tel. *277–5581*), practically next door at 547 West Fourth Ave.; or **Royal Hyway Tours** (tel. *276–7711*), 612 West Fourth Ave.— all of which are headquartered out of state; and **Eagle Custom Tours** (tel. *349–6710*), 612 West Fourth Ave., which prides itself on being a hometown outfit operating year round. We once went with Eagle to sites in South Anchorage (Alyeska, Portage Glacier, etc.). The tour itself was well designed, but our guide was not the greatest. Perhaps your experience will be better.

The **Alaska Wilderness Museum** (tel. *274–1600*), at 844 West Fifth Ave., which we mentioned in ''Sights and Sites,'' has its own Anchorage Wildlife City Tour. It includes a visit to the taxidermic museum, of course, and then a city bus tour that travels out in the country in search of some live specimens. The all-day excursion, including lunch, may run around $40. (An optional four-hour city tour alone might cost $25.)

Train tours to Denali National Park: As we've said before, anyone can hop on an Alaska Railroad car in Anchorage or Fairbanks and travel to Denali National Park—a wonderful scenic trip through the mountains and over the rivers—for a relatively modest amount of cash (see ''Transportation''). Besides that, between mid-May and mid-September there are two fiercely competing big-time tour corporations that gild the lily, perhaps, by tying onto these trains their own super-glitzy, full-length, glass-dome, double-deck, 60-passenger railroad cars. Everyone has reserved seats upstairs while the dining room and rest rooms are on the lower level.

They are the largest rail or land vehicles ever built for regular use, and everyone gets a great view. The seats are particularly large and plush, and the quality of meals and drink is approximately that of a luxurious ocean cruise. That may be because both of these companies are branches of luxurious ocean cruise lines, and many of these rail trips are filled or nearly filled with passengers who have arrived in Alaska aboard their vessels.

Be aware that unlike the seating arrangements in the ARR's own cars, about half the passengers must ride backwards on either tour operation. (You might try to reserve a forward-facing seat.) Although if you're a group of at least four, you can trade back and forth. And just as in an airplane, you may be allowed only small pieces of hand luggage in the special car after checking the larger suitcases. Smoking is allowed only in specific areas. Our advice is to sit on the east side of the car (on the left going north from Anchorage or on the right going south to Anchorage). The view is generally better and it's also the only place you can see the passing mileposts.

The first to set up this American Orient Express was **Tour Alaska** (tel. *276–7711*), whose Anchorage street address is 612 West Fourth Ave. It's a subsidiary of Princess Cruises, and it calls its Denali trip the *Midnight Express.* Usually the last two or three cars in the train, the new Ultra Domes, belong to them. One of their cars is at the very end, and they have an open-air observation platform on the back, an advantage for photographers.

The second outfit to hop on the rail bandwagon was **Holland America/Westours** (tel. *277–5581*), which also has the Gray Line concession in Alaska, and whose Anchorage address is the same as Gray Line at 547 West Fourth Ave. Calling its trip the *McKinley Explorer,* Holland America usually has its two or three glass-domed cars sandwiched between the stock blue-and-gold Alaska Railroad Vista Dome and the snazzy Tour Alaska Ultra Dome cars bringing up the rear. (It's amusing to see the contortions both tour companies go through in their advertising and publicity photos to show only their dome cars without showing the other guy's!)

Both companies offer a one-night Anchorage-Denali-Fairbanks deal (around $300 or so) or an Anchorage-Denali-Anchorage deal (maybe $325), which include a wildlife tour in the park. Holland America also has a two-night version for around $400, which is probably a better deal, especially since you really should stay at the park longer than a single overnight. At this writing, Gray Line will also sell one-way dome car space only, either between Anchorage and Denali (about $100) or between Denali and Fairbanks (maybe $50), but you'd better recheck again since this is the kind of policy that changes easily.

It's difficult for us to recommend one over the other in this edition, but you might like to find out where you're being put up at Denali. Tour Alaska usually chooses its own **Harper Lodge,** which is nicer; Holland America usually picks the **National Park Hotel,** which is a little more convenient (see hotel reviews in "The Alaskan Interior.") Tour Alaska also prepares its meals on board the train, whereas Holland America serves precooked meals. But Holland America claims it has a better suspension system to eliminate uncomfortable swaying "on other domed cars." (Sigh.) If you want to be sure to get in on either of these operations, you'd better book a long time in advance at the toll-free numbers we list in "Coming Into the Country" (be sure to ask for the latest fare specifics, too). Walk-in business is accepted, however, when there is room.

Gray Line also offers a two-day *Seward Explorer* from Anchorage that includes a Diesel Car (no dome) train trip to Seward, an excursion to Exit Glacier, a night in Seward, a cruise to Kenai Fjords, and a bus trip back to Anchorage, for around $250. A similar Homer Explorer includes a bus trip to Portage Glacier, then along the Kenai Peninsula to overnight in Homer, sightseeing in Homer, a marine tour of Kachemak Bay, and a flight back to Anchorage (or the reverse of all that). Figure around $350 per person in 1990 for that one. Both of these are likely to be excellent. Gray Line also has one-day train-bus tours to Seward for around $150, and a six-hour tour to the Matanuska Valley for around $30.

At least three cruises in Prince William Sound are operated out of Anchorage. We enjoyed the all-day 26 Glacier Cruise launched by **Phillips Cruises** (tel. *276–8023*), headquartered at 509 West Fourth Ave. The cruise disembarks from Whittier, so the whole enchilada includes a bus ride from Anchorage to Portage, an unusual experience when the entire bus is put on the train to Whittier (it's startling to see your driver standing and facing you to lecture while you continue to catapult through tunnel after tunnel), and then the catamaran *Klondike* cruise itself during which you do see at least 26 glaciers—perhaps more—with a hot lunch on board. (We also saw lots of sea otters, interesting birds, and terrific scenery in general.) Figure about $150 per person from Anchorage to Anchorage, although you could shave about $50 off that if you joined and left the cruise in Whittier. (If you want to call in advance from out of state, Phillips has its own toll-free number *(800) 544–0529*).

A more-expensive one- or two-day cruise experience featuring the famous Columbia Glacier in Prince William Sound is offered by **Glacier Tours** (tel. *276–1305*), 349 Wrangell Ave., aboard the *Glacier Seas*. The longer trip includes a bus to Valdez, overnight there, then the cruise to Whittier and the train/bus back to Anchorage (or reverse), at a cost of roughly $300. For the one-day tour you fly between Valdez and Anchorage, and that may run around $200. (The same tour is sold by Alaska Sightseeing and other umbrella booking services.)

The directly competing operation to the above is the **Columbia Glacier Cruises** (tel. *276–8866*), 547 West Fourth Ave., aboard the *Glacier Queen II*. It offers a similar itinerary at a similar price. This cruise is also sold by Gray Line, headquartered at the very same address. We have not taken either of these tours so we cannot compare them. We do know it's no longer possible to get very close to the face of the Columbia Glacier for technical reasons. Nevertheless, both are long-standing, well-respected corporations. (If you go, let us know.) There are also two sound trips via outfits headquartered in Valdez (see "Sides Trips" for details).

Yet another Prince William Sound cruise is aboard the small yacht *Denali* out of the isolated fishing village of Cordova. A package with round-trip Anchorage-Cordova air included is available from Anchorage with **Travel Enterprises** (tel. *276–2228*), at 614 West Fourth Ave.

Including meals and one night on the boat, it may run around $350 per person in 1990. (You have to get to Cordova first, and that must be by air or boat, since there is no land connection to the town.)

Raft tours: There are at least a couple of outfits who are itching to get you in a rubber raft for some fun on nearby rivers. One of the biggest is **Alaska Whitewater** (tel. *338–0471*), which offers white-water experiences on five different Alaska rivers, some of them for several days. The shortest is a half-day trip on the Eagle River, for around $60. (You'll get a brochure if you call or write them at P.O. Box 142294, Anchorage, AK 99514.) Also, **Alaska Greatland Adventures** (tel. *274–1222*), at 329 F St., Suite 218, has an all-day Kenai River Float Trip for $100 or so.

Winter tours: Specializing in dog-sled tours, **Chugach Express** (tel. *783–2266*) has experiences ranging from 20 minutes to three days. We took their short $25 Moose Meadow Tour once near Alyeska and had a good time getting a feel for what it's like to ride a dog sled. An all-day tour is about $100. And a popular three-day, two-night McKinley Adventure tour is around $400 or so per person, counting meals and lodging. (Call or write for a brochure at P.O. Box 261, Girdwood, AK 99587.) Similar tours are also offered by **Mush Alaska** (tel. *376–4743*), which will take you on a section of the historic Iditarod Trail. (Call or write for a brochure to P.O. Box 871752, Wasilla, AK 99687.)

Flightseeing: By this we don't mean long trips far into the bush, which we cover in a minute. **J & M Alaska Air Tours** (tel. *276–5422*), headquartered at 2015 Merrill Field Dr., has several arrangements, including an hour of flightseeing over the Anchorage area for about $150 per person (minimum 2), plus longer flights to Mount McKinley (about $175) and Columbia glacier (about $200), in twin-engine aircraft. Similar flights may be available from the **Anchorage Air Center** (tel. *278–9752*), at 2301 Merrill Field Dr.; **Airlift Alaska** (tel. *276–3809*), also at 2301 Merrill Field Dr.; or **Vernair** (tel. *258–7822*), at 1704 East Fifth Ave. Also, **Ketchum Air Service** (tel. *243–5525*), 2708 Aspen Dr., a single-engine float-plane firm with a long-standing reputation, takes off for sightseeing (or fishing trips) from the seaplane/skiplane harbor on the north shore at Lake Hood. Three-hour flights to Mt. McKinley or the Columbia Glacier will run around $200 per person. Several other bush and charter operations base themselves either at Lake Hood or at Merrill Field.

Helicopter flights are available from **Era Helicopters** (tel. *248–4422*), a corporation with choppers stationed all over the state but which is headquartered at 6160 South Airpark Dr. in Anchorage. Tour A-1, All Around Anchorage, lasts 25 minutes for around $100 per person. Tour A-2, Southcentral Perspective, is 55 minutes, includes a swing over the Chugach Mountains to Mt. Alyeska, for around $150. And Tour A-4, Glacier Extravaganza, adds up to 100 extravagant minutes of flying plus a 15-minute landing at the Knik Glacier for around $300 per person. **Alaska Helicopters** (tel. *243–1466*), parked at 6400 South Airpark Dr., takes off on at least three different whirlybird excursions starting at around $125 per person. (One combines gold panning and a visit to the tiny village of Hope, across the Turnagain Arm.) **Northwind Aviation** (tel. *276–6515*), at 2400 East Fifth Ave., also has chopper flights beginning at about $100 per passenger for a half-hour going whopp-whopp over Anchor Town.

Whether or not this qualifies as flightseeing is up to you, but *ballooning* has become a popular evening activity in the Anchorage bowl. The only company we know of that will lift you off on one of these silent, colorful globes is **Hot Air Affair** (tel. *349–7333*), 3605 Arctic Blvd. One-hour flights will be about $150 per person. We don't know much more about it. (If you take off in one of these, please drop us a line.)

Longer air tours out of Anchorage: Anchorage is usually the most efficient launching point and has more opportunities for major aerial tours into the Interior as well those into the Arctic, over to the Bering Coast, or out to Southwestern Alaska and the Aleutians.

MarkAir (tel. *243–6275*) has all-inclusive Top of the World tours via Fairbanks to *Barrow* and *Prudhoe Bay,* previously described under Fairbanks, "Side Trips." As a general guide, from Anchorage the one-day tour to Barrow (#560) or the overnight tour (#510) may run around $450 to $475. The combination Barrow and Prudhoe Bay tour (#585) will be more like $550. We took two major tours from Anchorage with MarkAir recently. One was an overnight tour to *Kodiak Island,* which included a hotel and a tour around Kodiak. As a guess, that tour may run about $350 this summer. The other was a somewhat more complicated excursion to *Katmai National Park,* which involved at least one night in the town of King Salmon (the Quinnat Landing Hotel) and then transferring to MarkAir's commuter line, Hermen's MarkAir Express, a float plane trip to and from Brooks Lodge in the national park. Figure a minimum of about $350 per person, and make sure they have you booked on the trip from Brooks Lodge to the Valley of the Ten Thousand Smokes before you leave. (We didn't, and there wasn't room on the bus for us, Gus.)

MarkAir also has a two-night tour 800 miles out to Dutch Harbor in the Aleutian Islands in a joint effort with **Aleutian Experience Tours** (tel. *522–1323*), headquartered at 3400 Kvichak Circle in Anchorage. With airfare, hotel, and guided *tours featuring nature subjects* as well as World War II memorabilia, the experience will total close to $1000 in 1990. We haven't taken this one yet, but it looks like a good one. Detailed late information on all MarkAir excursions can be had by calling their toll-free number from out of state, *(800) 426–6784.*

By the time you read these words, **Alaska Airlines** (tel. *243–3300*) will have begun some new one-, two-, and three-day all-inclusive tours to the Eskimo village of *Kotzebue* and the gold rush town of *Nome* on the Bering Sea Coast. Same-day tours from Anchorage to Kotzebue or Nome will run around $325, including tax. Two-day tours to both towns, including an overnight in either will add up to about $450. (Our tip: You'll see pretty much the same sights on either, but if you're a night person who enjoys a drink or two in the evening, choose the Nome overnight; if a good, comfortable room means more to you, choose the Kotzebue overnight version.) There's also a three-day variation with an overnight in each of the two cities for about $525. You can get the latest details or make bookings by calling Alaska Air Vacations in their Seattle office toll-free at *(800) 468–2248* or *(800) 426–0333*. This tour will probably also be sold by Gray Line and others as booking agencies.

The tour company we used for a trip far out into the Bering Sea to St. Paul in the Pribilof Islands has now gone out of business (Exploration Cruises and Tours). They had worked with **Reeve Aleutian Airways** (tel. *243–4700*), and at this writing Reeve Aleutian was setting up some excursions with Tanadusix, the Native corporation of the Pribilofs. From Anchorage, all-inclusive three-day, two-night tours could run close to $1000, and we predict that if you draw a good guide even casual nature lovers will find it well worth the outlay. Extremely dedicated birders, seal hounds, and flower fanciers may choose the four-day (about $1200) or six-day (about $1500) version. June through August are the only practical months for these tours; you'll have a good time during any part of this period, but the very best time for seeing everything is from late June to early July. From outside the state, you can reach Reeve toll-free at *(800) 544–2248,* and ask them to send their color brochure. Pribilof tours may also be arranged through **Midnight Sun Tours** (tel. *276–8687*), 600 Cordova St. in Anchorage. Midnight Sun has a toll-free number too *(800) 544–2235*.

An unusual *summer tour* from Anchorage via Nome to the Eskimo village of Gambell on *St. Lawrence Island* in the Bering Sea is offered by **Alaska Village Tours** (tel. *276–7568*), 1577 C St., Suite 200. Only 40 miles from the Soviet Union, this remote village considers itself culturally and linguistically tied more to Siberia than to Alaskan Eskimos. Visitors are treated to a peek at the subsistance culture and demonstrations of ivory carving, dancing, and story telling. The exact itinerary changes depending on several variables, and this may be the closest the average visitor can come to understanding such a community. There are several different arrangements, some combining a tour to Nome, and this may total about $600–700 from Anchorage in 1990. By itself the one-day tour to the island out of Nome may run around $250, but use these figures only as a general guide. (This tour also will probably be sold by Alaska Sightseeing or Gray Line.)

An *overnight flying Interior tour* out of Anchorage is also offered by **Wilbur's Custom Tours** (tel. *277–0511*), a branch of the "Family Airline." For around $500, Wilbur's will take you aboard one of its twin-engine Cessnas to a Yupik village on the Kuskokwim River for a walking tour, then on to Red Devil for an overnight stay and a tour of the old mercury mine in the morning before returning to Anchorage. We haven't gone, but the itinerary sounds interesting. Wilbur's also has several other air tours that may vary from year to year.

SPORTS

As far as spectator sports are concerned, for many in Anchorage it's the same as over much of Alaska: *baseball* in the summer and *basketball* in the winter. *Hockey* is also big in Anchorage, and of course the city avidly follows all college sports. By the way that's baseball, not softball around here. Anchorage has had two semi-professional teams, the Bucs and the Glacier Pilots, both members of the ABL (the Alaska Baseball League), although this may be distilled down to one team or the other soon. Home games are generally scheduled at the stadium in Mulcahy Park, across East 16th Avenue from the end of Cordova Street.

Basketball consists of college contests with local fans following the Pioneers of Alaska Pacific University or the Seawolves of the University of Alaska, Anchorage. The big basketball excitement takes place in November, at the college invitational tournament called the Great Alaska Shootout held at the **George M. Sullivan Sports Arena** (tel. *279–2596* for recorded information on the arena). Preseason exhibition games from Lower 48 NBA teams are also played here.

University contests in hockey, volley ball, swimming, etc., are also followed enthusiastically. *Mushing,* of course, is the official state sport; and during the winter several sled dog races are followed with interest, most notably the 1000-mile Iditarod, which ceremonially begins in Anchorage (the first Saturday of March), and the World Championship Sled Dog Race, which is part of the week-long Anchorage Fur Rendezvous (Fur Rondy) celebrations in February.

Believe it or not, there are two amateur *rugby* teams in town. The Coconuts and the Green Dragons are both affiliated with the Alaska Rugby League.

Participation sports: Visiting *fishermen* and *hunters* should be sure to check out the **Alaska Public Lands Information Center** (tel. *271–2737*) in the old post office on Fourth Avenue between F and G streets. Official information is also available from the Alaska Department of Fish & Game (tel. *344–0541*) at 333 Raspberry Rd. There are hunting seasons for sheep, goat, moose, black bear, water birds, and small game.

Nonresident hunting licenses are $60, and fishing licenses were still $10 the last we looked.

In the immediate area are about 23 streams and rivers plus several lakes, but remember that anything within easy weekend driving distance means you'll be competing for a good spot with half of Alaska's fishing population. You'll have a little more privacy if you opt for fly-in fishing out in the bush. Planes are chartered for about $200 an hour, which obviously would be $50 per person for a party of four. Recorded information on fishing conditions is available at tel. *349–4687.* The ACVB log cabin Visitor Information Center has lots of poop on hunting and fishing guide services. One such firm with a downtown address is **Adventure North** (tel. *276–0713*), at 1030 West Fourth Ave., a block west of the Captain Cook. Another outfit that seems well organized is **Jake's Alaska Wilderness Outfitters** (tel. *248–0509*), 3002 Barbara Dr. Also, some bush pilots act as fishing and hunting guides to wilderness areas with which they are familiar. It might be a good idea, too, to get in touch with the **Alaska Wilderness Guides Association** (tel. *276–6634*), a self-regulating organization. You can write the AWGA in advance at P.O. Box 89061, Anchorage, AK 99508.

There are four *golf* courses in the municipality of Anchorage, including one on **Elmendorf Air Force Base** and another at **Fort Richardson.** The public courses are **O'Malley's on the Green** (tel. *522–3322*), 18 holes, at 3651 O'Malley Rd.; and **Russian Jack Springs** (tel. *333–8338*), 9 holes, par 30, at Boniface Pkwy. and DeBarr Rd. And indoor golf—why not? Try **Par Tee Golf** (tel. *344–5717*) at 1307 East 74th Ave., off the Old Seward Highway. You might find about 50 *tennis* courts lobbed here and there around Anchorage in public parks. Five of these are near each other in the **Delaney Park Strip,** near Ninth Ave. and C St. For further information, tel. *264–4356.*

Bowling? Not as big as it used to be, apparently. **Center Bowl** and **Spare Room** (tel. *562–2695*) have amalgamated and now rack 'em up together at 3717 Minnesota Dr. *Swimming*: In addition to the pools for club members and guests at the Captain Cook, the Hilton, and the Holiday Inn, you'll find five indoor city public pools. For further information, tel. *786–1233.* During the summer, supervised swimming is also at **Goose Lake,** Northern Lights Blvd. and Providence Dr.; and at **Spenard Beach,** Spenard Rd. and Lakeshore Dr.; either about three miles from downtown.

With the 120-plus miles of public trails through the Anchorage Bowl available—including the scenic Coastal Trail—*hiking, biking, jogging,* and *running* are certainly popular. In the winter, of course, these turn into paths for *snowshoeing* and *cross-country skiing.* You can get a map from the **Municipal Parks and Recreation Department,** 620 West 10th Ave., Third Floor.

Skiing: The Anchorage area has one major combination downhill

(Alpine) and cross-country (Nordic) ski resort plus two more modest commercial operations. Visiting skiers who can schuss on the weekdays will find themselves in less competition for lift space, of course. The big resort, around which local boosters now hope to center the 1998 Winter Olympics, is the **Alyeska Resort** (tel. *783–2222,* but call *783– 2121* for the ski report). About 35 miles south of central Anchorage in Girdwood, it features wide open bowls, excellent trails, and good snow pack sometimes clear into June, with an average depth of more than 25 feet, and day and night skiing. Three double chairlifts accommodate experienced to intermediate skiers with a combined drop of 2800 feet. Two of these lifts are more than a mile long. A third is a new high-speed bubble chair from midway up the mountain to the glacier on the top. Two rope tows and a fourth chairlift serve novice skiers.

All-day lift tickets will cost at least $25 in 1990; figure another $20 if you need to rent skis, poles, and boots. Alyeska's 10-kilometer cross-country trail was designed by the Nordic Ski Club of the U.S. Ski Association. Owned by Japan's Seibu corporation, Alyeska is now in the midst of a giant expansion program that will see a large hotel built at the resort in about 1991 or 1992. A special ski bus called **The Lift** (tel. *276–1305*) leaves several locations in Anchorage in the morning for Alyeska and then returns in the late afternoon. Round-trip rides are around $10 (or perhaps $35, including your lift ticket.)

Less-experienced downhill skiers may prefer to try **Hilltop** (tel. *346–1446*), which has more bunny slopes, a single chairlift, and less expensive tickets (about $15). It's in Hillside Park off Abbott Rd., almost in midtown Anchorage, no more than 20 minutes' drive from anywhere in town, or you can get there on the People Mover. Lights are turned on for night skiing. There are also several Nordic trails.

A good compromise between the experts and the beginners is **Alpenglow** (tel. *522–3645*), at Arctic Valley, in the Chugach mountains about 30 minutes' drive (15 miles) from Anchorage. It has two chair lifts, a T-bar, a poma lift, and a rope tow. All but the rope tow serve intermediate to advanced terrain. From the top of the mountain at 3900 feet, it's a 1400-foot drop to the lodge. All-day lift tickets should be around $15 in 1990. This is the only Alpine ski area near Anchorage that gives free rein to *snowboards* (the winter version of a surfboard) on the slopes, and it is often open only on the weekends. Just like the big boys, however, you'll find a lodge, cafeteria, restrooms, ski patrol, ski school, and rental shop.

Nordic skiers should realize that with its extremely extensive system of trails, Anchorage considers itself the cross-country ski capital of the U.S. It has a climate cold enough to hold snow from November through March, but still mild enough to make outdoor activity fun. Trails are generally maintained by the Nordic Ski Club of Anchorage, which has thousands of members.

One terrific long route begins near the University of Alaska, continues through midtown along Chester Creek, and connects at Westchester Lagoon with the long and viewful Coastal Trail, extending as far as Kincaid Park (which has many intricate trails of its own). Beginning Nordic skiers, however, should probably try their ankles at **Russian Jack Park.** (Get a map at the chalet.) Many Anchorage ski trails, of course, are on the edge of the wilderness. Bears should all be asleep during the season, of course, but you can occasionally run across—hopefully that is not to say into—a moose.

SHOPPING

Like Fairbanks, shopping is big business in Anchorage, with many coming in from nearby areas and from far out in the bush to stock up on supplies. There are at least six enclosed shopping *malls*. You'll first see the attractive **Anchorage Fifth Avenue,** anchored by Penney's and Nordstrom, downtown between Fifth and Sixth avenues and C and D streets. The **Northway Mall** is rather far out in right field, on the other side of Merrill Field, where Fifth Avenue becomes the beginning of the Glenn Highway. That should not be confused with **Northern Lights Center,** a modest mall at the corner of Northern Lights Blvd. and Spenard Rd. The mighty **Mall at Sears** (which does, indeed, have a genuine Sears and Roebuck) is on the southwest corner of Seward Highway and Northern Lights Blvd. You'll find **University Center** not much farther south in the piece of triangular real estate formed by Old and New Seward highways and 36th Ave. Finally, **Dimond Center** is considerably farther south on the southwest corner of Dimond Blvd. and Old Seward Highway.

Although not strictly shopping centers, avid shop hounds will also want to note the locations of two large all-purpose stores—**Fred Meyer** (Freddie's) at 1000 East Northern Lights Blvd. (across from Sears) and at 2000 West Dimond Blvd. (at Victor Street), and **Carrs** in the Aurora Village Shopping Center at 1650 West Northern Lights Blvd. (corner of Minnesota Blvd.), at 1501 East Huffman Rd. (near New Seward Highway), and about a dozen other locations.

Local arts, crafts, and gifts: You'll find the products of local and bush Native artisans all over the place, and don't forget to look for those Made in Alaska bear labels or the silver-hand handicraft labels and others we've talked about. One store we liked is the Native-owned **Alaska Heritage Arts** at 400 D St., in the historic Club 25 Building, across from the police station. There you often find ivory carvers and other Natives at work in the store. Also check out **Alaska Native Arts** and Crafts in the Post Office Mall at 333 West Fourth Ave.; the **Alaskan Ivory Exchange,** at 700 West Fourth St.; and a real sleeper, the gift shop at the **Alaska Native Medical Center** at Third Ave. and Gambell St. **Boreal Traditions** in the Hotel Captain Cook, has some excellent pieces of crystal, ivory, brass, copper, and other media. There is also an attractive gift shop at the **D.J. Loussac Library** and another in the **Anchorage Museum of History and Art.**

Among the well-known *art galleries* in Anchorage are the **Stonington Gallery** at 550 West Seventh Ave., between E and F streets; **Artique, Ltd.** (which may be the city's oldest) at 314 G St., between Third and Fourth avenues; **Stephan Fine Arts,** in the Hilton and other locations; and the **Window Gallery** at 207 East Northern Lights Blvd. (You might want to keep an eye out for paintings and lithographs by Anchorage resident Jon Van Zyle, famous for his Iditarod posters.) *Antiques?* Look into **Remember When,** at 412 G St., between Fourth and Fifth avenues.

Fur shops include the **Anchorage Fur Factory** at 105 West Fourth Ave., and especially **David Green's** (tel. *277–95955*), at 130 West Fourth and at 423 West Fifth Ave. The **Alaskan Fur Exchange** is at 900 West International Airport Rd. And for super high-class European styles, **A.C. Bang** (tel. *258–6334*) in the Captain Cook is world renowned. We must admit, however, that we are much more partial to things made from fur that can be harvested without sacrificing the animal, and that would be only the qiviut and other items at the **Musk Ox Co-op** (tel. *272–9225*), the little brown building at 604 H St., corner of Sixth.

If you're just looking for something warm to wear, remember you can buy *Alaska parkas* and other well-insulated gear in department and specialty stores. You might check **Laura Wright Alaskan Parkys** at 223 East Fifth Ave., two blocks from the Sheraton (between Barrow and Cordova), where they like to call their Eskimomade parkas wearable works of art (where such varied customers as Elvis and the Emperor of Japan allegedly have been outfitted); or **Heritage North** on the upper level of Dimond Center. For *outdoor gear* in general, we also like to look around **Gary King Sporting Goods** at 202 East Northern Lights Blvd., between A and Denali streets; **Alaska Mountaineering;** at 2633 Spenard Rd.; **Barney's Sports Chalet,** 906 West Northern Lights Blvd.; or perhaps **REI,** in the Northern Lights Center. An excellent clothing store in general is **Lamonts,** with branches in University Center, the Northway Mall, and Dimond Center.

Frozen seafood: You can buy Alaskan seafood airpacked for travel at two or three places in town. One firm that may be pretty well organized is **Tenth and M Seafoods** (tel. *272–3474*), at 1020 M St. (at 10th Ave.) They usually have king crab, salmon, halibut, smoked salmon, prawns, scallops, shrimp, lox, and, believe it or not, squaw candy. Or they will pack and freeze your own catches for you too. (If you've tried these people or any similar business, we'd like to know how you got along.)

Photographic equipment and rocks? You'll find this unlikely film and jade combination at **Stewart's** (tel. *272–8581*), in an historic downtown building at 531 West Fourth Ave. Be sure to stop in to see this sourdough family operation.

Bookstores: You'll find a dozen branches of Alaska's famous **Book Cache** all over town, notably the headquarters store downtown at 436 West Fifth Ave., in the Post Office Mall at 333 West Fourth Ave., plus the major shopping centers. There are also **Waldenbooks** in the Anchorage Fifth Avenue Mall and at other malls. (And if you don't see copies of this volume in any Alaska book store, please complain!)

MISCELLANEOUS ADDRESSES AND PHONES

Surveyors who laid out the street plan about 75 years ago planned a perfectly square grid pattern—something that has somewhat fallen apart and caused some confusion with city expansion, since many of these streets are interrupted or have been renamed in some areas. Still, the low-numbered avenues begin downtown, and they run as high as 172nd Avenue about 20 miles to the south. Streets named with letters of the alphabet run north and south, and A Street divides the East and West avenues. For some reason, the alphabet streets are written by some in Anchorage with quotation marks around them: "A" Street, etc. They run from A to S, but with no J or Q streets, allegedly a Swedish influence. East of A St., the streets begin to be names of towns, areas, and other names associated with Alaska, also in alphabetical order—Barrow, Cordova, Denali, Eagle, Fairbanks, Gambell, Hyder, Ingra, Juneau, etc.; but eventually, like the best laid plans of mice and men, the system begins to break down after Orca Street.

Anchorage is now a big town, with about a dozen postal zip codes, all beginning with 995; the code for the downtown area is 99510. As in virtually all of Alaska, the telephone area code is 907. Local phone service is provided by the ATU (Anchorage Telephone Utility) and normal long-distance service is either by Alascom or the competing GCI (General Communications, Inc.). Most local phone numbers begin with a 2 or 3.

- Alaska Air Ambulance (tel. *258–EVAC*).
- Alaska Bridge Club (tel. *333–1827*), 2360 Commercial Dr.

- Alaska Department of Fish and Game (tel. *344–0541*, or recorded information tel. *349–4687*), 333 Raspberry Rd.
- Alaska Model Railroad Club (tel. *333–7147*), Boniface Center Mall.
- Alaska Pacific University (tel. *561–1266*), 4101 University Dr.
- All About Anchorage (recorded information) (tel. *276–3200*).
- Anchorage Convention & Visitors Bureau (tel. *276–4118*), 201 East Third St., Anchorage, AK 99501.
- Aurora Borealis African Violet Society (tel. *337–0957*).
- Bus information, People Mover (tel. *264–6543*).
- Cabin reservations, Chugach National Forest (tel. *271–2599*), 201 East Ninth Ave., Suite 206, Anchorage, AK 99501–3698.
- Challenge Alaska (Recreation for the Disabled) (tel. *563–2658*), 520 West 58th Ave., Suite C, Anchorage, AK 99518.
- Chamber of Commerce (tel. *272–2401*), 437 E. St., Suite 300.
- Cleaning World Coin-Op Laundry (tel. *345–2311*), 1120 Huffman (behind the Lucky Wishbone).
- Dental Society, 24-hour emergency service (tel. *279–9144*).
- Dudes and Dames Square Dance Club (tel. *333–8671*).
- Emergencies of all types (tel. *911*).
- Fire department (tel. *276–7232*).
- Humana Hospital (tel. *276–1131*), 2801 DeBarr Rd.
- Lucky Strike Bingo (tel. *274–6711*), Northern Lights Blvd. and A St.
- Mayor's office (tel. *343–4702*).
- Mountain View Car Wash (tel. *279–4819*), 3433 Commercial Dr.
- National Bank of Alaska (tel. *263–2500*), 446 West Fourth Ave.
- Poison Control (tel. *563–3393*).
- Police department (tel. *786–8500*).
- Rent-A-Mom, hotel child care (tel. *349–4463*).
- Road conditions (tel. *243–7675*).
- Salvation Army (tel. *276–1609*), 546 East 15th Ave.
- Time and temperature (tel. *844*).
- U.S. Post Office (tel. *266–3340*), Downtown Station, Post Office Mall, 333 West Fourth Ave.
- University of Alaska at Anchorage (tel. *786–1800*), 3211 Providence Dr.
- Visitor Information Center, ACVB (tel. *274–3531*), Fourth Ave. and F St.
- Weather forecast recording (tel. *936–2525*).

INDEX

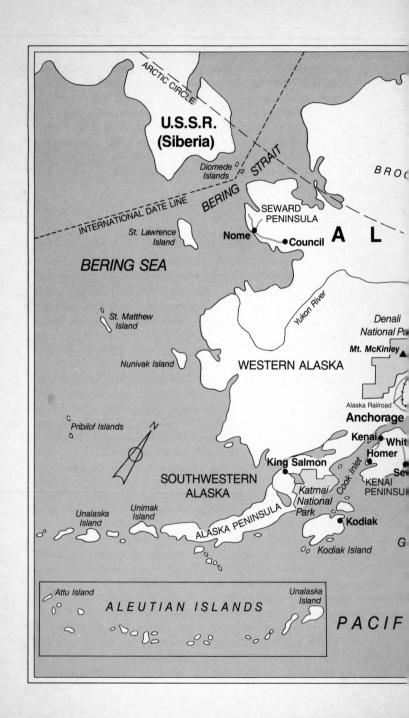

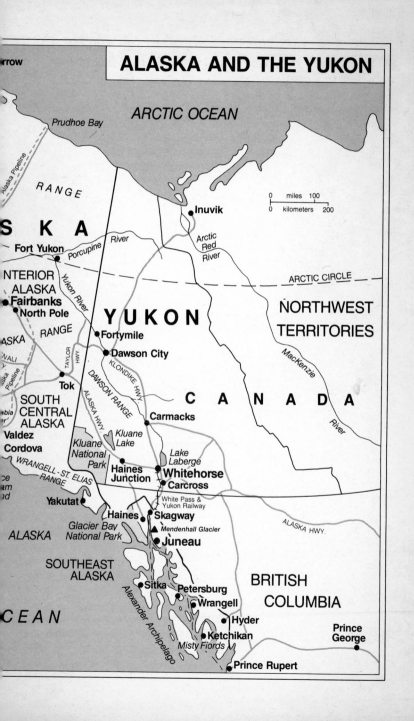

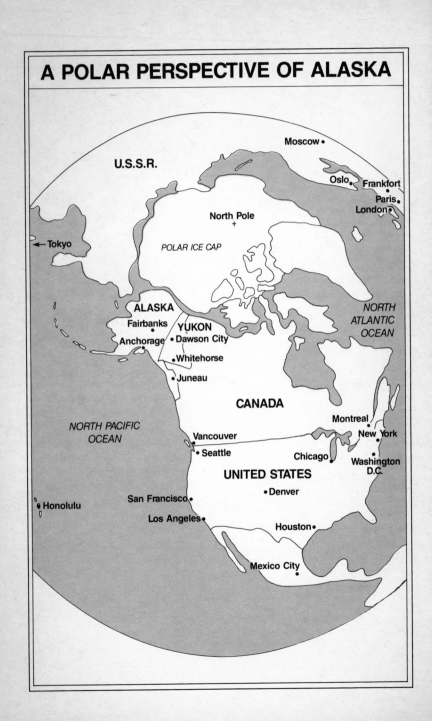

A POLAR PERSPECTIVE OF ALASKA

U.S.S.R.

Moscow •

Oslo • • Frankfort

Paris •
London •

← Tokyo

North Pole
+

POLAR ICE CAP

ALASKA

Fairbanks •

YUKON

Anchorage • • Dawson City

• Whitehorse

• Juneau

NORTH
ATLANTIC
OCEAN

CANADA

Montreal

New York

NORTH PACIFIC
OCEAN

Vancouver

• Seattle

Chicago •

Washington
D.C.

UNITED STATES

• Honolulu

San Francisco •

• Denver

Los Angeles •

Houston •

Mexico City •